Chinese Society

'This first rate collection will be indispensable reading for scholars of Chinese society. Each of the book's uniformly excellent well-written and substantive chapters open by providing enough historical background on its specific topic to make it comprehensible enough to advanced undergraduates as well as the general informed reader.'

The China Journal

'I would recommend to all students who wish to begin studying this country.'

China Perspectives

'Should be read by all serious scholars of contemporary China.'

Asian Affairs

This book, written by an interdisciplinary and international team of China scholars, uses the themes of resistance and protest to explore the complexity of life in contemporary China. Topics covered include:

*   labour and environmental disputes
*   rural and ethnic conflict
*   migration
*   legal challenges
*   intellectual and religious dissidence
*   opposition to family planning
*   suicide.

This new edition brings the text fully up to date, adding three new chapters on Falun Gong, Christianity and land struggles. *Chinese Society* provides a comprehensive resource for both undergraduates and specialists in the field and encourages the reader to challenge conventional images of contemporary Chinese society.

Elizabeth J. Perry is Henry Rosovsky Professor of Government at Harvard University. Her previous books include *Rebels and Revolutionaries in North China*, *Shanghai on Strike: The Politics of Chinese Labor*, *Proletarian Power: Shanghai in the Cultural Revolution*, and *Challenging the Mandate of Heaven: Social Protest and State Power in China*.

Mark Selden is Professor of Sociology at Binghamton University and Professorial Associate, Cornell University. His books include *China in Revolution: The Yenan Way Revisited*, *Chinese Village, Socialist State*, *The Political Economy of Chinese Development* and *The Resurgence of East Asia: 500, 150 and 50 Year Perspectives*.

ASIA'S TRANSFORMATIONS
Edited by Mark Selden

Binghamton University and Cornell University, USA

The books in this series explore the political, social, economic and cultural consequences of Asia's transformations in the twentieth and twenty-first centuries. The series emphasizes the tumultuous interplay of local, national, regional and global forces as Asia bids to become the hub of the world economy. While focusing on the contemporary, it also looks back to analyse the antecedents of Asia's contested rise.

This series comprises several strands:

Asia's Transformations aims to address the needs of students and teachers, and the titles will be published in hardback and paperback. Titles include

The Battle for Asia
From Decolonization to Globalization
Mark T. Berger

Ethnicity in Asia
Edited by Colin Mackerras

Chinese Society, 2nd edition
Change, Conflict and Resistance
Edited by Elizabeth J Perry and Mark Selden

The Resurgence of East Asia:
500, 150 and 50 Year Perspectives
Edited by Giovanni Arrighi, Takeshi Hamashita and Mark Selden

The Making of Modern Korea
Adrian Buzo

Korean Society:
Civil Society, Democracy and the State
Edited by Charles K Armstrong

Remaking the Chinese State
Strategies, Society and Security
Edited by Chien-min Chao and Bruce J Dickson

Mao's Children in the New China
Voices from the Red Guard Generation
Yarong Jiang and David Ashley

Chinese Society
Change, Conflict and Resistance
Edited by Elizabeth J Perry and Mark Selden

Opium, Empire and the Global Political Economy
Carl A Trocki

Japan's Comfort Women
Sexual Slavery and Prostitution during World War II and the US Occupation
Yuki Tanaka

Hong Kong's History
State and Society under Colonial Rule
Edited by Tak-Wing Ngo

Debating Human Rights
Critical Essays from the United States and Asia
Edited by Peter Van Ness

Asia's Great Cities

Each volume aims to capture the heartbeat of the contemporary city from multiple perspectives emblematic of the authors own deep familiarity with the distinctive faces of the city, its history, society, culture, politics and economics, and its evolving position in national, regional and global frameworks. While most volumes emphasize urban developments since the Second World War, some pay close attention to the legacy of the longue durée in shaping the contemporary. Thematic and comparative volumes address such themes as urbanization, economic and financial linkages, architecture and space, wealth and power, gendered relationships, planning and anarchy, and ethnographies in national and regional perspective.

Titles include:

Hong Kong
Global City
Stephen Chiu and Tai-Lok Lui

Shanghai
Global City
Jeff Wasserstrom

Singapore
Carl Trocki

Beijing in the Modern World
David Strand and Madeline Yue Dong

Bangkok
Place, Practice and Representation

Asia.com is a series which focuses on the ways in which new information and communication technologies are influencing politics, society and culture in Asia. Titles include:

Asia.com
Asia Encounters the Internet
Edited by K. C. Ho, Randolph Kluver and Kenneth C. C. Yang

Japanese Cybercultures
Edited by Mark McLelland and Nanette Gottlieb

Literature and Society is a series that seeks to demonstrate the ways in which Asian Literature is influenced by the politics, society and culture in which it is produced. Titles include:

Chinese Women Writers and the Feminist Imagination (1905-1945)
Haiping Yan

The Body in Postwar Japanese Fiction
Edited by Douglas N Slaymaker

RoutledgeCurzon Studies in Asia's Transformations is a forum for innovative new research intended for a high-level specialist readership, and the titles will be available in hardback only. Titles include:

1. Chinese Media, Global Contexts
Edited by Chin-Chuan Lee

2. Imperialism in South East Asia
'A Fleeting, Passing Phase'
Nicholas Tarling

Critical Asian Scholarship is a series intended to showcase the most important individual contributions to scholarship in Asian Studies. Each of the volumes presents a leading Asian scholar addressing themes that are central to his or her most significant and lasting contribution to Asian studies. The series is committed to the rich variety of research and writing on Asia, and is not restricted to any particular discipline, theoretical approach or geographical expertise.

Chinese Society,

Change, conflict and resistance

2nd edition

**Edited by
Elizabeth J. Perry
and Mark Selden**

RoutledgeCurzon
Taylor & Francis Group

LONDON AND NEW YORK

First published 2000
by Routledge
11 New Fetter Lane, London EC4P 4EE

Simultaneously published in the USA and Canada
by Routledge
29 West 35th Street, New York, NY 10001

Second Edition published
by RoutledgeCurzon 2003
RoutledgeCurzon is an imprint of the Taylor & Francis Group

Typeset in Baskerville by Taylor & Francis Ltd
Printed and bound in Great Britain by MPG Books Ltd, Bodmin

British Library Cataloguing in Publication Data
A catalogue record for this book is available from the British Library

Library of Congress Cataloging in Publication Data
   Chinese society: change, conflict and resistance / edited by
   Elizabeth J. Perry and Mark Selden.–2nd ed.
   p. cm. – (Asia's transformations)
   Includes bibliographical references and index.
   1. China–Social conditions-1976– 2. China–Politics and
   government–1976– I. Perry, Elizabeth J. II. Selden, Mark. III. Series.

   HN733.5.C444 2003
   306'.951–dc21   2003001261

ISBN 0–415–30170–X (hbk)
ISBN 0–415–30169–6 (pbk)

**To those who resist injustice,
whether loudly or softly**

Contents

Illustrations

Tables

Figures

Contributors

Geremie R. Barmé is a Senior Fellow in the Division of Pacific and Asian Studies, The Australian National University. His recent books include *In the Red, On Contemporary Chinese Culture* and *Shades of Mao: the Posthumous Cult of the Great Leader*. He was an associate director and co-writer of the documentary on the events of 1989 in Beijing, 'The Gate of Heavenly Peace'. His most recent book is *An Artistic Exile: a life of Feng Zikai (1898-1975)* and he was co-director and writer for the film *Morning Sun*.

Uradyn E. Bulag is Associate Professor of Anthropology at Hunter College and the Graduate Center of the City University of New York. He is the author of *Nationalism and Hybridity in Mongolia* and *The Mongols at China's Edge: History and the Politics of National Unity*. He is also co-editor of *Inner Asia*.

Peter Ho is Assistant Professor at the Environmental Policy Group of Wageningen University. He has published numerous articles on themes of institutional change, property rights, natural resource management, environmentalism, and rural development in China. He is co-editor of *Rural Development in Transitional China*. He is currently completing a book entitled *Institutions in Transition: Land Ownership, Property Rights and Social Conflict*.

Jun Jing is Professor of Sociology and Anthropology at Tsinghua University, Beijing. He is author of *The Temple of Memories: History, Power, and Morality in a Chinese Village*, and editor of *Feeding China's Little Emperors: Food, Children, and Social Change*. Much of his work deals with human suffering and social change. His current research is on the HIV/AIDS epidemic in China. He leads a Social Policy Forum in Beijing and is director of the Social Policy Research Institute at Tsinghua University.

Arthur Kleinman is an anthropologist and psychiatrist who is Rabb Professor of Anthropology at Harvard and Professor of Medical Anthropology and Psychiatry, Harvard Medical School. Kleinman has conducted field research in Chinese society for over 30 years, studying illness and health care in Taiwan (1968-79) and mental and social health problems in China (1978-present), including one of the first studies of survivors of China's Cultural

Revolution. He is currently engaged in research projects on suicide, depression, AIDS, and stigma in China.

Ching Kwan Lee is Associate Professor of Sociology at the University of Michigan, Ann Arbor. Her research interests focus on labor, gender, China and East Asia. She is author of *Gender and the South China Miracle* and is now working on a book on the remaking of the Chinese working class under the economic reforms.

Sing Lee is Professor at the Department of Psychiatry, The Chinese University of Hong Kong, and Lecturer at the Department of Social Medicine, Harvard University. He is a psychiatrist with an anthropological orientation. His research interests include eating disorders, the social construction of psychiatric diagnosis, neurasthenia, lithium therapy, suicide, and other mental health problems, stigma and social change in Chinese society.

Richard Madsen is Professor of Sociology and director of the Council on East Asian Studies at the University of California, San Diego. His books on China include *Chen Village under Mao and Deng* (co-authored with Anita Chan and Jonathan Unger), *Morality and Power in a Chinese Village*, *Unofficial China* (co-edited with Perry Link and Paul Pickowicz), *China and the American Dream*, *China's Catholics: Tragedy and Hope in an Emerging Civil Society*, and *Popular China: Unofficial Culture in a Globalizing Society*, co-edited with Perry Link and Paul Pickowicz.

Hein Mallee completed a PhD dissertation on "The Expanded Family: Rural Labour Circulation in Reform China" at Leiden University. He has worked for an NGO in China since 1997.

Minxin Pei is a Senior Associate and Co-director of the China Program at the Carnegie Endowment for International Peace in Washington DC. His main interest is the development of democratic political systems, the politics of economic reform, the growth of civil society, and legal institutions. He is the author of *From Reform to Revolution: The Demise of Communism in China and the Soviet Union*. He is completing a book, *China's Trapped Transition: The Limits of Developmental Autocracy*.

Elizabeth J. Perry is Henry Rosovsky Professor of Government and Research Associate at the Fairbank Center for East Asian Research, Harvard University. Her books include *Rebels and Revolutionaries in North China, 1845-1945; Shanghai on Strike: The Politics of Chinese Labor; Proletarian Power: Shanghai in the Cultural Revolution*; and *Challenging the Mandate of Heaven: Social Protest and State Power in China*. She is currently working on a book tentatively entitled *Patrolling the Revolution: Worker Militias and State-building in Modern China*.

Mark Selden is Professor of Sociology at Binghamton University and Professorial Associate, Cornell University. His China-related books include *China in Revolution: The Yenan Way Revisited, Chinese Village, Socialist State* (with Edward Friedman and Paul Pickowicz), *The Political Economy of Chinese*

Development and The Resurgence of East Asia: 500, 150 and 50 Year Perspectives (with Giovanni Arrighi and Takeshi Hamashita). He is presently completing a book on war and state terror in twentieth-century Asia.

Patricia M. Thornton is Assistant Professor of Political Science at Trinity College in Hartford, CT. She has published on the topics of popular protest and sectarian religion in modern and contemporary China and is completing a study of corruption and its implications for protest under late imperial, Republican, and Communist regimes.

Tyrene White is Associate Professor of Political Science at Swarthmore College, Swarthmore, PA. She has written widely on China's population policy and rural politics, and is co-editor, along with Christina Gilmartin, Gail Hershatter, and Lisa Rofel, of *Engendering China: Women, Culture and the State.*

Wang Zheng is Associate Professor in the Women's Studies Program and Associate Research Scientist at the Institute for Research on Women and Gender at University of Michigan. She is the author of *Women in the Chinese Enlightenment: Oral and Textual Histories*, and co-editor, with Xueping Zhong and Bai Di, of *Some of US: Chinese Women Growing Up in the Mao Era.*

David Zweig is Professor in the Division of Social Science, Hong Kong University of Science and Technology. His books include: *Freeing China's Farmers: Restructuring Rural China in the Reform Era, China's Brain Drain to the United States,* and *Agrarian Radicalism in China, 1968–1981.* His most recent book is *Internationalizing China: Domestic Interests and Global Linkages.*

Introduction

Reform and resisitance in contemporary China

Elizabeth J. Perry and Mark Selden

In the closing decades of the twentieth century, China defied the best predictions of development economists and Sinologists alike in compiling a stunning record of economic growth. This was accomplished in the face of formidable obstacles including inefficient state enterprises, ambiguous property rights, irrational prices, primitive transportation, and outmoded banking and securities facilities. Social and political obstacles, including instability born of the failures of the Great Leap Forward and the Cultural Revolution, deep political divisions, a legacy of rural poverty and low levels of education, constituted equally formidable challenges. Yet, whether measured in per capita GDP, exports, income or induction of foreign capital, China's sustained double-digit growth and rising per capita income from the late 1970s into the 1990s, was the world's envy. As a result, China was able to join a select group, including the East Asian Newly Industrializing Economies, which significantly improved their position in the world economy. And it did so at the very time when the former socialist economies of the Soviet Union and Eastern Europe were in ruins, even continuing its advance (albeit at a slower pace) into the twenty-first century while many other economies, including several high-flying East Asian economies, stumbled or languished.

These achievements were not the product of some clear blueprint designed at the outset; rather, Chinese leaders aptly liken their approach to economic reform to 'crossing a river by groping for stones' – or improvising as they go. While economists have marvelled at the growth achievements this flexible strategy has produced, rather less scholarly concern has been devoted to the social and political consequences and 'externalities' of the reform agenda, including galloping spatial and class inequality and environmental destruction, the explosive growth of a migrant labour underclass, mounting ethnic unrest, and loss of security and jobs for many state sector employees. Still less attention has been drawn to the conflicts that reform engendered, and the myriad arenas of resistance that have been its byproduct at every stage.[1] The emerging patterns of conflict and resistance should not simply be understood as responses to reform initiatives or the playing out of historic antagonisms; they have also stimulated and shaped significant dimensions of the reform programme itself.

China's reform is a multifaceted process whose key elements include greater latitude for market, mobility, modernization and internationalization. Viewed from the centre, these policies are intended to transform Chinese socialism in ways that will accelerate economic growth, bolster party authority, and strengthen China's international position. Viewed from the perspective of the diverse social forces promoting the reforms, they afford an opportunity to expand autonomy and facilitate a range of activities previously circumscribed by the party-state. From the multiple perspectives of those who are disadvantaged or disappointed by elements of the reform programme, however, the object is often to preserve the benefits and ideals of a bygone era. In sum, reforms generated both from above and from below have brought far-reaching, even cataclysmic, changes to the economy, society, politics and culture, changes that touch every citizen and extend to every corner of the land and beyond to redefine China's place in the world.

Diverse patterns of conflict and resistance are directly attributable to the reforms, yet they are frequently rooted in historic contests and display time-honoured beliefs and behaviours. Contention during the reform era has ranged from tax riots, labour strikes and inter-ethnic clashes to legal challenges, pro-democracy demonstrations, environmental, anticorruption and gender protests, local electoral politics, religious rebellion and even mass suicides. In addition to overt conflicts that directly challenge the power, authority and reach of the state, and increasingly that of capital as well, much everyday resistance is invisible.[2] It takes such forms as private acts of evasion, flight and foot dragging, which, in the absence of manifestos or marches, may nevertheless effectively enlarge the terrain of social rights. These acts, as well as direct legal challenges in growing numbers of court cases, persistently press at the margins of official power and raise the costs of state controls. In some instances, they may also strengthen the reform agenda, by demanding freer markets, political and social rights, legal guarantees and geographical mobility. The cumulative weight of these challenges has forced significant changes in law and social praxis in contemporary China, developments that have been largely missed by analysts whose vision is limited to the search for American-style democracy or who are dazzled by economic growth rates. The most striking of these shifts have taken place in economic, social and cultural realms, but the effects also extend to the political sphere.

This volume introduces contemporary Chinese society in the era of reform through examination of some of the dominant modes of resistance. Individual chapters trace the origins of different patterns of conflict to diverse sources: old and new, foreign and domestic, socialist and capitalist. Since much of this ferment is a product of the contemporary environment, we begin with a brief consideration of the main features of the reform effort.

Reform agendas and consequences

China's post-Mao reforms began officially with the Third Plenum of the Eleventh Party Congress in December of 1978, when the new leadership gave its blessing to the initial stages of the decollectivization of agriculture and the expanded scope of the market. Significant roots of reform can, however, be traced back to the years 1970–8, not only in the US–China diplomatic break-through and China's resumption of its place in the UN Security Council in 1970–1, but also in the rapid expansion of China's foreign trade, the agricultural modernization agenda from the 1970 North China Agricultural Conference, and the putative end of the Cultural Revolution with the 1971 death of Defence Minister Lin Biao, Mao's designated successor.

The centrepiece of post-Mao reform nevertheless was agricultural decollec-tivization and market opening, which proceeded by fits and starts between 1978 and 1982. Although land ownership continues to reside primarily in the village to this day, individual households were permitted to sign contracts that afforded them effective control over the management, output and marketing of agricul-tural production in exchange for payments in the form of crops and labour to the village, and taxes in kind to the state, as discussed in Peter Ho's chapter 4. China's thirty-year experiment in collective farming was in essence repudiated in favour of a return to family farming, officially styled the Household Responsibility System (HRS). With pressures from below from villagers and some cadres to expand the scope of market, mobility and household activity, and with increasing doubts at the centre concerning the viability of collective agriculture, in just a few years virtually the entire countryside had dismantled collective agriculture in favour of some form of household contracting that restored the primacy of the family farm. In 1984, these contracts were deemed valid for fifteen years; in 1993, they were extended to thirty years; and in 1998, President Jiang Zemin announced that contracts would remain in effect for at least an additional thirty years.

Alongside the HRS, the state sanctioned free markets, encouraged diversifica-tion of rural enterprises in the form of small-scale industry and handicrafts, relaxed restrictions on rural–urban migration, and substantially boosted state procurement prices for agricultural products in an effort to jump-start the rural economy. In each of these instances, the state now responded positively to pres-sures from below for the expanded scope of household and market that had built up throughout the era of anti-market collective agriculture. The immediate results of this policy package, which included far more than decollectivization, were a huge spurt in agricultural output and the first major gains in rural income since the start of the collective era a quarter of a century earlier. As farmers regained control of their labour power and the state relaxed prohibitions on markets and sideline production, rural labour and capital swiftly flowed in new channels and villagers experienced new earning opportunities.[3]

This did not constitute a complete break with the revolutionary era, however. Not only did land ownership continue to reside in the village, but there was also continuity in the managerial role of collectives, notably in directing rural industry and sideline production. The household economy had in fact never completely disappeared in Mao's China, as most families continued to cultivate individual plots of land at the margins of the collective economy. Hence founda-tions for reform existed in embryonic form throughout the countryside.

Perhaps the most dynamic response to the new opportunities presented by reform was the growth of township and village enterprises (TVEs) that mushroomed across the countryside. Many of the TVEs had their roots in earlier commune and brigade industries, but in the reform era under relatively open market conditions – including access to international markets and capital, and the infusion of migrant labour – they injected unprecedented dynamism into rural industry, notably in coastal and suburban regions. Over time, many of these collectively owned and operated enterprises have converted into share-holding companies (*gufen gongsi*) or private firms or joint ventures, including some with foreign investment.

Demand for labour mobility went hand in hand with pressures to relax the household registration (*hukou*) system that had segregated citizens by rigid categories designed to forestall rural-to-urban migration as well as to deter movement up the hierarchy of urban centres. Reform generally has allowed people the freedom to change their place of work and residence. But as 'outsiders' in the city or in richer agricultural areas, migrants face formidable official and unofficial restrictions in their new domicile and remain ineligible for many benefits enjoyed by those with legal urban registration. Despite the important contributions that migrant workers have made to China's economic growth, the state continues to view them as second-class citizens, a 'floating population' and a potential source of unrest, and denies them most of the benefits of urban registration. As their numbers soared into the range of fifty to one hundred million people in the 1980s, permanent urban residents also came to see the migrants as a source of crime and, increasingly, as a threat to their own jobs.

While economic and social transformations in much of the countryside were remarkably swift and far-reaching, urban industry proved more resistant to change. Because the state, rather than lower-level collectives, owned and operated the major urban factories, and depended heavily upon them as its primary source of revenue, it was wary of changes that might undermine its power economically and politically or call into question its important social base among the urban workers who had been among the major beneficiaries of the revolution. In particular, state leaders feared that moves which jeopardized the security and welfare benefits of workers at state-owned enterprises (SOEs), could precipitate widespread labour unrest. By contrast, villagers had enjoyed comparatively few state or other welfare benefits and were tightly controlled under the collective. From the late 1970s, as pressures mounted across the countryside to expand the scope of market and mobility and to curb the collective, workers in the city frequently resisted tendencies associated with reform as a direct threat to their income, security and prestige.

Comparable phenomena of reform pressures emanating from the rural collective sector, accompanied by a coolness towards reform in state enterprises and cities, were evident in Vietnam in the 1980s and 1990s. By contrast, Soviet collective farm workers, who had gained the security and welfare benefits of industrial workers, staunchly resisted reforms that would weaken or eliminate collective farming.[4]

The initial suspicions of Chinese labour proved prescient. Not only did reform bring few gains to SOE workers, it also meant that industrial labourers lost status to rising entrepreneurs and eventually that millions lost lifetime employment and even such welfare benefits as pensions that they had worked a lifetime to secure. Many who retained their jobs were required to sign contracts with their employers, frequently for five years, thereby severing the promise of lifetime employment. Neither the long-promised conversion of SOEs to share-holding corporations nor the forced bankruptcies of inefficient enterprises have yet to materialize fully, but with economic growth having slowed in recent years, massive layoffs have ensued nonetheless. Older and women workers have borne the brunt of dislocation and unemployment among SOE workers. Competition with joint ventures and private companies has further threatened the once hege-monic status of state industry.

The gap separating rich and poor, both between and within regions, has grown apace under the reforms. In contrast to industrial relocation to poorer and peripheral regions during the Mao era, Deng Xiaoping's reform heavily favoured coastal over inland areas with state investment and privileged access to international capital and markets. And in contrast to earlier class levelling, reformers promoted and exalted the new rich. Indeed, by the 1990s some analysts concluded that China in the course of a few decades had moved from the ranks of the world's most egalitarian societies to one of the most unequal in its distribution of income, wealth and opportunity.[5] Although Jiang Zemin's ambitious programme to develop the western interior was designed to redress this imbalance, few resources appear to have been allocated to the programme, and the coastal areas continue to outstrip most inland regions. Deng Xiaoping's famous adage that 'to get rich first is glorious', has left many of the less fortunate distraught, angry and wondering if their time will ever come. Such economic and social inequalities may be multiplied by distinctions of gender and ethnicity. In a context in which increased mobility and greater media access have height-ened awareness of income differentials and lavish conspicuous consumption, these disparities could prove explosive.

Reform has been accompanied by a relaxation of controls over economy and society in many, but hardly all, spheres. Indeed, in certain arenas the reach of the state has extended in the course of the reform era. To ensure that economic gains are not entirely consumed by an ever-burgeoning population, since the 1970s the state has imposed strict birth-control regulations, thus reaching directly into the nuclear family to regulate reproduction. In the face of an age-old preference for many children, especially sons whose responsibility is to assure the welfare of parents in their old age and continue the family line, the state acted vigorously to ensure that couples limit themselves to a single offspring. The single-child policy is fraught with profound implications and complications for a society whose core cultural values are based largely on kinship relations and an emphasis on the filial obligation to assure family conti-nuity through future generations, an act that requires a male offspring. The single-child policy achieved considerable success in the cities, where most families could rely on state or collective pensions to provide for them in retire-ment. But in the countryside, where no such welfare regime existed, the one-child policy posed agonizing choices for households, generating fierce resistance that took such forms as flight to give birth to a second or higher child, female infanticide and, at times, murder of cadres or family members of cadres who had imposed forced abortions or sterilizations. As Tyrene White demonstrates in chapter 8, rural-centred resistance would eventually force the state to relax the one-child policy to permit a second child when the first is a girl. Conflict and resistance surrounding the state's aggressive population control policies continue nevertheless.

It is commonly asserted that, despite far-reaching economic and social reform, China's political system remains frozen. Many of the contributions to this volume suggest otherwise. In part to alleviate the uncertainties and anxieties that accompanied head-spinning changes in both the economic and social arenas, the state initiated sweeping legal reforms. A revised constitution promulgated in 1982 was followed by codes that provide guidelines on a host of issues ranging from labour relations and intellectual property rights to the environment and commerce. A massive education campaign has been launched to publicize the new regulations. Mediation and arbitration offices, as well as the courts, have been beefed up to handle the escalating number of disputes in an effort to defuse conflicts that might otherwise produce violent confrontation. This is but one important sphere in which political and social relations are being redefined by a combination of state reforms and the expanded exercise of citizen rights, as chapters by Peter Ho, Jun Jing, Ching Kwan Lee, Hein Mallee, Minxin Pei, Wang Zheng and David Zweig reveal from diverse angles.

In keeping with its professed commitment to honour legal claims, symbolized by China's signing of international covenants on economic, social and cultural rights as well as on civil and political rights, the state has announced support for religious freedom (albeit only for officially recognized and registered groups), cultural autonomy for ethnic minorities (that is, for officially classified nationalities), and limited processes of democratization such as village elections. The results, however, are sometimes contradictory. Not all groups have experienced expanded religious or cultural space. As Uradyn E. Bulag shows in chapter 10, for minority nationalities facing pressures for assimilation, the reform era has brought the erosion of autonomous rights. The Chinese state has also enlarged the scope of official tolerance for intellectual activities in literature, the arts, scholarship and journalism. Yet the relationship of intellectuals to the state is no less ambiguous than it was during the Mao era, as discussed by Geremie Barmé in chapter 2. In practice, official guarantees are periodically circumscribed, at times harshly, primarily out of security concerns, but also in response to concerns over 'cultural pollution' – the importing of deleterious alien concepts and ideas that might undermine officially approved values. Suspicion of subversive, separatist, sectarian or even 'superstitious' activities has repeatedly elicited draconian state responses. The harsh repression campaign against the quasi-Buddhist sect, *Falun Gong*, follows decades of attempts to control unauthorized Christian and other religious activities as chapters 11 and 12, by Patricia Thornton and Richard Madsen respectively, detail. Nevertheless, the combination of broad new legislation, changing social relations, and the thrust and counter-thrust of resistance and repression has exerted a significant political impact. And what are arguably the three most far-reaching changes in politics and society are largely invisible. First, since the late 1970s, the state has abandoned the mass mobilization campaigns that were the hallmark of Chinese politics in the Mao era. Second, the state has withdrawn from direct control of large areas of the economy in both urban and rural areas, thereby sharply reducing its ability to dominate the lives of ordinary people. Third, it has permitted expanded migration and mobility.

The highly touted elections for village committees illustrate both the logic and limits of political reform. Centrally sponsored democratic elections have apparently been successfully conducted in about half of China's nearly one million rural villages. But in a context in which opposition parties remain illegal, and the nomination process is closely monitored by Communist officials, such grassroots experiments exert minimal influence on the basic structure of power. Moreover, party secretaries, not village committees, still rule the countryside. The Communist Party retains a monopoly over key instruments of control: propaganda, personnel, military and police. The small officially sanctioned minority parties cultivated by the Communist Party throughout the People's Republic are pledged to loyalty to the ruling party. Publications are restricted by an elaborate system of party censorship, while the official ideology remains Marxism–Leninism–Mao Zedong Thought guided in practice by theories and leadership principles associated with Deng Xiaoping and his successor, Jiang Zemin. And in the wake of the party's crackdown on the protests of 1989, it has moved aggressively to control signs of the emergence of political opposition, for example by banning attempts a decade later to register a newly founded China Democracy Party.

Despite significant changes, an apparent disjuncture remains between the free-wheeling economic expansion, on the one hand, and the still highly circumscribed political climate, on the other. Bustling stock exchanges, shimmering skyscrapers, and *au courant* electronic modes of communication have not broken the grip of the omnipresent security system. In the decade since 1989, despite a plethora of strikes, protests and everyday resistance, no large-scale political movements have challenged party rule. If threats to state power have grown in the course of the reform era, the state has repeatedly demonstrated its ability to stymie attempts to generalize resistance across time and space. In fact, the forces of repression have grown in tandem with modernization, internationalization, and the new prosperity *for some*. The institution of the armed police (*wujing*) augments the public security bureau in maintaining order, and an espionage service once reserved for international assignments is now being deployed domestically down to the county level.

Conflict, cleavage, and contention

It is not surprising that the current situation, in which Maoist precepts are often neglected in practice but rarely formally negated, has seen the emergence of a polyphony of conflict and contention – among and between state authorities and elements of the populace. Although Maoism shared many features with Leninism and Stalinism, it was also distinctive in its avowed egalitarianism and populism, and in the contentious mobilization politics that it fostered in such periods as the Hundred Flowers Movement of 1956–7 and the Cultural Revolution (1966–76). One important legacy of the era of revolution is a residual sense of entitlement and a repertoire of protest strategies which extend to even the most remote parts of the countryside and to people of diverse social classes and nationalities.

Of course, popular protest long predated the initiatives associated with Mao Zedong. Chinese history boasts a record of resistance and rebellion second to none. Whether we survey Imperial, Republican or Communist periods, we can find ample evidence of defiance and dissent shading into rebellion and revolution. An intriguing question, therefore, concerns the degree to which recent events build (consciously or unconsciously) on earlier precedents. To what extent do the wellsprings of conflict and resistance in China today draw on patterns and practices of bygone days? To what extent have they changed in response to the imperatives of the reform era?

One important basis of comparison concerns the social composition of the participants. While historians in the People's Republic during the Mao years celebrated the class nature of popular protest in China going back to the earliest recorded uprisings (third century BC), analyses of Imperial-era protests by Western and some Chinese scholars have demonstrated the significance of lineages, villages and religious communities in structuring patterns of resistance. A debate has recently developed over whether new forms of community began to emerge in the late Imperial and early Republican periods (and whether they have re-emerged in the post-Mao era), and whether they can best be understood as part of a nascent civil society or public sphere. Some stress a growing sense of citizenship among ordinary Chinese, particularly urbanites, as early as the final years of the Qing dynasty. Others argue that, under the influence of Western imperialism and domestic capitalism, a proto class consciousness developed that helped to fuel the Communist revolution and may be reappearing with growing class polarization of the reform era.[6]

In the post-1949 period, Mao insisted that class continue to command centre stage. Not only were land reform and nationalization of industry rooted in the logic of overcoming class exploitation, but Mao justified his Great Proletarian Cultural Revolution on the basis of the continued imperative of class struggle. The Cultural Revolution, however, was a class struggle of Mao's own distinctive formulation, one necessary to topple 'those in authority taking the capitalist road'; that is, the enemies of Mao and of socialism as he construed it.

In exploring the roots of cleavages and conflicts in the reform era, the authors of this volume break with stereotypical categories drawn from pre-land-reform society and from an era preceding the nationalization of industry to analyse anew the bases and structures of inequality within the People's Republic. They find that not only class, but also gender, ethnicity, generation and regional location constitute powerful sources of conflict and spurs to resistance in the reform era. These axes of contention intersect in ever changing and volatile ways. For example, as Wang Zheng and Ching Kwan Lee point out, large-scale layoffs of workers in state-owned enterprises in the 1990s were disproportionately directed against older women, while Hein Mallee underscores the discriminatory treatment of rural migrants to the city. Patricia Thornton notes the high rates of *Falun Gong* membership among elderly and laid-off workers, and Uradyn Bulag draws attention to the loss of Mongol autonomy within the reform framework. The chapters reveal how multiple intertwined factors shape social tensions and patterns of resistance.

This is not to suggest that the bases for conflict have been entirely reconfigured in the contemporary era. As Jun Jing, Peter Ho and David Zweig show, longstanding village and lineage loyalties continue to shape insurgent identities in rural China as social movements draw on themes and images sanctified by tradition even as they engage the consequences of reform. Patricia Thornton, Richard Madsen and Jun Jing demonstrate that popular religion and folk ideologies play pivotal roles in this process, with the beliefs and rituals surrounding local temples, churches, deities, spiritual masters, ancestral halls, and festivals often providing inspiration for collective mobilization. This may be the case even when the precipitant of protest, for example population relocation occasioned by the massive Three Gorges Dam project, is imbricated within a modernizing agenda associated with construction of the world's largest dam. In other words, traditional forms of contention are being revitalized in a new sociopolitical context framed not only by domestic reform but also by incorporation in global networks, sometimes creating new public spaces that are the product in part of new economic bases.

The recourse to claims rooted in history can take many forms. In the conflict between Mongols and Han Chinese, as Uradyn Bulag illustrates, the clash over land usage has been central for more than a century. Mongol pastoralism has long been pitted against Chinese agrarianism and, more recently, industrialism. To buttress their competing positions, both groups have staked claims to indigenous status in the area that is now Inner Mongolia. Countering Han Chinese claims to represent a modern 'civilizing mission', Mongols have turned to their own linguistic, cultural and historical traditions as wellsprings of resistance. Yet this longstanding dispute, which resonates with conflicts in other autonomous regions with large minority populations, has undergone substantial change in recent times as Chinese industries cast a covetous eye towards the natural resources hidden beneath the steppes and Mongols find themselves marginalized in the face of proliferating industries in their autonomous region. The widening economic gap between coastal cities and the interior provinces further inflames resentment that includes, but is not limited to, minority peoples.

Significant strains in contemporary popular protest can be traced back to Imperial- and Republican-era precedents. There are, however, compelling models much closer at hand. As Peter Ho shows, many of the land disputes that have recently erupted in rural China can be traced in large part to the structures and conventions of the collective era. Village communities now challenge earlier state and collective appropriation of their lands. Given the stark policy and value contrasts between the eras of revolution and reform, the former has come to stand as a convenient foil for many of the discontents of the latter, and protests often draw on themes and approaches honed during land reform, collectivization and the Cultural Revolution.

Thus, workers and women who find themselves disadvantaged by the industrial reforms are quick to remind authorities (with considerable irony) of Maoist slogans and promises: 'The working-class must lead in everything!' and 'Women hold up half the sky!' On occasion, as Ching Kwan Lee describes, workers even adopt Cultural Revolution style struggle tactics to press their demands against brutal or corrupt factory managers. And people of all classes, in bemoaning the rampant corruption of the present era, often recall nostalgically the high ethical standards and plain living of an earlier generation of revolutionaries.

The combination of seemingly ancient styles of protest with Maoist principles and practices can result in poignant and explosive expressions of discontent.[7] Take a case which occurred a few years ago in several provinces in Southwest China. A group known as the 'Heavenly Soldiers Fraternal Army' (*Tianbing dizijun*) recruited thousands of followers from more than one hundred villages. The group's leader, declaring himself a reincarnation of the Jade Emperor (a Daoist deity), practised shamanistic rituals of spirit possession and exorcism. His disciples pledged to fight for a new, divine regime free from social classes, authorities, grades and ranks, and the like. If the popular religious elements have a seemingly venerable pedigree, the commitment to rid China of all forms of inequality is an obvious throwback to Cultural Revolution rhetoric.

In another intriguing resistance movement, a 29-year-old peasant leader claimed to be Mao Zedong's son who had come to lead a rural uprising. The would-be Mao penned treatises on the 'thirty great relationships' (Mao Zedong had limited himself to ten) and assumed the titles of party chairman, military commission chair, state chairman, political consultative conference chair and premier, again surpassing Mao in the range of his official titles. He also sent letters to various government offices praising the radical ideas of the Gang of Four, attacking Deng Xiaoping's market socialism, and calling for armed rebellion, student boycotts and workers' strikes.

Even in what would appear to be the most 'traditional' of peasant uprisings, the slogans have a distinctly 'modern' ring to them. Take the case of a rebellion that got underway in the mid-1980s along the Yunnan–Guizhou border after its leader claimed – in the manner of Hong Xiuquan, commander of the Taiping Rebellion, the great millenarian uprising that rocked China in the mid-nineteenth century – that he had dreamed of an old man with a white beard who lent him a sacred sword. The contemporary insurgents slaughtered a chicken and swore a blood oath in the ancient manner of Chinese rebels, but alongside the age-old slogan of 'Steal from the rich to aid the poor', they emblazoned their battle banners with new mottoes: 'Support the left and oppose the right!' and 'Down with birth control!'

The syncretism of these recent movements is surely due in part to the quasi-religious dimensions assumed by the cult of Mao during the Cultural Revolution. Political rituals of that era, such as recitation of the *Little Red Book of Mao Quotations* and performance of loyalty dances, helped to blur the distinction between older forms of worship and new Communist practices. Moreover, collective loyalties fostered in that period can serve today as bases for resistance to higher-level state demands.

A theme that runs through many of the chapters in this volume is the pivotal – and often contradictory – role played by local authorities in relation to popular resistance. We find party officials articulating and defending the interests of retirees (Zweig), religious believers (Madsen) and land ownership rights (Ho) in their locality; union officials siding with disgruntled workers (C.K. Lee); birth control officials colluding with prospective parents (White); Mongol officials defending indigenous rights against the claims of Chinese migrants (Bulag); local officials leading villagers in demanding compensation from polluting enterprises (Jing), and so on. In short, while local officials frequently crack down on popular resistance, in numerous cases their leadership is instrumental in shaping, legiti-mating and articulating the demands of social movements, and in some instances in networking with state officials on behalf of local interests. It was, of course, precisely such leadership bifurcations that made possible the persistence and violence of the Cultural Revolution, and that lent strength to earlier rebel and revolutionary movements. Breaches in the loyalties of grassroots authorities are of enormous concern to the central government. Indeed, fears on the part of central leaders about renegade local officials help to explain Beijing's adoption of such policies as legal reform, anticorruption drives and village elections, which provide legitimate state-sanctioned channels to vent and adjudicate grievances. Yet, as Zweig reports, grassroots officials are often loath to respond to such insti-tutional initiatives. And as the *qigong* craze that nurtured *Falun Gong* clearly shows (Thornton), even central authorities may play a key role in encouraging beliefs and practices that are later deemed subversive.

The dramatic recrudescence of organized crime, often with police complicity, is another symptom of the contradictions and contentions that are products of reform. Active in both urban and rural areas on a scale unknown in the early decades of the People's Republic, criminal gangs oversee drug smuggling, traf-ficking of people, gambling and prostitution rings, extortion, robbery and more. The upsurge in such activities is attributable to several factors attendant upon the reforms: increased population mobility, high levels of surplus labour and unemployment, growing income disparities, access to previously unavailable economic resources, and declining civic values. Independent financial bases for criminals render government efforts at repression increasingly difficult – espe-cially when colluding officials also benefit.

Reform and the future of Chinese communism

Does the rich and multifaceted history of contemporary resistance, and the vast chasm between its revolutionary and pre-revolutionary origins on the one hand, and the emerging character of Chinese society on the other, augur the demise of China's reform-minded Communist Party? It is difficult to know whether 'liberal' initiatives, from economic reform to judicial reform to village elections, are serving to shore up, or to further erode, central government and party control. What is certain is that they are transforming the nature and terrain of state–society relations, leading some analysts to see the emergence of a 'soft authoritarianism' and even to speak of the advance of democratizing processes within the Chinese polity. Despite the fact that the Communist Party retains *de facto* veto and *de jure* power over the enforcement of laws and electoral results, reform measures have opened new space for expressing local interests and checking arbitrary abuses.

Particularly telling is the retreat of the state from direct control over many aspects of life and labour. The day-to-day economic activities of one billion villagers are no longer micromanaged by collective and commune officials, as people turn their energies to farming, industrial or sideline activities, undertake to organize family or joint enterprises or migrate far from home.

As Minxin Pei and David Zweig explain, legal reforms have set limits on state prerogatives at the same time that they have encouraged greater expectations about, and provided an institutional framework for, the protection of rights among the populace at large. The growing numbers of lawsuits filed against government and party officials in the 1990s are symptomatic of this emergent sense of entitlement. Moreover, the significant number of strikes and other clashes notwithstanding, labour and many other disputes are most commonly settled in newly established arbitration committees rather than in the streets. But laws, of course, are at least as useful to state authorities as to dissidents. The state security law, for example, sanctions the arbitrary arrest of anyone suspected of subversive motives, and efforts to create independent labour unions confront a legal structure that grants official unions a monopoly on representation.

Grassroots elections are also a two-edged sword for the state. State leaders hope that such procedures will help curb the corrupt excesses of local tyrants and thereby dampen the fires of rebellion in the countryside. Yet giving villagers an enlarged sense of their own political efficacy, and providing a public forum for open discussion of civic affairs, can also act to stimulate local resistance to higher-level dictates. At a 1999 local election monitored by the Carter Center, for example, voters vociferously protested a nomination process that they considered to have been rigged by party authorities.

While official elections have been closely watched in the West, the more important village activities are probably those sparked by the numerous new associations, ranging from religious and sectarian groups (Madsen, Thornton) to credit societies and cultural associations, that operate quite independently of the state. In the cities as well, as Geremie Barmé suggests, intellectuals who were preoccupied with issues of democratic transition and state authority in the late 1980s subsequently turned their attention to cultural discussions that seem quite removed from direct political confrontation. Yet such debates may of course also work to undercut party hegemony, as in the emergence of a 'new left' group that criticizes certain devastating social consequences of the reform agenda.

Internationalization

One of the most striking aspects of the reform era is the depth and multiplicity of China's engagement with the world. Whereas Cultural Revolution China was a relatively autarkic society, today China's links to the rest of the globe are extraordinarily dense. Foreign television programmes dominate the airwaves in even remote reaches of the countryside and American fast-food franchises dot the urban landscape. International capital defines leading sectors of economy and finance, and fuels China's explosive trade growth. Global fashions in everything from designer jeans to perfume to appliances make their presence felt in town and countryside alike. And pop music reverberates to the beat of Hong Kong and Taiwan musicians.

The implications of internationalization are far-reaching and contradictory. Access to the global market has placed fax machines, personal computers and Internet access within the reach of large numbers of people including intellectuals and activists, facilitating autonomous communication as well as contacts with foreign scholars, human rights organizations and the international media. It has also, however, simultaneously equipped the military and public security agencies with state-of-the-art electronic and communications technology. Thornton shows the significance of Internet technology to the growth of *Falun Gong* and other 'cybersects'. The new technology makes possible a growth in the information available to outsiders concerning Chinese domestic affairs while facilitating dissident communications. The expanded role of the international community in publicizing Chinese human rights abuses has been one outcome. But this does not begin to exhaust the implications. As Barmé indicates, the debates among domestic intellectuals and critics have been profoundly shaped by their exposure to international discourse, much of it via the Internet.

As foreigners assume a higher profile in China – whether as suppliers of capital and technology and purveyors of cultural and consumer styles, as human rights advocates, religious authorities, email correspondents, or simply as tourists – they inevitably alter the balance of power. Foreigners as well as Chinese sightseers streaming to religious centres, can trigger conflict within the state between public security officials concerned about maintaining social order and a cultural apparatus intent on promoting local traditions for economic as well as aesthetic reasons. The SARS epidemic has highlighted the challenges inherent in globalization. It has also triggered local protests by residents unhappy about the government's handling of the crisis.

Contradictions of reform

In short, the reforms have stimulated contradictory currents that elicit a melange of old and new responses. Strict birth control policies gave rise initially to tragic, yet historically familiar, practices of female infanticide and abandonment as desperate villagers sought to ensure that their one child would be a boy. However, as White shows, these tactics have been largely supplanted by new strategies such as sex-selective abortion, enabled by state-of-the-art ultrasound technology. Similarly, the protest against a dangerously polluting fertilizer factory, detailed by Jing, erupted only after a government medical team educated the villagers about the link between water pollution and birth defects. Sympathetic township officials not only sanctioned the worship of fertility goddesses to combat the pollutants, they also allowed village cadres to mobilize demonstrations forcing the fertilizer factory to solve the problems resulting from its wanton discharge of toxic waste and compensate the community for damages.

Relaxation of the household registration system, complementing the reform of agriculture and industry, has greatly complicated state control. Since the 1980s, migrant workers have provided the labour for many of the most productive and income-producing industries (Mallee). The option of flight from local authorities makes it much easier to evade the family planning policy (White). Migrant workers constitute a new source of labour unrest, notably in Special Economic Zones, like Shenzhen, where their numbers have skyrocketed (C.K. Lee). And the continued growth in the number of migrant workers at a time of rising urban unemployment brings into direct conflict the interests of urban and rural workers who once occupied different niches on the employment ladder, with migrants assuming jobs disdained by urban residents but also competing directly for jobs with laid-off urban workers (Mallee, Wang and C.K. Lee).

Whether using tested tactics from bygone days or innovative strategies of a new era, protests are seldom undertaken lightheartedly in contemporary China. The tremendous personal risk implicit in any confrontation with authority is a serious deterrent. Perhaps no action demonstrates this dilemma more poignantly than the ultimate recourse: suicide. In chapter 13 Sing Lee and Arthur Kleinman report that the number of suicides in reform-era China is extremely high. While the rate of suicides among certain categories of people almost certainly reached even more dizzying heights during the Cultural Revolution, the current figures – based for the first time on valid data – are of particular concern inasmuch as they indicate patterns rarely found elsewhere in the world. The victims fall into two high-risk groups: young, rural females, and elderly men and women. It cannot be determined on current evidence alone whether this is a new pattern or a continuation of one found in earlier Chinese history; but the contemporary precipitants of suicide do seem to be closely connected to local social problems brought on or intensified by the reform era.

Resistance, revolution and China's future

Along with rising per capita incomes and remarkable affluence for some, China's reforms and their attendant economic growth have brought anxiety and anguish to many. What does this situation augur for the future of state–society relations? Is Chinese society a ticking time bomb, about to detonate the Communist state?

Have the wide-ranging patterns of resistance and pressures for change from below generated a fundamental transformation in popular consciousness or in the state–society relationship? Or are the manifestations of discontent so small, scattered and (in some cases, literally) suicidal as to pose little threat to the survival of the political system?

Social science theories provide few signposts that allow us to specify with confidence the conditions under which social conflict may become politically destabilizing and even regime-threatening. Individual personalities and historical contingencies – factors that remain stubbornly immune to the best predictive efforts of social scientists – play a decisive role in translating popular unrest into political challenge or political and social transformation.

As this volume indicates, there is plenty of dissatisfaction in contemporary China, some of it attributable to grievances built up during the earlier Mao era, but much traceable directly or indirectly to the effects of the reform policies. The very economic successes of these policies have encouraged 'rising expectations' that could (*à la* Crane Brinton) not only spark protest but might ultimately prove revolutionary.[8] Moreover, the growing gap between greater and lesser beneficiaries of the reforms has clearly fostered among the less fortunate a sense of 'relative deprivation' (*à la* Ted Robert Gurr)[9] that generates not only individual frustration but may also, at times, lead to collective violence. If the economy were to suffer a sudden downturn after its steep gains of recent years, as eventually it surely will if history is any guide, it would then resemble James Davies' 'J-Curve'[10] – a situation said to be replete with revolutionary potential. And China's high-speed growth has produced deepening class polarization, the very outcomes that Karl Marx pinpointed as the prerequisites for resistance and revolution.

The chapters in this volume present evidence of all of these patterns at work, giving rise to diverse forms of everyday resistance as well as strikes, protests, riots and other types of organized and unorganized protest. Does this mean that China stands poised at the brink of revolution, auguring the overthrow of the Chinese Communist Party and a passage either into system disintegration and civil war or reunification under another political banner? The problem with the diverse theories sketched briefly above is that, while suggestive for analysing the psychological and material roots of protest, resistance, rebellion and revolution, none specifies the threshold point at which popular aspirations and grievances gain sufficient momentum to become politically threatening. Thus, however useful the theories may be in offering explanations for what occurred after the fact, and in drawing attention to areas of conflict and potential resistance, they offer little predictive value.

Approaches that focus on the state, more than the societal, side of the revolutionary equation (Charles Tilly, Theda Skocpol, Jack Goldstone, Mark Lupher)[11] direct our attention to critical issues of state capacity to administer and to repress. Revolutionary outcomes are contingent not only on social discontent, but also on the ability to mobilize people and resources effectively to exploit state weakness and ineptitude, and state capacity to counter such challenges. Here we move beyond the psychological to the political arena, but still without a clear vision – until we attain the vantage point of twenty-twenty hindsight – of the actual dividing line between state capacity and incapacity.

What is striking is the fact that for all the popular anguish and the variety and depth of contemporary protest, to date no significant organizational focus, whether enshrined in a political party or social movement, has emerged at the regional, national or even local level effectively to challenge Communist Party leadership. Moreover, the Chinese state has important residual strengths. In contrast, for example, to the Soviet-imposed regimes of much of Eastern Europe, China's Communist Party led a popular resistance against Japanese invasion en route to the founding of the People's Republic. And in contrast to the Communist-led regimes that collapsed or were overthrown in Eastern Europe in the late 1980s and 1990s, China's Communist Party can claim credit for several decades of rapid economic growth and income gains. The result has been growing international power and prestige as China assumes a wider role as a regional and in certain respects even a global power. This heightened international profile, in turn, strengthens the state's hand in dealing with certain types of protests; in the wake of 11 September 2001, for example, China gained US approval in its war against secessionist elements in Xinjiang, now labelled as Islamic 'terrorists'. And the initially hostile Bush administration has actively courted China's support for its 'war on terrorism' in general, and its attempts to counter Iraq and North Korea in particular.

Equally important has been the Communist Party's ability to absorb some of the most powerful complaints of its critics without yielding its grip on state power. The state has accommodated demands for expanding the market and the private sector as well as enlarging the scope of the legal system and sponsoring village elections. Nevertheless, far from quelling social protest, these achievements associated with the reform agenda have arguably stimulated it.

Recently, analysts have advanced a triad of concepts to account for the emergence of powerful social movements: political opportunity structure, mobilizational networks and collective action 'framing' (or cultural/symbolic interpretation).[12] This 'political process approach' has sensitized scholars to a wider array of relevant factors in generating social movements, ranging from the political climate and social connections to symbolic constructions. Like earlier theories, it offers scant likelihood of forecasting the outcomes of social protest. It does, however, draw attention, in assessing the salience of social movements, to the need to examine not only the nature and levels of discontent in society or the strength, resources and flexibility of the state, but also the concrete opportunities, organizations and outlook of would-be protesters.

The chapters of this volume provide insight into all of these dimensions. In terms of opportunities, we learn for example about ways in which ordinary people have taken advantage of new openings afforded by the legal reforms to press previously untenable claims against officials. In terms of organization, we discover the continuing importance of lineage and village membership in structuring a range of activities from environmental protests to tax riots, ethnic protests and demands for recognition of land rights, the honouring of pension agreements nullified by the privatization of industry and relocation compensation. In terms of outlook, we find that popular religion and historical myths, Maoist ideology and international discourse, sometimes intertwined in unexpected combinations, all play significant roles in inspiring and sustaining resistance, and in creating spaces autonomous from, and at times directly challenging, state power and discursive formulations (Bulag, Jing, Zweig, C.K. Lee, Thornton, Madsen, Barmé).

At present, these diverse strains of resistance take the form of single-issue conflicts over jobs (C.K. Lee, Wang), land (Ho, Zweig), reproduction (White, S. Lee and Kleinman), the environment (Jing), ethnic self-determination and equality (Bulag) and other matters of concern to a specific subset of the population. Resistance movements are for the most part small, local and isolated from one another, lacking interconnective ideological and organizational bonds. The fragmentation of the Chinese economy, with the decollectivization of agriculture and the increasing privatization of industry, has brought greater social segmentation as well. As the living and working conditions of various groups of Chinese citizens become increasingly heterogeneous, their relations to – and dissatisfactions with – the demands of state and market diverge accordingly. Consequently, the laments of laid-off workers do not readily resonate with the outcries of over-taxed farmers or the complaints of critical intellectuals, or the protests of minority nationalities or women. Facing very different dilemmas, these diverse groups among today's protesters frame their grievances and demands in distinctive terms that do not easily transcend the barriers of class, region, gender, religion, nationality or educational level. Still less has resistance taken the form of a significant political party or social movement that transcends a single locality, addresses multiple issues or offers a comprehensive ideological or organizational challenge to Communist Party rule.

New Social Movement theory (as developed by Alberto Melucci, Alain Touraine and others) celebrates the cultural creativity and tactical virtuosity born of such diversity.[13] The post-modern condition, they tell us, is inherently fragmented. Even globalization, indeed precisely globalization, breeds localization. At the same time, however, the annals of Chinese history stand as a reminder of the power of social cooperation. Alliances among previously disparate categories of intellectuals, farmers, workers, women, youths, minorities and so forth have served as the building blocks for influential protests, some of which eventually toppled the reigning order, from imperial rebellions through the revolution of 1911 to the Communist revolution of 1949.

To be sure, such mergers may harbour the seeds of hegemony in which 'liberation' from the ancient regime can mean an even more repressive and preemptive fate in the hands of the victors. A party that rides to power on the waves of mass mobilization, while claiming to represent the will of the people, may rule in the interests of a limited few. Nor is revolutionary victory any guarantee that a nation locked in the grip of poverty will improve its position within the hierarchical order of inequality of the world economy, still less that it will shake that international order to its roots. Nevertheless, diverse alliances are the *sine qua non* of politically consequential social movements. And the paucity of such connective webs in the case of recent Chinese protests bespeaks a fundamental weakness in their capacity to challenge state power beyond the realm of the single issues and local grievances that remain their strength.

Of course, the absence of ecumenical movements in contemporary China is hardly accidental. As astute students of their own history, Chinese leaders are perfectly aware of the dangers inherent in cross-class, cross-nationality and cross-regional associations. Since the founding of the People's Republic, attempts to forge such bonds have been dealt with swiftly and severely. The crackdown against *Falun Gong* that began in the summer of 1999 follows in the tradition of suppression efforts that include the suppression of sectarian movements in the early 1950s, the Anti-Rightist Campaign of 1957, the crushing of Cultural Revolution rebels in 1968, the closing of Democracy Wall in 1979 and the June Fourth Massacre of 1989, among others. In all of these instances, repression was a response to state fears that protest could give rise to inter-class and inter-regional connections, and in the case of *Falun Gong*, to international connections as well.

This is not to say that state–society relations have remained frozen throughout the duration of the Communist era. Far from it. The revolution itself generated fundamental social changes, destroying the power of landlord, merchant and industrial classes, undermining the status and influence of intellectuals, raising the status of the industrial working class while curbing its political autonomy and elevating the new cadre class, dividing city from countryside, and reorganizing agriculture on collective foundations as well as industry on state foundations, to the detriment of China's villagers. The socioeconomic transformations of the reform era have been equally powerful. Despite the survival of the single-party system, the situation today differs markedly from that which prevailed during the Mao era. And nowhere is this difference more obvious than in the realm of popular protest. A 1998 press account captured the distinction in an article whose headline read 'Emboldened Chinese take their complaints to the streets':

> About 200 demonstrators blocked traffic in the central Chinese city of Changsha this week protesting over not getting paid in the past six months by a local, formerly state-owned company. The police showed up to help unsnarl traffic, but not to intervene in the demonstrations.
>
> Last week 200 angry investors who lost their savings in a government-linked futures trading scheme marched to Tiananmen Square and demanded their money back. Police formed a line between them and the square, but allowed them to pass peacefully.
>
> … From striking cab drivers to disgruntled farmers, more and more people are taking their economic frustrations to the streets of China … Instead of beating and arresting protesters as they might have some years ago, officials seem more willing these days to accommodate, negotiate or simply pay them off. As long as demonstrators don't make personal attacks

against top leaders or demand political change, they are often free to vent their anger.[14]

As the chapters in this volume make clear, demonstrations are but one weapon in a vast arsenal of resistance and protest techniques that include legal challenges and silent pressures on the sociopolitical system in defence of enlarged claims by diverse groups. In recent years, incidents of worker protest have been legion, and in some instances the state has permitted and legitimated protest directed towards local officials and private capital even as it seeks to create non-confrontational channels for resolving conflicts.

Although popular unrest in China – in the twenty-first century as in the third century BC – *could* result in regime change or even revolution, it could also be managed by adept state leaders in such a way as to under*pin*, rather than under-*mine*, their rule. Jiang Zemin's ability to ride the waves and coopt or silence myriad protests in the course of his remarkable decade-plus tenure as General Secretary of the Chinese Communist Party reflects in large part his adroit handling of social protest.

Jiang's divide-and-rule approach to social unrest was already apparent before he took over the reins of central power. In the winter of 1986–87, when Jiang was still mayor of Shanghai, a wave of student protests swept across the city. The fuse for these demonstrations was a rock concert by the American group Jan and Dean, which had recently performed before a packed and appreciative crowd at the Shanghai Stadium. During their concert, the rock group invited members of the audience – most of whom were college students – to dance in the aisles and on the stage if they felt so inspired. When several students responded to this invitation with more enthusiasm than the Shanghai police could stomach, they were hauled outdoors and beaten. Fellow students, and then workers, soon poured into the streets to protest police brutality. On the mayor's order, barricades were erected at People's Square to discourage workers from entering the ranks of the student protesters. To defuse this potentially explosive situation, Jiang Zemin went in person to the university of the students who had been roughed up by the police to deliver an apology on behalf of the city government. He explained to an all-campus assembly that the police had mistaken the *students* for *workers*, which was why they had reacted so harshly! Even more surprising in this 'workers' state' was the fact that the professors and students in attendance apparently found nothing inappropriate in the mayor's explanation.

Jiang Zemin's strategy of divide and rule – successfully pitting one social group or one level of government against another – won him the attention of Deng Xiaoping. And, after being tapped for central leadership during the 1989 protests, Jiang Zemin put this strategy to effective use in dealing with a wide range of potential challenges. The state has dealt extremely harshly with movements (e.g., *Falun Gong* and the China Democracy Party) that boast a socially and regionally diverse membership, whereas it has shown considerable leniency toward conflicts – such as strikes by workers at a single factory or tax riots by farmers in a single village – that are more homogeneous in membership and locale. Indeed, the government has even endorsed and encouraged some single-issue protests (e.g., the student demonstrations against the US bombing of China's Belgrade embassy in the spring of 1999). Effective as these strategies have been, there is some question as to how long they can be sustained in the face of growing unrest – or indeed whether, in the absence of reforms that address the most pressing social grievances – Jiang's successors will be able to isolate and divide various groups of protesters.

Under the reforms, as the state assumes less responsibility for running the economy, it has become more willing to tolerate economic criticism and worker protest – so long as these remain localized and do not challenge central authority. Demonstrations over back wages, lost investments, the deprivation of retirement benefits and so forth are less apt to elicit harsh state repression and more likely to gain a sympathetic hearing from central authorities than was true in Mao's China. Only when such protests spill over state-sanctioned boundaries, as was true in the spring of 2002, when more than a dozen factories in Liaoyang went out on strike simultaneously, are they certain to draw swift and strong state suppression. Public outbursts serve as important signals to a government whose reform programme is very much a work in progress, seeking to navigate the shoals of sharply conflicting and potentially destablilizing class and group interests in a period of explosive social change.

The establishment in recent years of hundreds of thousands of arbitration committees to resolve labour disputes is an important sign of the state's attempt to regularize channels of economic conflict in the face of a firestorm of labour discontent among the former core of the working class, state sector employees. Advocates of reform in the All-China Federation of Trade Unions, the Ministry of Civil Affairs and other official agencies have argued that demonstrations, arbitrations and village elections not only provide a safety-valve for disgruntled citizens, but also serve as correctives to misguided policies and corrupt lower-level administration. Nonetheless, the Communist Party's virtual monopoly on power and the weak institutional foundations for citizens' rights to assemble and organize produce a situation in which the state periodically expands and contracts the terrain of protest and resistance.

The past 150 years of Chinese history, not least the half century plus of the People's Republic, has been a period of extraordinary contention. These years have witnessed the growth of diverse organized and unorganized challenges to state power, ranging from democratic, communist and anarchist movements to labour, peasant and nationality protests, and from religiously inspired uprisings to individual and private acts of everyday resistance. For their part, successive states have sought to maintain power by means of strategies ranging from fierce repression to cooptation and institutional adaptation. Periods of repression have often alternated with periods of relaxation, a pattern that has continued through the reform era.

China's reform leadership has presided over a time of rapid and far-reaching economic growth and equally profound social change. The pluralization of channels to wealth and power has given rise to new social formations and new political channels both independent of and interacting with the Communist Party. The party's willingness to welcome private entrepreneurs to its ranks is recognition of this rapidly changing sociopolitical scene. Diverse new social movements have responded to the imperatives of the day with new claims on the state and on private capital, some of which pose direct challenges to Communist Party rule. Like earlier regimes, China's reform leaders oscillate between the extremes of political repression and a willingness to tolerate local protest and social movements that do not directly challenge their own claims to power. But as they grope their way across the river of reform, the stones underfoot appear ever more slippery.

Notes

1   But see, in addition to the other contributions of authors in the present volume, Greg O'Leary (ed.), *Adjusting to Capitalism. Chinese Worker and the State* (Armonk: M.E. Sharpe, 1998); Xiaobo Lu and Elizabeth J. Perry (eds), *Danwei: The Changing Chinese Workplace in Historical and Comparative Perspective* (Armonk: M.E. Sharpe, 1997); David Zweig, *Freeing China's Farmers. Rural Restructuring in the Reform Era* (Armonk: M.E. Sharpe, 1997); Mark Selden, *The Political Economy of Chinese Development* (Armonk: M.E. Sharpe, 1993); Barrett McCormick and Jonathan Unger (eds), *China After Socialism. In the Footsteps of Eastern Europe or East Asia?* (Armonk: M.E. Sharpe, 1996); and Merle Goldman and Roderick MacFarquhar (eds), *The Paradox of China's Post-Mao Reforms* (Cambridge, MA: Harvard University Press, 1999).

2   See James C. Scott, *Weapons of the Weak. Everyday Forms of Peasant Resistance* (New Haven: Yale University Press, 1985) and *Domination and the Arts of Resistance: Hidden Transcripts* (New Haven: Yale University Press, 1990); Forrest Colburn (ed.), *Everyday Forms of Peasant Resistance* (Armonk: M.E. Sharpe, 1989).

3   On the nature and impact of the reform see, in addition to works cited above, Elizabeth J. Perry and Christine Wong (eds), *The Political Economy of Reform in Post-Mao China* (Cambridge, MA: The Council on East Asian Studies/Harvard University, 1985); Joseph Fewsmith, *Dilemmas of Reform in China. Political Conflict and Economic Debate* (Armonk: M.E. Sharpe, 1994); Barry Naughton, *Growing Out of the Plan. Chinese Economic Reform 1978–1993* (Cambridge: Cambridge University Press, 1995); Deborah Davis and Ezra Vogel (eds), *Chinese Society on the Eve of Tiananmen. The Impact of Reform* (Cambridge, MA: The Council on East Asian Studies/Harvard University, 1990); Stephan Feuchtwang, Athar Hussain and Thierry Pairault (eds), *Transforming China's Economy in the Eighties* (Boulder: Westview, 1988) 2 vols.

4   Mark Selden, 'After Collectivization: Continuity and Change in Rural China', in Ivan Szelenyi (ed.), *Privatizing the Land: Rural Political Economy in Post-Communist Societies* (London: Routledge, 1998); Benedict Kerkvliet and Mark Selden, 'Agrarian Transformations in China and Vietnam', in Anita Chan, Benedict Kerkvliet and Jonathan Unger (eds), *Transforming Asian Socialism: China and Vietnam Compared* (Melbourne: Allen and Unwin, 1999); Mark Selden, 'Pathways From Collectivization: Post-Socialist Agrarian Alternatives in Russia and China', in Barrett McCormick and Jonathan Unger (eds), *China After Socialism: In the Footsteps of Eastern Europe or East Asia?*

5   *China: National Human Development Report. Human Development and Poverty Alleviation 1997* (Beijing: United Nations Development Programme, 1998); Carl Riskin, Zhao Renwei and Li Shi (eds), *China's Retreat From Equality: Income Distribution and Economic Transition* (Armonk: M.E. Sharpe, 2001).

6   See, for example, the contributions to the symposium ' "Public Sphere"/"Civil Society" in China?', *Modern China*, 19 (3 April 1993); Jeffrey Wasserstrom and Elizabeth J. Perry (eds), *Popular Protest and Political Culture in Modern China*, 2nd edition

(Boulder: Westview, 1994); Deborah Davis, Richard Kraus, Barry Naughton and Elizabeth J. Perry (eds), *Urban Spaces in Contemporary China: The Potential for Autonomy and Community* (Cambridge: Cambridge University Press, 1995); Merle Goldman and Elizabeth J. Perry (eds), *Changing Meanings of Citizenship in Modern China* (Cambridge, MA: Harvard University Press, 2002). The debate was in part sparked by Jürgen Habermas's influential *The Structural Transformation of the Public Sphere: An Inquiry into a Category of Bourgeois Society* (Cambridge, MA: MIT Press, 1989) and by the movements of 1989 in China.

7　The following cases are drawn from Li Kaifu (ed), *Xingshi fanzui anli congshu – fangeming zui* (Compilation of Criminal Cases – Counter-revolutionary Crimes) (Beijing: Chinese Procuracy Press, 1992).

8　Crane Brinton, *The Anatomy of Revolution* (New York: Vintage, [1938] 1965).

9　Ted Robert Gurr, *Why Men Rebel* (Princeton: Princeton University Press, 1970).

10　James C. Davies, *When Men Revolt and Why* (New Brunswick: Transaction, 1997).

11　Charles Tilly, *From Mobilization to Revolution* (Reading, MA: Addison-Wesley, 1978); Theda Skocpol, *States and Social Revolutions* (Cambridge: Cambridge University Press, 1979); Jack A. Goldstone, *Revolution and Rebellion in the Early Modern World* (Berkeley: University of California Press, 1991); Mark Lupher, *Power Restructuring in China and Russia* (Boulder: Westview, 1996).

12　Doug McAdam, John D. McCarthy and Mayer N. Zald (eds), *Comparative Perspectives on Social Movements: Political Opportunities, Mobilizing Structures, and Cultural Framings* (Cambridge: Cambridge University Press, 1996).

13　Alberto Melucci, *Nomads of the Present: Social Movements and Individual Needs in Contemporary Society* (Philadelphia: Temple University Press, 1989).

14　*Baltimore Sun*, 20 November 1998, p. 34A. On the state's willingness to accommodate labour protesters, see also Philip P. Pan, 'An Experiment Begins', *Washington Post*, 5 November 2001, concerning a migrant worker's struggle in Tangxia, a small city not far from Wenzhou. Major protests were centred in the Daqing oil fields, the Maoist model of industry, Liaoyang and other industrial cities of the northeast that experienced large-scale layoffs. See the reports of the *China Labor Bulletin*.

Suggested reading

Ronald R. Aminzade *et al.*, *Silence and Voice in the Study of Contentious Politics* (New York: Cambridge University Press, 2001).

Thomas P. Bernstein and Xiaobo Lu, *Taxation without Representation in Contemporary China* (New York: Cambridge University Press, 2003).

Lucien Bianco, *Peasants Without the Party: Conflict and Resistance in Twentieth-Century China* (Armonk: M.E. Sharpe, 2001).

'China's Workers: Reform, Resistance and Reticence', *China Quarterly*, special issue, 170 (June 2002).

Edward Friedman, Paul G. Pickowicz and Mark Selden, *Revolution, Resistance and Reform in Village China* (forthcoming).

Doug McAdam, Sidney Tarrow and Charles Tilly, *The Dynamics of Contention* (New York: Cambridge University Press, 2001).

Elizabeth J. Perry, *Challenging the Mandate of Heaven: Social Protest and State Power in China* (Armonk: M.E. Sharpe, 2002).

Dorothy Solinger, *Contesting Citizenship in Urban China: Peasant Migrants, the State, and the Logic of the Market* (Berkeley: University of California Press, 1999).

1 Rights and resistance

The changing contexts of the dissident movement

Minxin Pei

Rights consciousness not only increases the frequency of resistance, but changes the forms of such resistance. The forms and tactics of democratic resistance have undergone significant changes since the late 1970s. While the dissident movement in the 1980s favoured direct and confrontational methods of resistance, the same movement in the late 1990s began to rely increasingly on indirect and legal means.

Although it is premature to evaluate the effectiveness of the new tactics, this chapter attempts to place the newly transformed dissident movement in political, institutional and social context. Rapid economic development has brought enormous changes to Chinese society and created a more hospitable environment for individuals to assert and protect their rights. Legal reform has opened a new legitimate political arena in which individuals, including political dissidents, can challenge the regime. Rising rights consciousness in Chinese society provides a social milieu within which invocations of rights are more likely to gain broad-based support. Finally, China's extensive and deepening integration into the international system in general, and its various commitments to international laws and institutions in particular, have placed leaders under new constraints and provided dissidents with new sources of moral support.

Oppression and resistance are symbiotic – one almost never occurs without the other. Even the most oppressive regime, such as the one portrayed in George Orwell's *1984*, fails to eradicate resistance completely. Although resistance – ranging from dramatic and sometimes violent confrontations with the authorities to 'everyday forms of resistance' may not succeed in overthrowing oppressive regimes, such acts of defiance help preserve individual dignity and set limits to oppression.[1] Those whose works celebrate resistance in all forms may have bolstered our faith in the strength of the human spirit. But at the empirical level, the scholarship on resistance has not shed much light on the precise relationship between oppression and resistance. We are not sure, for example, whether more oppression elicits greater resistance or vice versa; we know still less about the conditions that produce successful resistance.

This relationship poses an especially intriguing problem for social scientists because it is central to understanding the politics of reform in a liberalizing authoritarian regime. The most insightful contemporary observer of the French

Revolution, Alexis de Tocqueville, was perhaps the first to hint at a possible connection between declining oppression and growing resistance. In one of his most quoted passages in *The Old Regime and the French Revolution*, de Tocqueville wrote:

> The social order overthrown by a revolution is almost always better than the one immediately preceding it. Only consummate statecraft can enable a King to save his throne when after a long spell of oppressive rule he sets to improving the lot of his subjects. Patiently endured so long as it seemed beyond redress, a grievance comes to appear intolerable once the possibility of removing it crosses men's minds. For the mere fact that certain abuses have been remedied draws attention to the others and they now appear more galling; people may suffer less, but their sensibility is exacerbated.[2]

Tocqueville's formulation identifies a sudden change in the sensibility of the people as the cause for a dramatic fall in the public tolerance of the practices of the regime that used to be accepted with resignation. What Tocqueville called 'sensibility' seems very similar to 'rights consciousness' in the parlance of social scientists. Unfortunately, although he alerted us to the paradoxical effects of political opening by a softening autocracy, Tocqueville's own analysis overlooked other important issues on oppression and resistance: why rights consciousness rises quickly in an autocratic regime undergoing partial political opening; which specific factors contribute to this change; how changes in rights consciousness affect the forms and tactics of resistance; how changes in the balance of power or control of resources between the state and society may result from regime-initiated reform to produce a more favourable outcome in the contest between the regime and its societal opponents.

It is of theoretical and practical importance to raise these questions in analysing the changing relationship between the Chinese government and its citizens in general, and the evolving patterns of conflict between the ruling Chinese Communist Party (CCP) and its domestic critics in particular. For many students of Chinese politics have observed that, despite a considerable fall in the level of overt political repression since the late 1970s, resistance against the post-communist authoritarian regime persisted and may even have increased. In some cases, such resistance even took explosive and violent forms.[3] The most dramatic expression of resistance was, without doubt, the 1989 nationwide pro-democracy movement, with its focal point in Tiananmen Square, which posed the most serious threat to the survival of the regime in the post-Mao era. But the 1989 movement was a rare event (as was the violent repression unleashed by the regime in response). Most forms of post-Mao resistance did not directly endanger the existence of the ruling regime. There are few signs suggesting that popular resistance has reached such a level as to portend an imminent revolution. Nevertheless, despite the absence of revolution, China's limited reform has created enough public space to permit a small but tenacious dissident movement persistently to challenge the political legitimacy of the ruling regime.[4]

This chapter explores the factors that have indirectly contributed to the endurance, growth and change in resistance by China's pro-democracy activists. Such resistance must be understood in the overall context of the far-reaching institutional, socioeconomic and political changes that China has experienced since the 1980s. While no single cause should be credited with increasing the degree of rights consciousness of the Chinese people in general, including the dissident community, I argue that a multiplicity of factors has decidedly reshaped the contexts within which rights consciousness is engendered. More importantly, the changing contextual factors have not only influenced the emergence of new norms that give more specific meanings to certain rights, but have also reduced the institutional and structural barriers that previously impeded the full protection and exercise of such human rights, enabling resisters to adopt novel means of activism and defiance. In the first section of this study, I briefly discuss the idea of rights and the relationship between rights and resistance in the Chinese context. Then I trace the evolution of dissident resistance since reform began in 1979. Finally, I analyse the socioeconomic, legal, international and political–psychological contexts within which such resistance has been waged.

Rights and resistance

In theory, the relationship between rights and resistance appears straightforward: individuals or groups of individuals who feel either entitled to and/or endowed with certain fundamental rights may be expected to put up resistance when such rights are violated or perceived to be violated. The stronger the feeling of entitlement and/or endowment, the stronger the resistance. The more rights are claimed by individuals or groups, the more likely resistance will be triggered as government action infringes on them. In reality, however, the definition of rights, the degree of rights consciousness and the ability to secure rights are problematic and contingent on historical, cultural and political contexts within which such concepts are invoked. Students of Chinese politics and legal history, for example, have long noted some of the important differences in the meaning, nature, scope and utility of rights. According to Andrew Nathan, rights in contemporary China are derived from citizenship/membership instead of humanity, treated as programmatic goals instead of claims on government, restricted by state power, and unprotected by independent judicial review.[5] This restrictive conceptualization of rights creates apparent inconsistencies in rights practices. For example, even though Chinese constitutions grant extensive rights in theory, the state has maintained tight control over how these rights are exercised in reality.[6] The central goal of the extension of rights to individuals, moreover, is not the protection of individuals against the state, but the better fulfilment of duties to the state by individuals. This state-centred notion of rights, Nathan argues, is a product of Chinese obsession with a weak state since the mid-nineteenth century. Consequently, the strengthening of the state and the restoration of political order were viewed by Chinese rights thinkers as the more important collective goal.[7]

Other scholars have detected a strong influence of utilitarianism and collectivism on the Chinese conceptualization of rights. Chinese often conceive of rights as interests. An important political consequence of this conception is that political legitimacy does not derive from popular sovereignty but from the government's ability to serve the interests of the people. Another consequence is the inherent bias in this conception in favour of collective interests (rights) over individual rights (interests), especially if the two should come into conflict.[8] Thus, reciprocity becomes a central principle: an individual may possess and enjoy certain rights only to the extent that he or she has fulfilled certain duties to the community and the ruler.[9]

The conceptual differences between Chinese and Western notions of rights, however, must not be exaggerated. Even though such differences may influence rights practices, the extent to which rights are respected and protected may depend more on political conditions than on concepts of rights. In particular, the political milieu of a society may profoundly affect the degree of rights consciousness. Since rights consciousness is never static, individuals may assess the extent of the protection, exercise and enjoyment of rights on the basis of various political signals they receive from the governing elite, from the international environment, and from society in general. Therefore, the level of rights consciousness may be low when the possibility of rights protection and enjoyment is judged to be dim, and high when the same possibility improves. This reasoning may explain the paradoxical relationship between falling repression and rising resistance observed first by Tocqueville, whose insights provide a persuasive explanation for the patterns of repression and resistance in contemporary China.

If the Maoist era is identified with the most massive and systematic violation and curtailment of civil and political rights in Chinese history, the post-Mao reform era is a period in which the regime has tried to remedy its past excesses and has restored some basic rights to people. Formally, some of these rights were re-granted or reiterated in the revised Chinese Constitution (1982) and in many other laws. Informally, the regime has significantly expanded certain individual rights (such as most personal freedoms) while severely restricting some of the most important political rights (such as the freedom of political speech and association). Despite the limited nature of the improvement in the expansion and protection of rights, the enumeration of legal rights and promulgation of public policies have provided Chinese citizens important instruments of resistance against the government and its agents. The pioneering research by Kevin O'Brien and Lianjiang Li reported that peasants knowledgeable about specific government tax and procurement policies were able to protect their rights and interests more effectively.[10] Over time, out of China's new laws and policies have evolved implicit rules and norms that limit the scope and degree of oppression and abuse of power. For instance, persecution (such as imprisonment and physical abuse) of dissidents may occur routinely, but persecution of family members of dissidents has become almost taboo. This new norm enables family members of jailed dissidents to become open advocates of their personal causes, and to gain public and international support. Another newly established norm protects ordinary citizens who publicly protest against government administrative failures, abuse of power by lower-level officials, economic hardships and other shortcomings for which the government is held responsible (such as unemployment and financial scams). Citizens involved in these protests are not branded, as they once were, anti-government elements. Instead, their collective acts are frequently tolerated. They sometimes succeed in attracting official, even high-level attention and in obtaining at least a partial resolution of the problems that triggered the protests initially. This, together with increasing awareness of legal rights, may explain why collective protests by ordinary citizens increased dramatically in the late 1990s.

Dissident resistance in post-Mao China

Dissident movements in post-Mao China emerged and persevered in this dynamic environment. Democratic resistance accompanied Deng Xiaoping's reform in the late 1970s. To be sure, acts of defiance against the regime occurred during the Maoist era, such as during the Hundred Flowers Movement in 1957 and the early days of the Cultural Revolution. However, such collective, organized and public expressions of protest carried prohibitive costs and risks. Consequently, such modes of protest were favoured only in times of regime-sanctioned political campaigns or political turmoil.[11] In the post-Mao era, as the Dengist regime gradually loosened its grip on public political discourse and reduced the overall level of repression, political dissidents were emboldened to favour more organized and public forms of protest. In some instances, they tried to evoke new laws and procedures to legitimize their action.[12] Even though these tactics yielded mixed results and landed many dissidents in jail or exile, political dissent has gradually evolved, gained its own sources of support from within the fast-changing society, and become part of China's political landscape.

Dissident resistance: the early years

In the early years of reform, the embryonic dissident movement adopted a more direct and confrontational approach (though not comparable to that of the Red Guard groups of 1966–7), relying heavily on underground publications and mass demonstrations to challenge the Communist Party's monopoly of power. During this period (1978–89), the first sustained campaign of dissident resistance was the Democracy Wall movement in 1978–9. Although the movement initially began in Beijing, it soon spread to more than twenty major cities and continued for slightly more than two years. According to a veteran participant of the Democracy Wall movement, Hu Ping, underground publications mushroomed in these cities. At the peak of the movement, Beijing alone had over forty such publications, involving more than 2,000 people.[13] The crackdown on the Democracy Wall movement and the imprisonment of several of its main leaders (such as Wei Jingsheng and Xu Wenli) left the dissident community temporarily without leaders. In the hiatus between 1981 and 1986, dissident resistance was waged mostly under the protection of official covers. Pro-democracy activists were able to establish a presence on college campuses and in semi-official publications. Their intellectual influence was instrumental in fomenting the debate on political reform in the summer of 1986, which was soon followed by the student-led pro-democracy demonstrations that rocked several major Chinese cities at the end of 1986 and the beginning of 1987.

The 1986–7 movement was quickly crushed by the authorities, but with little bloodshed. Several political patrons of the liberal intelligentsia, such as CCP General Secretary Hu Yaobang and propaganda chief Zhu Houze, were dismissed. A handful of leading critics of the government (Fang Lizhi, the former vice-president of the Chinese University of Science and Technology) were blamed by the government for instigating student unrest and stripped of their party membership. In retrospect, however, the crackdown in early 1987 was both short-lived and limited in scope. The majority of liberal intellectuals and dissidents were unaffected. Two years later, they launched a third, and more costly, direct political challenge against the regime: the Tiananmen Square movement in the spring of 1989. The bloody end to the episode and, more importantly, the subsequent imprisonment and exile of many leaders of the Tiananmen movement dealt a severe, albeit temporary, blow to China's dissident community. In fact, it did not recover from the Tiananmen setback until the mid-1990s.

Dissent in the 1990s

The revival of the dissident movement in the mid-1990s may be attributed to many factors. Most importantly, the conservative attempt to reverse China's economic reform failed miserably and decisively in 1992 after Deng Xiaoping toured southern China and re-ignited economic reform. The decline of conservative elites and the strengthening of moderate reformers in Beijing created a more relaxed political atmosphere. Internal political considerations and external pressures led to the release of most of the leading dissidents (although some of the more prominent ones were forced into exile). Chinese society in the 1990s also became much more open and, as we shall see later, contained an increasing number of autonomous enclaves where resistance could be waged.

However, the renewed dissident resistance differed in important ways both from popular resistance by ordinary people (workers, peasants and urban residents) and from previous dissident resistance. Ordinary resistance in contemporary China seeks redress of routine instances of injustice for which victims hold the government and its agents responsible. Such resistance may take several forms. Individual acts of defiance may consist of filing petitions, staging sit-ins, lodging complaints, taking the government to court, or refusing to comply with official rules and policies.[14] While this type of resistance is observed daily and everywhere, there are no good data to measure its size, variety, causes and effects, chiefly because routine resistance seldom gets the type of media attention that is typically accorded to collective resistance by individuals and dissident resistance. A partial comparison between ordinary resistance and dissident resistance may thus be made by examining only the reported instances of resistance of both types. Official reports indicate that the number of collective protests was high – more than 32,000 incidents of significant size in 1999, even though only a small per centage of these incidents received media coverage (Table 1.1). News reports in the Chinese press and overseas dissident publications show that most such incidents were triggered by specific incidents, such as financial fraud involving relatives of senior government officials, non-payment of overdue wages, pensions and unemployment benefits, police brutality, and other forms of 'petty despotism'.[15] As a rule, ordinary resisters are likely to employ simple and direct forms of defiance. Their weapon of choice is street demonstrations, blocking major railways and highways, strikes, and even violent attacks on government buildings.[16] The targets of their protest are mostly local governments and state-owned enterprises. Rural residents are more likely to resort to collective protest and other direct or even violent means of defiance than urban residents, according to a survey of about 2,000 people by the State Planning Commission in 2001, even though the proportion of residents who chose such methods remained quite low. Among urban residents, about 12 per cent said that they would join collective petitions and another 2.4 per cent were willing to take part in strikes as preferred methods of seeking remedies for social injustice. By comparison, 20 per cent of the rural residents opted for collective petitions and 3 per cent indicated that they would join strikes.[17] But the risks of violent confrontation are high for ordinary resisters because their tactics focus on direct protest in public places and unavoidably come into contact with the police and security forces dispatched by the government to deal with them.

In comparison, dissident resistance was characterized by its peaceful nature. An analysis of the forty-nine reported instances of incidents from September to October 1998 (Table 1.2) shows that, as a sign of growing solidarity within the dissident community, nearly 40 per cent of the protest events were precipitated by the persecution of fellow dissidents. About 25 per cent of the incidents involved the declaration of rights and positions on major political issues. It should be noted that dissidents were also less fearful of waging organized resistance, as shown by the fact that attempts to register their opposition party and other groups comprised 20 per cent of the protest events. Even though most dissident protests involved a small number of participants (fewer than fifty),

Table 1.1   Rising numbers of collective protests, 1993–2000

Year	1993	1995	1997	1999	2000*
Number of collective protests of significant size	8,700	11,000	15,000	32,000	30,000

Source: Ministry of Public Security, Neibu canyue (Internal Reference), 10 August 2001, p. 18.

Note

* from January to March only

Table 1.2   An analysis of dissident resistance in September and October 1998
(49 reported incidents)

Causes of incidents	Number of participants	Type of participants	Forms of resistance	Targets/ intended audience
Persecution of fellow dissidents (20)	Fewer than 50 (35)	Known dissidents (39)	Open letter, appeals, declaration and protest (37)	Local government agencies
Rights/policy announcement (13)	50–100 (5)	Organized dissident groups (6)	Formal application (12)	Central government leaders (13)
Registration of opposition groups (11)	Unknown (6)	Family of members of dissidents (4)	Hunger strike (1)	Police/courts (10)
Declaration of candidacy (3)				International community and world leaders (6)
Other (2)				N/A (6)

Source: *Beijing Spring*, 63 (August 1998), pp. 100 other press accounts.

about one in five protests had over fifty participants. While street demonstrations were a favoured form of ordinary resistance, issuing open letters, appeals and declarations was the preferred tool of protest for dissidents. Filing formal applications was another frequently used tactic. Notably, dissidents eschewed the tactics of street politics and none of the protests was violent. Finally, dissident protests targeted not only central and local political leaders, but also an international audience. Chinese dissidents often appeal directly to world leaders (such as American Presidents Bill Clinton and George W. Bush) and representatives of international human rights organizations (such as the United Nations Human Rights Commissioner Mary Robinson) to seek their personal intervention.

This analysis suggests that Chinese dissident resistance towards the late 1990s was waged non-violently in the arenas of public relations and legal procedures. The immediate effects of dissident resistance were, however, not obvious, mainly because dissidents remained unable to expand their social bases of support or to mobilize workers and peasants. Even college students, who had been among the strongest supporters of the pro-democracy causes, had withdrawn from politics by the late 1990s. These adverse conditions did not appear to have discouraged the dissident community from continuing its resistance. Indeed, towards the end of the 1990s, Chinese dissidents had acquired more creative and sophisticated tactics, apparently to offset the disadvantages of the relative political and social isolation that was caused both by the regime's repressive measures and by a more consumerist and less politicized society. In the 1980s, Chinese dissidents tended to discuss and promote democracy at relatively abstract levels that appeared remote to the concerns of ordinary Chinese citizens. That elitist approach did not gain much sympathy or support from the working class even though it did attract significant support from the intelligentsia and college students (largely because these social elites were much more politicized in the 1980s than in the 1990s).

That is perhaps why, in the 1990s, the same dissidents began to pursue a two-pronged strategy: combining direct challenges to the regime with the adoption of certain populist causes (such as workers' rights, anticorruption and environmental protection) to gain public sympathy. Therefore dissidents continued to show their defiance directly, such as by declaring candidacy for local electoral offices (local people's congresses and village committees) and by attempting to register dissident groups.[18] Such efforts culminated in the formal declaration of the formation of China's first open opposition party, the China Democracy Party (CDP), in the summer of 1998. The 'provisional party charter' explicitly called for an end to the 'one-party dictatorship' of the Communist Party and advocated the promotion of justice, human rights, market reforms, freedom of religion and autonomy for ethnic minorities. Within four months, CDP claimed to have about 200 members in a dozen branches around the country (Guizhou, Henan, Beijing, Tianjin, Zhejiang, Shanghai, Liaoning, Jilin, Heilongjiang, Hubei and Shandong), and had secured broad and sympathetic international press in the USA and other democratic nations.[19]

The dissidents identified three political issues – corruption, patriotism and environmental protection – as top priorities that would enable them to galvanize public support as well as embarrass the government. Capitalizing on popular anger at rampant official corruption, some dissidents attempted to organize anti-corruption civic groups. In November 1998, a self-styled anticorruption fighter, Xiong Zhifu, announced a plan to visit several provinces to collect signatures on an anticorruption petition. After the former Politburo member Chen Xitong was secretly tried and sentenced to sixteen years in jail for corruption, seven dissidents in Zhejiang wrote an open letter to the People's Supreme Court demanding a live TV re-trial and a death sentence for Chen upon conviction. 'Corruption watch' groups established by dissidents sprang up in Hubei, Jiangxi and Gansu provinces.[20]

Sometimes dissidents packaged their protest activities as patriotic acts to embarrass the regime and reduce political risks. The most famous examples were their efforts to organize an unofficial movement to seek war compensation from Japan, to protest against Japan's occupation of the Diaoyutai Islands, over which China claimed sovereignty, and to demonstrate against the persecution of ethnic Chinese in Indonesia in 1998. In each case, the Chinese government was forced into a political dilemma because diplomatic considerations dictated a softer stance, which made it look weak and incapable of defending China's national interests. This created a rare opportunity for democratic resisters to score political points. While the Chinese government remained silent on the violence against ethnic Chinese in Indonesia in May 1998, forty-four dissidents signed a letter in July demanding that the Chinese government take a tough stand. In

August 1998, several hundred people staged demonstrations – the largest post-Tiananmen rallies – every day for two weeks in front of the Indonesian Embassy in Beijing to protest against Indonesia's treatment of ethnic Chinese. A written protest, signed by 240 people, was delivered to the Indonesian Embassy. It turned out that a quarter of the signers were relatives of the victims of the Tiananmen Square crackdown.[21] Embarrassing the government was an obvious objective. A hidden agenda of the dissidents was to use these unofficial patriotic events to develop an organizational base. This effort began with Bao Ge of Shanghai, who formed the 'All-China Alliance for Seeking Civil Damages from Japan', with several activists in Hubei, Fujian and Nanjing, in 1988. Its branch organizations sought, unsuccessfully, to register as civic organizations in Shanghai, Hubei and Nanjing. During the annual National People's Congress session in March 1993, Bao issued an open letter calling for a national referendum on the issue of seeking civilian war damages from Japan. Recounting this experience several years later, Bao said,

> On this issue (seeking war damages from Japan), we could hold public lectures at universities, conduct debates and invite international law specialists to answer legal questions. Eventually we would ask various places to send special petition groups to Beijing to ask the National People's Congress (NPC) to hold a national referendum on this important issue. This perhaps could have become an opportunity to rekindle China's democracy movement.[22]

Dissidents were also quick to champion the cause of environmental protection. After disastrous floods ravaged central China in August 1998, 309 prominent intellectuals and dissidents signed a letter openly blaming the government's policy for the floods. They called on the government to protect the environment along the Yangzi River, to publish accurate figures on the disaster (such as casualties and economic losses) and to punish the officials responsible for the disaster.[23] Fifteen dissidents donated 1,000 yuan to the flood victims.

The contexts of resistance

That Chinese pro-democracy activists were able to adopt various means of resistance owed significantly to the dramatic changes in the socioeconomic, legal and international context. Despite the tight control the regime maintained over the political sphere, market-oriented reforms and relaxation of restrictions on personal freedom provided dissidents modest but valuable resources to sustain their efforts of political resistance. Financially, some dissidents received support from overseas exiles and domestic private businessmen, allowing them to purchase much-needed equipment such as fax machines and personal computers. (The Chinese police claimed that the money for the Shanghai branch of the China Democracy Party – $1,000 – was sent from Fu Shenqi, an exiled dissident based in New York City.) Guo Ruoji, a professor of philosophy in

Nanjing who filed China's first lawsuit against the Communist Party, wrote his legal documents on an IBM computer which a private vendor sold him at a discount as a gesture of solidarity); the money paid for the computer was a $600 payment for an article Guo wrote for the Taiwan-based China Times Publishing Company.[24] Some dissidents operated commercial businesses to support themselves. Qin Yongmin, a Wuhan dissident, ran a small street stand. Peng Ming, who founded the China Development Union, was a successful private entrepreneur. Lin Hai, who was sentenced to two years in prison after he was convicted of illegally collecting and sending more than 30,000 email addresses in China to a New York based dissident Internet publication, owned his own software company in Shanghai.

Access to modern communications also enabled China's dissidents to maintain contact with each other and their overseas supporters. In 2000, China had about 144 million fixed telephone lines or about eleven per 100 people; in urban areas, there were about thirty telephone lines per 100 people. The number of cellular phones in use rose to eighty-four million in 2000. Access to the Internet also increased dramatically. In 1995, only about 7,000 users had Internet connections. An official report released in July 2002 claimed that the number of Internet service subscribers rose to almost forty-six million.[25] The increasing access to new information technologies has enabled the dissident community to become more effective in communicating its messages and persevering in its resistance, even in face of government repression.[26] Many dissidents had cell phones, personal computers, fax machines and even Internet connections. Qin Yongmin, a former skilled labourer who spent eight years in prison for dissident activities in the early 1980s, published a fax newsletter called *China Human Rights Observer* (the country's first human rights newsletter) at home. Before he was arrested on charges of 'subverting state security' and sentenced to twelve years in jail at the end of 1998, Qin was able to put out 362 issues.[27] Peng Ming claimed that he transmitted email notices to hundreds of people within China every day. Chinese dissidents frequently faxed their messages and political manifestos to overseas Chinese groups to gain exposure in the international media. For example, when a group of veteran dissidents, families of Tiananmen Square victims and former CCP officials issued two manifestos ('Declaration on Civil Rights and Freedom' and 'Declaration on Civil Rights and Social Justice') at the end of September 1998, they first faxed the documents to Chinese dissident groups in New York for translation into English and then posted them on the Internet.[28]

The spread of the Internet inside China gave dissidents a new and more flexible forum. In April 2000, a group of Shandong-based dissidents set up a website, <http://www.winwenming.net>, and was able to keep it running for three months before the police shut it down. In Sichuan, a computer scientist by the name of Huang Qi founded his 'tianwanxunren' website on 4 June 1999, using it to carry letters from ordinary citizens and exposés of corruption. He managed to keep his site in operation for a year before he was arrested by the authorities.[29] In 2001, a Beijing software engineer, Yang Zhili, established a website, <http://www.lib.126.com>, to post articles on political reform and democracy (he was soon detained by the police and his website closed).[30] Overseas dissident groups have also used the Internet to reach China's millions of netizens. *Dacankao* (*VIP Reference*), an Internet magazine published by a New York overseas Chinese group, claimed to be able to send its online publication to 120,000 Chinese email addresses every ten days.[31]

The potency of technologically enhanced resistance is most vividly illustrated by the case of *Falun Gong*, the spiritual movement declared an evil cult and banned by Beijing in July 1999 (see chapter 11). Even though the organizational network of *Falun Gong* was effectively destroyed after the regime launched a massive crackdown, cells of adherents of the movement were able to continue to communicate with each other through the use of cell phones and the Internet. This enabled them to mount occasional protests in Tiananmen Square to demonstrate their defiance against the government. Most important, the Internet provided *Falun Gong* a *global* stage. Websites set up and maintained abroad have become the rallying point for the movement in cyberspace. These sites post the messages from *Falun Gong*'s leader, Li Hongzhi, and other information about the movement that can be accessed inside China despite the government's efforts to block these sites. In late June 2002, *Falun Gong* managed to pull off a surprising – though perhaps illegal – technological stunt. Its followers used a powerful transmitter to jam the television signals broadcast by the government-owned Sinosat-1 for a full week and inserted their own video images of meditating *Falun Gong* followers for the millions of viewers in China to watch. This forced the government to shut down the entire satellite television network.[32]

The international context

One of the favourable contextual factors contributing to the increasing level of dissident resistance has been China's growing economic and political integration into the international community. Obviously, the post-Mao ruling elite pursued an 'open-door' policy primarily to gain Western investment, markets and technology; its expansion of political ties with international organizations and major Western governments also served to increase the status and respectability of the regime. While the economic and political gains of the 'open-door' policy were considerable, the regime has also paid a hidden price: its domestic behaviour has been subjected to the scrutiny and criticisms of most industrial democracies. While Beijing's leaders often reacted furiously to such outside pressures, China's growing economic and political ties with the international community indirectly, and sometimes directly, constrained its leaders' domestic policies and created new opportunities for dissident resistance.

There are numerous examples of how access to external material and moral support strengthened the dissident community. (However, only a few high-profile dissidents enjoy sustained overseas financial support while the vast majority of ordinary resisters do not receive such support.) Overseas dissident groups routinely send money to China-based dissidents, who frequently contact the foreign media and their overseas supporters to mobilize international pressures. For some leading dissidents, Western pressures have become an integral part of their resistance. In an essay published in December 1998, Xu Wenli wrote, 'Now, through the help and pressure of the international community, the CCP has recognized that human rights is a very serious problem, which has at times caused China to "lose face" and damaged its international image.'[33] Xu believed that Western coverage of the human rights conditions in China

> forced the Communist Party to gain a bit of understanding of the issue of human rights ... in particular, I believe that during Jiang Zemin's numerous visits abroad, he must have deeply felt the international criticisms and condemnation of the Chinese government on this issue ... he perhaps has made some commitments to Western leaders. Now it appears that there is some progress, for example, the CCP has pledged to sign the two international covenants on human rights ... we should take advantage of the opportunities the CCP is forced to give us.[34]

Inside China, well-known dissidents thus frequently timed their protest activities to coincide with important visits by major Western leaders to put the government in an embarrassing situation. Zhejiang-based Wang Youcai, a veteran of the 1989 Tiananmen Square movement, chose to announce the founding of the China Democracy Party the day before the arrival of President Bill Clinton at the end of June 1998. When the United Nations Human Rights Commissioner, Mary Robinson, paid her landmark visit to China in September 1998, leading dissidents openly challenged the government by requesting meetings with Robinson and attempting to present her with petitions for releasing jailed dissidents. Dissidents made similar attempts during the visits by British Prime Minister Tony Blair and French Prime Minister Lionel Jospin in October 1998.

In addition, China has signed a large number of international treaties and joined many international organizations since the late 1970s (Table 1.3). Most significantly, Beijing signed two critical human rights covenants under Western pressure – the international covenant on social, economic and cultural rights (in 1997) and the international covenant on civil and political rights (in 1998). According to the stipulations of the covenants, China would be required to report to the UN on its fulfilment of the covenant obligations within two years of their ratification by the Chinese National People's Congress. These, and other formal obligations under these treaties, may increasingly limit Chinese leaders' ability to impose repressive measures on pro-democracy activists and provide the latter with greater political legitimacy in their struggle. This potential has certainly not been lost on China's dissident community. A founder of the CDP, Wang Youcai, has claimed, perhaps a bit naively,

> Since the government has signed the international covenant on economic, social, and cultural rights and pledged to sign the international covenant on

civil and political rights, a large space has emerged for organizing an opposition party openly and through legal means.[35]

The battlefield of resistance has been effectively extended to the international diplomatic and legal arena. Dissident groups and families of imprisoned dissidents have learned to use the international media and political establishment to seek support. After Xu Wenli's imprisonment in late 1998, his wife travelled to the USA to work for his release. His daughter, a student at an American college, published an article in the Op-Ed page of the *New York Times* to highlight the Chinese government's persecution of her father. In some cases, international pressures forced the Chinese government to release individuals wrongfully imprisoned. For example, Song Yongyi, Gao Zhan and Li Shaomin, three Chinese-American scholars accused of espionage by Beijing, regained their freedom (in 1999 and 2001) after the international community, including many scholars on China, launched a well-coordinated rescue campaign. In recent years, overseas dissident groups and, since 1999, the foreign branches of the banned *Falun Gong* movement, have been able to organize sizeable protest rallies to 'greet' visits by senior Chinese government officials. On several occasions, their presence was so large and embarrassing that visiting Chinese dignitaries such as President Jiang Zemin, NPC Chairman Li Peng and Vice-President Hu

Table 1.3   International treaties/organizations China has signed/joined since 1980

1980	Signed convention on elimination of discrimination against women
1981	Signed convention on elimination of racial discrimination
1984	Acceded to seven International Labor Organization (ILO) conventions on labour inspection, wage protection, collective bargaining, forced labour, non-discrimination in employment and breaches of labour contract
1987	Accepted 1951 Hague statute on private international law
1987	Ratified 1973 UN convention on punishment of crimes against internationally protected persons
1988	Acceded to 1984 convention against torture and other cruel, inhuman or degrading punishment
1990	Acceded to ILO convention on equal pay for male and female workers
1990	Ratified ILO convention on consultations to promote implementation of labour standards
1992	Signed 1989 convention on the rights of the child
1992	Acceded to the 1952 Geneva convention on universal copyright
1992	Signed memorandum of understanding with USA prohibiting trade in products made with prison labour
1993	Signed 1971 Geneva convention protecting producers of phonograms against unauthorized duplication
1993	Ratified 1979 convention against taking of hostages
1993	Acceded to Bern convention on protection of literary and artistic works
1997	Ratified 1965 ILO convention on employment policy
1997	Signed international covenant on social, economic and cultural rights
1998	Signed international covenant on civil and political rights

Source: selected from Richard Baum, 'Globalization and Normative Convergence: The Chinese Case' (Department of Political Science, University of California, Los Angeles, 1998), pp. 7–8.

Jintao were forced to use side entrances to get into their hotels. An interesting, though incipient, trend is to use foreign legal instruments to harass visiting Chinese officials. *Falun Gong* groups in the USA filed civil suits against Li Peng in August 2000 during his visit to New York. Two senior provincial officials, the party secretary of Sichuan province and the deputy director of public security in Hubei province, were also sued in 2001 while travelling in the USA.[36]

The changing legal context

A notable trend in the pro-democracy movement in the 1990s was the dissidents' increasing use of China's evolving legal system in asserting rights and putting the government and the ruling party on the defensive. This important shift in the tactics of resistance was made in response to changes brought about by the post-Mao legal reform that gradually expanded individual rights, limited the repressive power of the state, and provided ordinary citizens with a limited set of legal tools to challenge the government. The institutional changes embodied in China's legal reforms were part of a complex process of political evolution in the Deng era. No longer a monolithic communist regime, the CCP-controlled party-state in fact consisted of groups and elements of diverse ideological persuasion. Indeed several open-minded reformers, such as Hu Yaobang and Zhao Ziyang, rose to the highest level of the power hierarchy inside the regime and used their office to promote a more tolerant political atmosphere. Several important institutional developments, such as the gradual strengthening of the National People's Congress and the initiation of village elections, occurred in this fluid political environment.

The growing influence of the NPC has accelerated the pace of reform in the legal system.[37] Official data show that the NPC issued 255 laws and eighty-four other pieces of legislation between 1979 and 2000.[38] Of these laws, the most important were the administrative litigation law, the civil procedure law, the revised criminal procedure law and the new criminal code that came into effect in 1998. Litigation – commercial, civil and administrative (suits filed against the government) – exploded as well, indicative of the growing importance of the legal system in resolving various conflicts (Table 1.4). China's professional legal community, which was almost non-existent at the end of the 1970s, grew rapidly in the same period. The number of licensed lawyers reached 117,260 at the end

Table 1.4 Growth of litigation in China, 1978–2000 (cases accepted by the courts of first instance)

Year	Commercial	Civil	Administrative
1978	–	285,000	–
1984	85,700	–	–
1987	367,156	1,213,219	5,240
1997	1,483,356	3,277,572	90,557
2000	1,297,843	3,412,259	85,760

Source: *Zhongguo falu nianjian*, various years; *Renmin sifa*, 4 (1998), p. 13.

of 2000.[39] Before a genuine democratic opening, China's emerging legal system may not become a full-fledged channel for resolving fundamental political conflicts between the CCP and its opposition. But the very existence of this channel and the increasing utility and importance of the courts in the lives of ordinary people should, in the long run, enhance the legal system's relative institutional autonomy and transform it into a political arena where democratic resistance is waged publicly and under certain legal protection.

To a limited extent, this has already occurred. In William Alford's view, China's legal reform forged a 'double-edged sword'. He observed that

> the regime has not only through its law provided a legal, moral, and political vocabulary with which those who wish to take it to task might articulate their concerns, but also has proffered these individuals a singular platform from which their concerns might be broadcast. In seeking to deploy formal legality for highly instrumental purposes, the regime has unwittingly handed its opponents a keenly honed instrument through which to seek to accomplish their own, very different ends.[40]

Indeed, as political entrepreneurs quick to detect the potential advantages embedded in the formal provisions of these laws, some Chinese dissidents took the lead in invoking the new laws, especially the administrative litigation law, to test the limits of the regime's tolerance of dissent. The first and most publicized lawsuit filed by a leading dissident scholar, Guo Ruoji, was a case in point. Guo, a professor of philosophy at Nanjing University, was stripped of his professorship and banned from travelling abroad by the Communist Party committee of his university in 1991. He promptly sued the Communist Party committee. His case attracted intense interest mainly because it was the first time the new administrative litigation law was explicitly used to challenge the power of the ruling party (although, technically, acts of the CCP were immune from administrative litigation). Both the Nanjing Intermediate Court and the Jiangsu Provincial Supreme People's Court ruled against Guo, but the professor believed that he had scored a moral victory. Writing about the experience later, Guo said, 'I knew that my lawsuit could not win in court, but it would certainly win morally. My suit was not filed to be read by the judges; it was meant for the people.'[41]

Several other dissidents filed similar lawsuits against the government and the CCP. In 1993, a professor at the People's University in Beijing, Yuan Hongbing, sued the university's CCP committee for banning a book he had edited, *The Tide of History*, which attacked leftist orthodox views. In 1998, a Wuhan-based dissident, Li Weiping, used the administrative litigation law to sue the head of the city's public security bureau for the illegal seizure of his passport. In the same year, a Beijing-based dissident, Peng Ming, filed an administrative litigation suit against the Beijing Municipal Civil Affairs Bureau for shutting down an affiliate of his private think-tank (the China Development Union) and confiscating its office equipment. Bao Ge, a former medical student in Shanghai who was sent to a re-education camp for organizing an unofficial movement to seek war compensation from Japan, claimed to have filed more than twenty suits against the government while in camp and against the agency in charge of the camp after his release. 'Each time I filed a suit, I made sure the press knew.'[42] Although none of the dissidents won their suits against the government, the very act of filing these suits achieved important political and symbolic victories. As Alford has perceptively noted,

> The mere act of filing a complaint enables litigants to juxtapose publicly the gap between the state's professed ideals and lived reality with a rare drama, clarity, and moral force – whether their goal be to attack particular individuals and institutions without appearing vengeful or to raise more systemic questions about legitimacy. Litigation further poses a profound dilemma for the authorities by requiring, in effect, that the state either provide the litigant a day in court to make his case or appear to be acting in hypocritical disregard of processes that it has labored hard to publicize.[43]

In using the legal system to resist the domination of the state, the Chinese dissident community merely borrowed a time-tested and proven political tactic widely adopted by resisters in other countries. 'Legal institutions are important sites for public performances of resistance by individuals and groups. Telling one's story in court, particularly a story of oppression, can be an important act of resistance.'[44] As an institution of the state, the court is often identified as an instrument of domination. But ironically, under certain conditions the court can sometimes be converted into a forum where acts of resistance may be performed at relatively low cost. Scholars of popular resistance have reported that

> people who are otherwise politically marginal go to court regularly to resist domination ... they skillfully manipulate legal rhetoric in courts and in a variety of other sites of oppositional practice ... although governments wield tremendous power to encode and enforce law, a crucial part of the power of law is its very contestability ... resisting state domination ... often entails seeking inclusion in legal institutions ... people regularly appropriate the terms, constructs, and procedures of law in formulating opposition.[45]

To be sure, Chinese dissidents have filed only a handful of lawsuits against the government and these suits had no direct impact on the protection of the rights of dissidents. But the knowledge and experience gained in making use of China's own laws against its rulers seem to have prompted a shift of emphasis – away from direct acts of protest to the skilful exploitation of existing political procedures and processes. Veteran dissident Xu Wenli has openly articulated such a change in tactics. 'We're using the law now, and they (the government) have never dealt with that before on such a scale.'[46] Xu sees great potential in exploiting existing institutional advantages under the current system:

Our actions should not be covert, but should be open and in conformity with the Chinese constitution. The tactics of so-called 'street politics' or demonstrations should be minimized or be used with great caution ... we must gradually shift from a 'street politics' approach to parliamentarianism. We must begin now to enter the process of instituting an electoral process and to strive for the participation of democracy activists in that process.[47]

Rights consciousness and resistance

Democratic resistance in China may be better understood as part of a broad trend of increasing rights consciousness among ordinary people. Such resistance is likely to occur more frequently and intensely and gain greater, although not necessarily overt or direct, popular support when the general level of rights consciousness is on the rise. There is evidence that suggests that rights consciousness has gradually risen in the post-Mao era. One of the manifestations of the rise is the number of complaints filed by consumers. In 1996 alone, Chinese consumer associations handled 526,975 complaints from consumers and were able to obtain 304 million yuan in compensation. By 2000, the number of consumer complaints received by Chinese consumer associations exceeded 706,000.[48] At the end of 1998, China's Internet subscribers used online bulletin boards to threaten a consumer boycott against government-owned Internet service providers for charging excessive monthly fees (although their campaign did not win an immediate victory). Another trend has been the increase in the number of lawsuits filed against violations of property rights and personal rights (such as libel, defamation and unauthorized use of personal portraits). As Table 1.5 shows, the number of personal-rights-related civil lawsuits rose by more than five times in twelve years (from 1988 to 2000). Although no official data are available, many ordinary citizens have filed collective and individual lawsuits under the administrative litigation law against government agencies for collecting illegal taxes and seizing their private property.

More systematically gathered data, mainly public opinion survey results, similarly show rising rights consciousness. In an extensive survey (financed by the Ford Foundation), Chinese legal scholars interviewed 5,461 individuals in six provinces in 1993 and published some of their findings in a landmark book titled *Zou xiang quanli de shidai: Zhongguo gongmin quanli fazhan yanjiu* (*Marching Toward the Era of Rights: A Study of the Development of Citizens' Rights in China*).[49] This study, the

Table 1.5   Civil lawsuits filed against violation of personal rights

Year	Number of lawsuits accepted by the courts of first instance
1988	2,434
1992	3,761
1996	7,467
2000	11,763

Source: *Zhongguo falu nianjian*, various years.

first of its kind undertaken in China, has several limitations, chief of which is its inability to correlate socioeconomic attributes with rights consciousness. Nevertheless, the study provides valuable insight into the current state of rights consciousness. One important finding of the study is that, indeed, popular Chinese conceptions of the source of rights are substantially different from those in the West. As Table 1.6 shows, far more respondents stated that some of the most basic rights are granted by the state rather than given at birth.

Nevertheless, there is evidence suggesting that rights consciousness, especially in the areas of property rights, personal rights, due process and legal rights, may have risen to relatively high levels. For example, nearly 80 per cent of the respondents in the survey agreed with the statement 'Private property is sacred and must not be violated' (*'siyou caichan shensheng buke qinfan'*).[50] Two-thirds of the respondents also opposed the suggestion that 'The government may confiscate private property under any circumstances in the national interest.'[51] About the same proportion of respondents also rejected the view that 'In a lawsuit involving an individual and a collective, the judgement should favour the collective.'[52] Chinese citizens also seemed to be more aware of their rights to due process. When asked whether a law enforcement agency could continue to detain a person for public security even if it was unable to determine his or her guilt or innocence, nearly 47 per cent of the respondents opposed such action while only 27 per cent of the 5,456 respondents supported it.[53]

Rising levels of rights consciousness are accompanied by increasing popular awareness of legal recourse. Contrary to the traditional perception that Chinese culture frowns upon confrontational litigation and prefers mediation, Chinese legal researchers reported that more than half of the rural respondents and 70 per cent of the urban respondents felt they neither gained nor lost face going to court to resolve conflicts with someone they knew.[54] More importantly, a very large proportion of ordinary citizens selected the legal system as a channel to seek recourse to official injustice. When asked what they would do if they were

Table 1.6   Conception of sources of basic rights*

Type of rights	Granted by the state and government	Given at birth
Security of life	32.38	8.15
Security of livelihood	36.95	1.34
Elect and dismiss officials	34.82	1.08
Work for wealth	23.38	7.45
Receive primary education	40.92	6.70
No mistreatment of the imprisoned	49.99	2.95

Source: Xia Yong (ed.), *Zou xiang quanli de shidai: Zhongguo gongmin quanli fazhan yanjiu* (Marching Toward the Era of Rights: A Study of the Development of Citizens' Rights in China) (Beijing: Chinese University of Politics and Law Publishing Co., 1995), p. 16.

Note:
* According to the Chinese constitution and laws, you enjoy the following rights. Where do you think these rights come from? Choose the principal source of rights – from the following choices. Numbers indicate percentage of respondents

attacked and injured by the police or local bullies, more than 60 per cent of the respondents stated that they would take their cases to judicial authorities and demand punishment. Only 5 to 7 per cent of the respondents would acquiesce. About 43 per cent would take the same action if they were attacked by their bosses or supervisors.[55]

Conclusion

The preliminary evidence presented in this chapter offers some support for Tocqueville's hypothesis that falling repression produces greater resistance mainly as a result of rising rights consciousness among the oppressed. In China's case, a small but resilient dissident resistance movement has been sustained since the late 1970s because of many important changes in the political, economic, social and international context within which the movement operates. These changes sometimes provided dissidents with direct means of resistance (such as access to material, legal and moral support). At other times, the impact of these contextual changes was less direct but no less real, and they created a more favourable political milieu for resistance. Operating within such a milieu, dissidents were likely to gain greater confidence, enjoy more influence and increase the effectiveness of their acts. Of course, as in most cases of resistance waged by relatively small groups, their acts of defiance such as making public declarations, petitioning the government, protesting against personal persecution and attempting to register opposition groups have failed to have an immediate and measurable effect. Rarely have they succeeded in visibly weakening the regime or directly changing public opinion or government policy. Over time, however, sustained dissident resistance, even in its most routine forms, may slowly sap an authoritarian regime's legitimacy, authority and prestige. At the most basic level, such acts reveal most vividly and publicly the vulnerability of the political authority of the regime. They demonstrate that even a government with a considerable repressive capacity may be brought to answer some of the most basic questions about its political legitimacy and governance record: why did it violate its own laws in imprisoning its critics; why did it stop unofficial groups from registering; why did it fail to protect the national interest; why did it fail to protect the environment; why did its own officials commit crimes of corruption?

In short, dissident resistance performs some of the most essential functions of political opposition in political systems where legal opposition does not exist. In the long term, dissident resistance may have important and more direct political consequences. It will likely produce demonstration effects encouraging ordinary resisters to imitate the tactics of dissidents in asserting their rights. Persistent dissident efforts may loosen up parts of the political system (the most likely point of entry is the legal system and the grassroots electoral process) and create more favourable political conditions for ordinary resisters. Dissident resistance may lead to the emergence of a freer media which will become a voice for ordinary resisters. Despite the government's ban on formal opposition parties such as the China Democracy Party, one should not dismiss the possibility that dissidents may eventually be able to forge direct links with ordinary resisters to develop a stronger and broader social base. Rising levels of social frustration and state–society tensions in China today should provide dissidents with more opportunities for reaching out to groups that have been victimized and neglected by the autocratic political process. Recent press reports indicate that some Chinese dissidents have begun to seek such ties.[56] If the history of dissident resistance over the last 25 years is to be used as a basis for judging its future potential, China's incipient opposition is likely to become more resilient, sophisticated and adept in challenging the regime as the conditions for democratic resistance further improve.

Notes

1 For the most illuminating account of ordinary resistance against domination, see James Scott, *Weapons of the Weak: Everyday Forms of Peasant Resistance* (New Haven: Yale University Press, 1985).

2 Alexis de Tocqueville, *The Old Regime and the French Revolution* (New York: Anchor Books, 1955), pp. 176 7.

3 See, for example, Craig Calhoun, *Neither Gods Nor Emperors: Students and the Struggle for Democracy in China* (Berkeley: University of California Press, 1994); Jeffrey N. Wasserstrom and Elizabeth J. Perry (eds), *Popular Protest and Political Culture in Modern China* (Boulder: Westview Press, 1994); Kevin O'Brien, 'Rightful Resistance', *World Politics*, 49, 1 (October 1996), pp. 31–55.

4 Dissidents are individuals who directly oppose the Communist Party's claim to rule and openly offer a political alternative. They are also referred to as pro-democracy activists because the political alternative they offer embodies democratic ideals and institutions. Their political objective distinguishes them from other protesters who are motivated by non-political issues.

5 Andrew Nathan, 'Sources of Chinese Rights Thinking', in R. Randle Edwards, Louis Henkin and Andrew Nathan (eds), *Human Rights in Contemporary China* (New York: Columbia University Press, 1986), pp. 125–6.

6 Nathan, 'Sources of Chinese Rights Thinking', p. 161.

7 *Ibid.*

8 Randall Peerenboom, 'Rights, Interests, and the Interest in Rights in China', *Stanford Journal of International Law*, 31, 2 (Summer 1995), pp. 359–86.

9 Wang Gungwu, 'Power, Rights and Duties in Chinese History', *The Australian Journal of Chinese Affairs*, 3 (January 1980), pp. 1–26.

10 Lianjiang Li and Kevin O'Brien, 'Villagers and Popular Resistance in Contemporary China', *Modern China*, 22, 1 (January 1996), pp. 28–61.

11 For most ordinary citizens, resistance was expressed through individual and non-public means. One of the most common forms of private resistance during the Cultural Revolution was to keep a secret diary in which the resister wrote what he or she really thought about the Maoist regime. An exception was the long essay on democracy and law jointly written and posted publicly by Li Yizhe in Guangzhou in the mid-1970s.

12 The protest against the Gang of Four in April 1976 was perhaps an exception. But, strictly speaking, that event should not be classified as a pro-democracy act.

13 *Beijing Spring*, 66 (November 1998), p. 3.

14 Ordinary resistance described here is different from 'everyday resistance' formulated by James Scott. In this chapter, ordinary resistance primarily targets political authorities, while in Scott's work everyday resistance is directed against non-political forces of domination.

15 The most high-profile case of financial fraud in recent years was the case involving Li Peng's elder son, who was accused by nearly 6,000 defrauded investors of participating in a commodities trading scheme that stole more than 500 million yuan from them. For a detailed description of the case, see *Beijing Spring*, 92 (January 2001), pp. 6–10.

16 USA-based dissident publications such as *Beijing Spring* and *China Spring* contain extensive coverage of such incidents of collective protest in China. Free-wheeling Chinese publications such as *Nanfang zhoumo* (Southern Weekend) and *Banyuetan neibuban* (Semi-Monthly Forum, internal edition) frequently carry similar stories.

17 Macroeconomic Research Institute of the State Planning Commission, 'Zhongguo gumin shehui xintai genzong fengxi' (Tracking Analysis of the Social Opinions of Chinese Residents) in Rui Xin, Lu Xueyi and Li Peilin (eds), *Shehui lanpishu 2002* (Social Blue Book 2002) (Beijing: Shehui kexue wenxian chubanshe, 2002), p. 20.

18 In September 1998, three dissidents in the Chaoyang district in Beijing announced their candidacy for the district's people's congress on a platform of workers' rights and anticorruption. *Agence France-Presse*, 21 September 1998. A member of the banned China Democracy Party in Zhejiang province ran for the chairmanship of his village, although his candidacy was blocked by local authorities. Another Beijing-based dissident, He Depu, was nominated by his fellow workers in late 1998 to run for the local people's congress. *Beijing Spring*, 68 (January 1999), pp. 103–4.

19 *Wall Street Journal*, 27 November 1998, A9.

20 *Beijing Spring*, 68 (January 1999), p. 102.

21 Reported in *USA Today*, 31 August 1998, p. 4A.

22 Ya Yi, 'Tuijin Zhongguo gongmin quanli yundong' (The Movement to Promote Citizens' Rights in China), *Beijing Spring*, 57 (February 1998), pp. 66–74.

23 Letter reprinted in *Beijing Spring*, 65 (October 1998), pp. 6–7.

24 Guo Ruoji, *Gongchandang weifa an ji shi* (Real Stories of the Communist Party's Violation of Law) (Hong Kong: Minzhu daixue chubanshe, 1997).

25 See China Internet Network Information Center's July 2002 report at <http://www.cnnic.net.cn/develst/2002-7/4.shtml>.

26 For an excellent study of how Chinese dissidents have taken advantage of the Internet, see Michael Chase and James Mulvenon, *You've Got Dissent* (Santa Monica: Rand, 2002).

27 *Agence France-Presse*, 18 November 1998.

28 *New York Times*, 30 September 1998, p. 3.

29 *Beijing Spring*, 88 (September 2000), p. 101.

30 *Beijing Spring*, 85 (June 2001), p. 100.

31 *Washington Post*, 5 December 1998, A20; *South China Morning Post*, 11 January 1999 (Internet edition).

32 See *Washington Post*, 9 July 2002, A 18.

33 Xu Wenli 'Democratic Movement in China', *China Strategic Institute Issue Papers on China*, 43 (3 December 1998).

34 *China Spring*, 172 (June 1998), pp. 30–4.

35 Wang Youcai, 'Ruhe zhujian quanguoxing gongkai fandui dang' (How to Organize an Open National Opposition Party', *Beijing Spring*, 65 (October 1998), pp. 42–3.

36 *Beijing Spring*, 89 (October 2001), p. 103.

37 See Michael William Dowdle, 'Constructing Citizenship: The NPC as Catalyst for Political Participation', in Merle Goldman and Elizabeth J. Perry (eds), *Changing Meanings of Citizenship in Modern China* (Cambridge, MA: Harvard University Press, 2002).

38 *Legal Daily*, 13 March 1997, p. 5; the data for 1993–2000 are the author's compilation according to information provided in *Zhongguo falu nianjian*, various years.

39 *Zhongguo falu nianjian* (2001), p. 1272.

40 William Alford, 'Double-edged Swords Cut Both Ways: Law and Legitimacy in the People's Republic of China', *Daedalus*, 122, 2 (Spring 1993), p. 62.
41 Guo Ruoji, *Gongchandang weifa an ji shi*, p. 27.
42 Ya Yi, 'Tuijin Zhongguo gongmin quanli yundong' (The Movement to Promote Citizens' Rights in China), *Beijing Spring*, 57 (February 1998), pp. 66–74
43 Alford, 'Double-edged Swords Cut Both Ways', p. 58.
44 Susan Hirsch and Mindie Lazarus-Black, 'Introduction', in Mindie Lazarus-Black and Susan Hirsch (eds), *Contested States: Law Hegemony and Resistance* (London: Routledge, 1994), p. 11.
45 Susan Hirsch and Mindie Lazarus-Black, 'Introduction', *Contested States*, pp. 1–10.
46 Quoted in *Agence France-Presse*, 28 September 1998.
47 Xu Wenli, 'Democratic Movement in China'.
48 *Legal Daily*, 15 February 1997, p. 1; *Zhonghua renmin gongheguo nianjian 2001* (Yearbook of the People's Republic of China 2001) (Beijing: Zhonghua renmin gongheguo nianjian chubanshe, 2001), p. 483.
49 Xia Yong (ed.), *Zou xiang quanli de shidai: Zhongguo gongmin quanli fazhan yanjiu* (Marching Toward the Era of Rights: A Study of the Development of Citizens' Rights in China) (Beijing: Chinese University of Politics and Law Publishing Co., 1995).
50 *Ibid.*, p. 376.
51 *Ibid.*, p. 353.
52 *Ibid.*, p. 383.
53 *Ibid.*, p. 464.
54 *Ibid.*, p. 42.
55 *Ibid.*, p. 37.
56 A member of the China Democracy Party in Hunan, Liao Baohua, spoke at a rally of laid-off workers in Changsha in June 1999. A labour activist and a veteran of the 1989 pro-democracy movement, Liao was credited for organizing another large protest rally at the end of 1998. *Beijing Spring*, 75 (August 1999), p. 100. A lawyer in Shaanxi province, Ma Wenlin, filed suits on behalf of local farmers against government officials over illegal taxes and corruption. After Ma was sentenced to fifteen years in prison in November 1999, more than 30,000 farmers signed a joint petition for his release. *Zhongguo shibao* (*China Times*, Taipei), 6 June 2002.

Suggested reading

On dissidents and the democracy movement

Ian Buruma, *Bad Elements: Chinese Rebels from Los Angeles to Beijing* (New York: Random House, 2001).

Michael Chase and James Mulvenon, *You've Got Dissent: Chinese Dissident Use of the Internet and Beijing's Counter-Strategies* (Santa Monica: Rand, 2002).

On legal reform

Stanley Lubman, *China's Legal Reforms* (Oxford: Clarendon, 1996).

Minxin Pei, 'Citizens v. Mandarins: Administrative Litigation in China', *China Quarterly*, 152 (December 1997), pp. 832–62.

On rural resistance

Kevin O'Brien and Lianjiang Li, 'The Politics of Lodging Complaints in Rural China', *China Quarterly*, 143 (September 1995), pp. 756–83.

On changing state–society relations in urban areas

Deborah Davis, Richard Kraus, Barry Naughton and Elizabeth Perry (eds.), *Urban Spaces in Contemporary China* (New York: Cambridge University Press, 1995).

On the state of reform

Merle Goldman and Roderick MacFarquhar, (eds.), *The Paradox of China's Post-Mao Reforms* (Cambridge, MA: Harvard University Press, 1999).

On dissidents and the Internet

Michael Chase and James Mulvenon, *You've Got Dissent: Chinese Dissident Use of the Internet and Beijing's Counter-Strategies* (Santa Monica: Rand, 2002).

2 The revolution of resistance

Geremie R. Barmé

China's economic reforms have not only been about the growth of an entrepreneurial business sector. The privatization of public debate, intellectual life and cultural activity has also unfolded over the past twenty years. Availing themselves of state resources, which were the product of plunder in the name of nationalization in the 1950s and 1960s, groups and individuals have arrogated to themselves both the *matériel* and the prerogatives to develop alternative intellectual and cultural activity in China. This culture, projected through the Kong-Tai (that is, the Hong Kong and Taiwan Chinese-language) media and international media, has achieved a global profile, construed as being representative of the latest version of 'New China'.

The present chapter reviews the incipient growth of these activities in the 1980s and their significance during the second radical phase of party-initiated reforms during the 1990s, and indicates ways in which resistance and compliance with cultural protocols have manifested themselves in the medium of the Chinese Internet since the turn of the millennium.

The chapter raises questions about the nature of resistance within the intellectual-cultural urban elites, and offers an overview of who is resisting what and why.

> Revolution. To revolutionize revolution; to revolutionize the revolution of revolution; to rev ...[1]

In late December 1991, Zhou Lunyou, a poet of the 'Not-not' school in Sichuan, produced a manifesto entitled 'A Stance of Rejection'. Written in response to what he saw as the cultural capitulation that had followed in the wake of the 4 June 1989 Beijing massacre, Zhou called on his fellows to resist the blandishments of the state. 'In the name of history and reality', he wrote,

> in the name of human decency, in the name of the absolute dignity and conscience of the poet, and in the name of pure art we declare:
>   We will not cooperate with a phoney value system –
> • Reject their magazines and payments.
> • Reject their critiques and acceptance.

- Reject their publishers and their censors.
- Reject their lecterns and 'academic' meetings.
- Reject their 'writers' associations', 'artists' associations', 'poets' associations', for they are all sham artistic yamen that corrupt art and repress creativity.

The stifling of cultural experimentation and intellectual debate that occurred in the wake of 4 June was neither as extreme nor as widespread as anti-liberals in Beijing had hoped (or, indeed, as overseas dissidents and exiles claimed). That purge came after a decade of radical economic policies that had undermined the ideological certainties of high socialism and fostered, among other things, an environment of intellectual and cultural debate outside the stifling confines of political agitprop. The scope and effect of the 1989 purge was circumscribed by many factors: a revulsion against Cultural Revolution style denunciations, internal dissension within the party, the impact of administrative reforms and weakening on the mechanisms of social and political surveillance, widespread public disinterest, political fatigue and opposition, as well as the stark economic imperatives of the party's own programme.

Zhou Lunyou's romantic call for resistance itself came at an intriguing and crucial moment for Chinese culture. It was on the cusp of Deng Xiaoping's vaunted 'tour of the south' of early 1992. During his inspection of economic reformist centres in Guangdong province, Deng made a series of speeches and comments that not only had a radical impact on the economic life of the nation, but also further transformed the nature of cultural dissent and intellectual opposition to the party.

In the years prior to Zhou's appeal to reject the state-sanctioned arts world, cultural practitioners and activists had evolved complex relationships with the official overculture that made any simple gestures of rebellion seem quixotic, if not nugatory. Egregious oppositionist acts, while sometimes meaningful, were generally also part of a larger, highly nuanced skein of activity that could not be easily classified in terms of clumsy dichotomies. Furthermore, from 1989, mainland Chinese cultural and intellectual discord more than ever before developed an international dimension. The 1989 protest movement and its bloody denouement served to globalize further the debate and dissent, a process that worked in tandem with the internationalization of the economy.

Hong Kong, Taiwan and international media attention was now fixated on the issues related to the 1989 protests and subsequent massacre, the fate of activists, any hints of a change in official government policy and the possibility of further mass unrest. Key participants in the movement escaped, or were subsequently sent, into exile, and while some continued agitating for political change in China, many more turned their energies to other, often business, pursuits from 1990–91. The Chinese government and its avowed opponents throughout the 1990s engaged in 'mimetic violence' against each other – rhetorical attacks, purges and dissident resistance – that entrenched their mutual opposition. Meanwhile, in the larger realms of intellectual, cultural and commercial life debate flourished. New Chinese-language forums (newspapers, magazines and semi-academic journals) strengthened an environment for discussion and contention within the 'Chinese commonwealth'. This involved mainland writers, as well as offshore and overseas commentators, in a direct dialogue about future scenarios for China and the region in a manner – as some pointed out – that was reminiscent of the 'internationalization' of political dissension in late-Qing China at the end of the nineteenth century, when the frustration of the 1898 reforms of the Guangxu Emperor had forced his supporters into exiled activism overseas.

The economic boom of the 1990s challenged thinkers and critics of all schools to re-evaluate the modern history of the Chinese party-state; it also drew scholars and activists into a series of discussions about the impact of the party's programme on issues of official corruption, cronyism, the growth of a new underclass, commodification-consumerism and globalization, as well as media freedom and democratization. Some of these issues were central to the inchoate protests of 1989; however, a decade later, they were being debated in the mainland media in unprecedented detail and with considerable candour.

In the 1980s vague reformist visions had been at the centre of much intellectual and political debate. During the 1990s the integration of China's economy into the global system (and the global system's infiltration into China), as well as the cut-throat commerce of the decade, confronted intellectuals and lent impetus to the revolution of resistance.

Also after 1989, the romantic posture of failed resistance achieved a certain social and commercial éclat. This was particularly true in the cultural sphere where transgressive activities – that is, actions that were 'naughty but not dangerous'[3] to the entrenched power holders and new elites – flourished. A number of successful careers in cinema, art, theatre and literature were launched on the basis of alternative cultural activity, sporadic state repression, and offshore investment in avant-garde cultural activities. The crushing of flagrant dissent gave these more anodyne activities a highly visible media profile. Non-official arts activists continued to plunder state resources in a fashion not dissimilar to the vampirization of state (that is 'public') sector assets by bureaucratic cronies and the super-rich. Film-makers and artists who joined the international exhibition and cultural carnival circuit during the 1990s, for example, were generally trained in state institutions, cultivated alliances with associates and used (or 'privatized') state and semi-official resources (equipment, locales, networks) to pursue their activities. The works of film-makers such as Zhang Yuan (director of MTVs and feature films such as 'Beijing Bastards' and 'East Palace, West Palace') and a slew of painters were in the artistic avant-garde of those diverting state resources to their private (and often profitable) ventures. The arrest or harassment of activists who attempted to organize a concerted opposition to one-party rule, or who petitioned the government to undertake democratic reform, to reassess the events of 1989, or at least to honour the national constitution, made clear that political confrontation, rather than image marketing, was regarded by the power holders as illegitimate and dangerous.

For a time after 1989, consumerism was viewed popularly, and among many segments of the political and intellectual elite, as possessing a near revolutionary significance[4] – and many of the most celebrated cultural fads drew upon revolutionary images.[5] The romance of resistance included now a belief that quotidian activities were the site of struggle and cloaked sociopolitical retail therapy (that is, shopping for new lifestyles and accessorizing the self in contradistinction to the official nation-state inculcated guise of identity). It was a development acceptable to economic reformers, the business elite, crony cadres, wannabe rebels, kids with 'tude, and the displaced literati, many of whose members felt they had been sidelined by economic developments and political stability in the 1990s. The rise of this discourse of consumer-as-revolutionary also dovetailed neatly with a liberal teleology that now saw the ascendancy of the middle class and the democracy of Taiwan as part of the overall trajectory of Chinese modernity, and not just as a hotly contested alternative. While ballot-box democracy might be deferred until a sizeable middle class existed, the republic of shopping could be realized immediately.

Along with cultural transgression, consumption was also a key zone for the affirmation of avant-garde scouts. Consumption directs desires and enlists resistance within itself as product promotion and placement usurp edgy non-mainstream, or state-sanctioned, phenomena. Cultural or social developments that once seemed antipathetic and threatening could, in the guise of marketing strategies or sound street commercial sense, be incorporated in the domain of product and purchase. Some might well claim that this does not necessarily 'make commodified resistance "packaged", tame or lame. It simply makes it tactical and potentially effective.'[6] But, effective for what? Arguments about shopper-as-rebel and promoter-as-revolutionary are certainly suggestive if the seditious subaltern or canny consumer was chiefly construed as existing and acting in some closed system embraced by the market-party-state. If viewed within the larger, multipolar environment of the Kong-Tai world, as well as in the thrall of the international media and transcultural sphere, however, the 'new ways and new things "to market", consume, subvert, rebel against or steal',[7] so noteworthy on the mainland during the 1990s, could also be appreciated in terms of promotion, positioning and redefinition of elitist norms in the guise of subaltern strategies. For the mavens of international academic theory, China was fallow territory, a 'blank page' as Chairman Mao would have it, on which new texts could be written or at least divined.

After 1992, it was initially the old 'Maoist-style' left[8] which, through internal lobbying and public propagandizing, continued to articulate most coherently a position of opposition to the reformist status quo. From the middle of the decade, however, a number of 'new-leftist' thinkers joined pro-party conservatives to respond both to the predicament of mainstream social and political thinking, and to the glaring inequities resulting from the economic libertarian agenda. Many of these thinkers – who were based both in the USA and China – emphasized the threats posed by the declining fiscal viability of the Beijing authorities and growing social inequities that had resulted from decentralization and marketization. They envisaged a range of dire scenarios that invoked the plangent fate of the former Yugoslavia or Soviet Union and grudgingly argued that a strong and economically competent Communist Party was perhaps, for the moment at least, a necessary bulwark against national collapse.

The post-1976 period of the officially-sponsored 'movement to liberate thinking' (*sixiang jiefang yundong*) from Maoist strictures was a time during which official ideology underwent a transformation that freed the authorities from past dogma while also providing a rationale for economic reform and new directions for social growth. In a retrospective analysis of the intellectual developments on the mainland over the two decades from 1978 to 1998, Xu Jilin, a leading scholar of twentieth-century intellectual history based in Shanghai, observed that the party's previous reliance on a utopian political programme was gradually replaced by theoretical justifications for the 'secular socialism' (*shisuhua shehuizhuyi*) of the economic reforms.

The process continued with a complex intellectual and cultural mutation that extended far beyond the earlier limited aims of pro-party revisionists. From the mid-1980s, the mainland experienced a cultural effervescence that was called by some 'another "May Fourth" movement', a 'Chinese Enlightenment'.[9] Like that earlier period of cultural and political debate and furore during the 1910s and 1920s, this post-Cultural Revolution 'New Enlightenment' was supposedly witness to an initial period of broad agreement among thinkers who rejected the old state ideology and propounded instead various alternative models for modernization. It was a period in which intellectual traditions were invoked, invented and reclaimed as part of intellectuals' attempts to define themselves within the Chinese polity and claim a role in its evolution. This supposed consensus, however, also contained within it a critical response to the various international discourses that were being introduced piecemeal through translation projects, young scholars studying overseas, conferences, seminars and a wealth of publications; and it was a response that carried also the seeds of a major reassessment of China's 1980s and 1990s fascination with the West (or global commercial and political culture) itself.

Moreover, the debates of the 1980s were influenced by an intermittent series of cultural and political campaigns, or purges, in particular the nationwide attacks on 'spiritual pollution' and 'bourgeois liberalization' in 1980–1, 1983–4, 1987 and 1989–90.[10] These administrative and ideological condemnations included attacks on Marxist-style humanism and the efforts by loyalists to construct a new rationale for the party beyond the confines of its economic programme. The purges more often than not had the effect of silencing establishment intellectuals (*tizhinei zhishifenzi*) and critics who stepped out of line, or resulted in their isolation within or banishment from its ranks. In conjunction with economic reform and more general social transformations, however, a semi-independent sphere of intellectual activity gradually blossomed, and it found outlets in the deregulated publishing market. At the same time, a revival of the educational sphere and academic standards saw a rapid increase in tertiary enrolments and a college-trained urban stratum that enjoyed unprecedented (in post-1949 terms, at least) access to information and a range of media. As a consequence, they provided a ready audience for the products of the *Kulturkampf.*

The period of the 1980s New Enlightenment was, to use Xu Jilin's description,

> A major historical turning point for Chinese intellectuals in that through cultural debate they gradually withdrew from and, in some cases, entirely broke free of the politico-ideological establishment and the state system of specialized knowledge production [that is, the strictures of official academia]. This enabled them to create intellectual spaces and attain a new cultural independence.

It was a kind of autonomy more akin to the situation that had existed prior to the founding of the People's Republic in 1949.[11]

While avoiding direct confrontation with the official ideology, these intellectuals in effect began to challenge its dominance in every field of thought. The public realm for intellectual debate was to flourish in the 1990s although the consensual environment shared by different schools of thinkers and cultural activists was ruptured first by the 1989 protest movement and the subsequent purge of elitist activists, and then again by the effects of the economic boom that followed in the wake of Deng Xiaoping's 1992 'tour of the south'.

In the 1980s, intellectual contestation had generally centred on debates about abstract ideas and theoretical issues in the belief that it was through cultural and national transformation that China would be revitalized. Educated urbanites long excoriated under Maoist cultural policy presumed that this new 'Enlightenment project' was their responsibility, and members of the intelligentsia were anxious to play the role of patriot-savant supposedly central to the identity of the traditional educated caste. Following the successes, and excesses, of the economic reforms during the 1990s, however, engaged intellectuals related their disagreements more directly to economic and political programmes, as well as to class or caste differences. In an age during which much of the 'capital accumulation', that is superficial economic prosperity, that had been the goal of earlier reforms and revolutions seemed to have been realized, the nature of this affluence and the inequities it presented now came to the fore as issues of pressing importance. The intelligentsia had, throughout the twentieth century, argued bitterly over the merits of a dizzying array of developmental theories, political programmes, economic systems and cultural paradigms. Now, at the century's end, debates and intellectual programmes began to revolve around not simply how to achieve power and prosperity, but the dilemmas of power and prosperity *per se.*

Economic wealth and the vision of a strong and prosperous China – or even the reverse, the looming menace of an economically imperilled, crisis-ridden and socially divided nation – made the debates about the history of modernity in China and the future it faced both relevant and urgent. Although past controversies had been launched from a common ground, and a general wariness of monopolistic party rule had existed among diverse cultural and intellectual worlds from the late 1970s, now questions were disputed on the basis of vastly different, even mutually exclusive, academic and theoretical frameworks, as well as social experiences.

While open intellectual debate in the style of the 1980s was quelled for a time after 4 June, the broader cultural sphere was witness to considerable resilience. During 1990 the pall of the Beijing Massacre still hung over artistic life. It was, however, also a time of considerable ebullience for alternative culture. For example, the rock 'n' roll scene enjoyed unprecedented activity and growth. Similarly, in 1989–91, independent painters developed on the diversity of the 1980s arts scene and began creating work that would gain an international audience and that, through high-profile exhibitions and reviews, came to represent more than any other aspect of mainland culture the face of the new 'New China' overseas. Despite a number of bans on authors directly involved in the 1989 protests, controversial younger novelists and poets who were not aligned with the establishment, along with essayists and cultural critics, published in leading provincial journals or, when the opportunity arose, in the pages of Hong Kong and Taiwan publications. And, just as Zhou Lunyou published his *cri de coeur* (quoted near the beginning of this chapter), Beijing TV aired 'The Editors', a sitcom set in a magazine editorial department that lambasted the official over-culture with unprecedented, and ill-concealed, glee.[12] Zhou's 'A Stance of Rejection' itself appeared in a samizdat poetry journal that subsequently ceased publication because its contributors found they could readily place their works in mainstream literary magazines.

The growth of these popular market spaces was not, as revolutionary vis-à-vis the ordained cultural order as many observers would claim. Nonetheless, the rise of a local rock and pop (dubbed by some 'Mandopop' – that is, Mandarin rock-pop)[13] scene, the mass publishing market with its plethora of entertainment and lifestyle journals, mainland commercial and party advertising, and so on, did constitute an active response by local culture producers to the incursion of off-shore cultural forms and capital. However, in the years following Deng Xiaoping's 1992 tour, during which he openly criticized 'leftist' thinking (that is, political opposition to the accelerated market reforms, the privatization of state industries, and so on), the most vocal and concerted attacks on the Communist Party's reformist agenda and its sociopolitical impact came not from the semi-independent intelligentsia, or fringe cultural figures, but from within the party itself.

The hostility of the official left, a group of establishment thinkers and writers who were derided by their public critics as 'red fundamentalists' (*yuan hongzhizhuyizhe*), also found expression in a number of public forums that had been created following 4 June. As they were routed by policy shifts and marginalized during the 1990s, many of the true believers decamped to institutions and publications on the fringes of power. Their journals covered both cultural and ideological issues and, throughout the decade, they produced a constant stream of criticism – and in many cases vitriol – aimed at the most divisive elements of the party's programme.[14] They also launched attacks on an array of ideological soft targets, in particular individuals whom they regarded as being dangerous revisionists, the chief object of their spleen being Wang Meng, the writer and former minister of culture (1986–9).

In 1995, the Australian-based Chinese journalist and oral historian Sang Ye questioned one retired high-level cadre about his views of the degeneration of the revolution and his opposition to the reform policies. He said that,

> starting with the Third Plenum of the Eleventh Party Congress in 1978, we have pursued a dangerous rightist policy. We've now gone so far to the right that we've abandoned the basic principles of Marxism and the objective rules of social development.
> ... [T]hings have reached a point that anyone with a conscience, anyone who cares about the fate of our nation, just has to weep at the dire predicament we are in.[15]

Retirees like this former minister muttered glum condemnations in private while some of their colleagues memorialized the Central Committee through secret petitions, but from the mid-1990s, a number of writers chose to speak out publicly against the market reforms that they argued were undermining what remained of both the ethos and the rationale of the revolution.

Their protests were aired in a media debate about what was called the 'humanist spirit' and 'kowtowing to the vulgar'. The burgeoning of mass-market popular culture led to despair among people who had only recently regained their faith in (and affirmed their identification with) the tradition of the Chinese literati-scholars, the political and cultural mandarins of the past. It was a self-identification that reinforced an abiding belief in the socialist dogma of the artist as prophet. Having borne witness to the decay of the cultural welfare state over the past decade, they now saw their own influence waning. They felt that writers who profited from the tide of commercialization were prostituting their talents and betraying the cause of a revived literati culture.

Among the most outspoken critics of the new marketplace and its advocates were two ex Red Guard novelists, Liang Xiaosheng and Zhang Chengzhi. They issued dark warnings about the effect that mass commercial culture was having on the 'soul of China'. As Zhang wrote in an alarmist hyperbole partially inspired by Samuel P. Huntington's writings on 'the clash of civilizations',

> After the war of the civilizations, they should at least find in the rubble of the defeated a few bodies of intellectuals who fought to the death. I despise surrender. In particular, in this war of civilizations, I loathe intellectuals who have made a vocation out of capitulation.[16]

Appeals for a moral rearmament that would find its ordnance in the Maoist past were part of a strategy used by writers such as Zhang to critique contemporary social, political and artistic realities. To question the status quo, the incursion of capital and the consumer tendencies of society was a shrewd tactic in an avowed 'war of resistance'. Opponents to this approach, however, were deeply suspicious of the presumption of intellectuals to harangue their fellows. Of these the most noteworthy was the novelist and essayist Wang Xiaobo (d. 1997), an important figure who perhaps, more than any other 1990s writer, represented the urbane scepticism of people both weary and wary of intellectual afflatus. 'I respect your high-sounding ideas,' he wrote, 'but I'm less than anxious to have them shoved down my throat.' Or, as he remarked on the habits of the educated caste: 'Chinese intellectuals particularly enjoy using moralistic paradigms to lecture others.'[17]

Indeed how useful or reliable were the tainted resources of high-socialist 'leftism', ones that were by the very nature of their place in contemporary Chinese life compromised and disingenuous? Was the objectivization of the past simply distorted and clouded by the subjectivist caste of those who lived and remember it, or needed to use it to justify themselves in the 1990s? Again, a number of writers were equivocal about intellectual grandstanding and instead turned their attention to the detail of the past, and attempted, through the writing of local histories for a general readership, to fill in some of the gaps of public knowledge.[18]

Not all critics of either the moral revivalists or the 'new leftists' (see below), however, were as phlegmatic as Wang Xiaobo. The ideological control of the party had been such that many had suffered, or continued to suffer, directly from its manipulations, or at the hands of the people's democratic dictatorship (the main organs of which were the police, the penal system, the armed police, the army and the judiciary). There were those who had been arrested for their unorthodox activities or views, denied publishing opportunities or chances to travel, or refused improved housing conditions and promotion, as well as those who had been jailed, harassed by the police and placed under surveillance. They were emotionally and intellectually determined to see the one-party state weakened and undermined, no matter what the cost. For them the marketplace was a welcome ally in their quest. They preferred an enfeebled party-state that permitted direct resistance even if it meant that the new dominant market might well make that resistance little more than cosmetic.

For some publishers and editors, trepidation about the continued ability of the Chinese Communist Part (CCP) to maintain national integrity, as well as to shore up its ideological and cultural hegemony, was virtually on a par with fears about the inundation of overseas capital and the multinational corporations that were energetically expanding into the Chinese cultural market. As one publisher remarked to me in late 1998: if you are a responsible intellectual you have to consider whether you are willing to live with the consequences of your opposition to the relatively free-wheeling status quo. Individuals like my interlocutor contemplated a future ruled by the kind of Great Leader that the American journalist P.J. O'Rourke encountered during his late 1990s 'worst of both worlds' sojourn in *fin-de-siècle* Shanghai, omnipresent amid all the frenzy of Shanghai is that famous portrait, that modern icon. The faintly smiling, bland, yet somehow threatening visage appears in brilliant red hues on placards and posters, and is painted huge on the sides of buildings. Some call him a genius. Others blame him for the deaths of millions. There are those who say his military reputation was inflated, yet he conquered the mainland in short order. Yes, it's Colonel Sanders.[19]

Modernization and prosperity had been central to the aspirations and public discourse not only of the Chinese intelligentsia but also to the concerns of the broader population throughout the twentieth century. When, during the 1990s, the economic reforms created a version of modernization as well as its attendant problems in the urban centres of the nation, the debates about it took a new turn.

If the 1980s saw intellectuals and broad segments of the population gradually breaking away from the thrall of the socialist nation-state to articulate visions of the society and its future at variance with the official world, in the 1990s, a gradual reformulation of controversies and issues that had first resurfaced in the intellectual and cultural worlds took place. The topics of political reform, Enlightenment values and modernity were now interrogated in more comprehensive terms and in relation to the history of modern Chinese history, conventionally dated from the Opium War of 1840.

A number of the key intellectual critics of the 1990s – as well as some of the most controversial participants in the debates – were themselves historians, or specialists in aspects of intellectual history. Their number included academics such as Xiao Gongqin, Lei Yi, Wang Hui, Xu Jilin, Qin Hui and Zhu Xueqin. They were thinkers who constantly shifted between their studies of sociopolitical issues of the past, the development of historical narratives during the century and an engagement in contemporary polemics. Although these individuals were attracted to different academic schools of thought, from the early 1990s, they were all active as media cultural commentators. Writers such as Xu Jilin recognized that even though the intelligentsia no longer enjoyed its previous prominence, there was still a place for the socially engaged cultural commentator.

> One can take on the role of observer, a person whose particular intellectual and cultural standpoint attempts an independent critique of various social phenomena. You try to participate actively in the cultural evolution of your world … and try to use the mass media to give voice to your conscience.[20]

After 4 June, various divisions within the intellectual and cultural worlds laid the basis for the conflicts of the 1990s. One group of intellectuals, academics, writers and propagandists tended to devote its energies to developing theoretical approaches and formulating practical policy strategies to serve the party-state, to participate in what was called 'systemic innovation' (*zhidu chuangxin*). Supporting the secular socialism of post-totalitarianism, these strategists and academic thinkers-cum-advisers concentrated their efforts on aiding the emerging market-socialist state to modernize, augmenting its efforts at legitimacy as well as helping it respond effectively to the problems that the reforms (as well as its disavowed utopian socialist project) had created. Their aim was to achieve some form of 'ideological hegemony' for themselves while also helping to buttress the legitimacy of the Communist Party.[21] Beyond the calculated goodwill and efforts of these image and policy consultants, non-aligned critics were more generally drawn to ponder the questions of whether the party leadership could renew itself effectively, or if it was simply fatally burdened with the political talents of what John Maynard Keynes would have recognized as 'third-generation men'.

Some thinkers who were not necessarily unconditional supporters of the status quo wrote policy papers both for the political and the new economic elites. Their motivations were complex, they combined a sense of duty to the nation-state with the hope of achieving a public profile while at the same time providing a rationale for the activities of (or a reasoned limitation on) the power holders. They were latter-day advocates of 'disinterested opinion' (*qingyi*), if you will.[22] The issues that many of these thinkers tussled with concerned the balance between equity and liberalism, market power and political stability, national sovereignty and global capital. Concocting strategies that could help the party renovate itself and possibly move towards greater plurality was, for many of these activists, the best way China could avoid going through another revolution and suffering the social dislocation, mass deprivation and political confusion that they felt would inevitably result. National crisis was not some distant or inchoate fear, but an overshadowing spectre reinforced both by China's history from the 1840s onwards and the more recent collapse of the former socialist countries to the West.

For many other writers, however, the fate of the party and its immediate future were no longer issues of particular relevance. Broad-based political, social and cultural criticism became one of the fundamental ways in which circumspect dissent was expressed throughout the decade. Authors of historical tracts, as well as publishers, took advantage of the commercial market to help fill in the 'white spots' of history and inform contemporary debates. By the late 1990s, as a range of analysts within China warned that the economic reform strategy in its present form had all but run its course, many publicly-active intellectuals – that is, academics and writers who engaged in the major intellectual and cultural disputes of the decade in the print media and at specialist forums – were tending to form into two camps. These were divergent, even opposing, groups in the debates surrounding the central issues of twentieth century Chinese cultural and political polemics.

In the 1990s, the formerly dominant state-sponsored ideology was going through further transformation; the fustian party credo still maintained a notional media hegemony, even though the actual pursuit of political cohesion was increasingly limited to party organs and official discourse. In administrative terms, the ageing and retirement of staunch traditional propagandists left the way open to a cadre of younger men and women who functioned more as party PR people than political watchdogs. The downsizing (or 'rightsizing') of the party apparat also meant that there were fewer reliable apparatchiki devoted to the persecution of clandestine or even egregious ideological errors. Added to this was the ravenous publishing market hungry for new books and periodicals, as well as the commercialization of transgressive thought. As a result, writers and thinkers had to contest openly for the approval of like-minded activists, a share of public attention, media success and even official approbation. All of these developments had a significant impact on the commercialized controversies of the 1990s such as the clash over humanistic values of 1993 onwards, the strife regarding the 'kowtowing to the vulgar' a few years later (mentioned earlier), and the furore surrounding pop nationalistic screeds such as *China Through the Third Eye* and *China, Just Say No!* As the decade drew to a close, a number of factors gave a focus to the last major intellectual clash of the century: a previously buoyant economy coupled with a looming fiscal crisis and social upheavals; concerns about the agendas of the entrenched party bureaucrats and its big business allies; US hegemony and the impact of global capital; and the effects these were having on the population at large.[23]

The mainland characterization, or even assumed self-description, of the two major opposing groups of independent intellectuals that developed from the mid-1990s was that they consisted of neo-liberals and neo-leftists, or to follow Xu Jilin's early 1999 appellation of the latter group, the new left-wing.[24] The initial public conflict between these schools of thought was sparked by Wang Hui, the editor of *Reading* and a prominent intellectual historian.[25] In a lengthy analysis of the post Cultural Revolution Chinese intelligentsia and its relationship to the question of modernity published in late 1997, Wang interrogated the ability of contemporary mainland thinkers to respond to the complex issues related to China's modernization and involvement in the global economy.[26] A year later, he further challenged his fellows by issuing a theoretical discussion of scientism, the accepted sociopolitical and historical paradigms of modernity, and the nation-state in twentieth-century Chinese intellectual history.[27] It was from the publication of Wang's 1997 essay in particular that the two polemical groupings developed contending public positions and thereafter engaged in a high-profile 'confrontation of caricatures'.

An extensive and widespread theoretical interest in liberalism had developed from the 1980s. This body of thought and theory was influenced by the introduction, or popularization, of the writings of a range of thinkers from John Locke and Jean Jacques Rousseau, to Karl Popper and F.A. von Hayek, as well as by the efforts of writers in Beijing, Shanghai and elsewhere to 'unearth' and write about Chinese proponents of liberal thought from earlier in the century.[28] By the mid-1990s, there was, as Xu Jilin observed, a de facto 'thorough-going victory of liberalism in the realm of popular ideas. The word "liberalism" itself had achieved a cultural cachet previously enjoyed by such terms as democracy and science'.[29] Writers of all backgrounds and persuasions, philosophers, historians, as well as literary critics, were gradually drawn in to considering the impact of these ideas and employing them, as well as other theoretical models, to come to terms with the vast changes China was experiencing.

Finding inspiration in particular in the neo-classical liberalism of von Hayek, thinkers and writers advocated the pursuit of an Enlightenment agenda: their concern was to see the project of modernization in China fulfil its promise to allow for independent thinking and democratic reform, as well as providing a legal framework for the protection of property rights and economic freedoms. As ideological policing waned for a time in 1997–98, writers in this camp gave voice to their opposition to the Communist Party and called for further market reforms. They talked directly of the need for a programme of political change, along with democratic and legal reforms, that would bring the nation into line with what they identified as accepted international practice.[30]

Many thinkers entered the fray, and their writings covered a range of positions that reflected a spectrum of opinion that actually belied the overall impression that there was agreement even within these avowedly opposing groups. A number of observers remarked that they thought the controversy between neo-liberals and neo-leftists rather bizarre, given the fact that, as they put it: 'In you there is a little bit of me, and in me there is a little bit of you' (*nizhong you wo, wozhong you ni*). Be that as it may, while the neo-liberals were more than willing to be identified as such, the neo-leftists generally shied away from the label of leftism; it was a reluctance influenced by the negative connotation that 'the left' had acquired in China due to its historical associations with the extremism of the Maoist past.[31] And here we should be mindful of the fact that all participants in the intellectual debates of 1990s China were functioning in an environment that was both less ideologically confrontational (the authorities were generally reluctant to interfere directly) and more commercially driven than ever before. In other words, well-articulated intellectual positions could accrue dividends in a range of ways within academia, the media, and in terms of public exposure and intellectual profile.

The symbiotic relationship of dissenting individuals and groups could also be evaluated in terms of both group dynamics and long-term 'outcomes' and credibility. A person's status and position during the next period of liberalization could be influenced if one did not perform in a manner acceptable to one's intellectual-cultural peers during the previous phase of activism and repression. While we should be alert to the need to avoid assertions that there was some crude collective mentality at the heart of this performative activism, it would nonetheless be naive to ignore the realities of group dynamics when considering the style as well as the content of cultural and political apostasy.

The thinkers identified as the left wing had first found their voice among overseas scholars and writers based in particular in the USA. Although they initially published their views in Hong Kong journals such as *Twenty-first Century*, which was founded in 1990,[32] gradually they came to enjoy overt support among mainland-based writers. Their stance, one particularly informed by their position in US academia, provided 'a vigorous critique of the liberal ideology of the West, and a call to transcend socialism and capitalism by developing a strategy for 'systemic renovation' based on China's particular path of modernization'.[33] Their credentials and post-colonial superiority did not impress everyone, however, and in 1995 the voluble philosopher Liu Dong dubbed their writings a product of a 'pidgin academic style'.[34]

As they gradually formulated a general position in the Hong Kong and mainland media from the mid-1990s, the left-wing writers were particularly attentive to what they saw as being the collaboration between the socialist state and international global capital. Some of their number analysed how intellectuals had been disarmed by their acceptance of an economic (and ideological) programme that would not necessarily lead to a real social and market liberalization, or a democratization that could be enjoyed by all equally. They stressed that the reforms were fostering extreme inequalities, inequities both of class within China and in relation to international geopolitics in which the mainland would be dominated by overseas capital. They pointed to a new form of mass dictatorship by a cartel of international capital, the super-rich oligarchy, or 'monopoly elite' (*longduan jingying*) of China and party cronies. And they warned that the liberal intellectuals would, by default, provide a cultural and historical justification for the power holders as this process unfolded.

If the neo-liberals championed the middle class and the 'level playing field' of the market, aiding (as their critics saw it) the interests of both domestic and international capital – and saw in the rise of the market the possibility for equitable modernization that would eventually benefit society as a whole – then the new left wing was deeply sceptical about the democratizing benefits of market reforms. They increasingly took a position in defence of 'mass participatory democracy' (*quanmian minzhu*), a vague formulation that notionally favoured the exploited masses and the rapidly growing underclass. As Cui Zhiyuan, an outspoken thinker of the 'new left' then based at the Massachusetts Institute of Technology, put it, 'The real struggle today is between reformers out for the people as a whole, and reformers out for themselves.'[35] Some on the left stressed the need for a stronger state that could effectively limit inequities, prevent domination by foreign/private capital and shore up national unity. According to the Qinghua University historian Qin Hui, an active participant in the debates, the irony of the situation was that both sides in this rhetorical stand-off should have been able to find common cause in opposing extremist positions; that is to say, the liberals should have concentrated on opposing authoritarianism, while the left-wing 'social democrats' should have been on guard against populism. Instead, they identified a common enemy in each other.

Something that added an edge to these acrimonious debates was the crucial issue of perceived political impotence. Communist Party monopoly rule effectively deprived participants in the rancorous intellectual exchanges from utilizing any direct political or systemic mechanism through which they could implement their ideas beyond exercising a measure of influence on party leaders. The hegemony of the one-party state both frustrated the intelligentsia and at the same time afforded them an unprecedented freedom to debate the abstract issues central to twentieth-century Chinese intellectual life. The left wing, while energetic in its critiques of liberalism and the market, was, until the time of writing at least, unenthusiastic about joining forces or openly advocating any concrete political programme or strategy to deal with what they perceived as being a parlous situation. Certainly, some of their number advocated a reinvigorated central government and putting a brake on the market and foreign capital, while expanding the state's redistributive role. Similarly, the spectrum of liberal thinkers actively advocated change within the context of the existing political system – and their demands in this context were not that different from those of the protesters of 1989, or the small number of public dissidents during the 1990s[36] – but they shied away from direct political action or the forming of public lobby groups.

Han Yuhai, a professor of literature at Peking University, became one of the most extreme public opponents of liberalism. His critiques were so splenetic that one was reminded of the 'gunpowder stench' (*huoyaowei*) of Cultural Revolution period denunciations. Han declared that the market liberals' support for social and political stability for the sake of economic development (and, theoretically, long-term societal transformation) was little more than a justification for market rapaciousness; it served to protect and further the interests of entrenched elites, mitigated against majority political participation and indeed frustrated attempts at bona fide democratization. In one particular screed entitled 'Behind the "Liberal" Pose', Han stated, 'liberalism has enjoyed ascendancy because it proffers a theoretical framework that allows right-wing politics to overcome its legitimacy crisis'.[37] Han insisted that the liberals were giving succour to the party-state and the status quo; stability was essential for economic prosperity, and the threat of a collapse in China was being used by *sui-disant* liberals as an argument against democratic rebellion, concerted and organized opposition, or radical resistance.

Han Yuhai proclaimed the so-called liberal intelligentsia of China to be bankrupt; they had lost any claim to legitimacy themselves and a role in the (presumably more democratic and egalitarian) future of the nation. But even for extremists such as Han, not all liberalism was bad – even if, as a label, it was useful for tagging one's opponents and condemning them holus-bolus. In the same article Han referred positively to Isaiah Berlin, the political philosopher whose death in 1997 was widely commented on in China, and who was recalled as a 'great herald of liberalism'. Indeed, in Berlin's writings we find a clear articulation of the issues that hound Chinese intellectual debate:

> Both liberty and equality are among the primary goals pursued by human beings throughout many centuries; but total liberty for wolves is death to the lambs, total liberty of the powerful, the gifted, is not compatible with the rights to a decent existence of the weak and the less gifted ... Equality may demand the restraint of the liberty of those who wish to dominate; liberty – without some modicum of which there is not choice and therefore no possibility of remaining human as we understand the word – may have to be curtailed in order to make room for social welfare, to feed the hungry, to

clothe the naked, to shelter the homeless, to leave room for the liberty of others, to allow justice or fairness to be exercised.[38]

Although both sides could quote Berlin at each other, the glaring disparity in the intellectual underpinnings of the groups made a dialogue between them problematic. The neo-liberals identified with the post-May Fourth tradition of cultural renewal in China and basically accepted celebratory views of the Western Enlightenment and late twentieth-century Euro-American market democracy. For their part, the neo-leftists generally drew on post-modernist, post-colonial and neo-Marxist theories, as well as on more conventional Marxism-Leninism and Mao Thought. Be that as it may, by the end of the decade, neither side was willing or perhaps even able to talk to the other.

Critics such as Xu Jilin were intent on maintaining independence from these two, notionally opposed, polemical camps. In 1989, Xu had written an essay on the 'vicious cycle of the May Fourth movement' in which he reviewed the history of the first decade of the reform era and expressed concern that the nation was entering another period similar to that of the May Fourth, when the opposing forces of iconoclasm and conservatism had led to bitter intellectual and cultural infighting. The strife of the 1920s had become endemic to public debates thereafter, and politicized academic life in China for decades.[39] Writing again in 1998, this time in retrospect on the intellectual history of the past twenty years, Xu concluded,

> A unified intellectual sphere in which people can engage in profitable dialogue no longer exists. The consensus of the New Enlightenment [of the 1980s] has collapsed, very much in the way that it did during the original May Fourth movement. Does this mean we are to experience some inescapable historical destiny?[40]

Although I would be tempted to question whether such a consensus ever really existed,[41] a nightmarish vision that predicted that the present would disappear in such a circular motion made for an appealing cultural trope. Confrontations could aid and abet ideological opponents in a media environment still circumscribed by the Communist Party. Indeed, the public clash of competing views tended to enhance extreme positions and led to 'a certain idiom of vituperation that belongs to the levels of escalation at which debate is no longer possible'.[42] During the late 1990s, each side became more extreme in its critique of the other; where a middle ground existed it was often undermined by rhetorical overkill. Both sides felt that their opponents were conspiring (*hemou*) with the authorities. Thus, 'leftists' were identified as being part of the party-state status quo; while 'rightists' were seen as serving the interests of international capital and new commercial elites within China.

In early 1999, a number of non-aligned Shanghai-based scholars including Xu Jilin gathered to discuss the contest between the new left and the new right. Xu in particular pointed out that there were traditional intellectual resources, a lineage of liberalism that dated back to the 1920s, that could perhaps help foster a new environment for rational disputation.[43] What was required was, and here Xu referred to the political philosopher John Rawls, an 'overlapping consensus', that is to say, an 'overlapping consensus of reasonable comprehensive doctrines'.[44]

Just where that consensus could be found could not easily be articulated in public. As Joseph Brodsky observed in an open letter to the former Czech dissident Václav Havel shortly after the latter's rise to political power in the early 1990s, 'in the police state absolutes compromise each other since they engender each other'. For one point of commonality among the disputants described above appeared to be a shared opposition to the one-party state as it was presently constituted. And although writers would meditate in their long analyses on the multifarious crises facing China, direct confrontation with the authorities was still limited to a small, and at times highly public and vocal, coalition of dissidents. Again, as Brodsky noted about dissidents in socialist Czechoslovakia, overt opponents to the powers-that-be were often a 'convenient example of the wrong deportment and thus a source of considerable moral comfort, the way the sick are for the healthy majority'.[45] Their existence cautioned others not to catch cold.

In the left-wing stance, however, there was also an explicit critique of the monism of globalization and liberalism current in China from the early 1990s. It was a critique that went back to the origins of the 1970s reform policy itself when the incipient economic policies were justified not only as a necessity, but as part of a continued effort to link the nation with the grand trends of market oriented developmentalism. The 1990s left wing questioned the new holism, the view that there was one programme or rationale that promised through its realization the resolution of the myriad of problems of contemporary life – political, social, cultural and economic. Thus the loose collective of Chinese left-wing thinkers came to articulate an opposition to democratic capitalism and the ideology of a universal civilization that John Gray identified as the 'last false Utopia of the twentieth-century': globalization.[46]

But to accept at face value the wholesale (perhaps even ritualistic) condemnation of liberals by writers such as Han Yuhai is easily misleading. Liu Junning, for example, was a prominent Beijing-based advocate of liberalism and the editor of the main liberal journal, *Res Publica* (Liu subsequently lost his job and travelled to the USA for an extended period of 'research' as an independent scholar). In his editorial introduction to a collection of essays on pre-1949 liberalism and the history of Peking University published at the time of the school's centenary in 1998, Liu noted that, although the Chinese intelligentsia had been captivated by holistic projects from the 1920s, when it came to the economic realities of their own environment they were often at a complete loss. Throughout the century they shared a scepticism regarding the role of free markets and the need for the growth of a strong middle class. For them 'the allure of totalitarian patterns of thought was paramount'. Liu argued that although the intelligentsia had at times shown itself to be passionately interested in cultural liberalism and a measure of political freedom, in regard to socioeconomic realities the disparate members of the nation's liberal thinkers had always 'been basically out of touch with their environment. They have never really been part of the normal Chinese community, rather they have been sequestered in an ivory tower.'[47]

Intellectuals debating these issues in the pages of learned journals, often employing the guarded language required by an environment of official censorship, was one thing. But change would not necessarily come from the refined 'wonking' of the chattering classes or *trahison des clercs*.[48] Dissidents felt that only popular agitation would allow disparate social forces to have a say in the direction and protection of their own lives, as well as in national politics. (See chapter 1.) Other non-aligned intellectuals and social activists attempted in a myriad of ways – through private, small-scale charity projects, covert foundation activities and so on – to engage actively in civic actions that would benefit their fellows. However, for those imbued with the ideologies of national salvation and participation, to be materially well-off but politically dispossessed, a member of the underclass or itinerant labour force, or being engaged but compromised within a system that would allow the acquisition of capital but maintained electoral disenfranchisement and political impotence, was deeply frustrating. The hope, follies and failure of 1989 and the quest for systemic change and political reform that was central to the concerns of thinkers, cultural activists, progressive politicians and people of conscience at the time remained issues central to the political agenda ten years on. Enforced political impuissance and the internecine warfare obsessed the intelligentsia, and for moderate thinkers such as Xu Jilin and his fellows, it was increasingly evident that when major changes did come the niceties of political discussion could once more be overridden by restive mass sentiment.

At the advent of the new millennium, as the Communist Party held its Sixteenth Congress in late 2002, here was the dilemma that the intelligentsia and cultural activists continued to face: was the role of the independent critic or feisty artist enough to satisfy participants in the bitter debates about the state of the nation and its future? Was the twentieth-century tradition of political agitation to remain obscured by the Communist Party's purges of the early 1950s, the repression of the Hundred Flowers, the 'mass democracy' of the Cultural Revolution, the crushing of the Democracy Wall dissidents, and the purges of the 1980s, as well as the bloodshed of 1989, and the quelling of dissidents in the late 1990s? Would elite intellectuals who proffered analyses of the nation's woes find fellowship with dissidents who were willing to confront the government, or workers and peasants whose outrage at exploitation led them to rebel? Or was the reconstitution of the intellectuals' mission something that encouraged circumspection and inactivity? Did international cachet count more for local street-cred? This 'cult of transgression without risk'[49] found adherents at all points of the political spectrum, while a cult that did not really transgress, such as that of the Buddho-Daoist *Falun Gong* meditation sect that was outlawed in mid-1999, ironically posed risks for its adherents, and was celebrated by many internationally as a misunderstood force for good. While Falun Dafa's pastiche of religious practice appealed to some, others cleaved to an electronic *deus ex machina*. (See chapter 11.)

For some – both in China and internationally – it has been an article of faith that the growth of a Sinophone intellectual and information-oriented web culture from the 1990s would herald the transformation of cultural protocols and even political possibility in the Chinese world. Webzine editors, writers, activists and default censors include some of the most prominent established 'independent' and 'critical intellectuals' active since the 1980s. Many participate in the web culture that they also critique and play a key role in mediating and shaping. Some have extended into cyberspace an intellectual stance and self-imposed role that has evolved in the complex arena of 'reformist-era' media (publishing, editing and writing, in particular, in the 1990s).[50] Many of its producers are guided by the notion that using cyberspace to discuss problems and issues in Chinese intellectual praxis will nurture a virtual civil society into being, one that they assume will see enlightened public opinion winning out in the end over ill-informed ideas and misconceptions essayed both by the official media and populist discourse in China. That this parallels a cluster of views within international cyber-discussion which sees the net as creating an open community of netizens who will obviate sociopolitical and historical boundaries is, perhaps, no coincidence. It goes without saying that this notion is akin to a guiding principle to which most producers of cybertexts subscribe, wherever they are physically located and whichever language they use.

An unprecedented openness and frankness seems to be apparent when one surveys the debates generated on the plethora of Chinese websites. In the years when web debate has flourished (roughly from 1999), a glut of electronic text has appeared on diverse topics such as the Cheung Kong *Reading* Awards of 2000, intellectual plagiarism, the awarding of the Nobel Literature Prize to the French-based writer Gao Xingjian, 11 September, the China tours of Jacques Derrida and Jürgen Habermas, to name but a few of these topics. The 'discussions' that have taken place around such current affairs issues and prominent intellectual tourists are textually uneven. Some authors publish under their own names while others assume pseudonyms, or both; some provide essay-length accounts, others script paragraph-length critiques, while some others contribute no more than a sentence or two, or lend support to or show disapproval of any one declared position through an appropriately worded subject heading. The unsolicited text-bite, as opposed to the media-massaged sound-bites generated by ordained experts, gives a currency to the kind of utterances previously sequestered in narrow specialist cultural journals while making public the private discussions of the culturally concerned.

In engaging with this new technologically enabled and enhanced mode of discourse, it is arguable that the mode of production (that is, cyberspace publishing via Internet technology) can and does determine (although one must also be wary of technological determinism) the contents of the resulting discourse significantly more than print technology did for what we now regard as conventional print texts. The speed at which an electronic text can be composed and posted to draw almost immediate responses, composed and published in like manner in mere minutes, appears at first glance to alter in a radical way the nature and function of discourse as it has operated within a conventional print medium. The proliferation of critical themes and targets in supra-border Chinese intellectual cyberspace offers its readers, among other things, the novel experience of observing and participating in spectacles of disagreement that reflect existing rivalries between individuals and intellectual 'factions' and in the range of current opinions circulating in Chinese intellectual cultural circles. There is a crucial difference between the economies that govern the production of conventional print and electronic publications, and the regulative controls to which these are subjected by publishers, the media authorities and the market-place.

Newspaper and journal editorial boards deliberate on what is suitable for publication, mindful of the often vague but sometimes quite pointed and specific guidelines that issue through the party-state chain of command, and what 'sells' (or in the case of academic journals, what is 'relevant' to the field's concerns, or indeed what can create a potentially rich new sub-area of inquiry) within the physical limits imposed by available page space, in accordance with publication deadlines and printing schedules that can be met only through reliance on a size-able number of support staff. The webmaster, web editorial team or list owner, however, skims through postings, forced by the sheer quantities and types of responses received to reach quick decisions on what to post. In the context of cyberspace 'freedom' from the spatial constraints of the printed page, electronic textual arbiters would seem to be generally inclined towards favouring an inclu-siveness as comprehensive as their websites are able to accommodate, while observing rudimentary protocols of discursive interaction derived from existing conventions that guide embodied exchanges in the seminar room or textual encounters in the pages of journals and newspapers.

But does the greatly accelerated rate of publication and access, increased space for plural commentaries and the transformed nature of what can be acknowledged as intellectual or critical discourse lead, as it were, *naturally*, to the emergence of an unprecedented degree of intellectual freedom and greater accountability? On the contrary, increased access to textual production and consumption, and a seemingly inexhaustible wealth of electronic publications on manifold themes and topics, might end up doing little more than shifting existing modes of intellectual discourse and well-established structures of intellectual authority into a new virtual realm of expanded combative interaction of a kind that first found market validity in the humanism debate of the mid-1990s.

For the China academic (that is, the ethnic or non-ethnic scholar of Chinese studies), on the net there is now the novel experience of seeing a virtual assem-blage akin to all that can be said on a given topic of interest displayed as a long list of subject headings. Indeed it will not be surprising to see prominent academic careers being forged in the coming years on the basis of interpretive mastery of issues debated on Chinese web forums. Perhaps a new research industry awaits us, one that harnesses techniques of empirical scholarship and textual analysis to the enterprise of charting an emergent virtual Chinese 'public sphere' whose perceived salient features could be variously represented, distilled as these are from the ongoing accrual of textual riches deposited at different sites, providing a republic of opinion in the guise of equal and equitable exchange with which to gauge the state of 'Chineseness', or at least to plumb the depths of concern and interest of the Chinese 'internal audience' of intellectual practitioners, at any given moment. For the Chinese cybertext reader and producer, the novelty of this particular form of low-risk but circumvented public participation in debates that were hitherto largely the exclusive province of select groups of elite intellectuals is tempered by considerations of the consequences that attend such participation.

* * *

In his 1991 manifesto, 'A Stance of Rejection', Zhou Lunyou had advocated cultural disengagement and disobedience. In the following years, market reforms as well as expanding areas of civil debate and social agitation blurred the simple cultural antagonisms of the past. By the end of the decade, the romance of resistance may still have appealed to observers of the mainland arts scene (both Chinese and foreign), but for prominent participants it was often easier to ignore the state than to resist the discreet charms of offshore capital. In the revolution of resistance, outspoken members of the intelligentsia, however, found themselves variously on the defensive and on the offensive, participants in and opponents to the reforms that had given them a new lease on life. At the *debut de siècle* the domain of intellectual politics on mainland China was quickened not by an overlapping consensus, but by issues and debates that divided and confronted at every turn.

Notes

1   Lu Xun, 'Xiao zagan', *Eryiji*, collected in *Lu Xun quanji* (Beijing, Renmin wenxue chubanshe, 1981), vol. 3, p. 532. From the translation by Simon Leys in his *The Burning Forest: Essays on Chinese Culture and Politics* (New York: Holt, Rinehart and Winston, 1985), p. 222. The first part of the quotation is:

> Revolution, counterrevolution, nonrevolution.
> Revolutionaries are massacred by counterrevolutionaries. Counterrevolutionaries are massacred by revolutionaries. Nonrevolutionaries are sometimes taken for revolutionaries, and then they are massacred by counterrevolutionaries, or again they are taken for counterrevolutionaries, and then they are massacred by revolutionaries. Sometimes, also, they are not taken for anything in particular, but they are still massacred by revolutionaries and by counterrevolutionaries.

2   Quoted in Geremie R. Barmé, *In the Red, on Contemporary Chinese Culture* (New York: Columbia University Press, 1999), p. 37. For more on the 'Not-not' poets, see Geremie R. Barmé and John Minford (eds), *Seeds of Fire: Chinese Voices of Conscience*, 2nd edition (New York: Hill and Wang, 1988), pp. 405–6; and 'Feifei zhuyi zhuanji' in *Jintian*, 3, 42 (1998), pp. 55–96.

3   This is W.J.F. Jenner's gloss on the term 'transgressive'.

4 After 1989, a number of dispirited cultural activists turned to money making in the south. It was a trend obvious in intellectual discourse from around 1992, at first particularly in Shanghai, where a number of intellectuals began playing the stock market and speculated on the real estate boom.

5 Evinced in the new Mao cult, revolutionary *karaoke* numbers, popular interest in pre-1966 feature films, and so on.

6 Michael Dutton, *Streetlife China* (New York: Cambridge University Press, 1998), p. 282.

7 *Ibid.*

8 That is, ideocrats who supported elements of traditional Marxist-Leninist-Maoist theory, although few of the public, or internal, pronouncements by these figures was 'Maoist' in the pre-1976 or high-Cultural Revolution sense of the word.

9 Xu Jilin, 'Qimengde mingyun – ershi nianlaide Zhongguo sixiangjie', *Ershiyi shiji*, 12, 50 (1998), pp. 4–13, at p. 5; translated by Geremie R. Barmé with Gloria Davies as 'The Fate of an Enlightenment – Twenty Years in the Chinese Intellectual Sphere (1978–98)', *East Asian History*, 20 (December 2000). For a detailed study of the 1980s' cultural foment, see Chen Fong-ching and Jin Guantao, *From Youthful Manuscripts to River Elegy: The Chinese Popular Cultural Movement and Political Transformation 1979–1989* (Hong Kong: Chinese University Press, 1997).

10 For an overview of responses to the intellectual and cultural ructions of the late 1980s, see Geremie R. Barmé (ed. and ann.), *On the Eve: China Symposium 89, Bolinas, California, 27–29 April, 1989*, 1996 cyberpublication at <http://www.tsquare.tv/film/Bolinas1.html>.

11 Xu Jilin, *op. cit.*, p. 6.

12 For the published version of this series, see Wang Shuo, Feng Xiaogang *et al.*, *Bianjibude gushi–youmo dianshi gushi* (Shenyang: Shenyang chubanshe, 1992, 2 vols.

13 'Mandopop' was promoted in competition to Canto pop, or Cantonese pop music from the mid-1990s. Mandarin-language rock/pop had flourished in Taiwan from the early 1980s with the success of singer-songwriters such as Lo Ta-yu (Luo Dayou).

14 Two leading oppositionist journals were *The Pursuit of Truth* (*Zhenlide zhuiqiu*) and *Currents in Contemporary Thought* (*Dangdai sichao*).

15 From the interview 'The Non-dissident', in Sang Ye, *Chairman Mao's Ark: The People on the People's Republic* (forthcoming), my translation.

16 Zhang Chengzhi, *Wuyuande sixiang*, ed. Xiao Xialin (Beijing: Huayi chubanshe, 1995), pp. 24–5, quoted in Geremie R. Barmé, *In the Red*, p. 308. Samuel P. Huntington's *The Clash of Civilizations and the Remaking of World Order* (New York: Simon and Schuster, 1996) had and continues to have an inordinate impact in China.

17 Wang Xiaobo, 'Zhishifenzide buxing', in his *Wode jingshen jiayuan: Wang Xiaobo zawen zixuan ji* (Beijing, Wenhua yishu chubanshe, 1997), p. 18; and 'Zhongguo zhishifenzi yu zhonggu yifeng', in his *Siweide lequ* (Taiyuan: Beiyue wenyi chubanshe, 1996), p. 21 respectively.

18 An example of this kind of work was the journalist Lu Yuegang's work on the state-induced famine in Fenghuo village, Shaanxi province. See Lu, *Daguo guamin* (Beijing: Zhongguo dianying chubanshe, 1998).

19 P.J. O'Rourke, 'How to Have the Worst of Both Worlds: Shanghai', in his *Eat the Rich: a Treatise on Economics* (New York, Atlantic Monthly Press, 1998), pp. 220–221. For a discussion of the impact of another US food giant, Ronald McDonald, in the north, see Yan Yunxiang, 'McDonald's in Beijing; The Localization of Americana', in James L. Watson (ed.), *Golden Arches East: McDonald's in East Asia* (Stanford: Stanford University Press, 1997), pp. 39–76.

20 Meng Meng (ed.), *1999 dubai (juan yi)* (Shanghai, Shanghai yuandong chubanshe, 1998), pp. 57–58.

21 Xu Jilin, 'Qimengde mingyun', p. 11.

22 The *qingyi* scholar-officials of the late nineteenth century were both spokesmen for public conscience and reformers of the status quo. See Luke S.K. Kwong, *A Mosaic of*

the Hundred Days: Personalities, Politics, and Ideas of 1898 (Cambridge, MA: Harvard University Press, 1984), pp. 68–73, esp. p. 70.

23 For an articulate presentation of these issues by well-informed mainland analysts, see Zhongguo zhanlüe yu guanli yanjiuhui shehui jiegou zhuanxing keti zu, 'Zhongguo shehui jiegou zhuanxingde zhongjinqi qushi yu yinhuan', *Zhanlüe yu guanli*, 5 (1998), pp. 1–17; Yang Fan, 'Zhongguo jingji mianlinde weiji yu fanweiji duice', *Zhanlüe yu guanli*, 5 (1998), pp. 18–27; and He Qinglian, *Xiandaihuede xianjing – dangdai Zhongguode jingji shehui wenti* (Beijing: *Jinri Zhongguo* chubanshe, 1998).

24 The terms in Chinese are *ziyouzhuyipai*, *xinzuopai* and *xinzuoyi* respectively.

25 *Dushu*, produced by Sanlian Publishing in Beijing, was founded by Fan Yong in the late 1970s and, for twenty years, was a leading forum for public intellectual discussion.

26 Wang Hui, 'Dangdai Zhongguode sixiang zhuangkuang yu xiandaixing wenti', *Tianya*, 5 (1997), pp. 133–50; translated by Rebecca E. Karl as 'Contemporary Chinese Thought and the Question of Modernity', in *Social Text* 55, 16, 2 (Summer 1998), pp. 9–44.

27 Wang Hui, 'Kexuezhuyi yu shehui lilunde jige wenti', *Tianya*, 6, (1998), pp. 132–60.

28 During the 1980s, prominent works on this subject were translated from English, and writers such as the journalist Dai Qing and Xu Jilin, among others, began introducing the reading public to the variety of liberal thought and leading pre-1949 liberal activists.

29 *Ibid.* Xu identifies the idolization of the Cultural Revolution period writings of Gu Zhun (both essays and diaries, for reactions to Gu Zhun's posthumous literary debut, see Ding Dong and Chen Minzhi (eds), *Gu Zhun xunsi lu* (Beijing: Zuojia chubanshe, 1998) and the best-seller status of the 1997 translations of von Hayek's *The Road to Serfdom* and *The Constitution of Liberty*, as well as the influence of *Res Publica* (*Gonggong luncong*), a journal edited by Liu Junning, as aiding the theoretical and public rise of liberalist thinking in China.

30 See, in particular, the introductory essays of Li Shenzhi and Liu Junning in Liu Junning (ed.), *Ziyouzhuyide xiansheng: Beida chuantong yu jindai Zhongguo* (Beijing: Zhongguo renshi chubanshe, 1998), pp. 1–5; and the essays by a range of prominent thinkers in Dong Yuyu and Shi Binhai (eds), *Zhengzhi Zhongguo: mianxiang xintizhi xuanzede shidai* (Beijing: *Jinri Zhongguo* chubanshe, 1998).

31 Xu, *op. cit.*, p. 13, n. 14. See also Ren Jiantao, 'Jiedu "xin zuopai"', *Tianya*, 1 (1999), pp. 35–46.

32 Based at the Institute of Chinese Studies, the Chinese University of Hong Kong, *Twenty-first Century* was edited by Liu Qingfeng and Jin Guantao. Throughout the decade this journal, which was increasingly available on the mainland, was one of the major forums for intellectual and cultural debate in the Chinese-reading world.

33 Xu Jilin, *op. cit.*, p. 11. These writers included, in particular, Gan Yang, Cui Zhiyuan, Sheng Hong, Wang Shaoguang and Hu Angang. For details of their early writings, see Xu, *op. cit.*, p. 13, n. 15. See also Xudong Zhang's introduction to 'Intellectual Politics in Post-Tiananmen China', in *Social Text* 55, 16, 2 (Summer 1998), pp. 1–8.

34 *Yangjingbang xuefeng*. See Liu Dong, 'Jingti renweide "yang jingbang xuefeng"', *Ershiyi shiji*, 12 (1995), pp. 4–13, and a response from Gan Yang, 'Shei shi Zhongguo yanjiuzhongde "women"?', *Ershiyi shiji*, 12 (1995), pp. 21–25.

35 Quoted in Erik Eckholm, 'Detour on Capitalist Road: Die-hard Maoist Collective', *The New York Times*, 7 January 1999.

36 For a range of the opinions regarding media freedom, as well as legal and democratic reform, see the 1998 volume of essays by leading liberal thinkers edited by Dong Yuyu and Shi Binhai, *Zhengzhi Zhongguo*.

37 Han Yuhai, 'Zai "Ziyouzhuyi" zitaide beihou', *Tianya*, 5 (1998), p. 17.

38 Isaiah Berlin, 'The Pursuit of the Ideal', in his *The Crooked Timber of Humanity: Chapters in the History of Ideas*, ed. Henry Hardy (London: Fontana Press, 1990), pp. 12–13. See

also David Kelly, 'The Chinese Search for Freedom as a Universal Value', in David Kelly and Anthony Reid (eds), *Asian Freedoms: The Idea of Freedom in East and Southeast Asia* (New York: Cambridge University Press, 1998), pp. 99–114.

39 See Xu's comments as translated in Geremie R. Barmé and Linda Jaivin (eds), *New Ghosts, Old Dreams: China's Rebel Voices* (New York: Times Books, 1992), pp. 345–50.

40 Xu Jilin, *op. cit.*, p. 12.

41 In regard to the 1980s, for example, one thinks of the overlapping but often antagonistic agendas of various intellectuals and cultural figures. There were also those dissidents, old and young, who rejected the elitist consensus entirely.

42 J.M. Coetzee, *Giving Offense, Essays on Censorship* (Chicago: University of Chicago Press, 1996), p. 134.

43 See, for example, Xu Jilin, 'Shehui minzhuzhuyide lishi yichan–xiandai Zhongguo ziyouzhuyide huigu', *Kaifang shidai*, 4 (1998), pp. 13–20; and Jerome B. Grieder, *Hu Shih and the Chinese Renaissance: Liberalism in the Revolution, 1917–1937* (Cambridge MA: Harvard University Press, 1970); Geremie R. Barmé, 'Time's Arrows: Imaginative Pasts and Nostalgic Futures', in Gloria Davies (ed.), *Voicing Concerns: Contemporary Chinese Critical Inquiry* (Boulder: Rowman and Littlefield, 2001), pp. 226–57.

44 John Rawls, *Political Liberalism* (New York: Columbia University Press, 1993), p. 43. See also, pp. 140, 144ff. The Qinghua University historian Qin Hui was, in particular, an advocate of such an 'overlapping consensus'. For a further discussion of this and related issues, see 'In Search of a "Third Way": A Conversation Regarding "Liberalism" and the "New Left Wing" by Xu Jilin, Liu Qing, Luo Gang, and Xue Yi', translated by Geremie R. Barmé in Gloria Davies (ed.), *Voicing Concerns*, pp. 199–226.

45 Joseph Brodsky, 'Letter to a President', written as a response to a speech by Václav Havel published in *The New York Review of Books*, 27 May 1993. For these quotations, see Brodsky, *On Grief and Reason: Essays* (London: Hamish Hamilton, 1996), pp. 215 and 214 respectively.

46 John Gray, *False Dawn: The Dilemmas of Global Capitalism* (London: Granta Books, 1998), pp. 3 and 191 respectively.

47 Liu Junning, 'Beida chuantong yu jinxiandai Zhongguode ziyouzhuyi', editor's preface to *Ziyouzhuyide xiansheng: Beida chuantong yu jindai Zhongguo*, p. 9.

48 Those whose interests, and jobs, were concerned with formulating policies such as the Anglo-American Third Way in the 1990s were called members of the 'wonking classes'. What they did was to 'wonk'.

49 This formulation comes from Pierre Bourdieu. See his *Acts of Resistance: Against the Tyranny of the Market* (New York: The New Press, 1998), p. 12.

50 For more on this environment, see Geremie R. Barmé, *In the Red*, pp. 46–8, and Gloria Davies, *Voicing Concerns*, pp. 18–21.

3 Pathways of labour insurgency

Ching Kwan Lee

Two decades of market reform have brought on their heels waves of labour insurgency. By the early 2000s, incidents of worker unrest by the massive unemployed population had become so routine that government and party leaders identified labour problems as one of the biggest threats to social stability, alongside tax revolts and land disputes by peasants. Indeed, state-led economic reforms have paradoxically undercut a major social base of regime support. As a result of large-scale planned layoffs of workers in the state industrial sector, many state workers have had to confront a drastic reversal of fortune within the past decade, from being 'masters' of their enterprises to becoming destitute unemployed. By documenting various forms of labour insurgency – ranging from everyday workplace resistance, petitions, work stoppages and strikes to public protests, violence, independent unionism and political movements – this chapter assesses the consequences of reform on labour and its relation with the state. The overall argument is that deepened reforms have triggered both a proliferation and an intensification of labour strife. The relation between reform and resistance is due, on the one hand, to heightened labour antagonism towards state officials, managers and capitalists; and on the other hand, to an opening up of new political and institutional spaces for interest and grievance articulation.

Renewed availability of arbitration institutions and promulgation of labour laws and social legislation invite more petitions, complaints and lawsuits from workers, resulting in dramatic growth of registered conflicts. Although workers have succeeded in extracting some concessions from the regime, the latter has been unrelenting in crushing certain forms of labour action. Thus, on the one hand, emergency funds have been doled out to localities hardest hit by unemployment and protests and a national re-employment campaign has been emphasized. On the other hand, however, the state has pressed ahead with large-scale ownership reform of state-owned enterprises and has shown its determination to repress any sign of independent unionism or political organization involving cross-class alliances between peasants, workers and intellectuals. It seems that as long as workers' actions are not politically-oriented but self-limiting to purely economic and livelihood demands limited to a single factory, the state tends towards tolerance and limited concessions. However, arrest and imprisonment of labour activists have continued to send a powerful message concerning what the state designates as a most forbidden path of resistance – organized political dissent.

Worker rebellion in a worker's state

This explosion of labour action occurs in the context of a sea change in China's socioeconomic system. In the Maoist era of state socialism, the working class as a whole made great strides vis-à-vis other social groups, notably the peasants, the bourgeoisie and the intellectuals in terms of political status, wages, welfare and employment security. Consistent with the Maoist development priorities, which placed dual emphasis on industrialization and public ownership, Chinese workers including both blue-collar and white-collar employees in urban China benefited from the 'urban bias' in resource allocation commonly found in developing countries. Maoist ideology also elevated workers vis-à-vis the intelligentsia and managerial cadres. The latter groups were required to engage in productive labour periodically, sometimes being sent to the countryside for this purpose, and their salaries were capped following the Cultural Revolution at only 10–30 per cent above those for the highest paid skilled workers. On the other hand, manual labourers were involved in managerial work through innovation and design campaigns, group decision making, group problem solving, and, during the Cultural Revolution, representation on revolutionary committees running factories. In material terms, despite a low wage system, workers' real wage levels in 1970 represented a 35 per cent rise above those of 1952. Periodic setbacks notwithstanding, the revolutionary regime made available unmistakable improvements in worker consumption – food, housing, medical care, education and training opportunities.[1] At the top of the labour hierarchy were the permanent workers employed in state-owned enterprises. In 1981, when reform began, this labour aristocracy accounted for 42 per cent of the entire industrial workforce and produced 75 per cent of total industrial output. Their employment conditions epitomized all that was superior about socialism: cradle to grave welfare, permanent job tenure, housing provision, life-long medical and pension benefits and guaranteed, superior wages. The next group down the industrial rank order consisted of workers in urban collectives, followed by temporary workers in state-owned enterprises and those in rural industries. All these workers were distinguished from those in the state sector by relatively inferior material conditions and political status.[2]

Even in the pre-reform period, when workers were economically dependent on enterprise paternalism, and were politically controlled by well-entrenched party networks extending to each factory shop floor, Chinese labour was not always the docile subject of a totalitarian state. Both state-inspired factionalism and economic inequalities rooted in the socialist industrial system have periodically propelled different segments of the workforce to assert political prowess and economic demands. Thus, post-1949 China can claim a history of proletarian rebellion and activism, notably in the strike wave of 1956–57, factional strife and protests during the Cultural Revolution in 1966–7 and workers' participation in the 1976 April Fifth Movement.

Seizing the opportunity of the Hundred Flowers Campaign, when Chairman Mao encouraged dissent from below to pre-empt larger-scale revolts similar to the Hungarian ones, workers displaced by the socialization of industries staged more than 1,300 strikes in Shanghai alone between the months of March and June in 1957. Launched most fervently by apprentices and temporary workers and those in joint ownership enterprises, striking workers demanded higher wages, better welfare, permanent worker status and guaranteed promotion.[3] The Cultural Revolution a decade later offered another political opportunity for labour struggles. Turmoil inside Chinese factories across the nation was partially shaped by factional cleavages created by the party's network inside the factories, distinguishing the royalists (comprised of loyal members of the party's organization, activists, party members, shop-floor leaders, model workers, etc.) from the rebels (including a diverse group of ordinary workers who were either victimized by the royalists or by factory managers prior to the Cultural Revolution, or those who had criticized the party). But labour conflicts during this period were also structured by deep-rooted occupational grievances and inequalities, with apprentices, the unskilled, irregular workers and younger workers figuring most prominently in making economic demands and joining rebel factions across the country.[4] Then, in the spring of 1976, mass demonstrations and riots with a strong contingent of worker participation broke out in more than forty places across the country. The backbone of this uprising was young workers, who had been the basis of mobilization during the Cultural Revolution but had been stigmatized for their bourgeois leanings. They used the occasion of commemorating the late Premier Zhou Enlai to express their dissatisfaction with the political persecutions and the injustices they suffered.[5]

Labour's loss in the reform era has occurred during a period of rapid and sustained economic growth. During the period 1980–97, China's gross national product grew at an average annual growth rate of 10 per cent. Industry, while maintaining the same 49 per cent share of national output, grew at an even more impressive annual rate of 12 per cent.[6] Real annual wage increases for urban employees between 1979 and 1996 averaged 4.4 per cent.[7] The influx of foreign investment and liberalization policies towards the private economy have created a national labour market, enhancing labour mobility and autonomy. Employment in these two sectors, which were non-existent at the beginning of the reforms, has mushroomed to an estimated 80 million, or 15 per cent of total by 1995.[8] A new class of rural migrant labourers has emerged in response to these employment opportunities and an estimated 100 million migrant labourers have left the countryside to enter towns and cities in search of non-agricultural jobs. Another important source of employment for these rural labourers is the burgeoning township and village enterprises employing some 170 million workers.[9]

Inequalities across regions, ownership sectors, industries and occupations are concealed behind figures of aggregate growth and prosperity. The stark fact remains that relative to other social groups, the core state working class has suffered drastic dislocation. Veteran permanent workers and retirees find their employment security, welfare benefits and workplace status vanishing. While a new generation of young migrant workers benefits from substantially improved income and status, when they find urban jobs they have to confront ruthless exploitation which harks back to the labour degradation of nineteenth-century industrial capitalism.

Almost every step along the path of market reform has amounted to a setback for state workers' status and livelihood. First came the reform for greater enterprise autonomy and director responsibility in 1984, paving the way for the ascendance of managers' dictatorial power over workers, the union and even the party. Then, the policy of 'labour re-optimization', first implemented in 1988, gave managers the power to render redundant surplus workers in state enterprises. Labour contract reform required that all employees sign contracts of varying duration with employers who now have a legal mandate to dismiss workers. By 1995, the permanent employment system was officially dismantled, giving rise to two groups of unemployed workers: the off-duty and the registered unemployed. What the state has euphemistically called 'off-duty' (or *xiagang*) workers are those who maintain 'employment relations' with the enterprise, potentially re-employable when business improves, and who receive livelihood allowances amounting to only a tiny fraction of regular income. The ' registered unemployed' workers are those who have completely cut off employment relations with the enterprise and are left to their own devices after receiving minimal unemployment allowances. These destitute workers now number more than twenty million nationwide.[10] Unemployment is further aggravated by the rise in the number of enterprise bankruptcies since the early 1990s. By 1996, 11,544 state owned enterprises had declared bankruptcy, and many more had applied for bankruptcy but not yet had their applications approved.[11] Finally, for those who are still employed in state factories, the enterprise welfare system has also been gradually eliminated and the retreat of this old system has outpaced the installation of a new nationwide insurance system.

The pattern of 'organized dependence' and paternalism characteristic of state–labour relations under state socialism has given way to a new despotism. State-sector workers who are unable to find alternative employment in private or foreign firms, including large numbers of unskilled, older and particularly women workers, are subordinated to a dictatorial management empowered by labour contract and enterprise reforms, and untrammelled by the party or the union.[12] With more than 40 per cent of state-owned enterprises operating in the red, workers' paycheques have not only dwindled, but these reduced wages now also have to pay for 'commodified' welfare services such as nurseries, clinics and housing which were, until recently, provided free or with substantial subsidies. For the millions of migrant labourers in the private sector, where state regulations are rarely enforced, despotism is all the more blatant.[13] Local governments, engaged in fierce competition for foreign investments, collude with foreign capital in undermining state labour regulations regarding contracts, minimum wages, overtime pay, rest days, total working hours and industrial safety. Under these oppressive and deteriorating employment conditions, Chinese workers have pursued a plethora of collective actions.

Labour disputes and arbitration

A new form of labour conflict has resulted from Chinese government efforts to institutionalize conflict resolution. In July 1987, the State Council revived the national labour dispute arbitration system, which had been abolished in 1955. By 1997, some 270,000 labour dispute mediation committees at the enterprise level, and 3,159 labour dispute arbitration committees at county, city and provincial levels had been established. These committees are constituted by a 'tripartite principle', with representatives from the labour bureau administration, the trade union and economic administrative organs, representing respectively the state, labour and the employer. In the past decade, enterprise mediation cases amounted to 820,000, while 450,000 cases of labour arbitration were processed. With the promulgation of the 1993 Regulation on Handling Labour Disputes and the 1995 Labour Law, the scope of arbitration and legal actions has been expanded in terms of actionable claims and coverage of enterprise types. The original dispute resolution process only covered contract disputes or cases involving termination of permanent workers in state enterprises. Since 1993, workers in private and collective enterprises can bring their grievances concerning wages, fringe benefits, occupational safety and health as well as termination of contract to obtain legal resolution.

This national hierarchy of labour dispute arbitration attests to the Chinese state's explicit recognition of large-scale growth in labour conflicts and the need to provide institutional channels for resolution in order to assure social stability. The emphasis is on pre-emption and mediation at the enterprise level, with arbitration at the local committee level. Submission of labour disputes to the civil court is the last resort. Workers have seized this institutional space to redress grievances and defend their rights, as disputes statistics register a staggering increase in the number of petitions and dispute cases. The explosion in arbitrated labour disputes followed the implementation of labour contract reform and the drastic rise in unemployment (Table 3.1). Also significant has been the increase in not just the number of cases but also the number of employees involved in 'collective labour disputes'. 'Officially defined as disputes involving more than three employees, collective disputes involved an average of 16.5 workers in 1992; by 1998, the figure averaged 37.1 and ranged as high as 45.1 depending on the type of enterprise.[14]

Beneath this aggregate rise in the volume of arbitrated disputes, certain patterns can be discerned, illustrating the focus and distribution of labour conflicts. First, the most contentious provinces in the 1990s have been Guangdong, Chongqing, Shanghai, Fujian and Jiangsu, regions which experienced particularly rapid economic growth. Shenzhen, with its huge contingent of migrant workers numbering more than six million by 2000, alone accounted for

Table 3.1   National total of arbitrated labour disputes, 1994–2000

Year	Arbitrated labour dispute (cases)	Arbitrated collective dispute (cases)	Employees involved
1994	19,098	1,482	77,794
1995	33,030	2,588	122,512
1996	47,951	3,150	189,120
1997	71,524	4,109	221,115
1998	93,649	6,767	358,531
1999	120,191	9,043	473,957
2000	135,206	8,247	422,617
2001	154,621	9,847	467,150

Source: *Zhongguo laodong he shehuibaozhang nianjian* (China Labour and Social Security Yearbook) (Beijing: Zhongguo laodong he shehuibaozhang chubanshi, 1995–2001).

one-tenth of the national total of arbitrated labour disputes in 1999. On the other hand, in terms of increase in arbitration, Sichuan, Inner Mongolia, Tianjin, Gansu, Shanxi, Xinjiang all registered triple digit rates in 1995, reflecting perhaps the rapid deterioration in employment conditions among workers in the state-owned sector. Second, in terms of ownership type, taking the year 1996 as an example, state-owned enterprises account for 34 per cent of arbitrated disputes, while foreign invested, collective and private enterprises respectively account for 21 per cent, 26 per cent and 10 per cent of the total of 48,121 cases, involving 189,120 employees respectively. Third, most disputes are economic in nature, with wages, welfare and social insurance payment the most common (50 per cent) causes of conflicts, with another 30 per cent or so about contract termination and dismissal. Wage arrears are particularly pronounced in private and foreign-invested firms.[15]

Most of these dispute cases originated in petitions by employees. They succeeded in redressing their grievance in 50–80 per cent of cases depending on the locality and the orientations of local labour officials. However, the protection of workers' rights is still wanting, as follow-up studies have revealed many examples of discrimination against the plaintiffs after disputes were formally settled. In a county in Beijing, for instance, of the 441 employees involved in disputes in 1993–94, 66 per cent were later dismissed by employers. Moreover, the tripartite principle in the makeup of enterprise mediation committees is often violated. In Hubei, in the enterprise committees studied, management and union representatives always outnumbered worker representatives, who were also mostly appointed rather than elected. Thus, it remains to be seen how effective and genuine these different levels of labour dispute arbitration mechanisms are in protecting workers' rights in the reform era.

Work stoppages and strikes

The entire twenty-year period of reform has been punctuated with incidents of work stoppages and strikes of varying durations throughout China. As reform deepened in the 1990s, strikes occurred more frequently, involving more workers, and affecting enterprises in more ownership sectors. Although the demands workers made were predominantly material ones, economic grievances some-times evolved into political critique of regime legitimacy.

Under the regime of Deng Xiaoping, the first wave of strikes emerged in the autumn of 1980. The ascendance of the Polish Solidarity Movement embold-ened Chinese workers, already dissatisfied with years of wage stagnation and inadequate housing, to take action. Some twenty to thirty strikes reportedly occurred in the last quarter of 1980 in the central Chinese industrial cities of Wuhan and Taiyuan. Additional strikes were reported in 1980–1 in Shanghai, Tianjin, Kunming, Manchuria, and cities in Hubei and Shanxi, involving coal miners, steel workers, tool-and-dye workers, and workers in machinery and elec-tronics factories. One noteworthy incident at the Taiyuan steel mill in December 1980 was sparked by demands for better housing, rights to family reunion for workers living apart from spouses, and election of worker representatives to sit on management committees. Demands turned more political as steel workers joined in. The local press reported that, a

> 'minority of workers' … labeling themselves 'the poorest workers in the world,' called for 'breaking down the rusted door of socialism,' the right to decide their own fate, the end to dictatorship, and the overthrow of the system of political bureaucracy.[16]

Poland's Solidarity seemed to have the greatest impact on Shanghai, where the call for independent unions was a recurrent theme in a number of go-slow and strike incidents in 1981. When such demands proliferated across the country, coming from as far as Xinjiang, the Chinese government reacted by striking the 'freedom to strike' clause from the revised 1982 Constitution. Legal ambiguity notwithstanding, Chinese workers have remained adamant in using strikes to defend their rights and welfare throughout China's reform transition. In recent years, labour and legal scholars in China have reportedly reached a consensus that China's membership in the World Trade Organization should soon lead the government explicitly to legalize this labour right recognized by all major inter-national conventions.[17]

The late 1980s witnessed another period of volatile labour relations, as state workers' discontent intensified due to anxiety fuelled by rising unemployment, widening income gaps between managers and workers, and corruption. These grievances resulted from reform measures aimed at increasing efficiency and competitiveness of state-owned enterprises. Between 1986 and 1988, labour contract reform, the bankruptcy law and the regulation on labour re-optimization were enacted one after another, threatening workers' employment security and livelihood. Coupled with record high inflation rates, climbing to 18.5 per cent in 1988 and 25.5 per cent in 1989, worker frustration reached a zenith.[18] The official All China Federation of Trade Unions (ACFTU) counted ninety-seven strikes in 1987, and over a hundred in 1988. The largest took place in a cotton mill in Zhejiang province: 1,500 workers participated. The longest occurred in the Northwest Medical Instruments Plant in Xi'an, lasting more than three months from 1987 to 1988. In the first quarter of 1989 in Shanghai alone, the official union handled fifteen strikes, touched off by worker grievances regarding bonus allocation and lay-offs. Thousands of People's Liberation Army soldiers were reportedly sent to occupy the Daqing oilfields to quell a labour stoppage demanding higher wages and better treatment.[19] Then, in May and June 1989, workers in Beijing, Shanghai and other cities left the confines of factory gates, and their collective action took the forms of public protests, independent unionism and political mobilization. Despite the deadly crackdown of the Tiananmen Movement, with workers receiving the heaviest sentences, strikes have become an increasingly routine method of labour resistance. For instance, internal reports compiled by the Department of Public Security recorded a national total of 480 strikes in 1992, 1,870 in 1995, and 1,740 in the first nine months of 1996.[20] Since the mid-1990s, when plant closures, mass layoffs and delays in pension payment occurred, strikes have given way to public protests as unemployed and retired workers can no longer threaten to withdraw their labour.

Besides veteran workers left jobless by the restructuring of the state industrial sector, labour militancy in the 1980s and 1990s was also fuelled by a new generation of factory workers who waged their own struggles against exploitation in private and foreign-invested companies. Concentrated mostly in the Special Economic Zones (SEZs) in southern coastal provinces, migrant worker discontents centred on poor working and living conditions, low wages, wage arrears and degrading management practices.[21] As early as 1986–7, Shenzhen (the first SEZ in China) witnessed at least twenty-one strikes in foreign-funded enterprises and the local trade union received about 1,000 worker complaints. Incidents were triggered by harsh treatment, low wages, wage arrears, extremely long hours of work and unreasonable disciplinary practices involving meal times, toilet breaks and holidays. A typical incident reported by the Chinese press revealed that a Hong Kong owned toy factory forced young women workers to work up to eighteen hours a day seven days a week without adequate overtime pay and no time off on Sundays. Thirty women went on strike after one pregnant woman collapsed from exhaustion.[22] Even though statistics on work stoppages and strikes are always incomplete underestimations, the unmistakable trend is one of increased volume. In Shenzhen alone, where sixty-nine strikes and work stoppages were recorded from June 1989 to the end of 1990, there were 250 such cases in 1992. In Guangdong as a whole, between 1994 and 1995, there were 182 strikes involving more than 400 people, accounting for 28 per cent of all strikes in the province in that period that came to official attention. Chinese labour researchers have noted a trend of contagious strikes among companies in the same locality.[23] For instance in 1993–5, a series of strikes were staged by workers in the Japanese-owned plants of Canon, Mitsumi, Sanmei and Panasonic in Shenzhen and Zhuhai SEZs. Runaway inflation reaching as high as 20–27 per cent in these cities caused economic distress among migrant workers who demanded wage hikes of 30–35 per cent to maintain their livelihood. These work stoppages and strikes varied in duration, from a few hours to several days, and involved up to one to two thousand workers in large factories.

Based on their experience in handling fourteen strikes in Xiamen SEZ in Fujian province, two labour officials summarized the characteristics of these incidents as short-lived, economically motivated episodes. However spontaneous they may have been, 'very soon organizers and leaders would emerge from among the foremen, line leaders or shop floor heads'. They also pointed to the importance of native-place ties, noting that eight out of the fourteen strikes occurred in factories with an unusually high proportion of workers coming from the same locality, forming regional cliques. 'As relatives or native-place locals, they share strong exclusionary sentiments and solidarity which can easily lead to collective rebellions.'[24] Other reports of similar incidents elsewhere revealed more ambiguous effects of localism in worker resistance. During a go-slow in a Korean factory, workers remarked that regional divisions among them undermined the unity needed for a strike, saying 'if there were no migrant workers, we would be on strike already'.[25]

Striking workers demonstrated a certain level of organizational ability, as accounts of these incidents mention organizers writing open letters and printing leaflets and flyers to mobilize workers. One commonly used tactic was calling up journalists and news agencies about their actions, in efforts to arouse public attention and sympathy for their struggles.

A notable feature in most of these strikes is the ambiguous and conciliatory role played by the local ACFTU and Labour Bureau officials. Trade union officials admitted that their double role was one 'of supporting the foreign investors, but also monitoring whether the management is abiding by the labour laws'. Thus, the Zhuhai ACFTU criticized the 1993 strike at the Canon plant. In a number of cases where striking workers demanded the setting up of enterprise unions, local ACFTU officials urged consultation with management before endorsing their establishment. Union officials were also helpless in defending workers during strikes in foreign-owned enterprises, when local public security personnel were often called into the compounds by management to intimidate strikers. Although unionization rates among foreign-invested enterprises allegedly reached 40 per cent by the end of 1994 in Guangdong, most of these ACFTU approved unions were led and staffed by management personnel who were mainly responsible for collecting union fees, and organizing birthday parties and recreational events. At the same time, these union leaders were also salaried shop floor supervisors or section heads in the factory administration.[26]

Protests, demonstrations and violence

In the spring of 1989, the mobilization of workers into street protests, many with support and approval from work unit leadership and the official union, raised the spectre of labour mobilization against the state. In mid-May 1989, marching workers in Beijing hoisted banners bearing the name of their enterprises including the Capitol Steel Corporation, the main factory of the Beijing Internal

Combustion Engines, Beijing Lifting Machinery Factory, etc. At one point before the declaration of martial law, the ACFTU also joined the demonstration with its own banner and even made a 100,000-yuan donation to the student hunger strikers.[27] One observer remarks that this 'distinctive Chinese pattern of [work-unit] protest has come to mirror the distinctive Chinese pattern of work-unit control'.[28] Labour protests in the post-Tiananmen decade witnessed a heightened tendency for workers to go beyond the confines of their workplace. Bringing their protests into public view, they were often joined by other disgruntled segments of the local community. Labour activism thus not only underlines the erosion of state power at the grassroots level, and a shift from the enterprise to the state as their target of challenge, it also has the potential to become a rallying point for community-based activism.

In 1995 alone, by official reckoning, protest marches involving more than twenty people rose to a record high of 1,620, including more than 1.1 million people and occurring in more than thirty cities.[29] One scholar reported a four-fold increase in collective protests (including but not restricted to those by workers) from a total of 8,700 in 1993 to 32,000 in 1999.[30] Grievances that sparked these public protests reflected the predicaments of debt-ridden state enterprises under reform. Worker opposition was directed against wage and pension arrears, inadequate unemployment and medical allowances, embezzlement of funds by factory managers, plant mergers, and restructuring and relocations which disrupted their lives. Among the first of its kind, the large-scale protest staged by workers in the Chongqing Knitting Mill in November 1992 proved to be representative of similar incidents in the province of Sichuan and other impoverished provinces throughout the 1990s. When this large state enterprise went bankrupt and cut back on pension payments to retired workers, workers took to the street, demanding the 'right to subsistence'. Retirees led the procession and pleaded tearfully to the riot police, arguing that their pension payment was their rightful share of the surplus value they generated for the state over the years, and that the state and the enterprise had no right to withhold their repayment. Workers on the job also demanded state guarantee of their basic right to live. After five days of confrontation, the authorities conceded to workers' demands: pension payment would not be cut, while workers on the job were retrained or assigned to new jobs by the enterprise.[31]

Subsistence rights occupied top priority in the slogans found in many other demonstrations, revealing workers' desperation and outrage.[32] 'We Want To Work', 'Our Children Want to Go to School' (in a Chengdu shoe factory protest in July 1997),[33] 'We Want Jobs' and 'We Want Food' (in a textile mill protest in Baicheng, Jilin in October 1995), 'We Don't Demand Fish Or Meat, Just Some Porridge', and 'Not A Yuan In Six Months, We Want Rice to Eat' (a protest in Changsha in November 1998).[34] Corruption was also a major complaint as there were slogans targeting the cadres: 'Down With the Newly Emerging Nobility' and 'Eradicate the New Bureaucratic Bourgeoisie' (a petition rally by chemical workers in Shenyang in March 1994).[35] In a protest in Ningxia, banners read 'We Need to Eat, We Need to Exist' and 'Save the Factory, Save the People'.[36]

Most noticeable among these slogans were those heard at a 5,000-strong protest march in April 1994 in Anshan, the capital of China's iron and steel industry: 'Workers As the Masters of the State', 'Down With the New Born Bourgeoisie', 'Yes to Socialism, No to Capitalism' and 'Long Live the Working Class'.[37] Reappropriating what used to be ideological statements from the party-state to launch their political critique, workers' demands have gone beyond strictly economic ones to directly challenging the legitimacy of a self-proclaimed socialist state.

In an illustrative incident, the city of Nanchong in Sichuan was the scene of a massive spontaneous labour uprising. Certain features of the incident could be found in numerous other labour protests, which resembled milder versions of this one. The state-run Jialihua silk factory used to support 10,000 workers, who suffered pay cuts and lay-offs as company revenue plunged beginning in the early 1990s. Disgruntled by management's extravagance in hard times, workers held the general manager hostage as he prepared for an official 'inspection tour' in Thailand with his wife.

> They loaded Huang [the manager] into the back of a flatbed truck and forced him into the painful and demeaning 'airplane position' – bent at the waist, arms straight out at the sides. Then they marched 10 kilometers through the rain to downtown Nanchong and paraded him through the street ... just like the Cultural Revolution ... Workers from other factories joined the spontaneous demonstration ... 20,000 people took part ... The day-long parade ended at the city government building ... Workers blocked the government gates, refusing to let officials leave. They took turns making speeches. The stand-off lasted 30 hours, and ended peacefully with the promise of pay ... The government ordered the local branch of the state-run Industrial and Commerce Bank of China to lend enough money to Jialihua to cover back wages.[38]

Acts of vengeance like those in the Nanchong incident, and even violence, have characterized many labour actions, as furious laid-off workers and retirees blamed managers for corruption, profiteering, abuse of power and plundering of state assets. Physical assaults and kidnapping of managers by angry workers were reported in various provinces. In Liaoning, from January to July 1988, there were 276 reported incidents in which managers were beaten up and a total of 297 managers injured. In the provincial capital Shenyang, a study revealed that 54 per cent of managers had been threatened by force or blackmailed.[39] Cases of suicides and attempted murder were also reported: in Fujian, an unemployed worker poured gasoline over himself and ignited a fire after grabbing two officials responsible for imposing fines on his peddling business. The worker died and the officials were seriously burnt. In many other sit-ins and demonstrations, workers broke through police blockades and occupied main roads and railways, bringing local and inter-provincial traffic to a standstill. In addition, officials have also been alarmed by the rise in violent crime committed by laid-off workers and migrant workers, especially in provinces where unemployment rates are high. Public security officials have found that laid-off workers were ganging up to commit armed robberies and other violent crimes such as murder, sabotage and theft. Large-scale factories, steel mills and mines have been particularly hit by upsurges in crime. Some 1,900 illegal purchasing centres, involving more than 300 gangs, were found to be buying steel and metal products and raw materials that workers had stolen from factories.

By the end of the 1990s and into the early 2000s, many workers had come to see ineffective state policies, and ill-enforced laws and regulations as the cause of their plight. The increasing assertiveness of state sector workers has been marked by an emergent discourse of legal rights which appeals to the regime's own promotion of 'ruling the country by law'.[40] Irregularities in the handling of enterprise bankruptcy perpetrated by rampant corruption of officials at the local level have left many workers without even the legal severance payment or pension. The wave of protests in old industrial bases in the spring of 2002 was workers' reaction to central government policies intended to tackle the severe unemployment condition. Re-employment centres were set up nationwide in 1998 to provide laid-off workers with allowances for an 'in-centre' term of three years. When this policy expired at the end of 2001, as many as 22.3 million workers were 'released into society' with scant prospect of finding jobs. Then, starting in November 2001, Zhu Rongji designated Liaoning as the testing ground for a new social security reform. The most controversial part of the scheme was to allow enterprises to give a one-off payment to workers deemed redundant. Enterprises would then no longer be financially responsible for workers' welfare and pension. Many disgruntled workers were infuriated by the low rate of compensation or the lack of any compensation at all.

Available accounts indicate that most protests originate at enterprises. The prevalence of work-unit mobilization is due to workers' perception of firm-specific interests and possible resolution, the ease of communication among workers in the same enterprise sharing the same residential quarters, and workers' fear of official retaliation against cross-unit organization.[41] Importantly, there have been occasions when single-factory agitation spread to other factories and disgruntled employees in the same locality, and even reports of sympathy protests in the same industry in different parts of the country. The series of worker protests in the north-east and the petrochemical industry in the spring of 2002 illustrated the potential for localized and dispersed activism to develop into more coordinated unrest. The Liaoyang incident began with one factory, the Liaoyang Ferro-Alloy Factory, which had gone bankrupt in November 2001, and where workers accused the management and the local city officials of corruption, illegal handling of bankruptcy procedures and two years' default wage payment. Thanks to city-wide unemployment, which residents claimed to have reached a staggering 70 per cent, workers from different factories with similar grievances came to know each other in their petition drives to the city government. In early March 2002, when the commonly assumed culprit, the former mayor and current head of the local legislature, went on television to proclaim that 'there were no unemployed' in the city, furious workers, first from six factories and then from as many as twenty, marched in the streets, shouting 'Hooligan Government', 'Remove Gong Shangwu' (the former mayor), and 'We Want to Eat'. After four worker representatives were arrested and charged with 'illegal gathering and demonstrating', they added the demand to release their co-workers.[42] The scale, the cross-factory mobilization and the political demands of the Liaoyang protests were an alarming reminder to the authorities that market reform and corruption can together produce structurally disadvantaged groups that hold the government politically responsible for mass economic dislocation. Protests subsided after the arrest of labour leaders and after the government had paid 50 per cent of the back salary and an instalment on the severance pay owed workers. This 'carrot and stick' or 'divide and conquer' technique has become a common strategy deployed by the regime in dealing with worker unrest. In the same month, as many as 50,000 laid-off workers in the Daqing oilfield, in another north-eastern province, staged three weeks of street protests against managers cheating workers with 'unfair severance packages'. Thousands of armed security forces sealed off part of the city where workers had reportedly sustained their protests for two months. Most significantly, in April, hundreds of oil workers in Lanzhou, Gansu in northwest China blockaded roads to protest a low severance pay offer of about 1,000 yuan per year worked. They were reportedly inspired and emboldened by the unrest in Daqing, and overseas activists suggested that workers in the oil industry had their own personal and family ties across the country due to government-organized transfers between oilfields. Smaller protests in this old industry in eastern Hebei and Shandong reportedly broke out after the one in Daqing, but they quickly collapsed under government pressure.[43]

Even though workers may not have formal horizontal organizations to coordinate their actions, their shared grievances and the geographical concentration of unemployment and plant closures provide a social and ecological unity for mass rebellion. Local officials, who were the initial target of many protests, have become supporters and even organizers of collective action. When a Sichuan munitions factory failed to pay wages, managers led 300–400 elderly retired workers to march downtown, forcing authorities to pay pension arrears. Leaders and cadres of the impoverished inner and northeastern provinces allegedly tried to hold Beijing hostage over the proliferation of labour unrest, in an attempt to demand more central funding for economic development and social insurance payment. In 1998, an extra 3,000 million yuan was allocated to these provinces as emergency funds.[44] In most cases, public security looked on and cordoned off the protest areas, but arrests were not widespread. One reason for official toleration may have been the central authorities' intention of establishing 'safety valves' whereby protesters could let off steam without targeting the top leadership. More recently, government concessions have become so common that workers have entered into a rather 'ritualized' exchange with local officials: demonstrations, especially those taking place before important holidays, for example National Day or Chinese New Year, are occasions for pressuring the government to dole out emergency pay-outs.

Geographical variation in the volume of protest dovetails with the uneven regional consequences of reform for Chinese workers. One writer has remarked that the provinces that experienced the most turmoil were mostly interior provinces in central China, including Sichuan, Hunan, Shaanxi, and Henan.[45] These provinces have a high concentration of strategic and heavy industries as a result of the Communist Third Front industrialization and relocation inland of enterprises in the 1960s and 1970s, when heavy industries were moved to the interior to avoid possible attacks by the USA and Soviet Union. Now,

> of the provinces occupying the top thirteen ranks in turmoil, eleven … have more heavy than light industrial firms … These firms share some common characteristics: producer-goods industry, obsolete equipment, excessive consumption of energy, autarky and an underemployed and poorly-educated workforce.[46]

In addition, the three northeastern provinces – Liaoning, Jilin and Heilongjiang – are also prone to worker unrest due to heavy reliance of local economies on state firms, coal mining and steel production, sectors which have suffered most from economic liberalization.

Although worker insurgencies have concentrated on coal mining, steel and textile industries, labourers in other economic sectors are also poised to engage in collective and public actions. Sanitation workers in Beijing, hawkers in Shenzhen, and taxi drivers in Beijing, Luzhou (in Sichuan), Changsha, Zhuhai, Shenzhen and Shaoguan (in Guangdong) have protested against low wages, unreasonable hikes in fines and licence fees, and arbitrary punishment meted out by police. Many of these service workers are former laid-off workers from state-owned enterprises, or migrant workers from poverty-stricken rural areas. The most serious turmoil occurred in April 1998, when direct sales agents across the country rioted after a government ban on direct sales firms. At least ten people were killed and more than a hundred were injured when these agents demanded refunds. Many of the ten million sales personnel involved in direct marketing were laid-off workers who had to use their savings to pay for training and deposits before joining the companies. Likewise, in November 1998, when the government closed down a number of financial services firms for fraudulent practices, hundreds of workers marched through the streets of Beijing, Zhengzhou and Xinhui. These worker investors, some of them unemployed, were lured by the promise of interest payment as high as 30 per cent a month, and some had invested their life savings with these firms.

Overall, only some of these collective protests, demonstrations and strikes have been effective in bringing concrete improvements in workers' livelihood. As mentioned previously, central and local authorities occasionally responded to workers' demands by providing emergency relief funds, or by postponing and revising plant closure or relocation decisions. So far, it seems that localized economic demands by retirees and unemployed workers in the state sector have been most successful in soliciting sympathetic government responses.[47] Yet, once political demands were made, international media exposure spread the news and cross-factory mobilization occurred, as in the spate of protests in 2002, the regime responded with swift and decisive crackdowns, arresting and jailing organizers. The course of enterprise restructuring and market reforms, coupled with China's huge reserve of surplus labour, will likely see a significant segment of the working class continuing to suffer from a wholesale commodification of its labour power, well before a societal system of insurance and labour regulation will be effectively in place to protect workers' rights.

Independent unionism and political movements

Organized dissent, among all forms of popular resistance, has provoked the most severe repression by the Chinese state. The ferocious crackdown on the religious sect *Falun Gong* is most illustrative of the regime's suspicion of any organized capacity of society that rivals its own. On the labour front, similarly harsh treatment has been meted out to activists who dare to pursue independent and cross-class mobilization of workers. The beleaguered official union, ACFTU, has proved to be too weak a bureaucracy to protect workers' rights under the combined onslaught of economic reforms and the government decisions to cut back sharply on state enterprise. The 1992 Union Law may have boosted the ACFTU's legal status, and was indicative of top union leaders' striving for a more autonomous role from the party-state. But numerous surveys undertaken by the ACFTU indicate widespread disillusionment among rank-and-file workers: over 64 per cent of workers in the state sector turn not to the ACFTU but to informal networks for support when their rights are encroached upon. More often than not, official unions are controlled directly by management. Moreover, transmission of funds from lower level unions to the ACFTU has frequently been blocked due to financial difficulty or estrangement of grassroots enterprise unions. In 1993, for instance, the national ACFTU was able to collect only 38 per cent of mandated contributions.[48] Finally, the laying off of tens of millions of state workers means the loss of the bulk of the ACFTU membership, long the core of Communist Party power. These unattached and underprivileged workers have become a potent source of rebellions and protests, and perhaps constitute the most serious threat to the party's monopoly on power.

The emergence of autonomous trade unions and their alliance with intellectual and human rights dissidents are most politically unsettling to a regime which still proclaims itself the embodiment of the dictatorship of the proletariat. The reform era has marked a period of unprecedented ferment in organized labour dissent in the history of post-1949 China. Political challenge climaxed in the 1989 Democracy Movement, although mobilization for independent unions and cross-class political coalitions have been found both before and since. Demands for forming independent unions à la Polish Solidarity first emerged in 1981 in Shanghai, Hangzhou, Tianjin, Wuhan, Xinjiang, Anshan, Nanchong, and

Zhengzhou. In Chongqing, a mimeographed pamphlet entitled *The Chongqing Democratic Trade Union* accused the provincial ACFTU of being 'a docile instrument of the Party'. In response, the Chinese government decided to allow more workplace democracy by setting up worker congresses in Chinese state enterprises.[49] The next round of struggle for autonomous unions took place in April 1989. Taking advantage of students' agitation and a rebellious social climate, several dozen young workers who gathered to talk politics in Tiananmen Square gave birth to the Beijing Workers' Autonomous Federation (BWAF). Claiming a registered membership of 20,000 workers before the military crackdown, the BWAF became a model for fifteen other independent unions set up in other major cities. WAFs were organized in Tianjin, Harbin, Shenyang, Huhhot, Xi'an, Wuhan, Nanjing, Shanghai, Jinan, Hangzhou, Suzhou, Changsha, Shaoyang, Fuzhou and Guangzhou during the two months between April and June 1989.[50] Of lasting significance may be the political consciousness of WAF leaders and the tradition of democratic movements they draw on and keep alive. Walder and Gong have stressed a strong strain of 'working-class populism' in the rhetoric and collective mentality of the Beijing WAF – disrespectful of intellectual authority, doggedly independent, inclusive of and open to all ordinary citizens, capable of linking the idea of working class struggle with the language of democratic opposition to political oligarchy. Thus, not only did this independent union movement demand price stabilization, the right to change jobs, an end to discrimination against women workers, investigation of official incomes and privileges, but it also consciously engaged in a 'fight for democracy', a struggle for the right to 'supervise the Communist Party', and the right to supervise the legal representatives of the company in state and collective enterprises.[51] Elsewhere, Elizabeth Perry has observed a tradition of democratic movements, fuelled by worker-student nationalism, which began with the May Fourth Movement in 1919 and continued throughout the Civil War years. In 1989, it was the students' exclusionist and elitist attitude towards ordinary workers which set limits on the potential for an urban coalition of citizens.[52] After the bloody crackdown in June, workers were treated more ruthlessly than any other group and several were swiftly executed or sentenced to life imprisonment for 'counter-revolutionary sabotage'.[53]

Relentless suppression by the Chinese state of autonomous unionism has since been met with an equally persistent resolve on the part of some labour activists to keep alive the radical tradition of the 1989 uprising. In 1991, there were reports of a government crackdown on some fourteen underground labour organizations with memberships ranging from twenty to three hundred in the capital alone. In the post-Tiananmen decade, several underground unions and initiatives have surfaced, thanks to their strategy of maintaining international connections and communication: the Free Trade Unions of China, the League for the Protection of the Rights of the Working People, the Hired-hands Workers' Federation, and the China Development Union, among others. Although workers are represented among the core members of these groups, dissident intellectuals – mainly students and university lecturers – account for the majority of organizers. Many of them had participated in the 1979 Democracy Wall Movement and the 1989 Movement, and shared the goal of incorporating an independent union movement into a broad-based political opposition to the Chinese Communist Party regime.[54] In 1997, seizing the opportunity of China's signing of the United Nations Convention on Economic, Social and Cultural Rights, dissidents wrote open letters urging Chinese workers to exercise their right to free association and to unite against massive lay-offs. They also published and distributed bulletins to workers, released petitions for workers' rights, set up nationwide networks of activists, and even attempted to register their organizations with the Ministry of Civil Affairs. Appealing to unemployed and migrant workers (and peasants in some cases), and supported by Chinese dissident communities living overseas, activists of these nascent associations increasingly frame labour interests in terms of human rights concerns.[55] As the volume of protests increased, reports circulated about underground networks of labour activists working as 'consultants' to protesting workers and succeeding in delaying factory closures imposed by local governments. During the course of the Liaoyang and Daqing protests, workers formed their own provisional unions to represent their interests.[56] Not surprisingly, however, arrests, convictions and imprisonment of labour activists have also continued unabated in different parts of China.

The road ahead

Social conflicts between various sectors of labour on the one hand, and enterprise management, local officials and the state on the other have been sharpened by market reforms. Deepened integration into the international economy, most prominently marked by China's new membership of the World Trade Organization since 2001, will bring additional pressure on the urban and rural labour markets in the years ahead. The government warned in 2002 that the official unemployment rate is likely to triple over the next four years to top twenty million. At the same time, an estimated 150 million surplus rural labourers will enter cities in search of jobs.[57] With intensified lay-offs of state sector workers and proletarianization of migrants, we are likely to see even more labour unrest in the years ahead. But this does not necessarily mean the rise of a nationally organized labour movement. This chapter has shown how rice-bowl issues have combined with a reappropriation of Marxist and Maoist rhetoric of exploitation and inequality to unite a broad spectrum of veteran labourers in the state sector. Their common interests and cultural frames for action have their roots in almost forty years of state socialist rule with its claims of worker mastery. The young generation of migrant workers share widespread degrading and inhumane treatment, many of them employed in the private sector. Yet, these two generations of workers are not ready allies in forming any class-based movement. Divided by localistic origins (local workers versus outside workers), residential registration (rural versus urban *hukou*), age (young versus middle-aged and older workers), and historical experience with the state, these two groups of workers have very different interests and identities in today's market economy.[58]

China has yet to witness the emergence of a labour movement, if movements are defined by 'collective challenges by people with common purposes and solidarity in sustained interaction with elites, opponents and authorities'.[59] Most episodes and pockets of resistance documented in this chapter lack effective social and organizational networks to transform them into sustained challenges. Under reform, Chinese workers and ordinary citizens alike no doubt enjoy greater personal autonomy and a widening public sphere,[60] as market mechanisms and economic decentralization have gradually unravelled their webs of dependence on official units. Yet, the strong grip of the state is also evident in the organization and leadership formation of these newly emerging societal and civic associations.[61] Attempts to form opposition political parties or independent unions are ruthlessly crushed. The political opportunity structure remains decidedly exclusionary and closed to organized dissent from below.

Yet, instead of suggesting that these weaknesses predetermine a stymied course of development for labour insurgency, I want to highlight some of the potential inherent in this seemingly weak form of resistance. Sociologists studying social movements by disadvantaged groups have pointed out that their lack of organizational capacity does not necessarily preclude effective disruptive capacity. Organized resistance poses the classic problem of being cooptable into normal politics, and in communist or authoritarian regimes it invites the most ferocious crackdown due to the obvious threat it presents to the elaborately organized regime. *Falun Gong*'s structural isomorphism with the Chinese Communist Party is a case in point. Sidney Tarrow has perceptively noted along with others that the weak in repressive centralized political systems have a crucial weapon: they have 'a great deal in common'. Not that their interests or constraints are homogeneous, but at least they have a common target. In addition, 'repressive states depress collective action of a conventional and a confrontational sort, but leave themselves open to unobtrusive mobilization; a signal for solidarity that becomes a resource when opportunities arise'.[62] Dissent of such an unobtrusive, such a diffuse and local nature can take many forms, from social memories and private criticisms, to work-unit based protests and city-wide demonstrations.

One critical factor affecting the possibility of widening the political space for organized labour dissent hinges on elite alignment. Two of the most astute observers of Chinese labour politics agree on the importance of elite cleavage for labour activism. Reviewing the trajectories of labour strife since 1949, Elizabeth Perry concludes that

> Chinese labour activism has, for the better part of a century, been characterized by a complex blend of bottom-up initiatives and top-down mobilization … [W]e should not underestimate the extent to which contemporary labour protest is likely to feed into the projects of rival political leaders.[63]

Andrew Walder likewise underlines the interaction between divided elite and social groups:

> The 'Tiananmen protests' was emphatically not a case where an autonomous protest movement from below rose up to challenge and incapacitate a communist regime ... Instead, 'Tiananmen' is a classic case in which nascent protests interact with a divided elite and party-state apparatus ... with impulses for protests from below.[64]

As Sidney Tarrow notes, a political opportunity structure may become conducive to sustained collective action during times of shifts in ruling alignments, influential allies or elite cleavages. These conditions have strong precedents in contemporary Chinese politics. And when these conditions do mature in conjunction with labour agitation, those forms of unobtrusive struggle and public resistance documented above may prove to be constitutive elements of a 'repertoire of contention' for a Chinese labour movement powerful enough to challenge the government's monopoly of power. But there is an alternative scenario which bears on the development of labour politics. This has to do with the effectiveness of the state in addressing workers' needs, interests and rights in the reform process. If the state, either locally or via a national programme, can successfully institutionalize a new social security net to guarantee the economic survival of the massive unemployed population and put in place a law-based system for labour arbitration and conflict resolution, motivation to rebel collectively will be dampened. We have seen how failure to meet the livelihood, pension and severance payment demands of state-sector workers in the northeast spawned radical reactions, and how in the process economic grievances were transformed into political ones. On the other hand, local initiatives in Shanghai have allowed a more stable market transition for the state workforce. A similarly open future awaits the young generation of migrant workers. In Shenzhen, for instance, which leads the country in the volume of arbitrated labour disputes, migrant workers are increasingly conscious of their legal rights and savvy in using the arbitration and court systems to fight against employers' violation of the law. Yet, without responsive government and a law-based judiciary, workers have few alternatives but to resort to non-institutionalized channels of protests and demonstrations, if they believe the system is biased in favour of the rich and powerful.[65]

Notes

1   Charles Hoffmann, *The Chinese Worker* (Albany. State University of New York Press, 1974).
2   Andrew Walder, *Communist Neo-traditionalism* (Berkelcy: University of California Press, 1986), chap. 2.
3   Elizabeth J. Perry, 'Shanghai's Strike Wave of 1957', *The China Quarterly*, 137 (March 1994), pp. 1–27.
4   Andrew G. Walder, 'The Chinese Cultural Revolution in the Factories: Party-State Structures and Patterns of Conflict', in Elizabeth J. Perry (ed.), *Putting Class in Its Place:*

Worker Identities in East Asia (Berkeley: Institute of East Asian Studies, University of California, China Research Monograph, 1996), pp. 167–98; Elizabeth J. Perry, 'Labor's Love Lost: Worker Militancy in Communist China', *International Labor and Working-Class History*, 50 (Fall 1996), pp. 64–76; Elizabeth J. Perry and Li Xun, *Proletarian Power: Shanghai in the Cultural Revolution* (Boulder: Westview Press, 1997).

 5 Sebastian Heilmann, 'The Social Context of Mobilization in China: Factions, Work Units, and Activists During the 1976 April Fifth Movement', *China Information*, 8 (Winter 1993–1994), pp. 1–19.

 6 Renhong Wu, 'China's Macroeconomy: Review and Perspective', *Journal of Contemporary China*, 7, 19 (1998), pp. 443–58.

 7 *China Labour Statistical Yearbook 1997* (Beijing: China Statistical Publishing House, 1997), p. 6.

 8 Fei-ling Wang, 'Floaters, Moonlighters, and the Underemployed: A National Labor Market With Chinese Characteristics', *Journal of Contemporary China*, 7, 19 (1998), pp. 459–75.

 9 *A Statistical Survey of China 1998* (Beijing: China Statistical Publishing House, 1998), p. 32.

10 For the different types of 'unemployed' workers, see Dorothy Solinger, 'Why We Cannot Count the "Unemployed"', *The China Quarterly*, 167 (September 2001), pp. 671–88.

11 Russell Smyth, 'Toward "the Modern Corporation": Recent Developments in the Institutional Reform of State-owned Enterprises in Mainland China', *Issues and Studies*, 34 (August 1998), p. 121.

12 Ching Kwan Lee, 'From Organized Dependence to Disorganized Despotism: Changing Labor Regime in Chinese Factories', *The China Quarterly*, 157 (March 1999), pp. 44–71.

13 Dorothy Solinger, 'The Chinese Work Unit and Transient Labor in the Transition from Socialism', *Modern China*, 21 (April 1995), pp. 155–83.

14 Virgina Harper-Ho, 'Labor Dispute Resolution in China: Implications for Labor Rights and Legal Reform', JD thesis, Harvard Law School (June 2001), p. 40.

15 *Laodong Zhengyi Chuli Yu Yanjiu* (Labour Disputes: Handling and Research) (1995, 1996, 1997), various articles; see also *Chinese Labor and Social Security Yearbook*, from 1995 to 2001 (Beijing: Zhongguo Laodong he Shehuibaozhang Chubanshi).

16 Alan Liu, *Mass Politics in the People's Republic* (Boulder: Westview Press, 1996), p. 105; Jeanne L. Wilson, ' "The Polish Lesson": China and Poland, 1980–1990', *Studies in Comparative Communism*, 23 (Autumn/Winter 1990), p. 263. See also, Chen-chang Chiang, 'The Role of the Trade Unions in Mainland China', *Issues and Studies*, 26 (February 1990), pp. 92–93.

17 Chang Kai, 'China's Entry into WTO and Legislation on Labor Standards', *Hong Kong Journal of Social Sciences*, 21 (Winter 2001), pp. 41–65.

18 Shaoguang Wang, 'Deng Xiaoping's Reform and the Chinese Workers' Participation in the Protest Movement of 1989', *Research in Political Economy*, 13 (1992), pp. 163–97.

19 Quoted in Elizabeth Perry, 'Labor's Battle for Political Space: The Role of Worker Associations in Contemporary China', in Deborah S. Davis, Richard Kraus, Barry Naughton, Elizabeth J. Perry (eds), *Urban Spaces in Contemporary China* (Cambridge: Cambridge University Press, 1995), p. 315.

20 *Cheng Ming* (Hong Kong) (March 1993), p. 19, (April 1994), p. 21 and (December 1996), p. 11, and FBIS-CHI-96–077, 29 (19 April 1996).

21 Anita Chan, *China's Workers Under Assault: The Exploitation of Labor in a Globalizing Economy* (Armonk: M.E. Sharpe, 2001).

22 Leung Wing-yue, *Smashing the Iron Rice Pot: Workers and Unions in China's Market Socialism* (Hong Kong: Asia Monitor Research Center, 1988), pp. 155–8.

23 Shi Meixia *et al.*, 'Causes and Policies Regarding Spontaneous Incidents in Labor Relations', in Labour Science Institute of the Labour and Social Security Bureau

(ed.), *Report of Chinese Labor Science Studies 1997–1999* (Beijing: Zhongguo Laodong Shehuibaozhang Chubanshe, 2000), pp. 166–216.

24 Lin Zhengong and Chen Yulin, 'Sanziqiye gongren taigongbagong de tedian he duize' (Characteristics and Handling of Slow-downs and Strikes by Workers in Foreign-invested Enterprises), in *Zhongguo Laodong Kexue*(Chinese Labour Science), 89 (May 1993), pp. 33–5.

25 China Labor Education and Information Center, *The Flip-Side of Success: The Situation of Workers and Organizing in Foreign-invested Electronics Enterprises in Guangdong* (Hong Kong: China Labor Education and Information Center, 1996), p. 11.

26 Anita Chan, 'Labor Relations in Foreign-funded Ventures, Chinese Trade Unions and the Prospects for Collective Bargaining', in Greg O'Leary (ed.), *Adjusting to Capitalism* (Armonk, New York: M.E. Sharpe, 1998), pp. 122–49; China Labor Education and Information Center, *The Flip-Side of Success*; Leung Wing-yue, *Smashing the Iron Rice Pot*, p. 175.

27 Elizabeth J. Perry, 'Labor's Battle for Political Space', pp. 318–19; Andrew G. Walder, 'Urban Industrial Workers: Some Observations on the 1980s', in Arthur Lewis Rosenbaum (ed.), *State and Society in China: The Consequences of Reform* (Boulder: Westview Press, 1992), pp. 103–20; Lu Ping, *A Moment of Truth: Workers' Participation in China's 1989 Democracy Movement and the Emergence of Independent Unions* (Hong Kong: Hong Kong Trade Union Education Center, 1990); Jonathan Unger (ed.), *The Pro-democracy Protests in China: Reports from the Provinces* (Armonk: M.E. Sharpe, 1991).

28 Andrew G. Walder, *'Urban Industrial Workers*, p. 116.

29 FBIS-CHI-96–077, 29 (19 April 1996).

30 Minxin Pei, 'China's Governance Crisis', *Foreign Affairs* (September–October 2002), p. 96.

31 *Cheng Ming* (April 1993), p. 37.

32 Chen Feng, 'Subsistence Crisis, Managerial Corruption and Labor Protests in China', *The China Journal*, 44 (July 2000), pp. 41–63; William Hurst and Kevin J O'Brien, 'China's Contentious Pensioners', *The China Quarterly*, 170 (June 2002), pp. 345–60; Yongshun Cai, 'The Resistance of Chinese Laid-off Workers in the Reform Period', *The China Quarterly*, 170 (June 2002), pp. 327–44.

33 *China Labor Bulletin*, 37 (July–August 1997), p. 5.

34 *South China Morning Post*, 18 November 1998.

35 FBIS-CHI-94–072, 28 (14 April 1994).

36 *South China Morning Post*, 20 September 1998.

37 FBIS-CHI-94–108, 19 (6 June 1994).

38 *Far Eastern Economic Review*, 26 June 1997, p. 15.

39 Shaoguang Wang, 'Deng Xiaoping's Reform', p. 187.

40 Ching Kwan Lee, 'The Revenge of History: Collective Memories and Labor Protests in Northeastern China', *Ethnography*, 1, 2 (December 2000), pp. 217–37.

41 Ching Kwan Lee, 'From the Specter of Mao to the Spirit of the Law: Labor Insurgency in China', *Theory and Society*, 31 (April 2002), pp. 189–228.

42 John Pomfret, 'With Carrots and Sticks, China Quiets Protesters', *The Washington Post*, 22 March 2002; Erik Eckholm, 'Leaner Factories, Fewer Workers Bring More Labor Unrest to China', *The New York Times*, 19 March 2002; Jasper Becker, 'Workers in a State of Disunion', *South China Morning Post*, 23 March 2002; Ming Pao China Team, 'Signs of Emerging Independent Trade Unions', *Ming Pao*, 28 March 2002.

43 Philip P. Pan, 'China's Seething Workers: Oil Industry Layoffs Spark Widespread Demonstrations', *The Washington Post*, 24 April 2002.

44 *South China Morning Post*, 6 December 1995; *Ming Pao*, 24 July 1998.

45 Alan Liu, *Mass Politics in the People's Republic*, p. 124.

46 *Ibid.*, p. 124.

47 Elizabeth J. Perry, 'Introduction' in her *Challenging the Mandate of Heaven* (Armonk: M.E. Sharpe, 2002).

48 Feng Tongqing, 'Workers and Trade Unions Under the Market Economy: Perspectives From Grassroots Union Cadres', *Chinese Sociology and Anthropology*, 28 (Spring 1996).
49 Chen-chang Chiang, 'The Role of the Trade Unions in Mainland China', pp. 92–93.
50 Lu Ping, *A Moment of Truth*.
51 *Ibid.*
52 Elizabeth J. Perry, 'Casting a Chinese "Democracy" Movement: The Role of Students, Workers, and Entrepreneurs', in Jeffrey N. Wasserstrom and Elizabeth J. Perry (eds), *Popular Protest and Political Culture in Modern China*, 2nd edition (Boulder: Westview Press, 1994), pp. 74–92. David Strand traces a tradition of public critique to the post Taiping Rebellion nineteenth century in his 'Protest in Beijing: Civil Society and Public Sphere in China', *Problems of Communism* (May–June 1990), pp. 1–19.
53 Lu Ping, *A Moment of Truth*, p. 19.
54 Trini Wing-yue Leung, 'Labor Fights for Its Rights', *China Perspectives*, 19 (September/October 1998); *South China Morning Post*, 9 October 1998.
55 *New York Times*, 24 December 1997; *South China Morning Post*, 28 December 1997.
56 For labour activists in Zhengzhou, see 'Fighting to Organize', *Far Eastern Economic Review*, 6 September 2001 and 'Working Man Blues', *Time Magazine* (Asia edition), 1 April 2002. For Liaoyang and Daqing unions, see Ming Pao China Team, 'Signs of Emerging Independent Trade Unions', *Ming Pao*, 28 March 2002.
57 *The China Daily*, 29 April 2002.
58 Ching Kwan Lee, 'From Organized Dependence to Disorganized Despotism'.
59 Sidney Tarrow, *Power in Movement: Social Movements, Collective Action and Politics* (Cambridge: Cambridge University Press, 1994), pp. 3–4.
60 See for examples, Deborah Davis *et al.* (eds), *Urban Spaces in Contemporary China*.
61 Tony Saich, 'Negotiating the State', *The China Quarterly*, 161 (March 2002).
62 Sidney Tarrow, *Power in Movement* (New York: Cambridge University Press, 1994), p. 93; and Zhou Xueguang, 'Unorganized Interests and Collective Action in Communist China', *American Sociological Review*, 58 (February 1993), pp. 54–73.
63 Elizabeth J. Perry, 'Labor's Battle for Political Space', p. 325.
64 Andrew G. Walder, 'Does China Face an Unstable Future?', in Maurice Brosseau, Kuan Hsin-chi and Y.Y. Kueh (eds), *China Review 1997* (Hong Kong: Chinese University Press, 1997), pp. 344–45.
65 An illuminating legal case in Shenzhen is reported in Philip P. Pan 'Chinese Workers' Rights Stop at Courtroom Door', *Washington Post*, 28 June 2002.

Suggested reading

Anita Chan, *China's Workers Under Assault: The Exploitation of Labor In a Globalizing Economy* (Armonk: M.E. Sharpe, 2001).
Elizabeth J. Perry, *Challenging the Mandate of Heaven* (Armonk: M.E. Sharpe, 2002).
Elizabeth J. Perry and Li Xun, *Proletarian Power: Shanghai in the Cultural Revolution* (Boulder: Westview Press, 1997).
Jackie Sheehan, *Chinese Workers: A New History* (London: Routledge, 1998).

4 Contesting rural spaces

Land disputes, customary tenure and the state[1]

Peter Ho

The explosiveness of rural land ownership

> Granting land ownership to the natural village will create a shock (*yinqi zhendong de*). It is not beneficial for social stability. Such a proposal by that bunch of scientists in the Academy of Social Sciences is unrealistic. Their research is too remote from reality.[2]

When the people's communes were dismantled in the mid-1980s, the party and some international observers trumpeted this as the 'second land reform'. After more than three decades, the use right to rural land was once more returned to the tiller through lease, although land ownership remained in state and collective hands. This hybrid tenure system of privatized land use, on the basis of state and collective ownership, attracted much international attention. Neo-liberal economists cautioned that an economy based on state ownership of the means of production could not sustain long-term, stable growth. In their view, privatization is a *conditio sine qua non* for the market economy. This premise, enshrined in the 'Washington Consensus' became the guiding principle for many of the social engineering programmes of the World Bank and the International Monetary Fund in the former Soviet Union and the East-bloc countries.[3]

However, the dynamic performance of China's rural economy since the 1970s has undercut these ideas. Scholarly attention to China's hybrid tenure system soon shifted to the security of the land lease contracts issued to farmers. The rationale behind these studies is that security of land use rights is essential if farmers are to invest.[4] Viewed in broader perspective, however, studies of reform processes have shown that there is no blueprint for the economics of transition. Reforms need to be weighed in light of a given society's economic structure and history, rather than being pursued – or worse, imposed – on the basis of a universal blueprint. Ownership is among the most critical issues in transitional economies because of both historical reasons and contemporary implications. In China, land reform was used to rally social support for the Communist revolutionary cause. Hence, a new land reform, or the privatisation of ownership, remains one of the most explosive issues in Chinese society.

It is obvious that collective land ownership[5] in China is shrouded in vagueness. If we delve into the past, we see that land ownership – after several years of intense debate in the central leadership – was finally vested in the lowest collective level: the production team.[6] While the locus of land ownership during the collective period (1956–78) was clear, the level of land ownership subsequently has been vague. The implications of this fact for social stability in China are the main focus of this chapter.

Contested ownership: main argument, definitions and methodology

For tax purposes, both the Republican and Communist governments attempted to delimit village communities, resulting in frequent redrawing of boundaries, renaming of villages and merging of hamlets into larger territorial units. Collectivization with a three-tier system of basic administration – the people's commune, the production brigade and the production team – and subsequent decollectivization in the mid-1980s have complicated the situation. With exceptions,[7] we can state that the commune has become the present township/town (*xiang/zhen*), the brigade the administrative village (*xingzhengcun*), and the team the natural village (*zirancun*), which is also called the villagers' group (*cunmin xiaozu*). Note that the brigade and administrative village are administrative units controlling natural villages, yet may also simultaneously be natural villages themselves. As such, they claim ownership to land within the traditional village borders, which will be shown below (see also Fig. 4.1).[8] While the brigade or administrative village in many regions is comprised of multiple natural villages, in some instances it coincides with the natural village. Although the natural village – in its capacity as the production team – held formal land ownership rights, it possessed no real power over land. For example, the power to transfer ownership to another community or to the state, or even to determine what crops were grown, rested with the commune and higher administrative levels (the county and above). In short, the natural village was unable to safeguard the interests to the land that its inhabitants tilled and lived on. During the collective period, land was frequently requisitioned from the natural village in the name of economic development. If the commune decided to build a pig farm, or the brigade wanted to establish a small industrial enterprise, village land was simply expropriated. As formal requisitioning procedures were seldom followed and appropriate financial compensation even less seldom provided, this was the origin of many land disputes. During the National People's Congress debates over the draft for the 1998 Revised Land Administration Law, some delegates explicitly called for the clarification of collective rural land ownership.[9] Yet, when the revised law was finally promulgated, this issue was intentionally evaded by leaving the term 'collective' undefined. For this reason, I introduce the term 'deliberate institutional ambiguity' to describe China's land rights system.[10]

It should be noted that the deliberate institutional ambiguity does not necessarily have a negative impact on society. A majority of farmers support the status

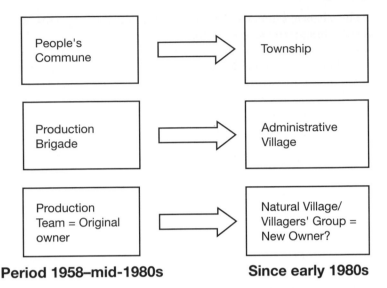

Figure 4.1   Changes in ownership of rural collective land

Source: Drawn by Zhao Heng.

quo,[11] and, despite a legal system bound by conflicting and unclear rules, conflicts that fundamentally challenge the present ownership structure are infrequent. No widespread claims for private, common or other forms of rural land ownership have arisen since decollectivization in the early 1980s. In addition, the ambiguity of collective rural land ownership has provided leeway for wide regional experimentation with property rights.[12] Above all, there is no evidence that the hybrid and ambiguous property rights structure has hampered agricultural development. In this respect, institutional indeterminacy is the 'lubricant' on which the system runs. the ambiguity of legal rules allows the land tenure system to function at the current stage of economic reforms.

The vague land ownership structure has, however, created ample opportunity for the trampling of villagers' and collectives' legitimate rights by the local and central state. Scholars have documented many instances of 'territorial theft' from villages to construct office and apartment buildings for the ever-expanding cities (see chapter 5); imposed land leases, sometimes without the knowledge of the farmer as contracts are issued for several households at once; and erratic land policy changes resulting in the victimization of farmers.[13] Indeed, leaving ownership deliberately ambiguous could give rise to large-scale social conflict, a risk the Chinese government can ill afford. I highlight three legacies of the collectivist past that may give rise to land disputes. First, the incoherent legal framework and lack of the rule of law. Second, the absence of a national land survey. And finally, the state's failure to recognize customary claims over the control and ownership of land. These legacies plague China's current land administration and lie at the heart of many contemporary land ownership disputes. This chapter examines the sources of conflict and speculates on the implications for future land tenure reforms.

The cases are drawn from the two-volume *Encyclopedia of the New Land Administration Law*, edited by Liu Xinhua, and the compilation of administrative cases released by the Supreme People's Court in 1997.[14] The cases recorded and summarized here date from the early 1990s. Since then, two important developments have taken place in land legislation: 1) the replacement of the 1989 State Land Administration's Suggestions on the Assessment of Land Titles (hereafter, the 1989 Suggestions) with the 1995 Regulations on the Assessment of Land Ownership and Use Rights (hereafter, the 1995 Regulations) and 2) the proclamation of the 1998 Revised Land Administration Law.[15]

Land theft or requisition? Sources of conflict

Although land ownership was formally given to the lowest collective level (the team) by party decree after 1962, in cases where higher collective levels or the local state stole land from the village, the seeds were sown for protracted disputes. During the collective period, these disputes were often suppressed. However, they returned with a vengeance after the start of the economic reforms. With growing commercialization and galloping urbanization since 1978, the value of land has risen steeply and a semi-clandestine land market has emerged. In the years 1997–98 alone, revenues from transferred land increased 78.1 per cent over the preceding year to 13.2 billion yuan.[16] The higher economic stakes brought conflicts over land to the fore.

In the drive for economic development that marked the history of the People's Republic of China, land was frequently requisitioned from teams and brigades without any formal procedures or without proper compensation. In many cases, the word of higher-level cadres was law: once their approval was secured – including oral commitments – economic projects, such as the construction of a silk farm, water reservoir or plantation, could proceed. Under collectivism the legal framework was weak and inconsistent. Until 1982 there were no formal rules pertaining to land requisition of the collectives. Moreover, from the establishment of the collectives in 1955, the state failed to register collective land holdings. In the history of the People's Republic two events decisively affected the land holdings of the natural village: Land Reform in the 1950s and the Four Fixes Movement (*si guding*) in 1962, which enshrined the team as the basic unit of accounting. The term 'Four Fixes' refers to the granting of permanent ownership of labour, land, animals and tools to the production team in 1962. To date, the Supreme Court and the Ministry of Land Resources consider these two events the basis for the assessment of land title.[17] However, Land Reform and the Four Fixes Movement were not accompanied by a national cadastre. During Land Reform some villagers were issued land titles, but this was never done systematically. Moreover, many of these titles were lost or destroyed in the subsequent decades of collectivization and political and social upheaval when ownership of land in fact passed from households to collective units.[18]

The final explosive issue giving rise to land conflicts is the question of customary land rights. Like other developing countries, Chinese rural communities face great difficulty in having customary land rights, which are largely unwritten, recognized by the state.[19] On a different level, the problem of recognition pertains to a cultural clash between a rapidly industrializing society and an agrarian society based on a tradition of the 'rule by man'.[20] The controversy over the term 'customary law' reflects the intangibility and fluidity of tenure by custom. Motion defined customary law as 'unwritten law established by long usage'[21] but what is long? In England, custom only has legal force if it has existed for so long that 'the memory of man runneth not to the contrary'. Curiously, the limit of human memory was fixed at the date of the accession of Richard I in 1189.[22] In examining the sources of conflict over the ownership and control of land, several essential features of Chinese current legal culture must be borne in mind: the fragmentation of law, the dependency of the courts on local government and the subordination of law to policy; in short, the blurred distinction between judicial and administrative powers. Chinese courts have to perform a complex juggling act with conflicting and often unverifiable claims, intervention by the local government and faint hope of rectifying the wrongs of the past. On the one hand, villages have repeatedly fallen victim to land theft from higher administrative levels, which calls for justice. On the other hand, over time considerable investments have been made in the stolen land while new customary land rights have emerged. This makes it all the more difficult 'simply' to return the land to the original owner. The court cases described below highlight this dilemma.

See you in court: legal cases on land disputes

Economic development[23]

The cases in this subsection illustrate two points. First, under collectivism the 'theft of land' was possible because the legal framework was incomplete and inconsistent. Second, during the collective period land requisition from the village was effected by administrative rather than legal measures.

Shiqiao Commune in Hubei Province built a small reservoir in 1959, which was expanded one year later. In 1963, the party branch of the Hubei Provincial Water Conservancy Bureau issued a directive that ordered the transfer of the reservoir's ownership and capital assets to the county. The reservoir and its land thereby became state property. In 1965, the Bureau of Water Conservancy planned another expansion of the reservoir and requested land from the county. The Xiangyang county magistrate orally conveyed to the bureau his decision to requisition 210 *mu* of land from the Third Villagers' Group of Hongdao Administrative Village for the purpose. No formalities for land requisition were ever completed.

Decades later, a series of conflicts erupted between the villagers' group and the state water reservoir. In March 1993, the county government issued a document which marked the land as 'disputed area'. This strengthened the villagers' group in its conviction that the land was indeed its property and it started to petition the authorities. A month later, however, the county bluntly ruled that the land was state owned according to the 1989 Suggestions. In response, the villagers' group filed a lawsuit challenging the county ruling. The county asked that the plaintiff's claim be dismissed 'to safeguard the correct enforcement of the state's laws'. [24] Of specific interest is the county's claim that the villagers' group could not legally enjoy collective ownership, and thus was not entitled to act as a legal person. Instead, ownership should have rested with the administrative village under which jurisdiction the villagers' group falls.

The court, however, ruled that the villagers' group could own land. This decision was based on the State Land Administration's interpretation of article eight on collective ownership of the 1986 Land Administration Law: 'The land originally owned by the team belongs to the farmers' collective of the agricultural collective economic organization of the corresponding villagers' group.' The court read this interpretation as meaning that 'there are two kinds of collective land ownership: ownership by the villagers' committee *and* ownership by the villagers' group or production team' (emphasis added).[25] In addition, as there was only an oral commitment by the county head, while no requisition procedures had been followed, the court ordered the land returned to the villagers' group.

A second case, related to the first, concerns the dispute between a commune and three brigades. In 1975, Shifo Commune in Shandong expropriated a total of 170 *mu* of land from Xulou, Weihai and Qianchenhai Brigades to set up a pig farm. Typically, no land requisition procedures had been followed, nor had any compensation been paid. Since 1978 the three brigades have petitioned the commune authorities to return the land and compensate them for financial losses. An agreement was signed between the commune and the brigades in 1980. The agreement stipulated how much land had been requisitioned and at what price. It also determined that the land belonged to the pig farm, but would be sold back to the brigades at the purchase price in the event that the farm was to be disbanded. The brigades were partly paid in cash and partly in kind. With the demise of Shifo Commune and subsequent change to a township in 1983, the pig farm was disbanded. From then on, the land was used for forestry. In 1990, the trees were felled and one-third of the land was leased for agriculture to farmers from Hanzhuang village for a period of thirty-five years. At that point, disputes between the township and the three administrative villages erupted. The county government intervened on several occasions. In 1988 and 1991 directives were issued stating that the land was owned by the township (*gui xiang suoyou*). In the end, the villages filed a case against the township and county governments.

The villages claimed that the land was theirs because the commune had requisitioned it without their consent and the land use had been changed in violation of the 1980 agreement which stipulated that ownership was to be sold back to the village if the farm was disbanded. The county invoked the 1989 Suggestions to prove that the land belonged to the township. According to these regulations, a change in the level of collective land ownership is possible for the establishment of enterprises. For land in use between 1962 and 1982 this is effective if an agreement has been signed, if approval from the county, township and village authorities has been obtained, or if the ownership structure of the user has changed.[26] As an agreement had been signed and compensation paid, the land belonged to the township, the county claimed. The township authorities added that land use had not changed: its former forestry activities were geared to animal husbandry and the farm had not been dissolved. The director, the buildings and pigsties were still there. Lease for agriculture was permitted, the township stated, as it owned the land.

The county court ruled that the disputed land belonged to the township. The villages appealed to the intermediate court of Liucheng Prefecture, which annulled the verdict of the lower court and decided that the ownership of the disputed land should be allocated to the three villages. This decision was taken on three grounds: 1) the three villages' land had been appropriated without formal approval and appropriate procedures; 2) land use had been changed with the demise of the pig farm and the lease for agriculture; 3) the law had been inappropriately applied to sustain the 1988 and 1991 county directives which vested land ownership in the township.

The legal miasma of the past has created the courts' dilemmas of the present. A major problem is the nature of collective ownership. As explained in the introduction to this chapter, collective ownership was intentionally left undefined in law because of the central government's fear of large-scale social conflict. The land ownership of the team (natural village) has remained ambiguous since the start of the economic reforms. In particular, in the urbanized, coastal regions where land prices have soared, legal indeterminacy has been used to deny land ownership by the natural village. During the revision of the 1998 Land Administration Law, Zhejiang Province went so far as to suggest altering the land tenure structure stipulated in the Sixty Articles to abolish the natural village's land ownership rights.[27] Zhejiang officials reasoned that collective ownership by a higher level would facilitate urban and spatial planning. However, the village would thereby be robbed of the possibility of fighting against forced land requisitions. With the current boom in land prices and the frenzy for real-estate development, the natural village and its inhabitants will be stripped of their legal rights if they lose the authority to represent collective ownership.

Against this backdrop, the first case is no less than a landmark. Xiangyang county used the ambiguity of the law to delegitimize the Third Villagers' Group as the legal owner of land. Significantly, the court read the law as saying that the villagers' group *can* enjoy ownership of land and not merely the right to use and management. If, through higher appeals, Xiangyang county were to bring the case to the Supreme People's Court, it could become a crucial test of the legal and political limits of China's land tenure. There is a paucity of laws and regulations covering areas other than ownership. As a result, courts have no recourse but to rely on administrative measures of uncertain legal status. This problem is illustrated in the second case. The main question here is whether land appropriation from three villages by Shifo Commune constituted a legitimate act of land requisition. According to Chinese law, land requisition is carried out for purposes of state construction only, in which case ownership is transferred from the collective to the state. Under the past and current legal framework this is the sole condition under which collective ownership can change; there are no legal rules under which various collective levels can transfer the ownership of land among themselves.[28] For this reason, the 'land requisition' by the commune was illegal. Furthermore, the 1980 agreement, which arranged to sell land ownership back to the original owners in the event that the enterprise was disbanded, was also unlawful as it stipulated a sale of encumbered land ownership.[29] Since the 1988 revision of the Constitution, only the non-commercial transfer of the use right to rural land is allowed. This issue is still heatedly debated and there is no reference to it in the latest amendment to the Land Administration Law.

Yet the appropriation of land for township and village enterprises is widespread throughout rural China. Therefore the silence of the Land Administration Law on this issue is problematic. The court cannot but resort to the interpretation of administrative regulations issued by the executive branch of the state – the 1989 Suggestions. However, as these have not been reviewed, debated and passed as law by the National People's Congress (NPC), nor issued by the State Council as binding rules for implementation (*shishi tiaoli*), nobody knows their exact legal implications. In fact, the rules applied here do not even have the status of an administrative regulation (*guizhang*) but are merely 'suggestions'.

No cadastre, a disaster!

The cases here illustrate the consequences of China's lack of a cadastre. They also concern customary tenure.

In 1992, X Village filed a lawsuit against Y Village for a dispute over 257 *mu* of land located on the Daozhai Mountains between the two villages. In Republican times, this land housed a Nationalist Army military depot. Before collectivization X Village used this land for sideline activities, but it became the common property of both villages during the 1950s. In 1966, the prefecture wished to construct a silk farm on the common land. A requisition certificate was signed between Y Village and the silk farm, but not with X Village because no agreement could be reached. Some time later, X Village consented to the expropriation for which it received a financial compensation of 1,000 yuan – a pittance.

In 1980, the county government planned a new county capital and requisitioned land including that of the silk farm. The county informed the two villages of the upcoming expropriation, which they understood as a renewed requisition – in other words, the county assumed that it was the owner of the tract. The villages appealed to the county to recognize their ownership and grant appropriate compensation. The county ignored the requests and proceeded with the construction. In reaction, thirty farmers from Y Village demolished the new buildings. After two years of conflict, the county appointed an investigation team, which concluded that the land had been requisitioned in 1966 with the agreement of both villages. Therefore, they were entitled neither to claim ownership nor to demand compensation.

But Y Village kept appealing to the authorities. In 1985, the county stated that the land rights of the disputed plot had always been unclear. Therefore, the land should be equally divided between the two villages and once more requisitioned against compensation. The conflict between the villages and the county then changed into a boundary dispute between the two villages. In court, X Village claimed ownership to the land on the basis of the texts of two stone stelae (one from the Kangxi period in the seventeenth century and another engraved in 1922). Y Village responded that even before liberation it had used the land for animal husbandry, agriculture and brick production.

The court adopted the county's verdict and ruled that the land was commonly owned by X and Y Villages, because written land titles were lacking. This meant that the land had to be equally divided between the two villages and re-requisitioned. X Village appealed to the prefectural court, which ruled that the county had violated the law. By recognizing the villages' dual ownership to the disputed land, the county had illegally returned the land to the original owners, while it was actually state-owned. According to the 1986 Land Administration Law, 'collective land that is requisitioned by the state for construction is owned by the state; the unit that uses the land [in this case: the silk farm] only enjoys the right to use'.[30] Therefore, the county's land appropriation from the silk farm was not a matter of changing ownership but of changing use rights. The villages' claims for ownership and compensation were declared unfounded.

The following case concerns the struggle over rights to newly formed land. The case is especially interesting because – to my knowledge – it is the first documented case on riparian rights in China. What are riparian rights? Suppose a tract of land borders a river or lake and the title mentions the water body as part of the boundary, then the owner may claim what are called riparian rights. These usually include the use of the water for boating, fishing and swimming. As Frank Emerson Clark wrote in his authoritative 1939 *Fundamentals of Law for Surveyors*, 'water bodies [can] make especially troublesome boundaries' because they 'shift as streams meander, lake levels fluctuate, and coasts erode'.[31]

Bolin and Xiaqu are two villages located on the northern bank of the Weihe River and extending south to the Shanghai-Lanzhou railroad in Gansu Province. Along the river there was a stretch of common land that was jointly cultivated by farmers from the two villages. After a large flood in 1954,[32] this land was lost to the water. During the Four Fixes Movement in 1962 Bolin and Xiaqu exchanged two equal plots of land situated north of the railway track. The boundary between the plots was the 305 landmark east of the Jiashigou Canal. As the land as far south as the railroad had been washed away by the flood, nothing was agreed on its boundaries. In 1972, Xiaqu built a dam upstream. The dam diverted the Weihe River southwards and a stretch of wasteland surfaced at the northern bank. Xiaqu claimed that the boundary for this land should follow the boundary north of the railroad: the 305 landmark east of the Jiashigou Canal. Bolin maintained that the boundary should be the 1,384 kilometre stone of the railroad. Neither village could furnish any written evidence to support their claims.

In 1990, Xiaqu Village filed administrative litigation with the Beidao county government. A year later, the county pronounced:

> Through examination of maps of land requisition for the Shanghai-Lanzhou railroad before the founding of the People's Republic and through on-site investigation, it is confirmed that the boundary between the two villages at the time of the Four Fixes Movement ran from Jiashigou to the north of the railroad.[33]

For this reason, the county decided that the boundary north of the railroad would also apply to the new land south of the railway (see grey area in Fig. 4.2). The land east of the 305 landmark would be allocated to Bolin, the land west of it to Xiaqu. Bolin did not agree and took the case to the county court. Bolin responded that the boundary laid down in documents from the Republican period was not a fair standard for demarcation. In their words:

> The Weihe River is not a stream that can be fixed to its riverbed. Some years it flows southwards, some years northwards, flooding and damaging arable land. As early as Land Reform, cooperativization and collectiviza- tion, this tract was forestland, yet it became riverbed during floods ... [U]sing maps ... that date from before the founding of the People's Republic of China cannot explain the natural changes of 30 years.[34]

The court confirmed the evidence put forward by Bolin Village that 'before 1954 there was land south to the railroad and east of the 1384 kilometer marker stone of the Shanghai-Lanzhou railroad, which was commonly tilled by Xiaqu and Bolin Villages' But the court also stated that 'the title to this disputed land has not been determined since either Land Reform or the Four Fixes Movement in 1962'.[35] The verdict of the Beidao government, which determined that both villages held title to the land, was annulled and the county was ordered to pay legal costs.

In both cases, local government attempted to resolve land disputes that derive from long-term use without clear ownership. In the first case, the county proposed to reverse the problematic requisition of the past through renewed requisition with equal financial compensation for each village. However, this action only led to a new dispute over boundaries between the villages. There are several issues at stake. First, as the prefectural court also noted, the silk farm was by law not entitled to act as a claimant because it enjoyed only the use right to land and not ownership. Instead, the requisition should have been handled by

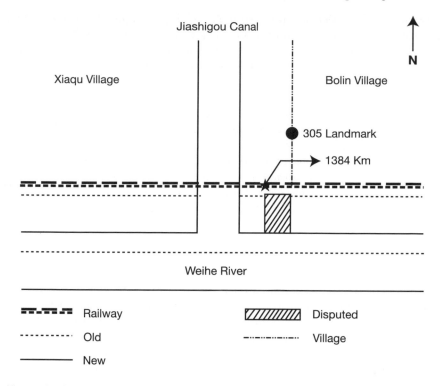

Figure 4.2 Schematic map of a dispute over riparian rights

the prefecture as the representative of the state. Second, after requisition the change in land titles from collective to state ownership should have been regis-tered with the county as the then current regulations stipulate.[36] Lastly, in a case in which the plaintiff's evidence is limited to stone stelae without detailed boundary descriptions and maps, while the defendant merely relies on oral history, the county's ruling is probably the best option.

In the second case, the local government sought a Solomonic judgement. This conflict is far more complex than the first: the disputed land alternatively submerged and resurfaced, and the land was tilled by two villages, neither of which could establish ownership. It is also a legal test case; its complexity exposes the legal shortcomings in adjudicating ownership issues pertaining to newly formed land that must be addressed to safeguard the interests of the state, the collective and the individual.

Who owns land that accrues from shifting river flows? The tract disputed by Bolin and Xiaqu is land that was naturally formed through a change in the river's course. This is a typical case of riparian rights: a void area in China's legal system today. The second fundamental problem is the lack of written evidence that could be used as a standard in adjudication. For its judgement Beidao county could rely only on maps of the Republican era. However, the use of historical documents to prove title is not uncontested. As the commentary on this case stated: 'The Beidao government used land material of the old system [society] as evidence to arbitrate in a land dispute forty years after liberation. We feel that a verdict on such basis is wrong.'[37] According to law, the basis for the assessment of land titles is Land Reform and the Four Fixes Movement, as 'all land deeds before Land Reform are invalid'.

There are great difficulties in taking land deeds issued during Land Reform and the Four Fixes Movement as the basis for collective ownership today. The registration of land titles during Land Reform was fragmentary at best, and many of these titles were lost over time. Moreover, during Land Reform, the land was generally distributed to individual households and not the village as a whole. All privately owned rural land was transferred to the collective with the establishment of the Higher Agricultural Production Cooperatives in 1956.[38] The Four Fixes Movement should have led to the registration of the production team as the basic owner of land as the Sixty Articles stipulated.

However, as the recorded cases demonstrate, systematic land registration was the exception rather than the rule. The illegal requisition of village land by higher administrative levels led to further ambiguity over ownership of collective land. For these reasons, the state called for the first nationwide registration of collective land in 1984. Due to the minefield it uncovered, however, it was halted at the level that mattered most: the natural village. It is certain that in the event of a national cadastre, China could not avoid taking into account the historical claims that predate Land Reform and the Four Fixes Movement. In the case of claims based on customary tenure, the situation is even more complicated.

Customary rights, silent rights[39]

The terms 'customary rights' or 'traditional land tenure' have the ring of a dim and distant past – something that has existed for so long that, as defined in one instance noted above, 'the memory of man runneth not to the contrary'. From the two cases reviewed here, we will see that entitlements do not necessarily have to date back centuries to be marked as 'customary'. Moreover, customary entitlements are – in China's context – often associated with the rights of ethnic minorities, such as the forest rights of mountain tribes in Yunnan, or the grazing arrangements of Mongols and Kazakhs in Inner Mongolia and Xinjiang, which are framed in terms of community rather than individual ownership rights. In the near future, with growing pressures from capital, China will encounter great difficulties in the assessment of customary land titles, not least because of their unwritten character. The challenge to the Chinese state is to grant fair recognition of such claims that can satisfy both state and collective interests, rather than simply to suppress differences.

The following case was not decided in court, but arbitrated by the Shaanxi Provincial Bureau of Land Administration. In 1984, Beiying Village occupied 361 *mu* of steppe from a farm of the Air Force Telecommunication College. The village claimed this land was ancestral steppe (*zuyi tandi*).[40] According to the village authorities, farmers had long tilled and afforested the land on the basis of a land permit issued during Land Reform. In addition, the village furnished land tax statistics and a clarifying map drafted in 1951 by the Goutai Administrative Region (which administered Beiying Village at the time). The material demonstrated that Beiying Village paid tax on over 500 *mu* of steppe, which included the disputed land. Lastly, the village cited a map of the Yellow River Water Conservancy Committee that showed the disputed plot falling outside the jurisdiction of Xi'an City, to which the air force's farm belonged. The farm, on the other hand, claimed that the disputed tract had always been public land (*gongdi*) and was commonly used by the Shaanxi Province financial, forestry and educational departments. In 1951 – with consent of the Shaanxi Provincial Bureau of Agriculture – the land was transferred to the farm for use. The transfer of use right was formally approved by the Shaanxi and Xi'an Party Committees in 1965. Party decisions generally took precedence over government decisions, an outcome that was particularly common during the collectivist period. The Shaanxi Bureau of Land Administration ruled that the disputed land is state owned and that the air force farm holds the use right. For its illegal occupation of land, Beiying Village had to be penalized. But in light of the substantial village investments in afforestation, no redress was imposed. Instead, the air force farm was ordered to pay 20,000 yuan for the fruit trees which then would belong to the farm. The verdict was based on the following considerations: 1) the land permit issued during Land Reform, which the Beiying Village authorities alluded to but did not present, was not found in archives; 2) the land tax statistics and accompanying map do not indicate whether the disputed tract was part of the land for which tax was due – neither is it clear whether the village paid taxes on land owned or leased; 3) the map of the Yellow River Water Conservancy Committee was drafted for the construction of the Sanmen Gorge Reservoir and not for the assessment of administrative boundaries, and therefore could not be admitted as evidence; 4) the farm's claim that the use rights were formally transferred in 1965 could not be corroborated.

The second case, too, concerns a land dispute between a village and a state institution. On Zechongqiao Mountain in Liuzhou City (Guangxi Province) lies a forest of around 550 *mu* that is contested by the Sanmenjiang State Forest Farm and Niucheping Village of Liudong Township. Since Land Reform no land title has been issued. In 1953, villagers sowed pine seeds on the mountain, followed by the planting of saplings the next year. In 1955, part of the land was used by the villagers for shifting cultivation. In that year, workers of the state forest farm planted fir trees on the land. The trees were carefully maintained and protected by villagers and foresters. In 1960, the East-is-Red Commune (later Liudong Township) carried out a general survey of the afforested land and had it registered as property of Niucheping Brigade. Three years later, after the proclamation of the Sixty Articles, Niucheping Brigade granted the forest's ownership to the fourth, sixth and seventh production teams (*huafen gei xiaodui suoyou*).[41] During the same period, the state forest farm strengthened its claims to the land. In line with regulations of the provincial forest bureau, the disputed plot was included in the farm's regional planning of 1954 and 1963. In addition, the Forest Mapping and Survey Institute drew maps of the area in 1973 and 1984.

By the late 1970s, the trees had matured and conflicts erupted over the mountain forest. For years, the conflict simmered despite repeated mediation by the Liuzhou City government. In 1991, the city authorities issued a verdict that assigned ownership of half of the tract to Niucheping Village and the other half to the state, while the use rights were granted to the state forest farm. The Sanmenjiang State Forest Farm did not submit to the verdict and filed suit against the city government. The farm claimed that peasants from Niucheping had illegally felled trees on the land since the late 1970s. Not only was the plot included in the farm's regional planning, but the farm was still formally responsible for forest protection on the Zechongqiao Mountain. The defendant, the Liuzhou City government, retorted that the title to the forest had never been assessed, although the land was used and managed by both claimants. Because the claimants could not furnish any evidence to prove title, the city government requested the court to sustain its verdict to 'prevent a continuation and worsening of the conflict'.[42]

The court ruled that both the 1960 land title registration of Niucheping and the forest farm's 1954 and 1963 regional planning were illegal, because they had not been approved by the county government and relevant departments. For this reason, the Liuzhou City verdict was sustained by the court and deemed 'factually clear, and a correct use of the laws and legal procedures'.[43] A later appeal to the higher court by the village and state forest farm was dismissed.

Land resources claimed by customary right include forest, grassland and wasteland – which does not imply that there are no customary claims on agricultural land. Most such claims are in the frontier zones inhabited by ethnic minorities that use these resources in common under customary regulations. Moreover, in those areas even land long occupied or colonized by Han peasants, forest, grassland and wasteland is generally common property – owned and used by the village community.[44] With the proclamation of the 1954 Constitution, forest, grassland and wasteland were formally nationalized, unless collective ownership could be proven, which implies that the burden of proof lies with the collective. The reverse situation applies to rural land, which is considered collective unless state ownership can be proven. This principle forms the legal basis for state and collective ownership and has been enshrined in the 1954 Constitution and the respective amendments to date.[45] The administrative measures proclaimed by the State Land Administration take the Constitution's basic principle of legal proof for state and collective ownership one step further. The 1989 Suggestions and the 1995 Regulations stipulate that 'land that has not been *legally* (i.e. according to the 1950 Land Reform Law and the Sixty Articles) allocated to farmers during Land Reform and the Four Fixes Movement is state-owned'.[46] The problem is that the common property aspect of customary entitlements is frequently regarded as 'nobody's property' by the state. It was therefore rare during Land Reform and the Four Fixes Movement for titles to forest, grassland and wasteland to be issued to farmers and collectives, still rarer where the (local) state considered these natural resources to have been national property since 1954. In other words, in the eyes of the state, forest, grassland and wasteland are state owned unless proven otherwise. In the eyes of Chinese villagers, this land is owned by the community, which faces the impossible task of proving that decades-long use of land is sufficient to claim 'customary right'. The two cases in this subsection painfully highlight this issue.

Both Beiying and Niucheping Villages claim wasteland on the basis of land use before Land Reform. The steppe and forest farms – as state representatives responsible for the management and development of national resources – counter the villages' claims and maintain that the disputed areas are state owned. Exactly how the land became state owned is unclear, because no official land requisition was carried out. Certain, however, is that state institutions invested considerable human and financial resources in land development. So simply reinstating the village's oral history claim to ownership is unacceptable to the state and the legal authorities. By again looking at the 1989 Suggestions and 1995 Regulations we can see how potentially explosive the situation is. The stipulation that land is state owned unless registered as collective during Land Reform or the Four Fixes Movement provides the state with a powerful instrument to brush away all customary land claims. If this rule were to be rigorously applied it would set off a firestorm of social conflict, putting the state on a collision course with the residents of virtually all minority areas. This issue is discussed in more detail in chapter 10. It is no surprise that the newly Revised Land Administration Law has shrouded this issue in vagueness rather than adopting the stipulations of the 1995 Regulations.

In dealing with customary entitlements, the judiciary and executive powers walk a thin line between safeguarding the state's interests and social justice. The solutions adopted by the courts and local governments in the two cases described above refrain from implementing the extreme measures possible under the 1989 Suggestions and 1995 Regulations. Instead, the formal verdicts are a veiled recognition of villages' customary claims. In the first case, the local government attempts to effect some sort of retroactive land requisition by demanding financial compensation from the state farm. However, whether this compensation comes anywhere near the real value of the requisitioned land can be questioned. In the second case, the local government and court steer a middle course through an equal division of the disputed land between the village and the state farm.

Concluding remarks: caught between historical heritage and social justice

How can (local) government and courts strike an equitable balance between unclear historical land claims and the imperatives of social justice? This requires scrupulous passage through a minefield of irreconcilable interests: villages' land has been 'stolen' as a result of a weak legal culture, while those that profited have in some instances invested substantial resources in the 'stolen good'. The root problem, however, is that for decades land has been used and developed by governments *and* villages precisely because ownership has been unclear. For the People's Republic there will be no easy answer to this complex matter. In this respect, the Chinese state is in the same boat as other governments struggling with indigenous and pre-colonial land claims.

For the Chinese state there are several critical issues. Local governments have frequently sought to deny the land ownership rights of the natural village altogether. At a time when land prices are booming and land ownership cannot be verified beyond doubt nor dealt with in transparently equitable ways, the highest responsibility of the central state must be to safeguard the legal interests of the weakest: the villages, farmers, herders and minority nationalities. Yet such a stance, while consistent with state goals of stability and unity, flies in the face of developmentalist priorities and the powerful business and state interests that see the opportunity to reap large profits and presently appear dominant in the Chinese polity.

From the first case discussed we can see how the courts can play a crucial role in establishing jurisprudence that confirms the natural village as the basic legal owner of land – as stipulated in the Sixty Articles. To date, however, procedures for the establishment and the status of case law to support this position are still fragmentary and weak.

A second problem that derives from unclear land laws and regulations is related to the level of collective ownership and changes therein. Under the past and present legal frameworks, the level of collective ownership cannot be changed. But during the collective period, team land was often requisitioned for the establishment of commune or brigade enterprises. Many current township and village enterprises were established in this way. Over time it became increasingly unclear what collective level could claim ownership to the land on which an enterprise was built. The heart of the problem is that the National People's Congress has not addressed critical issues clarifying the nature, and the level, of collective ownership.

In the absence of a national land cadastre, and there is no indication that the Chinese state is contemplating so vast, costly and controversial an undertaking, assessment of title must be adjudicated on the basis of historical claims. According to the current laws, the validity of claims is limited to land deeds issued during Land Reform and the Four Fixes Movement. However, because land was never systematically registered, claims that predate Land Reform will continue to be contested. This question is intertwined with the state's willingness to take seriously villages' and minority nationality's territorial claims under customary tenure.

The present legal principle that forest, grassland and wasteland are state owned unless proven collective property, with its grave implications for depriving minority peoples of customary rights, is surely untenable in the process of title recognition and registration. However, the common ownership of natural resources – not necessarily limited to a single village community – and the unwritten character of customary rights make them difficult to authenticate within the evolving legal framework. Laying the burden of proof on the collective is a strong legal instrument with which customary claims can be brushed aside. The attempts by the State Land Administration (and present Ministry of Land Resources) to strengthen the principle of 'state-owned unless proven collective' have created a potentially explosive situation. The local government and courts walk a thin line between the protection of the state's interests and meeting the collectives' demands for social justice. Yet, from the cases reviewed here, it can be seen that the local government and courts are capable of making independent judgements. Their verdicts may be regarded as implicit recognition of customary claims without sacrificing economic interests.

Into the present, the central government has maintained a rather passive stance by intentionally leaving land ownership issues fuzzy. By upholding such 'deliberate institutional ambiguity' it hopes to allow sufficient leeway for local experimentation with new property arrangements conducive to development, while simultaneously avoiding large-scale social conflict. If local practices prove feasible they can subsequently be institutionalized, a method utilized by the state in the early years of land reform and decollectivization in the 1970s and early 1980s. As the economic reforms and commercialization advance, the number of land claims will rise substantially. These will pose a formidable challenge for the Chinese judiciary and executive authorities.

Notes

1 I would like to thank Shi Wenzheng, Eduard B. Vermeer, Mark Selden and the land rights jurists Ellen-Roos Kambel and Herman Slaats for their helpful comments on an earlier version of this chapter. This research was funded by the European Union-China Academic Network (ECAN).

2 Interview with Li Sheng, Senior Official within the Directorate General for Political Reform and Law of the Ministry of Agriculture, 3 March 2002.

3 See, for example, Alice H. Amsden, 'Bringing Production Back In: Understanding Government's Economic Role in Later Industrialization', *World Development*, 25, 4 (1997), pp. 469–80.

4 James Kai-sing Kung and Shouying Liu, 'Farmers' Preferences Regarding Ownership and Land Tenure in Post-Mao China: Unexpected Evidence from Eight Counties', *The China Journal*, 38 (July 1997), pp. 33–64; Shouying Liu, Michael R. Carter and Yang Yao, 'Dimensions and Diversity of Property Rights in Rural China: Dilemmas on the Road to Further Reform', *World Development*, 26, 10 (1998), pp. 1789–806.

5 For an excellent introduction on land ownership in China from the 1950s until the early 1990s, see Mark Selden and Aiguo Lu, 'The Reform of Landownership and the Political Economy of Contemporary China', in Mark Selden (ed.), *The Political Economy of Chinese Development*, (Armonk: M.E. Sharpe, 1993).

6 The team was identified as the primary accounting unit. Article 21 of the Sixty Articles stipulated that 'all land within the limits of the production team is owned by the production team. [...] Collective forest, water resources, and grassland, are all owned by the production team'. See C.S. Chen (ed.), *Rural People's Communes in Lien-chiang* (Stanford: The Hoover Institute, 1969) or the excerpts in M. Selden, *The People's Republic of China. A Documentary History of Revolutionary Change* (New York: Monthly Review, 1978), pp. 521–6). For a detailed description of the leadership's discussion on the level of collective land ownership, see Peter Ho, 'The Clash over State and

Collective Property: The Making of the Rangeland Law', *The China Quarterly*, 161 (March 2000), pp. 247–9.

7 For example, such exceptions occurred if the former commune consisted of two levels instead of three. As also written in article 2 of the Sixty Articles: 'The organisation of the commune can consist of two levels: the commune and the team; but it can also consist of three levels: the commune, the production brigade and the production team.' See Chinese Communist Republic, 'Nongcun Renmin Gongshe Gongzuo Tiaoli Xiuzheng Cao'an' (Revised Draft of the Work Regulations of the Rural People's Communes), 27/9/1962, in Zhongguo Renmin Jiefangjun Guofang Daxue Dangshi Yanjiushi (ed.), *Reference Material on the CCP*, p. 137.

8 There is to date no evidence that administrative villages also claim ownership of the larger territory under their jurisdiction, which includes several natural villages.

9 See Boyong Li, 'Quanguo Renda Falü Weiyuanhui guanyu 'Zhonghua Renmin Gongheguo Tudi Guanlifa (Xiuding Cao'an)' Shenyi Jieguo de Baogao' (Report on the Results of the Review of the 'Land Administration Law of the People's Republic (Revised Draft)' by the Law Committee of the National People's Congress), Speech at the 4th Session of the Standing Committee of the 9th National People's Congress, 24 August 1998, p. 3.

10 See Peter Ho, 'Who Owns China's Land? Property Rights and Deliberate Institutional Ambiguity', *The China Quarterly*, 166 (2001), pp. 402–7.

11 Many studies have provided empirical evidence for this. See, for example, James Kaising Kung and Shouying Liu, 'Farmers' Preferences regarding Ownership and Land Tenure in Post-Mao China: Unexpected Evidence from Eight Counties', *The China Journal*, 38 (July 1997), pp. 33–64.

12 Guangming Huang, 'Xin Tudi Geming' (The New Land Revolution), *Nanfang Zhoumo*, 14 June 2001, p. 1.

13 Peter Ho, 'China's Rangelands under Stress: A Comparative Study of Pasture Commons in the Ningxia Hui Autonomous Region', *Development and Change*, 31, 2 (March 2000), p. 394; and Peter Ho, 'The Four Wastelands Auction Policy: Removing the Rural–Urban Divide or Another Commandist Mass Campaign?', *China Information*, 14, 1 (2000), pp. 1–37.

14 Xinhua Liu (ed.), *Xin Tudi Guanlifa Quanshu* (Encyclopedia of the New Land Administration Law) (Beijing: Zhongguo Wujia Chubanshe, 1998), vols 1 and 2; Zuigao Renmin Fayuan (ed.), *Renmin Fayuan Anli Xuan – Xingzheng Juan: 1992–1996* (A Selection of Cases from the People's Courts – Volume for Administrative [Cases]: 1992–1996) (Beijing: Renmin Fayuan Chubanshe, 1997). Legal terms have been translated according to: Shutong Yu and Jia Wen (eds), *Xin Han-Ying Faxue Cidian* (A New Chinese-English Law Dictionary) (Beijing: Falü Chubanshe, 1998).

15 See the State Land Administration's 1995 Regulations on the Assessment of Land Ownership and Use Rights, in Jianhong Sun (ed.), *Tudi Quanshu Shiwu Zhinan* (Practical Compass on Land Titles) (Beijing: Zhongguo Dadi Chubanshe, 1998), pp. 282–93; and the State Land Administration's 1989 Suggestions on the Assessment of Land Titles, in Zhongguo Tudi Guanli Zonglan Bianji Weiyuanhui (ZTGZBW) (ed.), *Zhongguo Tudi Guanli Zonglan* (An Overview of Land Management in China) (Beijing: Falü Chubanshe, 1992), pp. 68–71.

16 State Statistical Bureau, *China Statistical Yearbook* (Beijing: China Statistical Press, 1999), p. 233.

17 See, for example, the review of the Supreme People's Court on 'The Use of Policies and Laws for the Land Dispute between the Villagers' Committee and the Villagers' Group', in Hongyi Xiang (ed.), *Tudi Quequan Shiyong Shouce* (A Practical Manual for the Assessment of Land Title) (Beijing: Zhongguo Dadi Chubanshe, 1996), p. 293.

18 The original idea of the Four Fixes was to transfer from the larger brigade or commune to the production team permanent use rather than ownership of labour,

land, animals and tools. The formal basis for the Four Fixes Movement was the Sixty Articles.

19 A large literature is available on this issue, captured under key words such as 'common property resource management', 'common pool resources' and 'legal pluralism'. See, for example, Daniel W. Bromley, *Making the Commons Work: Theory, Practice and Policy* (San Francisco: Institute for Contemporary Studies Press, 1992).

20 The Chinese discussion of 'rule by man' is described in Ronald C. Keith, *China's Struggle for the Rule of Law* (New York: St Martin's Press, 1994), p. 12.

21 A.W. Motion cited in R. Rowton Simpson, *Land Law and Registration* (Cambridge: Cambridge University Press, 1976), p. 220.

22 *Ibid.*, pp. 220–1.

23 Case drawn from Zuigao Renmin Fayuan (ed.), *Renmin Fayuan Anli Xuan – Xingzheng Juan: 1992–1996* (A Selection of Cases from the People's Courts – Volume for Administrative [Cases]: 1992–1996) (Beijing: Renmin Fayuan Chubanshe, 1997), pp. 334–40 (second case) and pp. 341–7 (first case).

24 *Ibid.*, p. 343.

25 *Ibid.*, p. 344.

26 See Suggestions on the Question of the Assessment of Land Titles, in ZTGZBW (ed.), *Zhongguo Tudi Guanli Zonglan*, pp. 69–70.

27 'Remarks on the "Land Administration Law (Revised Draft)" by Relevant Units and Personnel of Zhejiang Province', in Renda Fazhi Gongzuo Weiyuanhui (ed.), *Zhonghua Renmin Gongheguo Tudi Guanlifa Shiyi* (An Interpretation of the Land Administration Law of the People's Republic of China) (Beijing: Falü Chubanshe, 1998), p. 366.

28 See '1958 Measures on Land Requisition for State Construction'; '1982 Administrative Regulations for Land used for Building Construction in Villages and Towns'; and the '1982 Regulations on Land Requisition for State Construction', in Xiang (ed.), *Manual for the Assessment of Land Title*, pp. 108–28.

29 About this, a Chinese jurist remarked that at the time of the transfer, the Sixty Articles were still valid and stipulated: 'The land owned by the production team ... can by no means be rented or sold' (article 21). See Xinhua Liu (ed.), *Xin Tudi Guanlifa Quanshu*, vol. 1, p. 900, in which this case is also described.

30 Article 24 of the 1986 Land Administration Law in: Nongyebu Zhengce Tigai Faguisi (ed.), *Nongyefa Quanshu* (Encyclopedia of Agricultural Laws) (Beijing: Zhongguo Nongye Chubanshe, 1994), p. 557.

31 Frank Emerson Clark cited in Mark Monmonnier, *Drawing the Line: Tales of Maps and Cartocontroversy* (New York: Henry Holt and Company, 1996), p. 123.

32 The original text states 1984. However, the text is corrupt, as it later talks about 1954. From the context it is also clear that the year 1954 is meant here.

33 Xinhua Liu (ed.), *Xin Tudi Guanlifa Quanshu*, vol. 1, p. 910.

34 *Ibid.*, p. 911.

35 *Ibid.*, p. 912.

36 Article 14 of the 1958 Regulations on Land Requisition for State Construction, in Xiang (ed.), *Manual for the Assessment of Land Title*, p. 111.

37 Xinhua Liu (ed.), *Xin Tudi Guanlifa Quanshu*, vol. 1, p. 913.

38 Article 13, Exemplary Regulations on the Higher Agricultural Production Cooperatives, in *ibid.*, p. 131

39 First case drawn from Xinhua Liu (ed.), *Xin Tudi Guanlifa Quanshu*, vol. 1, pp. 1039–41. Second case drawn from Zuigao Renmin Fayuan (ed.), *Cases from the People's Courts*, pp. 450–54.

40 Literally 'sandy land inherited from the ancestors.' The term *tandi* literally means 'sandy land' but is best translated as 'steppe' or 'sandy waste'.

41 Zuigao Renmin Fayuan (ed.), *Cases from the People's Courts*, p. 452.

42 *Ibid.*

43 *Ibid.*, p. 454.
44 One only needs to think of the colonization of state forest reserves in former Manchuria by rural collectives. An instance of a recently developed common property of forest is described by Emily T. Yeh, 'Forest Claims, Conflicts and Commodification: The Political Ecology of Tibetan Mushroom-Harvesting Villages in Yunnan Province', *The China Quarterly*, 161 (March 2000), pp. 264–78.
45 A chronological listing of the Constitution's stipulations on natural resources is given in Wenzheng Shi, *Caoyuan yu Caoye de Fazhi Jianshe Yanjiu* (Research of the Construction of a Judicial System for Rangeland and Pastoralism) (Hohhot: Neimenggu Daxue Chubanshe, 1996), pp. 37–38.
46 Article 1 of the State Land Administration's 1989 Suggestions on the Assessment of Land Titles and the State Land Administration's 1995 Regulations on the Assessment of Land Ownership and Use Rights, Xiang (ed.), *Manual for the Assessment of Land Title*, pp. 312 and 351.

Suggested reading

Jean Chen and David Wills, *The Impact of China's Economic Reforms upon Land Property and Construction* (Aldershot: Ashgate, 1999).

Peter Ho, 'Who owns China's Land? Property Rights and Deliberate Institutional Ambiguity', *The China Quarterly*, 166 (2001), pp. 402–7.

Hu Wei, 'Household Land Tenure Reform in China: Its Impact on Farming Land Use and Agro-Environment', *Land Use Policy*, 14, 3 (1997), pp. 175–86.

James Kai-sing Kung and Shouying Liu, 'Farmers' Preferences regarding Ownership and Land Tenure in Post-Mao China: Unexpected Evidence from Eight Counties', *The China Journal*, 38 (July 1997), pp. 33–64.

Shouying Liu, Michael R. Carter and Yang Yao, 'Dimensions and Diversity of Property Rights in Rural China: Dilemmas on the Road to Further Reform', *World Development*, 26, 10 (1998), pp. 1789–806.

Nicholas K. Menzies, *Forest and Land Management in Imperial China* (London: St. Martin's Press, 1994).

Mark Selden and Aiguo Lu, 'The Reform of Landownership and the Political Economy of Contemporary China', in Mark Selden (ed.), *The Political Economy of Chinese Development*, (Armonk: M.E. Sharpe, 1993).

Anthony Walker, *Land, Property and Construction in the PRC* (Hong Kong: Hong Kong University Press, 1991).

5 To the courts or to the barricades

Can new political institutions manage rural conflict?

David Zweig

Introduction[1]

Rapid economic development is highly destabilizing, and in China today accelerated economic growth is generating widespread protests. Newspapers worldwide – in Hong Kong, New York and even China – are replete with detailed stories of villagers joining together in various types of protests, some of which end in violence. As Huntington warned, if political demands overwhelm weak political institutions, political participation can trigger 'political decay'. But why do rural protests appear to be so frequent? What strategies do rural citizens employ to promote their interests? Can rural China's legal and political institutions manage rural conflict?

Intensified commercialization and commodification of land, labour and agricultural products, rapid urbanization, enormous capital construction and public works projects, and rural industrialization, are all occurring within the context of an emerging and poorly regulated market, a nascent legal and tax regime, a pliant environmental monitoring system, and a political system that favours the interests of powerful officials and the *nouveaux riches*, and often ignores or suppresses, rather than responds to, social grievances. Breakneck economic growth has been accompanied by environmental degradation and the economic and health costs it entails, excessive or illegal taxes imposed by local cadres, widespread official corruption, failures to fulfil business or contract obligations, and the frequent confiscation of collective rural land which is then resold by governments and developers at astronomical profits.[2] The result has been to mobilize large numbers of citizens to take collective action. Yet widespread demands by citizens for social justice and conflict resolution challenge the capacity of state institutions that remain rather ill equipped to manage (rather than simply suppress) these higher levels of popular political participation. Can China's new, and still weak, political institutions manage this burgeoning demand for political and legal action and attain political legitimacy? What is the likelihood that popular discontent will give rise to massive social unrest that could imperil the political system? In essence, will economic development lead to political modernization or political decay?[3]

The emergence of new political institutions

Since 1978, a new set of political and legal institutions have emerged to manage some of this burgeoning demand for responsiveness and political involvement. Elections for village leaders, the introduction of contract law and an increased role for the courts in adjudicating conflicts under the Administrative Litigation Law, and petitions to higher level officials, as well as a more aggressive investigatory role for journalists and television, have helped villagers express their grievances, influence local economic decisions and seek redress for unfair cadre behaviour. Some of these institutions emerged autonomously from society and were then borrowed by the state, while others were introduced by a state deeply concerned that rural demands for change and the rapaciousness of local cadres could trigger massive rebellions.

The current effort to establish Villagers' Committees, based on direct elections of popular representatives first emerged from Guangxi province to fill the yawning power vacuum that had emerged in rural China after decollectivization. By 1988, following several years of heated debate, leaders of the Chinese Communist Party (CCP) became convinced that direct elections for Villagers' Committees and particularly for the director of these committees, as well as the shift of economic authority to those committees, would strengthen the state's political power, placate villagers' concerns that local taxes were being misappropriated and stabilize rural society. The leadership still saw the local CCP secretary and party branch as the core organization for controlling village politics, but by allowing the villagers' own elected representatives to manage village finances, it hoped to increase legitimacy in the countryside.

'Public petitioning' has emerged as a new norm, supported by central elites, through which citizens can challenge local bureaucratic decisions and cadre corruption.[4] Under this procedure, higher levels are informed of corrupt behaviour by local officials so that festering issues can be resolved independently of the courts, thereby preserving rural legitimacy. Such actions conform with historical Chinese preferences for mediation over litigation, preferences reinforced by the fact that rural litigants live in close proximity to each other and a final, clear-cut legal decision in favour of one claimant can have long-term influence on intra-village relationships.

Since the mid-1980s, the Chinese government has tried with some success to introduce 'rule *by* law', if not the 'rule *of* law', by encouraging Chinese citizens to take grievances against cadres to court. Initially, as rural China shifted from plan to market, and many goods and services previously allocated by fiat moved onto the market, villagers and cadres often broke agreements in response to sudden changes in market prices or supplies. To prevent social unrest within villages, the state introduced the idea of rural contract law and offered citizens the chance to take their disputes to court for mediation or resolution.[5] In 1990, the state also introduced the Administrative Litigation Law, institutionalizing the process by which individuals and collectivities sought legal redress for a wide array of issues, including abuses by public security officials, and other zoning, land and real estate related abuses.[6]

Public participation and political demands in changing times can tax any political regime. Pressure on China's system is all the greater since local cadres see the emergence of new legal and political institutions as a challenge to their ability to manipulate the system to their advantage.

Moreover, the outcomes of poorly regulated economic development can trigger widespread collective action. Rivers that are polluted by rural industry affect the lives of thousands of people. This became apparent in the summer of 1998 when cadres allocated investment funds to rural industry or widespread wining and dining, and not to building dykes. Floods inundated millions of acres of land and homes in Yangtze valley regions. As urbanization expropriates the land around major cities or along new highways, villagers have common cause to unite to protect their land and livelihood. The fragile nature of the Chinese market and legal system also invites much unscrupulous business activity, which can have large-scale political or legal ramifications. For example, when a vegetable seed company in Shandong province was unable to meet its payments, 4,200 producer households in thirty-six townships across sixteen counties jointly petitioned the county government.[7]

How effective are the new institutions? Do they resolve villager–cadre problems and mitigate social unrest and the need for collective political action? Or are villagers still forced to adopt more informal, extra-legal forms of collective action?

This chapter uses two different sources of data to examine the relationship between economic development and political change. First, it analyses a series of articles about rural petitioning and protests that appeared in *Minzhu yu fazhi* (Democracy and Law; hereafter, *MZYFZ*). Second, it presents two related cases of villager resistance in a city in coastal China. While by no means statistically representative of rural conditions throughout China, the articles in *MZYFZ* reflect the types of problem resulting from unregulated economic development in rural China, while the suburban cases illustrate the crisis gripping much of suburban China confronting rapid urbanization.

Data from *Minzhu yu Fazhi*

In the absence of systematic data on protest activity across rural China, I collected all examples of political or legal action by individuals and collectivities against state and local officials reported in *MZYFZ* between 1988 and 1997. Of the thirty cases, twenty-six appeared in the journal between 1993 and 1997, two in 1991, one in 1990 and one in 1989.[8]

I subdivided the main issues that triggered these protests into five categories: land related cases, unofficial taxation (*luan shou fei*), administrative or business-related problems, cadre abuse of power, including administrative power and election fraud, and wrongful attacks on cadres or resistance to what seems to be fair state policies.

Of the thirty cases, six (20 per cent) related to land issues (see chapter 4). In three cases, cadres illegally requisitioned and sold collective land, keeping a large amount of the proceeds for themselves. Here the incredible value of suburban and urban land becomes apparent, as in one case where 1,738 *mu* (one *mu* is one-sixth of an acre of one-fifteenth of a hectare) of land was sold to the state for 40 million RMB (renminbi also known as yuan).[9] With the stakes so high, it is no surprise that cadres threaten villagers (and their representatives) who bring illegal cadre behaviour to the attention of the courts. In addition, with land perceived as a collective asset that was being privatized and plundered by cadres, the anger of villagers propelled them to take collective action.

A case from Shantou, Guangdong province, where cadres stole over 24 million RMB, is particularly interesting. Although villagers petitioned over 1,000 times over many years because they had received very little personal compensa-tion for land requisitioned by the state, they were constantly thwarted by township-, district -and municipal-level officials who protected the local cadres. When letters to the provincial government did not bring results, villagers went to Beijing. This case involved many new political and legal institutions: villagers hired lawyers but they were beaten by thugs hired by the village cadres; village elections took place, but they were manipulated by village cadres to protect their positions, while villager petitions over electoral fraud, backed up by their team of lawyers, triggered no response; and villagers contacted the media – in this case, *Minzhu yu Fazhi* – whose investigating journalist was threatened with physical violence.

A second source of protests, the imposition on villagers of local taxes (*luan shou fei*), involved seven of thirty cases (23 per cent). For Bernstein, excessive taxa-tion is the core of rural unrest.[10] The scale of these burdens can be quite high, reaching over 20 per cent of per capita income in one case.[11] Some burdens arise when cadres seek to develop the local economy – build a road, a power plant or some other modern facility. With the level of taxation set by the state at only 5 per cent of villager per capita income, local government lacks the tax base for costly public works.[12] Cadres may then force villagers to contribute more to the local state. In one county, cadres who wanted to build an electric power plant 'to promote development' demanded that each male villager donate twenty days of labour while women give ten days.[13] Or instead villagers could give three RMB per day – 90 RMB per household – which would have brought the county 12 million RMB.

On the other hand, some cadres simply stole the funds or used force to gain them. In one case, cadres broke into villagers' homes and threatened them,[14] while in another they contracted out tax collection to collection agencies. While cadres often extort funds through tax schemes for their own benefit, there are many areas of rural China where poverty precludes the possibility of substantial tax revenues.

A third set of cases reflects the types of business problem that emerge during incipient market development. These five cases included the selling of fraudulent products, the mistreatment of migrant workers, and one instance where villagers who had been compelled to raise seed for the township seed company were paid in IOUs when China's economy slowed dramatically in 1990.[15] The villagers, however, having been forced to grow the seeds, felt that they should not bear the burden of a downturn in the macroeconomy, so they sued the township company, its parent at the county, and the village government that had made them turn over their seed. Despite efforts at reconciliation, the villagers insisted on full repayment, and in the end won their case.

Not all examples in these thirty cases result from poorly regulated economic modernization. Ten cases (30 per cent) involved cadres or police who beat villagers, stole money or used their political authority in unethical ways unrelated to business, taxes or land. Several cases involved election fraud. Nevertheless, these abuses led villagers to file petitions or sue officials themselves, or turn to other citizens or relatives to file petitions on their behalf. Finally, three cases involved what the journal presented as unfair attacks on cadres by citizens who either violated state policies – in this case the one-child policy – or who suspected (incorrectly) that cadres had been stealing money when the collective's income increased but the villagers' income did not.

Several common characteristics emerge from these stories (Table 5.1). Unregulated economic development can trigger collective action. Of twenty-four cases that specify the actor, eighteen (75 per cent) involved collective action, while six involved individual actions. Despite the emergence of household farming, and contrary to rational choice arguments that private farmers are generally incapable of collective action,[16] most cases described in *MZYFZ* involved collective action. Why? First, many of these incidents had an impact on dozens of families within a single village or on villagers in more than one locality, leading to a united response. Second, the cost of filing petitions, in terms of capital and time, may lead villagers to pool monies quickly in order to seek group redress rather than pursuing an individual course. Third, there is security in numbers, given the political risks of challenging the state and the potential for revenge by cadres.

Despite the state's effort to promote petitioning as a peaceful, system-supportive means of conflict resolution, many petitions are initially rejected by higher-level authorities, forcing villagers to include civil disobedience as part of their repertoire of protest activity. In nine of twenty-five cases (31 per cent), the initial petition was rejected or delayed for a long time by upper-level authorities, while in twelve cases (41 per cent) local officials resisted the decisions taken by their administrative superiors and the courts, and sometimes continued to do so even as the story was being written. For example, when villagers approached a semi-governmental organization (called the Democratic Progressive Association – *Minzhu cujin hui*) in 1988, which published reports of this case in their newspaper, the problem remained, triggering another investigation in 1994. Similarly, many local cadres resist villagers' claims, threaten them or simply ignore the court's decision. By dragging out these affairs or threatening villagers, the state and its agents increase villager anger and frustration, and encourage the violence that has become part of the process by which villagers seek redress.

In fact, winning a case is not always the best solution as cadre revenge may negate a victory in court.[17] According to one article, family members said that:

Table 5.1 Content of 30 Cases of Protest Actitivity, 1989–1997

(1) Nature of political action*		(2) No. of cases involving public media	(3) No. of cases with petitions to higher level officials	(4) No. of cases that went to court	(5) No. of cases involving lawyers	(6) No. of cases already resolved as of 1997	(7) No. of villagers favoured in resolved cases	(8) No. of government cadres favoured in resolved cases	(9) No. of cases unclear in resolved cases	(10) Actors favoured by article*	
Collective	Individual									Villagers	Government cadres
22	7	14	23	13	8	20	14	4	2	19	8

Source: Cases reported in *Minzhu yu fazhi,* 1989–1997.

Note:

* When number of cases does not total 30, missing values were either not applicable or unclear.

'No matter whether you win or lose, you lose. You still have to live here and the township government won't forgive you.' The cases show the aggressive role the media plays in bringing cases of cadre abuse to light. Some villagers wrote letters to newspapers or magazines – other than *MZYFZ* – seeking help; the media then investigated. Particularly if the case stalled – either because higher-level officials were protecting their underlings or because officials passed the case back down for resolution to the very lower-level officials who perpetrated the abuse in the first place – gaining the attention of national newspapers was critical to triggering a serious investigation by higher-level officials. Newspapers, as well as *MZYFZ* itself, apparently follow up on old stories to see if problems reported remained solved or emerged anew.[18] The media can be an effective weapon of protest because middle-level officials fear adverse publicity. However, some journalists put their lives at risk, as abusive cadres and public security officials were not averse to using physical threats to warn the journalists off.[19] The large amounts of money involved in some of these cases give cadres strong incentives to resort to violence if it becomes necessary to protect their interests.

These cases and additional scholarly literature suggest that villagers are developing a strong 'rights consciousness' and consider using the law to their own advantage. No doubt, this journal promotes the use of the courts as a mode of conflict resolution. Survey data suggest that villagers rarely see going to court as a preferred means of resolving their conflicts with officialdom.[20] Nevertheless, of the total cases reported in *MZYFZ*, thirteen of thirty (43 per cent) made it to court, and in eight of those cases (61 per cent) villagers hired either a lawyer or legal worker. In several cases, villagers studied national laws before presenting their cases. One villager testified that according to provincial regulations he should have paid 12 RMB in local taxes, but the township demanded over 75 RMB. These findings, therefore, support Li and O'Brien's contention that many villagers now carry out 'policy based resistance'.[21] Also, in two of the cases, newly emerging democratic institutions played important roles in resolving these problems. In one case, overtaxed villagers protested to the city people's congress, which dismissed the party secretary from his position as a people's representative.[22] In another case, villagers took their concerns to the branch of the Democratic Progressive Association, which intervened on their behalf. Villagers also turn to the media, asking them to help bring these court cases to light.[23] By reporting such successful cases, *MZYFZ* encourages villagers to turn to such organizations.

The journal did not of course always take the villagers' side. While it favoured the villagers in nineteen cases, it supported government cadres in another eight. Interestingly, when one looks at the cases that were resolved, fourteen of the twenty occurred in cases in which the article clearly favoured the villagers, while only four of the cases were resolved in favour of government cadres. In this way, the journal encourages people to follow the legal path.

Urbanization, land markets and the politics of protest

One component of China's modernization – urbanization – as well as the marketization or commercialization of suburban land, has generated enormous levels of conflict over the past few years. As cities modernize, they eat up suburban land; since the mid-1980s, cities have expanded at a furious pace. Moreover, following Deng's southern trip in 1992, the 'zone fever' that swept China accelerated the pace with which cities have swallowed up their suburban rural land.[24] Also, city mayors are rapidly turning suburban land, formerly owned by rural collectives and managed by individual households, into bedroom communities. Commercialization of suburban and rural land is one of the most incendiary issues in Chinese society today. Among 236 cases filed under the Administrative Litigation Law collected by Pei, fifty, or 21 per cent, were over land use, urban zoning and real estate.[25] Why?

First, the process of urbanization mirrors the reforms in general, where economic changes, commercialization, new opportunities and the generation of wealth occur before the establishment of new economic and legal institutions that regulate the creation and distribution of these new market opportunities. Thus, the formal legal framework needed to manage the emergence of a land and suburban housing market, as well as the informal norms that could moderate political and economic confrontations, are only beginning to develop. Land laws are easily ignored by cadres and business interests, and much of the confiscated land is simply used as collateral for getting loans from the bank; after that, the land is left to lie fallow.[26] Because the market has outpaced the consolidation of legal institutions – such as land and real estate laws – enormous political problems have emerged as market and economic dynamisms leave political institutions constantly striving to catch up with reality. Huntington's conundrum, where demands for participation are greater than political institutionalization, is clearly at work.

Second, the financial stakes are enormous as the real property value of land at the time it is taken over by the local government is unknown; its value materializes only after it is zoned for suburban housing, or as the surrounding infrastructure, such as new roads and housing units, is developed. Yesterday's patch of tomato fields is tomorrow's three-storey townhouse or sixty-storey office tower. According to the 1986 Land Management Law, the price to be paid for land could not exceed twenty times the average annual output value of the land.[27] According to *MZYFZ*, this growth in the value of suburban land attracts much corrupt activity.[28] In one case reported in *Ming bao* (Hong Kong), cadres collected 2.8 million RMB renting out 240 *mu* of land of which only 350,000 RMB (12.5 per cent) was distributed to the villagers.[29] Rapaciousness mounts as city officials see land sales as the last source of capital to shore up shrinking tax bases,[30] while managers of development companies (and their allies in the city or district governments) make millions selling housing units that have cost them perhaps 5–7 per cent of the land's ultimate market value. Thus, powerful urban interests in China's opaque political system are scurrying to extract their share of wealth before a more stable, transparent system emerges.

Urbanization can bring benefits both to villagers and cadres. For some rural residents, urbanization means the shift from rural to urban household registration; this rise in status has psychological, educational, social, political and financial benefits.[31] Cadres, too, benefit as their locality's status rises within China's administrative hierarchy due to the shift from rural to urban space. For example, rural cadres can become state officials with retirement pensions and much higher salaries if their land is swallowed up by the expanding city. Also, if cadres behave fairly, the entire village can benefit. For example, a village in Wuhan's suburbs has grown wealthy by developing its own land and distributing that wealth to all members of the collective.[32]

But for many suburban villagers, the disappearance of their land causes their world to spin out of control. Nationwide reports tell of frequent confrontations between villagers and the police or the army. Major protests occurred in October 1998 in Guiyang, capital of Guizhou province, as villagers from Tongzi county marched on the provincial capital to protest against the low level of compensation they received after being forced off their land to make room for new urban housing.[33] When a well-connected developer failed to pay villagers for land he had acquired, they blocked the construction site and put up huts to stop the work. After police arrested four villagers, 300 peasants marched into Changsha and surrounded the provincial government buildings.[34] Star TV, viewed in Wuhan on Saturday 5 December 1998, showed violent clashes between villagers and the army over land confiscation.

The following section examines the political and legal ramifications of urbanization that emerged in a suburban community in a city in central China.

The case study

Sitting in the home of a former brigade cadre, now an official in a newly established street committee (hereafter, *jiedao*), the widespread impact of urbanization became clear. While he spoke of the court case he had just completed to win back land transferred by the city government to a neighbouring township, land whose value had increased fifteen times in two years, his friend piped up with his story. He and fifty-two other families in August 1998 had battled the director of the district's urban planning and construction bureau (*chengjian ju*), who, after knocking down their homes, tried to resettle them in apartment units built in a renovated factory. But without sunlight and adequate facilities, he and his neighbours revolted. I then discovered that the former brigade official's 72-year-old father had been a leader of a group of 108 rural retirees who had fought to save their pensions and their health care benefits, which were cut off because of the simultaneous occurrence of land transfers and the redistricting of the suburban boundaries. Their strategies involved both formal, legal activity and various degrees of civil disobedience.

In the following section, I will tell the story of two separate but related cases of villager resistance over land, while in an analytical section I will relate these events to the patterns discovered in *MZYFZ*.

The facts of the case

The case began in 1992, when the city's government decided to widen the streets within the city core and build new housing for urban residents. With the approval of the province, the city took over some rural land. At that time, too, the city formally terminated two administrative villages, Village A and Village B (both former production brigades), and incorporated them into District No. 1 under the city government. In June 1993, both brigades' long lives as rural units became history.

With the district becoming a bedroom community and the two brigades' administrative status in limbo, their farm land was transferred to the city Land Bureau, which paid the two brigades' superior administrative unit, the Township, 33 million RMB for the land. Also, nine *mu* of land belonging to Brigade A was transferred to the Township. Several brigade factories built since the mid-1970s were knocked down, but one clothing factory and a department store, formerly the property of Brigade A, were given to the Township, while District Government No. 2, above the Township, kept Brigade A's restaurant. The Township, however, was expected to use part of that 33 million RMB pay-out to care for the residents of Village A because, as a very prosperous rural community, Village A had given all its retired commune members retirement and health care benefits. With the brigades' territory now incorporated into the city, the Land Bureau sold the land to several development companies under District No. 1's urban planning bureau (*chengjian ju*). To make room for the new apartments and posh town houses that would line the streets of this new housing development, villagers' homes were to be levelled and the villagers relocated into new apartments nearby.

Incorporation into the urban sector brought villagers some benefits. First, their rural residence permits (*hukou*) were turned into urban residence permits, fulfilling a lifelong goal for many rural residents. Second, based on the square footage of their homes – including the area of the second and third storeys – villagers received an equal amount of square footage in new apartments. Most villagers got three to four apartments, while some got as many as seven flats. Most villagers moved into one or two flats, sold a third and rented the rest, allowing them a life of leisure as rentiers. Without land to tend, older villagers were expected to retire or find jobs in the private sector, while their children – teenagers and young adults – were all offered jobs in state-owned firms or a one-time pay-out of 10,000 RMB.

Around 1994 or 1995, urban boundaries were redrawn and, while Village A became an urban Street Committee (*jiedao*) under District No. 1, the Township remained in the countryside under District No. 2. Suddenly the Township announced that it no longer had the obligation to pay the retirement benefits of the 108 citizens of Village A, although it had received 33 million RMB for the land formerly held by Villages A and B, as well as some of Village A's property. The old villagers of Village A then sued the Township and took their case to the civil court (*minjian ting*) in the city's Middle Court. Although eventually they lost the case, the city government pressured the Township to turn over 300,000 RMB to help cover their retirement costs.

Several years later, after Village A became part of a larger Street Committee, it, with the support of the District No. 1, sued the Township in the city's Administrative Court (*xingfa ting*). The court, however, while publicly recognizing that 'the living standards of the villagers in Village A had gone down since they had lost their land',[35] refused formally to accept the case and passed it back down to the three districts, with a copy to the city government, insisting that they settle out of court. The terms of the final mediated settlement (*minshi tiaojie shu*) were as follows:

- The Township, in two instalments over three months, had to pay the Street Office 300,000 RMB, with 200,000 going to Village A and another 100,000 RMB going to Village B.
- The Township had to return the factory and the department store to the Street Office (Village A).
- Of the 36,760 RMB in legal fees accrued by the Street Office, the Township had to pay 30,000 RMB. Village A had to pay 3,380 RMB.
- The Street Office received the nine *mu* of land that had been taken from Village A.
- Village A had to persuade the villagers to give up their remaining claims to small plots of land and let the developer demolish the remaining homes in the village, facilitating the areas' continued urbanization.

When some people in Village A expressed dissatisfaction, the Middle Level Court which had refused to hear the case warned officials in the Street Office that if they did not sign the mediated settlement and end all claims immediately, they would get nothing.

Listening to the participants

While the articles in *MZYFZ* help clarify the broader macro-issues involved in these cases, we need to hear the stories of the participants themselves to see how urbanization affected their lives and how they viewed the process of resistance in which they engaged. As we will see, the views of the actors in this drama differ dramatically, based upon their own interests. What may be one person's calamity is another's opportunity. For officials, development, modernization and urbanization are buzz words connoting new sources of revenue and capital, new opportunities, and new forms of prestige. For villagers, whose land and homes are taken away, and who find the state's compensation insufficient and its behaviour exploitative, urbanization is an unwelcome intrusion that forces them onto the road of protest or resistance to get fair compensation for their homes.

The 108 retirees[36]

At risk was long-term security, particularly their retirement and health care benefits. Since 1958 these commune residents had contributed their labour, energy and intelligence to turning Village A into a wealthy suburban brigade. In the 1980s, due to its industrialization, Village A became one of a handful of rural collectives in China that awarded its members with retirement certificates (*tuixiu zheng*), promising them retirement payments (*yang lao jin*) until death. For some, these payments were high: former employees of the brigade administration received 150 RMB per month; benefits for simple fieldhands were 30–40 RMB per month. More importantly, argued one retiree, with most of them close to 70, their great fear was that the high cost of long-term medical care brought on by disease or infirmity would bankrupt their families. By a sleight of administrative hand, the collective wealth that should have sustained those benefits, and protected them in their old age, was transferred to the Township, then whisked away entirely when Village A left the countryside and the Township joined urban District No. 1. In the words of one informant, 'when they redrew the boundaries, we lost our benefits'.

But these older villagers, who had fought the party's 'class enemies' in the 1950s and 1960s, built a war chest, with each retiree contributing 30–40 RMB. They elected ten representatives, composed of 'older people who could talk well'. While each representative had the right to speak, the group had an informal leader who, through personal ties, found a lawyer who sued the Township in the city's Middle Court.

In retrospect, the group's lawyer erred in filing the case with the civil tribunal (*minjian ting*), rather than the administrative court (*xingfa ting*), since they were suing a government office, not other citizens. But in China it remains extremely difficult for civilians to win cases against officials, what many call *min gao gong*. According to Pei, the government wins twice as often as civilians, and the citizen's likelihood of success decreases if the case is brought against a local government.[37] Also, while the resources they lost were collective property, they were demanding individual compensation. In the eyes of local residents and officials, their strategy from the start was doomed to fail. Nevertheless, although it refused to hear the case, the court's 'opinion' (*sifa jianyi shu*) was that the income of the rural residents bringing the suit 'had really dropped'. It referred the report to the three suburban district governments and the city government to be resolved out of court.[38]

Buoyed up by a somewhat favourable decision – 'we felt good because the opinion showed the government's concern' – the representatives embarked on a deeply frustrating effort to find some government bureau or official who would resolve the case. Everywhere they confronted 'buck passing' (*ti pi qiu*), not solutions. The city government's General Office would not solve the problem, but stamped a letter approving their visit to the city's Land Bureau, which after hearing their plight 'put off our case again and again'. Several weeks later, in the winter, the representatives went and, in classically traditional form, bowed outside the door of the Administrative Litigation Bureau of the city government, pleading for assistance. Members of both the city's and Village A's police force brought the aged supplicants home. Frustrated by government inaction, the 108 retirees fanned out all over the city, visiting various district governments; but since the Township had been allocated the property, the land and the money by a government decision, other levels of government refused to intervene.

Civil disobedience became their only option. Organizing a month long sit-in at the restaurant that had been taken from Village A, they dug in for a long struggle. Were they afraid? 'No! Old people are not afraid to resist. You want to arrest us, well it's not easy; you want to control us, well that's not easy either' (*zhua, ye zhua bu zhu; guan, ye guan bu zhu*). Emboldened by the original court opinion which showed the city's moral support for their cause, they carefully avoided giving the Public Security Bureau any pretext for arresting them. 'We behaved well when we went to the city government. We knew that we were making a fair [*heli*] request, so we told everyone not to curse in public.' But as each government office sent them off with no resolution, their anger grew. 'Eventually we made trouble [*nao shi*]. Without making a little trouble, we would have had no results. We had no choice.'

As the strike dragged on – some retirees slept in the restaurant all night, making it impossible to open for business – the city government was forced to respond, instructing the Township to make a one-time payment of 300,000 RMB to the villagers. And in an effort to put the case behind them, and without mentioning the 108 veteran commune members, the city government, echoing the court's finding, announced that 'the remaining problem of a shortfall in people's livelihood' (*shenghuo bu zhu de yiliu wenti*) was now solved. The 108 veterans accepted the decision and quickly abandoned their collective action, even though they did not get their long-term health benefits. Why? 'We got the money, so there was no need to continue to make trouble.' The funds were then transferred to the government of District No. 1 to be managed by the Street Office.

In some ways it was surprising that the 108 retirees gave up the struggle so quickly, as the 300,000 RMB will not go far. By late 1998 almost half had been used up, although ninety-five veterans remained alive and in need of some financial support. Perhaps they felt that this already was a large sum of money; or they knew that since they had lost the legal case, this was the best deal they could get. Several years later, the Street Office decided to resurrect the legal challenge and go after the nine *mu* of land, another financial payment, and some of the enterprises awarded to the Township.

The fifty-three homeowners

It began spontaneously. To turn the lake beside their homes into an amusement park for urban residents moving to the suburbs, the homes of fifty-three rural families, which sat below the city's Western gate, were demolished in early 1997. The residents were expected to find temporary housing for two years while the development company, under District No. 1's urban planning and construction bureau (*cheng jian ju*), built them new homes. To cut costs, the urban planning bureau tried to push the homeowners into flats constructed in an old renovated factory, but when the homeowners saw this they immediately went en masse to the development company to protest.

> Under law, the company was supposed to sign a contract with us, but they refused. District No. 1's bureau of urban construction was responsible for this situation; they were supposed to set us up and guarantee us standard (*biaozhun*) homes. But this was a terrible place: no air, no sunlight. All fifty-three families refused to move in.

Each family contributed 150 RMB to a kitty, selected six representatives, and drafted and signed a document (*weituo shu*) entrusting the six to represent the group's interests in solving this problem.

> Without the *weituo shu*, it was not legal, and we wanted to do everything legally (*guo you xing wei*). This way we knew that we could step over the boundaries of what was acceptable behaviour a little bit … We called this group our 'representative small group' (*daibiao xiaozu*), and it was a short-term organization just for this purpose.

The man selected to lead the group was a middle-level administrative cadre, a party member who managed an office of six to seven people, 'so he knew how to organize things'.[39] He and his family lived in this village and were directly affected by these events. According to one observer, during confrontations with the party secretary of the bureau of urban construction he demonstrated a strong spirit, standing head to head with him. 'When Party Secretary XXX banged the table and warned us that our behaviour was illegal, this man banged the table back and accused him of not caring about the people.'

The six representatives first petitioned the Administrative Litigation Bureau of the city government, which told them that their complaint was fair (*heli*). The bureau then called District No. 1's Administrative Litigation Office and told them to give the delegation a fair hearing, which they did. In fact, the district's Administrative Law Office sent a car to bring the complainants to their offices. But the villagers had few illusions about receiving any swift response.

> We knew that petitioning was of no use, but we also knew that we had to go through that process or else we could not justify using other tactics. So we went to the Administrative Litigation Office of the city government. But we also knew that we needed to 'grab on and not let go' (*zhua bu fang*) or else they would not give in.

Events would prove their cynicism well founded as both the development company and the party secretary of the urban construction bureau refused to meet with them. Deciding that civil disobedience was necessary, sixty residents, led by their representatives, descended on the bureau of urban construction and occupied its offices for three days. They had dug in for the long haul, bringing their own food, which they prepared in the office's small kitchen, and despite the oppressive summer heat, many passed the night in the offices. In their own words, they 'suffered greatly' (*hen xinku*). But after the bureau's employees went home that first night, leaving only the protesters, they realized that they needed to escalate the confrontation. The next morning, after the office workers returned, the villagers barricaded the door, locking themselves and the office workers inside. They then demanded that the deputy director of the bureau call in the party secretary of the urban planning bureau to negotiate with them. But when he appeared the next morning, he brought along fifteen police officers in a failed attempt to intimidate the protestors.

Were they afraid, I asked?

> Not at all! This was a fair request of the masses [*qunzhong de heli yaoqiu*]. We told our people – don't swear, don't break public property, but when the police came and told us not to make trouble, we didn't let them take us away … We wouldn't leave because we knew that the party secretary wouldn't come again. We told the police that we had been trying to find the party secretary for days, but he had been ignoring our complaints.

The homeowners carried out a multi-pronged attack. While some occupied the government offices, others went to the provincial television station and persuaded it to send a camera crew to film the sit-in. The province's television station filmed the protest and the renovated factory, and interviewed specialists on these problems. They also filmed the villagers' protest banner whose slogan – 'We trust that the government will return our homes to us' (*xiangxin zhengfu huan wo zhufang*) – was calculated to shame the government by showing that the home-owners had faith that the government would do the right thing. The district government's propaganda department, which is part of the same media-related 'system' or *xitong*, sought to persuade the TV station not to air the report, but the station agreed only to give the government time to solve the problem first. In fact, the title of the show – 'After a knot is tied, you still need someone to undo it' – was selected to pressure the city government to solve the case, which it did, allowing the news story to end with a shot of the party secretary shaking hands with the homeowners' representatives.

The struggle had not been an easy one. After the party secretary failed to have them arrested, the protestors forced him to telephone the district govern-ment, which sent a representative who asked for fifteen days to study the problem. To the delight of the homeowners, fifteen days later the district govern-ment agreed to build them new housing. However, the government asked for a year to prepare that housing, which meant that the villagers would ultimately have waited two years for their new homes. Still, all these problems had not harmed the legitimacy of the government in the eyes of this rapporteur.

> Overall I still trust the government. It has been making many new laws and I trust these laws. What I do not trust are many people in the government,

in fact, I hate them … People with power don't do things according to law; this is quite prevalent. The law is good, but people don't follow it, and this is particularly a problem in smaller government bureaux where there is no one to check [*jiandu*] on how the laws are being implemented.

The role of local leaders

A key force supporting the 108 retirees' efforts to regain their economic security was the former deputy party secretary of Village A who became party secretary when the old brigade secretary retired in 1992. As a native son, with relatives dotted all over the village – his father was one of the 108 retirees and his best friend lived in one of the fifty-three homes that were knocked down – he defended the villagers' interests. He also understood the need for a double-barrelled attack that combined legal process and civil disobedience.

From his perspective, sit-ins and protests were necessary because the main bottleneck to resolving the case was the fact that the city's Middle Court would never make a legal judgment that challenged, let alone overturned, a formal decision taken by the city government. While some court researchers who investigated the 108 retirees' complaint had apparently believed the village would win its case, 'I doubted it', he said.

> The original decision to take the land was made by the city government, which had received permission from the province, so this was a government decision based on official government documents … The courts can't overturn such government decisions. So the court promulgated a statement that 'the land and property could be used only for development, and no unit or individual could expropriate it', but this was really the same as not giving us any result.

Because of the sit-ins and constant harassment by the 108 retirees, the Township could not run the factory nor could the district run the restaurant. So, 'returning the factory was an easy decision for the Township because although it had sent people to manage the factory, no one listened to them'. In fact, the old people had surrounded the officials and screamed at them, asking 'why have you taken our land?'

Discussing the cases

What do these cases tell us about the nature of rural collective action and even the possibility of the emergence of a mass movement? First, there are clearly two sampling biases here. The cases in *MZYFZ* reflect a more civil process of resistance and conflict resolution than exists in most parts of the country. After all, the magazine's purpose is to promote a legalistic conflict-resolution culture. Bernstein reports numerous cases of violent protest where villagers burned government and constabulary offices and beat employees. Reports by human rights groups in Hong Kong tell of two cases of tax resistance and anticorruption protests that ended in police beating villagers to death.[40]

Second, there are significant differences between the conditions faced by our suburban protagonists and villagers in more distant localities. The former had relatively easy access to higher-level government officials, the mass media, and the courts. Nevertheless, in both situations, urbanization and economic change are creating major conflicts among villagers and the state, increasing the need for protests. Also, the strategies adopted by suburban villagers and their more distant cousins, especially their reliance on modern political and judicial institutions and a willingness to resort to civil disobedience when those institutions fail to deliver justice, is not an uncommon phenomenon in the 1990s.[41]

Both sets of cases are consistent with Li and O'Brien's assertion that formal petitions to higher-level officials have increased dramatically since the late 1980s.[42] In the city suburbs, as well as the journal articles, we see villagers using petitions aggressively to defend their individual and collective interests. The 108 retirees believed strongly that there were good officials in the system who would respond to their just petitions, and in the end the courts and city government did respond to their complaints. In fact, the state seems to support petitioning not only because it invites villagers to seek redress within legal bounds, but also because it informs the state of grievances generated by cadres in the countryside, making it an important channel for the upward flow of information. On the other hand, one of the leaders of the fifty-three homeowners was quite cynical about petitioning, seeing it only as a necessary step to protect themselves from recriminations by the police. The only really effective, strategy, he believed, was public protest. Clearly, political reforms and the creation of important new political and legal institutions have increased the channels for formally presenting grievances; however, the most effective strategy seems to combine petitions with protests, thereby attracting the upper level's attention, while at the same time threatening the authorities with civil disobedience unless they respond to the petition.

Villagers today are far more aware of their legal rights than they were ten years ago and more willingly assert those rights, in large part because the state encourages them to do so. Increased communication, such as newspapers, magazines and word of mouth, have informed villagers about official regulations, creating more 'policy based resistance' using government laws to challenge cadres who misbehave.[43] Journals, such as *MZYFZ*, generally support villagers' claims (nineteen versus eight in the thirty cases reviewed), which may encourage them to petition and use the courts more frequently. No doubt, lawyers are beyond the financial means of most villagers, while in the case of the 108 retirees, hiring a less expensive but less skilled lawyer may have hurt their case. Only the Street Office could afford the 30,000 RMB needed to take the case to court properly. Still, in the case study above, villagers cited laws and court decisions to justify continuing their case. For the 108 retirees, the courts' recognition that 'their income had really dropped' made them believe that the government, if pressed, would help. One of the fifty-three homeowners stressed the existence of laws that supported their claims; the trick was to force cadres to follow, not ignore, the laws.

Interestingly, in neither of the two cases did the Administrative Litigation Bureau or the courts hand down a judgment favourable to the plaintiffs. Initially, the courts refused to overrule the city government, which had made the original decision to expropriate the land and transfer the village's resources to the township. But that failure simply angered the villagers even as it encouraged them to move on to the next stage – civil disobedience. Changing the political or legal context, and opening new channels for pursuing grievances, encourages citizens to seek redress. Yet, if local governments and cadres persist in the old authoritarian leadership styles, there is greater likelihood of conflict than if villagers' expectations had not been raised or if villagers see no new opportunities for pursuing their interests.

The mix of strategies adopted by these villagers reflect an ability to integrate modern legalistic 'repertoires of contention' with a more historically grounded or extra-institutional strategy of protest and resistance.[44] Villagers understood the legal bounds that had to be maintained and that violence would trigger a police response; they reasoned that if they avoided damaging property or swearing at government officials, it would be difficult for the state to use force against them. Therefore, they combined legal procedures with civil disobedience – in both cases sit-ins – or what they called 'making trouble' (*nao shi*).

The Chinese media has emerged as a critical resource in the villagers' struggle for social justice.[45] This role is not completely new. In 1977–9, the reformers orchestrated a series of 'Letters to the Editor' in national and provincial newspapers, which attacked 'leftist' cadres who promoted 'agrarian radicalism' and triggered investigations by correspondents or work teams who defrocked recalcitrant Maoists holding sway in the villages and townships.[46] In the 1990s, the media was a more independent collaborator in the struggle against cadre corruption and misdeeds, at times triggering angry responses from the bureaucrats they attacked. For example, after it reported how an armed force of cadres and police, demanding funds for education, shot one villager who resisted their extortion, party officials in Luoding City accused the *Guangzhou Daily* of meddling in matters outside its jurisdiction.[47] Similarly, a journalist in Tongzhou county, northern Jiangsu province, who helped a village party secretary draft a letter to the *People's Daily* protesting excessive tax burdens, was fired for his efforts due to pressure from local party authorities.[48] Analysts of social movements have long recognized that media support is critical if a social movement is to remain sustainable. [49]

With most households outside impoverished areas of rural China having their own television sets, television is becoming an important ally of resistance as well. Suburban villagers understood the potential of this medium, though they were surprised to discovery its potency. In the words of one activist, 'our general summary of these events was that the television station had a big impact. The government is very afraid of the publicity.' Thus the fifty-three homeowners sent delegates to the provincial TV station which filmed their protest and the poor housing they were being pushed into. And, despite efforts by the district government to stop them from broadcasting their story, outside observers from the TV station felt that once the story had been taped, neither the district nor the city government could have killed it. In fact, he argued, 'If district officials had asked them not to run it, they would have been more likely to run it the next day.' The media helped solve the case by informing district officials that the TV station would withhold broadcasting the report until district officials resolved the case.

Local village elections, another institutional innovation that could manage the negative consequences of development, did not play a very great role in resolving these cases.[50] Almost half the cases in *MZYFZ* involved problematic activity by cadres at the township level or above, placing them beyond the electoral reach of the villagers.[51] Still, villagers do directly elect representatives to the township people's congresses which today may be playing an enlarged role in supervising township cadres' activities.[52] Second, cadres who steal public funds or extort taxes from villagers are clearly not averse to manipulating elections. Finally, if the misconduct was carried out by the branch party secretary, it again was not subject to electoral politics.[53] Nevertheless, protests by villagers following electoral fraud did prompt investigations by higher-level officials, and have become one more arrow in the villagers' quiver of rural resistance.

Villagers lack, however, strong independent civic organizations which could help them deal with the negative effects of development. Despite the image of a powerful party/state, the CCP feels deeply threatened by society, and moves to suppress most permanent independent organizations. Some villagers are turning to historically grounded organizational structures, such as lineage groups or religious organizations, as a means of dealing with an intrusive state. But the state's coercive institutions have little patience for religious based anti-state behaviour. In the cases reviewed here, villagers implicitly recognized that while they could organize to press their claims, long-term autonomous organizations would not be tolerated. Both groups in our case studies dissolved their elected 'representative small group' once the issue was resolved. But if organizing to develop a petition is allowed, and if the petition fails – and many initially do – villagers are quick to establish organizations, replete with leaders and funds, to protect their rights against incursions of the state or abuses of power.

A final resource available to the 108 retirees in their challenge to the Township was the support of the local urban government which saw the nine *mu* of land as a critical opportunity for its economic development. Thus the successful case was litigated in the name of the Villagers' Residence Committee by a professional lawyer, whom the Street Office paid 30,000 RMB, a sum of money far beyond the capabilities of the villagers. Government-to-government cases go to a different tribunal in the city court, and resolving them in favour of a formally constituted citizens' organization – in this case the Residents' Committee – may be less threatening to the state than resolving a case in favour of a self-organized group of citizens who challenge a formal level of the government.

Conclusion

As economic development proceeds, affecting wider and wider spheres of society, it produces negative side-effects, or what we may call 'political externalities' of economic development. These spill-overs of development – such as environmental degradation, breakneck urbanization, massive jumps in the value of suburban land, excessive local taxation, or the movement of capital into development or infrastructure projects – move the sociopolitical system into unchartered waters, where economy and society meet in an often unregulated space. Within this sphere, given the opaque nature of the administrative system, winners and losers are often determined by their relative personal and administrative power, not by their legal entitlement, creating remarkable levels of social tension. But society, too, has power, especially if people act collectively. And as we have seen, the arbitrary acts of officialdom do fire up the ire of villagers, sometimes triggering a powerful social backlash.

Herein lies China's current political and social dilemma – the confrontation between an emerging 'rights conscious peasantry' and rapacious or entrepreneurial bureaucrats. The state's role then is to respond to these 'political' externalities of rapid development and manage the conflict generated by them. But to date, weak laws regulate those interstices between the economy and society, while early stages of the emergence of a political culture conducive to the rule of law can only partially mitigate the conflicts emerging under China's partially reformed economy. If cadres anticipate that they will be punished by the state or successfully challenged by society, these new norms could help reduce cadre abuses, while strengthening villagers' preference for legal forms of conflict resolution. Perhaps the central state has shifted its loyalties somewhat, from cadres, particularly unethical ones, to society and villagers, so long as they eschew violent protests. Nevertheless, recognizing the volatility of a situation of rapid social change and economic growth together with new rights consciousness, the state seeks to define legitimate means of conflict resolution that preclude independent political organizations, and yet channel behaviour arising from that consciousness into its new political and legal institutions. The cases in *MZYFZ* document this shift.

Nevertheless, villagers remain frustrated by the ability of the bureaucracy to deflect their claims. The rule *of* law remains weak; instead rule *by* law, while strengthening the villagers' resolve and ability to challenge cadre malfeasance, remains prey to administrative power, which can manipulate (or undermine) the justice distributed by a new legalistic system. And to the extent that what are perceived as just verdicts are not forthcoming, villagers will still adopt extra-legal forms of civil disobedience and collective protest, combining them with legal challenges to injustice.

With continued rampant cadre corruption and manipulation, rural China is likely to remain fertile soil for widespread protest and social unrest that could threaten the stability of the Communist regime.

Notes

1 Funding came from a Direct Allocation Grant, Research Grants Council of Hong Kong. Research assistance was provided by Yiu Keung and Dr Mak Hung Fa.
2 Rapid growth has also generated enormous income inequality, which also generates instability. However, while weak income tax laws are a problem for China, this issue is outside the framework of my analysis.
3 Samuel Huntington, *Political Order in Changing Societies* (New Haven: Yale University Press, 1968).
4 Lianjiang Li and Kevin J. O'Brien, 'Villager and Popular Resistance in Contemporary China', *Modern China*, 22, 1 (1996), pp. 28–61.
5 David Zweig, Kathleen Hartford, James Feinerman and Jianxu Deng, 'Law, Contracts and Economic Modernization: Lessons from the Recent Chinese Rural Reforms', *Stanford Journal of International Law*, 23 (Summer 1987), pp. 319–64; and David Zweig, *Freeing China's Farmers: Rural Restructuring in the Reform Era* (Armonk: M. E. Sharpe, 1997), chap. 6.
6 Minxin Pei (1997), 'Citizens vs. Mandarins: Administrative Litigation in China', *The China Quarterly*, 1, 52 (December), p. 840.
7 'Si qian jia nong hu zhuang gao "bai tiao"' (4,000 Rural Households Sue Over IOUs), *Zhongguo nongmin* (China's Peasants), 3 (1995), pp. 45–7.
8 Before 1993–94, the journal's articles were more philosophical than concrete; afterwards, the content seems to have changed; hence the larger number of articles since 1993. This shift also reflects the increased flow of information about legal proceedings that has emerged in the past decade.
9 *MZYFZ*, 9 (1993), pp. 2–6.
10 Thomas P. Bernstein, 'Instability in Rural China?', in David Shambaugh, (ed.), *Is China Unstable? Assessing the Factors* (Washington, DC: The Sigur Center for Asian Studies, July 1998), pp. 93–110.
11 *MZYFZ*, 11 (1996), pp. 18–20.
12 Thomas P. Bernstein and Xiaobo Lu, *Taxation without Representation in Rural China: State Capacity, Peasant Resistance, and Democratization* (Cambridge: Cambridge University Press, 2002).
13 *MZYFZ*, 6 (1991), pp. 4–8.
14 *MZYFZ*, 11 (1996), pp. 18–20.
15 *MZYFZ*, 14 (1996), pp. 10–11.
16 Robert H. Bates, 'Macropolitical Economy in the Field of Development', in John E. Alt and Kenneth A. Shepsle (eds), *Perspectives on Positive Political Economy* (Cambridge: Cambridge University Press, 1990), pp. 31–56.
17 Pei cites an article which quoted a Chinese citizen who said that one could 'win once but lose the rest of his life'. See Minxin Pei, 'Citizens vs. Mandarins', p. 841.
18 *MZYFZ*, 1 (1997), pp. 22–3.
19 *MZYFZ*, 9 (1993), pp. 2–6.
20 Data from a survey I conducted in four counties in Anhui and Heilongjiang provinces in 1999 show that villagers who took political action to redress some grievance chose going to court only 1.1 per cent of the time. See 'Democratic Values, Political Structures, and Informal Politics in Greater China', in *Peaceworks* (Washington, DC: United States Institute of Peace, July 2002).
21 Lianjiang Li and Kevin J. O'Brien, 'Villager and Popular Resistance'.
22 *MZYFZ*, 7 (1996), p. 13.
23 *MZYFZ*, 1 (1997), pp. 22–3.
24 David Zweig, *Internationalizing China: Domestic Interests and Global Linkages* (Ithaca, NY: Cornell Series in Political Economy, Cornell University Press, 2002), chap. 2.
25 Minxin Pei, 'Citizens vs. Mandarins', p. 849.

26 David Zweig, *Internationalizing China*, p. 98.
27 Mark Selden, *The Political Economy of Chinese Development* (Armonk: M. E. Sharpe, 1993), p. 198.
28 *MZYFZ*, 23 (1996), p. 40.
29 *Ming bao*, 17 May 1998.
30 Interviews carried out in the suburbs of a city in central China, October 1998.
31 See chapter 6.
32 Ning Lingling's MA thesis at Huazhong Normal University focuses on this village.
33 Kai Peter Yu, ' "Cheated" Villagers Take Dispute into Streets', *South China Morning Post*, 8 November 1998, p. 5.
34 'Farmers Abandon Protest over Land after Threats', *South China Morning Post*, 2 October 1998, p. 6.
35 It issued what my informants called a *sifa jianyi yishu* or legal opinion.
36 According to Elizabeth Perry, the number 108 may be apocryphal, as this was the number of good bandits/rebels in the classic Chinese novel *Water Margin*. In my conversations with people in this community, however, there was no reference to this novel or traditional protests.
37 Minxin Pei, 'Citizens vs. Mandarins', p. 845.
38 Chinese courts commonly dismiss cases without rendering a verdict, or pass cases to lower level officials for mediation, resolution through informal means, or other forms of out-of-court settlement. See Minxin Pei, 'Citizens vs. Mandarins', pp. 842–43.
39 Some rural protest leaders are cadres who take the interests of the villagers to heart. See chapter 9 and Thomas P. Bernstein, 'Instability in Rural China', p. 99.
40 ' Chongqing zhenzhang ji gongan da si liang nongmin. Nongmin caiqu shiwei kangyi' (A Town Leader and Public Security Forces in Chongqing Beat Two Peasants to Death; Peasants March in Protest) (Information Centre of Human Rights and Democratic Movement in China, 17 December 1998); and John Pomfret, 'Beijing's Law and Order Problem', *International Herald Tribune*, 19 January 1999, p. 1.
41 Still, in my four-county survey, only 2 per cent of the villagers' political strategies for resolving grievances involved joining in a public protest, a finding replicated by Li Lianjiang's nationwide survey (personal communication with the author).
42   Lianjiang Li and Kevin J. O'Brien, 'Villager and Popular Resistance'.
43 Kevin J. O'Brien and Lianjiang Li, 'The Politics of Lodging Complaints in Rural China', *The China Quarterly*, 143 (September 1995), pp. 756–83.
44 Tilly defines 'repertoires of contention' as 'learned cultural creations that emerge in political struggle'. See C. Tilly, *The Contentious French* (Cambridge, MA: Harvard University Press, 1986), pp. 390–91.
45 In my four-county study, villagers took 5.5 per cent of their grievances to the mass media.
46 David Zweig, *Agrarian Radicalism in China, 1968–1981* (Cambridge, MA: Harvard University Press, 1989).
47 'Chinese Peasants Have a Tough Row to Hoe', *Asia Times*, 16 August 1997.
48 *China Focus* (October 1998), p. 3.
49 Doug McAdam, John D. McCarthy and Mayer N. Zald, 'Introduction: Opportunities, Mobilizing Structures, and Framing Processes – Towards a Synthetic, Comparative Perspective on Social Movements', in D. McAdam, J. D. McCarthy and M. N. Zald (eds), *Comparative Perspectives on Social Movements* (Cambridge: Cambridge University Press, 1996), pp. 1–20.
50 In my four-county survey, villagers with grievances turned to the Village Committee and its director in only 20.6 per cent of the cases. They approached the party secretary or the party branch in 27.4 per cent of the cases.
51 Bernstein stressed this factor as a reason why elections could not solve the problem of 'random fees' (*luan shou fei*). See Thomas P. Bernstein, 'Instability in Rural China?'

52 Personal communication with Elizabeth J. Perry, January 1999, following her visit to observe township elections in China.
53 This may not hold true in future as experimental elections for party secretary are being carried out in parts of rural China. See Lianjiang Li, 'The Two-Ballot System in Shanxi Province: Subjecting Village Party Secretaries to a Popular Vote', *The China Journal*, 42 (July 1999), pp. 103–18.

Suggested reading

Thomas P. Bernstein and Xiaobo Lu, *Taxation without Representation in Rural China: State Capacity, Peasant Resistance, and Democratization* (Cambridge: Cambridge University Press, 2002).

Stanley B. Lubman, *Bird in a Cage: Legal Reform in China after Mao* (Stanford: Stanford University Press, 1999).

Minxin Pei, 'Citizens vs. Mandarins: Administrative Litigation in China', *The China Quarterly*, 1, 52 (December 1997).

Mark Selden, *The Political Economy of Chinese Development* (Armonk: M.E. Sharpe, 1993).

David Zweig, *Freeing China's Farmers: Restructuring Rural China in the Reform Era* (Armonk: M.E. Sharpe, 1997).

6 Migration, *hukou* and resistance in reform China

Hein Mallee

Between 1960 and the early 1980s, China experienced very low levels of rural–urban migration. This was the product of a strict system of residential controls, reinforced by central dominance over urban employment and housing, and by state rationing and distribution of daily necessities. During the reform era, this changed rapidly and by the late 1980s rural–urban labour migration had assumed huge proportions. While not denying the role of the state in structuring these processes, this chapter emphasizes the role of millions of migrants in bringing about change, at times pressing state policies to the limits.

With the dismantling of collective agriculture, the restoration of household farming and the revival of private marketing in the early 1980s, coinciding with acute urban labour shortages, pressures from enterprising rural migrants gradually eroded many of the control mechanisms. More often than not, local authorities could barely stay ahead of developments adjusting the regulations in the wake of unauthorized migration. Nevertheless, if the registration system can no longer prevent migration, it remains crucial in differentially structuring life chances across the administrative divide of urban and rural residential categories.

Introduction

Among the most profound social and economic changes in the reform era has been the veritable explosion of rural labour migration and the formation of large migrant populations in the cities and throughout the dynamic industrializing coastal regions. This change is all the more spectacular for the fact that, up to the late 1970s, the Chinese state so tightly restricted population mobility. Rural labour migration in the reform period is a story of gradual erosion of state control over movement, and the emergence of a volatile situation pivoting around migrant rights in a context that continues to privilege the city over the countryside, urban over rural residents. It is the story of how the state has attempted to continue its domination over migrants and of how migrants have resisted these attempts.

One of the critical axes of friction is rural–urban. Migrants are villagers in the city. This chapter is about migrants *as migrants*. From the perspective of power and domination, migrants have two important characteristics. First, they are outsiders. As newcomers, and especially because their legal position is at best ambiguous, they are easily exploited. They have little leverage to make claims on public resources. Indeed, their position is precarious in ways analogous to the plight of illegal aliens in many other countries. Second, migrants are members of two worlds. They work and live in one (urban) world, but socially and economically they retain important ties with their home community. In nearly all cases, these ties are sealed through remittances even for those who have lived in the city for decades. But some migrants may sojourn in the cities for several years before returning to their home communities. Such ties and the institutions that evolve around them are an important resource for migrants. The structure of this chapter largely follows from these two points: Sections Two and Three survey changing patterns of migration. These examine state attempts to enforce the outsider status of migrants and mounting challenges to this system of privilege and hierarchy. Sections Four and Five describe those aspects of migrants' daily lives that are most susceptible to state intervention and analyse how they resist such intervention, in particular through self-organization.

Migration control on the eve of reform

In the decades prior to reform, China rigorously controlled rural–urban and intra-urban migration. Since the late 1970s, this system has been gradually eroded and adjusted. There are two factors that explain the situation in the late 1970s. The first has received considerable attention in the literature: the development strategy predicated on restricted urbanization followed since the 1950s. It is less often recognized that a strong cultural-political preoccupation with preventing 'chaos' (*luan*) also lay behind migration policies. That is, the state viewed rural–urban migration as a *public order issue* and population registration fell within the purview of the Public Security departments.[1]

During the 1950s, China adopted a heavy industry led development strategy. In a situation of relative international isolation (even allowing for substantial assistance from the Soviet Union) and a weakly developed industrial base, the investment funds needed for this costly industrialization programme could only be found in the agricultural sector. The rural surplus was channelled into industry by means of a state-controlled distribution system, differential pricing of agricultural and industrial products, and collectivized agricultural production.

In the 1950s, China also witnessed rapid urban growth as a result of high levels of migration from the countryside. Confronted with economic crisis and famine in 1960 as a result of the failure of the Great Leap Forward, the Chinese state opted sharply to restrict entrance into the cities, implementing the *hukou* system (household registration system, HRS) (Mallee 2002). In addition, the state presided over forced rural migration of twenty million workers in the years 1961–62, and a programme of sent-down urban youth numbering some seventeen million, in the years 1964–78. China thus entered a period of low net urban migration, brought about by the strictly enforced HRS (forcefully propped up by central control over employment and housing, and especially by rationing of basic necessities including food) and rustication of large groups of urban residents.

Under the HRS, every citizen was required to register at his or her place of permanent residence. Transfer of registration required official approval, and, with the exception of state-initiated transfers, this was rarely forthcoming, particularly in cases involving moves from the countryside to urban areas, or from smaller to larger urban places. Apart from restricting changes of permanent residence, the regulations strictly limited even temporary stays in cities. While initially conceived as an instrument for migration control, the HRS soon developed into a social institution which divided Chinese society into spatial hierarchies whose sharpest division was between 'agricultural' and 'non-agricultural' *hukou* status. This hierarchy defined citizen claims on state resources, creating a fundamental cleavage between people 'eating state grain' and those growing their own grain. The essential difference between these two groups was their different relation to the state: the peasants basically depended for their livelihood on their own labour and the fluctuating harvests, while the state cared for almost every aspect of the welfare of holders of urban registrations including lifetime employment, subsidized housing and food, education, medical care and pensions. The high cost of this benefit package explains why the state tightly controlled access to urban *hukou. Hukou* status was inherited from one's mother, and, except for rare state-initiated transfers, it was virtually impossible to change an 'agricultural' to a 'non-agricultural' *hukou* in the years 1960–78.

Although, generally speaking, people with a 'non-agricultural' *hukou* were far better off, the HRS also inconvenienced many urban people. Urban places were divided into different categories and movement from smaller to larger cities was rarely sanctioned. Combined with the rigidity of the labour system, which assigned people to jobs regardless of their family situation and made transfers difficult, this forced millions of married couples to live permanently apart in different cities, often only able to meet once or twice a year. Another problem occurred when members of a family had different types of *hukou*. A rural woman who married an urban worker or whose husband changed from 'agricultural' to 'non-agricultural' status did not qualify for an urban registration and would not be allowed to live with him in the city. The same applied to their children.

The second heritage of the pre-reform period concerns maintenance of public order. Urban life was rigidly controlled, with work units and neighbourhood committees dominating most aspects of city life. Migrants did not fit neatly into this system and security officials viewed them as 'rootless' people prone to 'antisocial' or criminal behaviour. Labour migration, posing a potential threat to social and political stability, was conceptualized primarily as a public order issue. But whether viewed as a fiscal or as a public security issue, the state found powerful reason to exercise tight control.

From the mid-1950s onwards, migrants were dealt with by the Public Security Departments. Already during the 1950s, the authorities branded the rural-to-urban migration flows triggered by industrialization as 'blind' migration. State action and regulations were directed towards preventing 'spontaneous' (*zifa*), 'disorderly' (*wuxu*) or even 'chaotic' (*luan*) mobility, and towards turning these into 'organized' (*you zuzhide*) channels. Just as the Chinese state would not tolerate autonomous organizations (unregistered religious groups, unofficial labour unions, opposition political parties), and either destroyed or coopted them, it would not tolerate autonomous 'movements' and 'crowds'. From the state's point of view, people without, or far removed from, their organization or village are unaccountable, untraceable, hard to control.[2] Although the more extreme strand of this type of thinking gradually lost ground during the reform period, the basic tenet that migrants pose a potential threat to public order remains a powerful undercurrent in the official discourse about labour mobility (see Box 6.1). Many of the adaptations and alterations of the *hukou* system during the 1980s and 1990s were attempts to bring migration back into the scope of state control.

Box 6.1:   The battle of words

The public discourse about migrants and migration has been dominated by an urban/state perspective. This highly political labelling game serves to identify migrants as outsiders, as a problem, *to put them in their proper place.* James Scott (1990) points out that acts of description are politically loaded, and draws attention to euphemisms. In this vein, the 1958 *hukou* regulations demand that migrants have a 'proper reason' for staying in the cities. Those who are unable to do so end up in 'detention stations' to be 'mobilized', 'persuaded' or 'educated' to return to the countryside.

The term *mingong*, today the most common designation for rural labour migrants, can be found as early as the regulations of the 1950s. *Mingong* are not 'full' workers, *gongren* (with all its ideological implications), because the *gong* is qualified by *min*, which may come either from *nongmin*, peasants, or from *renmin* (the people *at large*, but anyway not part of the inner circle). In either case, it is clear that these people work, but that they cannot claim the superior 'worker' status. During the 1980s, this term, with all its implications, naturally fitted the newly emerging migrant population in the cities.

Other labels are simply demeaning. Migrants are 'blind vagrants' (*mangliu*), because they are 'chaotic' or 'disorderly' (*wuxu*). When there are many of them, migrants become an irresistible 'wave' or 'tide' (*mingongchao*). Once they have children, they become 'excess birth guerrillas' (*chaosheng youjidui*). The foundation of this discourse is the dichotomy contained in the *hukou* system. No matter how long migrants stay in the cities, they remain a distinct legal category. This leads to the migrants' identification as 'floating population' (*liudong renkou*) in surveys, and as *mingong* in daily speech.

At the end of the 1970s, the *hukou* system divided Chinese society into two large segments: about 16 per cent labelled as 'non-agricultural' was eligible for state benefits, while the great majority of Chinese fell in the 'agricultural' category. Individuals, most of whom lived and worked in cities, obtained 'non-agricultural' *hukou* by securing a state job or by gaining entrance to a university. But such cases were rare for rural people: in one village in Guangdong, on average only one man was able to change to urban registration every five years. Among women, this was only one every fifty years (Potter 1983). Officially approved movement mainly concerned people who were assigned new jobs, who were transferred to other places, and, in some instances, the family members of such people. In the countryside, the only large-scale legally sanctioned migration involved young women who moved to the villages of their husbands, transferring their household registration at marriage.

Yet even in these years inventive farmers skirted restrictions and moved around both the countryside and cities, earning income at the margins of legality but almost always retaining rural registrations. Xiang Biao (1998) recounts how farmers from Wenzhou used the chaos of the Cultural Revolution to move in small bands to other places to work as carpenters or shoe menders. They avoided the larger cities and the eastern part of the country, where controls were stricter. Travelling to county seats and suburban areas in Inner Mongolia and throughout the north-west, they went from house to house offering their carpentry skills, constructing furniture and making repairs. Sometimes they had to hide in pigsties and cow sheds to avoid detection. When arrested and sent back to Wenzhou, many simply set out again. By the second half of the 1970s, they had begun to draw on personal connections to set up businesses in larger urban centres. Other villagers obtained temporary employment in state enterprises, working at a fraction of state wages and without benefits or job security.

Migration and control in the reform era

If migration on the eve of reform was negligible, by the second half of the 1980s scores of millions of rural migrants were working in China's major cities and rural industrial zones. It is common to describe this process of change as a sort of 'cork out of the bottle' phenomenon. In this view, decades of migration control had led to enormous pent-up urbanization pressure. As soon as the authorities relaxed some of the controls over population mobility (the 'cork'), enormous migration currents were unleashed. The term 'migrant flood' (*mingongchao*), which gained currency in the 1990s to describe rural labour migration, fits in well with this type of explanation. This view of the causes of migration also underwrites the continuing emphasis on control of migrants by the state and the reluctance to bring about fundamental reform of the *hukou* system. While it is true that a number of milestones in the recent history of Chinese migration are marked by liberalizations of the *hukou* system, it is wrong to depict the government as the main initiator of change. In many cases, it is more accurate to describe the changes in regulations as adaptations to a situation that was already changing rapidly on the ground. The initiative of migrants, their ingenuity in finding loopholes, in evading, bribing and stretching the limits were at least as important in bringing about change as was government action. Perhaps, rather than migrants reacting to changes in official regulations, it was the various government agencies that trailed behind social reality and at best reactively adapted and adjusted. (Relative) freedom of movement was not granted; it had to be *conceded*. It was *won*. However, while changes in regulations are published in the *State Council Gazette* and further spread by the media, the countless minor acts of migrant resistance that were instrumental in bringing about the change by their very nature go largely unrecorded. The account of the main developments of the reform period that follows in this section draws extensively on the official 'transcript'. It is therefore important to keep in mind that the best evidence of active migrant resistance is the fact that over the last quarter century migration took place on a vast scale.

The growth of migration and its underlying causes

The door to the cities was initially opened by a special group of people. During the 1960s and 1970s, especially after Mao's personal 1968 call, some seventeen million urban youth had been sent 'up to the mountains and down to the villages'. The permanence of the move was powerfully expressed by the fact that all were stripped of their urban registrations. This rustication movement was deeply resented by many of the youths and their families. The political changes that followed the death of Mao and the fall of the 'Gang of Four' fuelled expectations that they might after all be allowed to return. After the Party's Third Plenum of 1978, the returned youths petitioned the authorities to restore urban residential rights, putting up posters, organizing demonstrations and sit-ins, and disrupting rail traffic. In 1979, the great majority were allowed to return to their home cities or at least restored to 'non-agricultural' status in local towns in a brilliant example of successful resistance to the state by a well-organized and determined group.

The return of millions of (no longer young) city dwellers put pressure on urban employment and welfare systems. A number of early reform measures, such as the encouragement of small-scale private entrepreneurship and the *dingti* system that allowed a parent working in a state enterprise to retire, transferring his or her job to a child, were primarily aimed at solving the returnees' problems. Investigations of the 'floating population' (i.e., people whose official registration was elsewhere) during the 1980s usually found a large proportion to be family members of urban dwellers, who were prevented by the *hukou* system from officially settling down in the cities. Some of these were returned youths, others were spouses or children from 'mixed' agricultural-urban *hukou* marriages, and yet others were aged parents who had come to the cities to retire with their children. So, the initial growth of the 'floating population' was closely related to the history of forced resettlement and the rigidities of the HRS. Enterprising farmers and rural entrepreneurs, however, were quick to grasp new opportunities opened by the weakening of social and political control, and over the course of the 1980s the non-official urban population gradually came to be dominated by rural labour migrants.

This labour migration was facilitated by a number of broader changes in rural and urban areas. With decollectivization, farm families regained control of household labour. Underemployment was a serious problem and rural families were eager to secure the cash remittances of members employed outside agriculture and the village. Although the early rural reforms boosted farmers' incomes considerably, the difference between them and urban dwellers was still large, and after the mid-1980s, this gap began to grow again.

The growth of migration was not only propelled by supply: in urban areas there was a strong demand for the kinds of products and services that migrants provided. Increasing numbers of farmers began to sell their products in the cities, at first stealthily and illegally, trying to stay one step ahead of public security forces. This quickly changed. In Beijing, official farmers' markets were established in the suburbs in April 1979, and extended to the city districts the next year. Migrants also began to run other businesses, selling clothes for example. The ban on long-distance trading, before 1980 still regarded as 'opportunistic profiteering', was also lifted. Within a few years, this revival of marketing not only improved urban consumption levels, but it also made it possible for farmers to stay in the cities for longer periods without rationing coupons for daily necessities.

Migrant employment was not limited to small-scale peddling and services. With China's economy booming, urban enterprises faced mounting labour shortages in textile and machine-building industries, in construction, in urban sanitation and others. The state's response was to ease provisions for temporary residence, which enabled labour shortages to be overcome without committing the state to the costs of providing costly services for a growing urban population. This solution also gave enterprises much greater flexibility, as temporary workers are easy to dismiss in times of economic slump. This shows that not only rural migrants resisted state control of movement, but that employers – in the early years still government agencies and state-owned enterprises – were also instrumental in bending the rules and bringing about change.

The new labour migration not only brought farmers into large urban centres, but from the second half of the 1980s, rural industry (usually called Township and Village Enterprises, TVEs) also began to grow and absorb large numbers of rural workers.[3] Increasingly unencumbered by state control and fuelled by a tax regime that encouraged local governments to invest in industry, these TVEs filled a niche that state-owned enterprises (SOEs) could not reach. Rural industry soon became the most dynamic segment of the industrial sector, flexibly responding to macroeconomic growth with expansion, and fuelling export growth. The proportion of rural workers engaged in non-agricultural pursuits grew from just over 10 per cent on the eve of reform to almost 30 per cent in the mid-1990s. Regions where TVEs were concentrated, around major cities and in southern Jiangsu and Guangdong's Pearl River Delta, became major destinations for migrants, as labour demand exceeded local supply.

Rural labour migration thus increased steadily during the 1980s. Throughout the Third World, rural–urban mobility mainly takes place in the form of chain migration, and China is no exception. Earlier migrants provide information and assistance with moving, finding jobs and accommodation to later migrants from their own villages, thus linking specific origins with specific destinations. Networks that facilitated later mobility began to emerge. In the early 1980s, for example, small bands of migrants arrived in the capital and began to settle in what later became known as 'Zhejiang Village'. However, most labour migrants in the major cities during these years probably came from the suburbs and adjacent counties.

As networks spread, linking up more and more villages with the cities, labour migration began to develop a momentum of its own. Refuting the idea that migration rates are a simple function of macroeconomic growth, in the late 1980s migration increased rapidly, in spite of government retrenchment policies and economic slump. The annual increase from 1989 to 1993 was about 25 per cent. Surveys indicate that by the early 1990s between fifty and sixty million rural migrants were working outside their townships. The growth of rural labour migration continued in the 1990s, but at a more modest rate. By the mid-1990s, the total migrant population was probably about eighty million people.[4] In most major cities and rapidly developing rural industrial belts, sizeable migrant populations had developed, often accounting for 10–20 per cent or more of the total population.

The causes of the levelling off of migration growth are many, but together they represent what one might call a maturing of the migration system after an initial period of rapid and sometimes chaotic growth. Networks of migration chains had spread throughout most of China and migration income had become an important part of the livelihood strategies of families in many villages. They evolved patterns of labour and income that depended on both agriculture and migration. The composition of migration streams had also begun to change. Rural labour migrants now dominated the urban non-official population. While sex ratios differ strongly by industry (with the export processing industries in the Pearl River Delta employing mostly women and the construction sector mainly men), there seems to have been an increase in the proportion of female migrants. To some extent, this may be related to a growth of the migration of entire families, with increasing numbers of migrant children in cities (see below). In the major areas of origin, local governments actively promoted labour migration and set up mechanisms to help migrants find employment and to mediate conflicts. Governments in the receiving areas also evolved more effective measures to deal with migrants. Such measures accept the need for outside workers and try to smooth the process, while at the same time denying them full citizen status. Nevertheless, the realism of local authorities in regulating migration was periodically punctuated by draconian measures such as the demolishing of Zhejiang Village (see Box 6.2) and by the formal exclusion of migrants from a large number of specified occupations in cities such as Beijing and Shanghai.

Box 6.2: 'Seesaw warfare': the turbulent history of 'Zhejiang Village'

In 1983, small bands of migrants from Zhejiang province began to arrive in Fengtai district, on the fringes of Beijing. Many of them had already spent years away from home, earning a living by making clothes or furniture, and had gradually ventured into the larger cities. They came from Wenzhou, an area with a long history of emigration to Europe and a tradition of small-scale entrepreneurship. They set up small businesses in the capital as they had in other places. By 1986, several thousand Wenzhouese lived in the area, which began to be known as 'Zhejiang Village'. The village began to play an important role in the north China textile market, especially after the introduction of leather jackets in 1989. From that time, the flow of people from Wenzhou assumed a mass character. Gradually a bipolar community (Wenzhou–Beijing) took shape, as factor markets (labour, cloth) developed in Wenzhou, serving the Village. By 1994, Zhejiang Village covered twenty-six natural villages in Fengtai district, with about 14,000 local residents and 96,000 migrants. Of the migrants, about 50,000 were from Zhejiang. Most others were employed in the workshops of the Wenzhou entrepreneurs, coming from Hebei, Anhui, Sichuan, Hubei and elsewhere.

While the Wenzhou migrants at first mainly engaged in dispersed 'guerilla warfare', from the mid-1980s, 'seesaw warfare' became the main mode of conflict with the state. Local authorities resorted to periodic clean-up campaigns in 1986, 1989 and 1990, but each time the migrants retreated to the outer suburbs of Beijing or neighbouring Hebei, where they weathered the storm. In November 1995, after a particularly harsh newspaper report drew the attention of the central government, the authorities made a concerted effort permanently to uproot and destroy the village. A special 'headquarters' was formed, and a 'battle campaign' launched. About 80,000 migrants were forced to leave and forty-six large residential compounds (*dayuan*) were torn down. However, by March 1996, the first migrants had begun to trickle back into the area and began to set up stalls on the rubble where once the vegetable market had stood. A year after the 'campaign', two *dayuan* began to arise again. The seesaw war had come full circle.

Sources: The work of Xiang Biao provides a full record of the village (Xiang 1998, 1999; Ma and Xiang 1998).

Changes in the regulatory framework

The hukou *system in rural towns*

Most experimentation with changes in the *hukou* system took place far from China's major cities, in small rural towns (*zhen*). The reform of the registration system in rural towns fit in a wider strategy of modernization of agriculture and gradual diversion of the rural population to local centres. Facing the spectre of massive migration to the largest cities, in the early 1980s, the state called on villagers to *litu bulixiang,* 'leave the land but not the countryside'. Farmers were urged to take up non-agricultural occupations in the villages or in small rural towns. To this end, small town migration was liberalized in late 1984. Villagers who had obtained jobs and accommodation in towns were allowed to settle there officially, and enjoy the same rights as the original town dwellers, on condition that they provide their own grain. They would be registered as holding an 'urban registration with self-supplied grain' (*zili kouliang chengzhen hukou*). The new policy premise was that these farmers would solve their employment, housing and food problems themselves. Only then would the state register the successful migrants as urban residents. As welfare entitlements of small town residents are far less generous than those in large cities, the costs to the state of such formal registration were low. Moreover, the provision that these townward moving farmers provide their own grain marked the first severing since the famines of the early 1960s of the link between grain supply and urban registration. Although five to six million peasants used this opportunity to settle in towns, by the late 1980s the experiment died a quiet death. Apart from implementation problems, perhaps most important was the fact that grain harvests had been disappointing since the start of the programme following the bumper harvest of 1984. It appears that, in spite of the many changes, central planners were still too sensitive about urban grain supply to continue experimentation (Mallee 1994).

In this context, it is interesting to see how such new state initiatives were immediately hijacked and used for other purposes. A study of towns near Shanghai indicates that, at least in the beginning, the new registration was used to solve the problems of mixed *hukou* families by giving the 'agricultural' members (mostly women) official urban status. Over half of the people who received the new registration were already living in these towns at the time it was introduced, and 35 per cent had lived there since before 1981. Women constituted up to 80 per cent of the new registrants in the first year of the scheme and 84 per cent had relatives in the towns, in most cases including a spouse. In other areas, the registrations mainly went to the 'agricultural' spouses of rusticated youths who had settled in local towns. Thus, rather than attracting new migrants to towns, the urban registration with self supplied grain recognized a *fait accompli* and helped alleviate the family plight of some who suffered most from the rigidities of the HRS.

Over the course of the following two decades, liberalization of registration in rural towns surfaced a number of times, usually as part of a wider discussion about reforming the *hukou* system. Encouraged by good grain harvests, the government in the early 1990s first raised retail prices of grain and finally abolished the subsidized rationing system. The simultaneous elimination of grain subsidies to urban residents reduced pressure on state budgets. After grain coupons were abolished, calls for reform of the HRS became louder. In November 1993, the Third Plenum of the Fourteenth Central Committee announced that the registration system in small cities and townships would be gradually reformed. It was only in 1997, however, that concrete measures were announced. In a number of pilot sites, people with agricultural registrations with stable jobs and over two years of residence in a county seat or rural town would be given a permanent urban registration. Since that time, the media has periodically announced that the HRS is about to be abolished or fundamentally reformed. The *China Daily* in 1998, for example, claimed that 'revolutionary changes are expected in China's rigid system for registering permanent residence'. In late 2001 and early 2002, there was another wave of similar announcements in the press, prompting a senior official in the Ministry of Public Security to warn that the registration system still played a vital role in China, and that complete dismantling was not on the agenda. However, the core of the introduced changes was still basically the conditional granting of official registration to people with stable jobs and residence in rural towns, a reform that had already been experimented with in the mid-1980s. The change is an *ex post facto* recognition of migration, since people eligible for registration need to have lived in town for a certain period. So rather than enabling new migration, the reforms are primarily an adjustment of registration rules to actual practice.

Temporary urban residence

As more people began to travel and larger numbers of migrants accumulated in the cities and peri-urban areas, the inconveniences of the *hukou* system became even more evident. To travel, one often needed to carry one's *hukou* booklet and a letter of introduction, and stays in cities needed to be reported to the police within three days. Police approval for stays of more than three months was required and seldom given. A number of changes were introduced from the mid-1980s onwards to accommodate the increase in population mobility. The most important of these was the relaxation in 1985 of restrictions on temporary urban residence. A system of temporary residence permits was introduced that became the basis for the permits still in use today (see below). It was also no longer illegal for outsiders to rent rooms or apartments in cities. A national identity card eventually began to replace the *hukou* booklets and introduction letters for travellers and labour migrants. Invariably, the authorities were responding to increasing population mobility. The 1985 regulations on temporary residence, for example, begin by noting the growth in population mobility between regions and between city and countryside, and explain that the regulations are being issued to 'respond to the development needs of the situation and to convenience the lives of the masses'. Here again, regulatory change lagged behind developments in society. Such change did fit in with a conception of urbanization that emerged during the first half of the 1980s, in which the formally registered population, which was heavily subsidized by the state, was kept as small as possible, while urban labour needs were met by relying on cheaper, 'temporary' migrant workers.

Change of registration status and special groups

In spite of the fact that migrants were denied local 'non-agricultural' registrations and had to remain 'temporary' residents, throughout the 1980s, the 'non-agricultural population' (NAP) had been rising.[5] From 1968 to 1978, the NAP had never exceeded 16 per cent of the total population, but by 1989 it topped 21 per cent. This increase of over five percentage points in just over a decade greatly worried the authorities, as it considerably exacerbated the financial burden of state subsidies to the urban population. Theoretically, change from 'agricultural' to 'non-agricultural' registration status was controlled by rigorous procedures, but in practice many loopholes existed that were readily exploited by clever migrants and unofficial long-term urban residents such as 'mixed *hukou* marriages'. But at the same time, the state manipulated access to 'non-agricultural' status. At different times, special regulations on change to the NAP were issued for miners, highly qualified intellectuals, military officials, relatives of overseas investors, etc. This selective use of privileged urban registration status enabled the state to cultivate groups of strategic importance (Mallee 1995). In short, the growth of the non-agricultural population was the result not only of ingenious individuals, but also of the institutional interests of various bureaucracies.

In 1989, the central government cracked down on *hukou* transfer. The State Planning Commission took charge of *hukou* change policy. The NAP dipped below 20 per cent of the total population, the first real decrease since 1977. However, by 1995, the NAP had again grown to almost 24 per cent of the total population. In recent years, the authorities have regularly declared that the registration system is moving away from ascriptive status towards registration according to occupation and actual residence. Indeed, the rules have been changed to make it easier for couples to live together and register in the same place. Under certain conditions, it is now possible for children to be registered in their father's place of residence – potentially the beginning of the end of the maternal inheritance of *hukou* status. However, this is still a far cry from total removal of the institutional *hukou* barriers that prevent the majority of rural dwellers as well as tens of millions of rural labour migrants from obtaining the same treatment as official city residents.

Commodification of urban registration

During the late 1980s, the HRS underwent a steady 'commodification': 'non-agricultural' registration status gradually became a commodity that could be bought with money. *Hukou* sales started to gain momentum in 1991, when the region around Dezhou in Shandong publicly announced the prices to obtain urban residence. The next year, *hukou* 'auctions' spread over most of the country, and received considerable media attention.

> [A]t places where the transaction 'to change agricultural household registration' to non-agricultural household registration' [took place], long lines formed, traffic was blocked, there was a hubbub of voices, and bends occurred in the lines. Peasants in surrounding villages and townships filled

satchels and flour bags with money they had earned by their blood and sweat and had saved for several years to conduct a transaction in which 'agricultural household registration was changed to non-agricultural regis-tration.'[6]

The wave of registration sales prompted the Ministry of Public Security in May 1992 to issue an order strictly prohibiting the practice. That October a county secretary and thirty other officials were dismissed and brought to trial for 'arbi-trarily changing registrations from agricultural to non-agricultural'. The *Sichuan Yearbook 1993*, on the other hand, candidly reports that the 'non-agricultural population' in 1992 had grown relatively rapidly, and that half of this was due to the practice of 'economic registrations' (*jingji hukou*). Whatever the central government's stance, the temptation for local governments to raise money in this fashion is large.[7]

Summing up the changes of the reform era, a number of observations can be made. First, rural labour migration greatly increased and 'floating populations' came to account for one quarter to one-third of the total population in most cities. Second, without the migrants, the economic boom of this period would not have been possible. Third, the migrant population in the cities came to be more and more dominated by rural labour migrants rather than by relatives of official urban residents. Fourth, the hukou system changed, for example with the increasing availability of purchased *hukou*, but the essential distinction between urban and rural population remained intact. While no longer capable of preventing migration, *hukou* still plays an important role in determining claims to public resources, and thus continues to shape life chances across the urban–rural divide. Despite increasing calls for fundamental reform, the essence of the HRS – entitlements based on ascriptive status – remained intact.

The effectiveness of the HRS (and associated mechanisms) was gradually eroded by the evasion, non-cooperation, resistance and bribery of millions of migrants. The situation is aptly summarized in the often-quoted saying *shang you zhengce, xia you duice* (there are policies on high but those below have countermea-sures). At the same time, increased migration was sometimes also in the interest of specific local government organs, officials and employers, either because it made cheap labour and services available, or simply because it increased the opportunities for institutional revenue raising and personal corruption. The more adaptations and exceptions there were made, the harder it was to enforce the system, the more corrupt it grew, and the easier it became to evade it. We observe a dialectical relationship between migrants' resistance and migration control. Over the course of the reform period, migration increased, thereby eroding the controls, which in turn made migrating easier.

Migrants and the state

Rural labour migrants are not a uniform entity. Three main groups can be distinguished by occupation. In the major cities, the largest group consists of construction workers. Virtually all unskilled and semi-skilled construction is done by rural migrants, mostly young males, organized in teams along native place lines. Many teams are run by or associated with the authorities at origin. The construction workers work long days, and usually eat and sleep at the construction site. Their daily lives are often highly regimented, with strict rules about leaving the site. A second major group consists of industrial workers, not only in the large cities, but also in industrialized parts of the countryside. In some industries, such as textiles and electronics, young migrant women predominate. Larger factories usually offer accommodation and food, and most industrial workers lead disciplined and isolated lives. The third main group consists of self-employed migrants and those working in small enterprises and households. This includes peddlers, traders operating market stalls or counters in shops, garbage collectors and waitresses, as well as domestic workers and sub-contractors of agricultural land on the outskirts of the cities. In comparison to the first two groups, these migrants are in much more frequent interaction with the local population, and many come into direct contact with the authorities.

In core city areas, where migrants are relatively small in number, the main interface between them and the state is the local police station and the neighbourhood committee. On the urban fringe, where migrants sometimes even outnumber the local population, management capacity is extremely limited, with staff being allocated on the basis of the number of permanently registered residents. Here, semi-official management organs and corruption, irregular arrests, and even harassment and violence are pronounced.

When migrants face the representatives of the state and the established population, they usually rely on 'invisible' resistance, yield, or attempt to take refuge elsewhere in order to weather the storm. A number of incidents, however, illustrate the pent up frustration beneath the surface. In 1986, 400 migrant traders in Tianjin's Hexi District surrounded and beat up tax officials and public security officers. In March 1994, fed up with paying one fee after another, migrant traders in the Muxiyuan Light Industrial Wholesale Market (inside Beijing's Zhejiang Village) went on strike. They sustained the strike for a week until the authorities met their demands. Such open conflicts are relatively rare, however. We will look at permits, forced repatriation, and housing as some of the specific contact points between migrants and the state, from the angle of conflict and resistance.

Permits and certificates

By the mid 1990s, the temporary residence permits (*zanzhuzheng*) introduced in 1985 had become fairly well established. Over two-thirds of migrant workers held one, preferring registration to the semi-illegal status associated with non-registration. Lacking the necessary certification considerably increases the vulnerability of an already marginal group. Being caught without papers often means being sent to a detention centre (see below), a risk that most migrants will not take. Among dependants, however, non-registration is much more common.

The main reason for evading registration is the cost: typically, applying for a permit costs 1 to 5 yuan, and a monthly management fee of 10 to 20 yuan is levied.

In early 1990, the authorities began to consider using work permits to control rural out-migration. Initially, this took the form of a 'labour migration permit' to be obtained at place of origin and a 'work permit' at place of destination. After 1994, the Ministry of Labour unified this procedure for inter-provincial migration. Both at origin and destination, procedures need to be followed to obtain a legal work permit. In practice, only a fraction of the migrants (less than one-quarter in one study) actually obtain these papers and two-thirds do not even know about the most recent rules (Research Group 1997). One study found that migrants on average paid over 60 yuan, both at origin and at destination; in extreme cases, the amount was several hundred. Thus, rather than giving labour migrants a well-defined legal status, the work permits merely expose them to additional fees. Most migrants apparently find employment without cards and permits. Peddlers, small traders and service providers similarly need operating permits to ply their trade. This group is usually visually present in the streets and avoiding the police is difficult. In addition to the threat of the detention centres, they sometimes face confiscation of their wares, carts, etc. As well as requiring documentation of labour migrants, many of China's big cities restrict their legal scope of activity. Concerned about employment of the registered population, Beijing and Shanghai, for example, list several scores of occupations from which outsiders are barred.

An area that has received much media attention concerns the fertility behaviour of migrants. While most scholars now agree that overall fertility will decrease with the growth of rural–urban migration, in many urban areas, migrants account for the great majority of 'excess births' (as defined by China's family planning policies).[8] (See chapter 8.) This is an aspect of mobility that brings out the inability of the *hukou*-based system to control the behaviour of mobile people, since the responsibility for such control is divided between the places of origin and destination and coordination is difficult. Women of child-bearing age are required to obtain a Family Planning Certificate from the authorities in their place of *hukou* registration. This forms the basis for a 'contract' between the authorities in the receiving area and the women, who then are issued a certificate that enables them to obtain other necessary papers. In both places, they need to pay deposits in order to obtain the certificates.

Such deposits and other fees levied on migrants have proliferated over the years and in many areas have become an important source of institutional income, as well as an opportunity for corruption. In late 2001, the situation apparently became so bad that the State Development Planning Commission issued a decree formally forbidding these kinds of fees. Only the cost of residence permits is allowed to be recovered from migrants and should not exceed 5 yuan. The Special Economic Zone of Shenzhen estimated that this measure would cost it over 1 billion yuan per year in revenues. Half a year after the decree, it became clear that localities were evading the restrictions by adding banned fees on to water and refuse-collection charges or by precharging migrants. Labour migrants remain easy prey for unscrupulous officials.

Detention and deportation

All Chinese cities have 'detention stations' (*shourongzhan*), where a variety of people unwanted in the city are kept before being sent 'back' to the countryside. The definition of 'unwanted' has varied considerably since the 1950s, but in 1986, the detention station in Guiyang City contained the following people: 1,972 'blind vagrants' (*mangliu*), 74 beggars, 27 swindlers, 86 thieves, 82 pick-pockets, 111 people who had been cheated, 14 people who had come in contact with the authorities, 5 people engaged in 'chaotic' sexual relations, 8 prostitutes, 2 gamblers, 3 woman traffickers, 7 fortune tellers, 8 people released from reform through labour, 23 mentally ill and 84 retarded and handicapped people. The numbers and categories of people detained in the stations, jointly run by the police and the department of civil affairs, increased through the 1990s and labour migrants are increasingly a target for detention.

Detention and deportation of people lacking the necessary papers (the 'three without' population, *sanwu renkou*) is still common. Usually it takes the form of sweeping 'clean-up' campaigns, in particular when a large public event is about to take place. In the run-up to the celebration of the fiftieth anniversary of the People's Republic, in late 1998, Beijing announced plans to remove one million migrants from its jurisdiction. Similar sweeps accompanied Beijing's bid for the Olympic Games a few years later. Migrants, however, have learned how to cope with the phenomenon. A professional beggar woman in Beijing said: 'We usually know beforehand when a campaign is coming and then we stay inside for a while.' In some cases, deportation means that the people are actually taken back to their place of origin; in others, they are simply dropped outside the city or provincial borders. It is an expensive and largely ineffective measure. Sometimes the deportees manage to get back in town before the officials who accompanied them return! It has become very common, however, for relatives of detainees to bail them out and it seems that many stations detain migrants simply in order to generate income. Detainees must work to pay for the cost of detention or to be released, and living circumstances are appalling (HRIC 1999).

Housing

Migrants have made quite diverse housing arrangements. Construction workers usually live on the work sites and industrial workers in dormitories provided by the factories. A 1994 Beijing study found 470,000 people living at construction sites and 430,000 on the premises of work units. Domestic workers, on the other hand, often live in the homes of their employers. Where weather conditions permit, small traders and peddlers not infrequently spend the night on the streets and in marketplaces next to their wares. Similarly, people working in shops, restaurants and service workshops simply spread their mattress on the floor once the customers are gone and the doors have been closed. One way that migrants resist control by the authorities is by frequently changing their living quarters. Especially in areas where migrants are numerous and accommodation is readily available, this tactic enables migrants to maintain some distance from the officials of the state.

In 1985, as part of the loosening of the control over temporary residence in cities, renting accommodation by migrants was officially sanctioned for the first time. The largest concentration of labour migrants in most cities is on the fringes of the central city districts. In these zones, where city gradually merges into countryside, finding accommodation is usually easier, official control less strict and commuting distances to downtown areas not prohibitive. Local farmers soon discovered that their land yielded much more income when it was occupied with rented-out rooms than when it was cultivated with crops. By the late 1980s, migrant enclaves had emerged on the periphery of most large Chinese cities. And even when there are no clearly identifiable settlements on the rural–urban fringe, migrants often account for a considerable proportion of the *de facto* population, sometimes even equalling or surpassing the number of original residents. In Shanghai, for example, most migrants live in the 'remote wards', i.e. the outskirts of the city proper, 41 per cent in 1986 and 65 per cent in 1993. The clustering of migrants in certain areas is not only a simple function of housing availability and larger social space in certain urban areas. Banding together on the basis of home area ties also makes life easier for migrants by providing ready access to information, employment, credit, and assistance in daily affairs, as well as mental comfort from contacts with familiar people in a familiar language.

Migrant organizations

The main organizing principle of migration chains is the reliance on kinship and native place ties. An investigation of 500 labour migrants at Beijing railway station in 1989, showed that 95.4 per cent had fellow villagers who had migrated and provided information (Mallee 1996). One study (Research Group 1997) categorizes 75.6 per cent of moves as being facilitated by various forms of self-organization.

Organization does not cease once migrants reach their destination. Facing discrimination and official harassment, many migrants seek comfort and protection in groups. Research Group (1997) reports that most migrants band together when going out for a stroll, shopping or watching videos 'because going out alone is not convenient, you easily get bullied [*shou qifu*]'. Informal groups also are important in providing migrants with mental comfort, through contacts with *tongxiang* [people from the same home area]. A 1993 Beijing survey found that 76 per cent of the migrants interviewed had regular contacts with more than two *tongxiang* other than their family, and over half had contacts with over five *tongxiang*. A 1994 survey found that almost three-quarters of the migrants received help from *tongxiang* when they fell ill or met other problems. In factories in the south, migrant workers form small mutual help groups. They stand in for sick fellow workers, lend each other money and fight (in the streets or with the boss) if necessary (Gao 1994).

Organization helps migrants to defend their turf and to cultivate relations with the authorities. Beggars, for example, are often led by a boss who protects their interests (as well as his own). In Wuxi county in 1993, a full-scale battle ensued between two competing groups of Anhui loaders, involving close to a hundred people and leaving one dead and five seriously wounded (Research Group 1997).

The form and degree of internal organization of migrant groups differs greatly. Some are small, loosely structured and lack clear leaders. At the other extreme are groups such as a large organization of transport workers in Wuxi, which was tightly organized, with strict rules governing work and leisure, with advanced division of labour and equipment, under the strong leadership of one person. However, regardless of their functions and internal structures, all are organized by native place, kinship and occupation.

A number of coordinated action by migrants have given rise to new institutions. These include a variety of markets, some of which supply migrants with daily necessities, others of which buy goods produced or collected by migrants. In most cities, specific migrant labour markets have emerged. Such markets are subject to continual monitoring and periodic suppression by the authorities.

One of the most tangible examples of migrant institutions are the migrant 'work shed' schools (*gongpeng xuexiao*) (Han 2000). The emergence of such schools is related to the changing nature of the migrant population, with a growing proportion of families. In the Beijing migrant survey of late 1997, for example, it was found that about one-third of the migrants consisted of families. In particular, small operations in commerce and services, which often need two workers, were characterized by family migration. As a result, 2.9 per cent of the migrant population, or almost 70,000 individuals, were children of school age (those aged under 15 accounting for 7 per cent). Like most aspects of urban life in China, the schooling system is based on *hukou*. School facilities and funding levels are tied to the number of school-age children with local registration. When children of migrant workers were refused access to local schools, or required to pay very substantial fees, in many places, migrants set up their own schools, inviting teachers from their home areas. From the early 1990s, migrant schools began to appear only to be subject to regular suppression by the authorities. But no sooner were schools closed down than they reopened again somewhere else. By the late 1990s, the overall policy had changed from one of active opposition to a more ambiguous one that did not formally recognize the schools but allowed them to operate. Currently, migrant children are allowed to enter public schools, but only if there is capacity and with payment of high fees. They can also go to commercially run private schools ('aristocrat schools'), which are extremely expensive. The most common solution is to turn to migrant-run schools. Because of their ambiguous legal status, migrant schools rarely make long-term investments in their facilities and most such schools are in a bad physical state (which accounts for the usual designation *jianyi xuexiao*, 'simple' or 'makeshift' schools). By the end of 2000, there were an estimated 200 such schools in Beijing, many of them institutions run for profit. In sum, the active pursuit of education by migrant families and groups has had two broad outcomes. On the one hand, the authorities and public school system have somewhat softened their attitude towards migrant schools. The fundamental, *hukou*-based discrimination, on the other hand, has led to the emergence of a separate educational sector, catering for the needs of migrant children.

The attitude of the authorities towards migrants' self-organization is ambiguous. On the one hand, informal organizations can be used to control migrants. This is the case in many larger work units, where migrant leaders are asked to shoulder responsibility for the behaviour of a whole group. Sometimes local authorities cultivate personal relationships with individual migrant leaders as in Wuxi, where one powerful migrant headed an organization of several hundred transport workers and monopolized most work in the harbour (Research Group 1997). On the other hand, there are many examples in which migrant organizations are denied state recognition (Li 2001) or are suppressed. Analogous to the semi-legal status of their members, migrant organizations are engaged in a continuous balancing act, compromising between interest representation and breaking the (unclear) limits set by the authorities.

Conclusion and prospects

Among the most important developments of the two decades of reform is the emergence of large-scale labour migration. On the eve of reform, there was very little mobility except for state-arranged moves. By the end of the twentieth century, eighty to a hundred million people were working or living far away from their place of permanent registration. Like many other changes in post-Mao China, the story of this mobility is often told in terms of state-initiated changes. Such an account is not entirely implausible, as the Chinese state did dismantle many controls on population mobility. Such changes, in particular in the mid-1980s, were in line with the general policy reorientation of the time, one more open to markets, mobility, manoeuvre and migration. This chapter has shown, however, that the relation between institutional reform and social change is complex, and it has emphasized the pressures for change and creative initiatives of migrants in shaping outcomes.

During the initial reform years, a number of structural changes took place that facilitated mobility. The most important of these were the restoration of production management to the farm households, an acute urban labour shortage and the growing role of markets in supplying daily necessities. In this situation, inventive and entrepreneurial rural migrants gradually stretched the limits of the possible. The foundations were laid for the mobility networks which over the years would become the main channel for large-scale rural labour migration. Faced with increasing mobility, the authorities were impelled to reconsider basic aspects of rural development and urbanization policies, and to adjust the *hukou* system and associated controls to the changing situation. Sometimes, such changes were in line with the particular interests of local government organizations and officials. In this way, the limits were widened and growing numbers of migrants gained new space to test these limits further. Thus mobility gradually eroded the controls, making possible yet more mobility. However, the proliferation of new regulations – exceptions, special cases and exemptions – made the system ever more liable to corruption.

Despite all the changes, the core of the *hukou* system has not changed. The division along rural–urban residence lines is less clear cut, but Chinese society by and large can still be divided into a large 'agricultural' segment and a much smaller 'non-agricultural' one, and glaring differences remain in entitlements between the two. The worst excesses have been trimmed away, and in rural towns, where the entitlement gap was never very large, experiments with easier access to urban registration have been resumed. Still, the large majority of migrants is denied urban citizenship. The HRS has become less transparent and more open to corruption, as personal connections and money play decisive roles in determining people's chances in life. Rural people continue to suffer severe disadvantages.

Prospects for the future are mixed. On the one hand, while bringing no revolutionary change, if the recent changes in the HRS are implemented well, they will benefit migrants, particularly the more successful ones, as well as the official urban population. On the other hand, employment prospects since the late 1990s have been very bleak. For the first time in more than a decade, TVEs are no longer absorbing workers and major layoffs have been experienced among state-sector workers in large cities. (See chapter 3.) Laid-off workers inevitably compete for jobs that have been the preserve of rural migrants. Moreover, migrants are more likely to be seen as a threat to urban dwellers' livelihoods. Finally, positive adjustments of the *hukou* system have been accompanied by exclusionary measures: large cities restrict migrants' employment options; migrant schools continue to be the object of forced closures; and 'repatriation' campaigns periodically disrupt migrant lives. After two decades of reform, the authorities are still trying to come to grips with rural labour migration.

Notes

1 See Scott (1998) concerning state aversion towards 'chaos' and the importance of mechanisms such as population registration to 'read' society.

2 James Scott's analysis (1990) of parades and mobs, of anonymity and of spontaneity, is illuminating in this context.

3 Labour migration to other rural areas has also grown in importance, especially for poor communities outside established migration streams. For reasons of space, we cannot deal with this phenomenon here.

4 Surveys invariably refer to the 'floating population', which includes all people in a place who are not registered locally. Thus, in addition to the rural labour migrants, the figures also include tourists, people attending training courses or conferences, medical patients, business people, etc. Furthermore, some studies (in particular those undertaken by the Public Security Departments) also add the daily population flow. Therefore, many of the figures are inflated.

5   Note that throughout, 'non-agricultural' (in quotation marks) refers to *hukou* status, not to actual occupation. There was also a strong increase in people engaged in non-agricultural occupations due to the growth of rural enterprises and labour migration, but this is only very partially reflected in the *hukou* figures.
6   JPRS-CAR-94-050-56.
7   See Solinger (1999) on this unclear attitude of the central government.
7   Migrants are also routinely accused of using their mobility to get away with transgressions of family planning regulations (the denigrating term used for these people is 'excess birth guerillas' (*chaosheng youjidui*), which conveys an impression of deliberate, planned violations).

Bibliography

Mobo C.F. Gao, 'On their Own, the Plight of Migrant Workers in South China', *China Rights Forum* (Fall 1994), pp. 4–7, 28.

Han Jialing, 'Beijingshi liudong ertong yiwu jiaoyu zhuangkuang diaocha baogao' [Investigation Report on the Situation of Compulsory Education of Migrant Children in Beijing City], unpublished report (Beijing, 2000).

HRIC (Human Rights in China), *Not Welcome at the Party: Behind the 'Clean-up of China's Cities – A Report on Administrative Detention Under 'Custody and Repatriation'*, HRIC Arbitrary Detention Series, no. 2 (September 1999).

Li Ling, 'Towards a More Civil Society: *Mingong* and Expanding Social Space in Reform-era China', *Columbia Human Rights Law Review*, 33, 1 (2001), pp. 149–88.

Liu Dawei and Wang Qiang, 'Survey Report on the "Difficulty in Recruiting Labour" in Beijing Municipality', *Chinese Economic Studies*, 21, 4 (1988), pp. 45–63.

Laurence J.C. Ma and Xiang Biao, 'Native place, migration, and the emergence of peasant enclaves in Beijing', *The China Quarterly*, 155 (1998), pp. 546–81.

Hein Mallee, 'Reforming the *Hukou* System: The Experiment with the "Urban Registration with Self-supplied Grain"', in Dong Lisheng (ed.), *Administrative Reform in the People's Republic of China since 1978* (Leiden: International Institute for Asian Studies 1994), pp. 100–20.

——, 'China's Household Registration System under Reform', *Development and Change*, 26, 1 (1995), pp. 1–29.

——, 'In Defence of Migration: Recent Chinese Studies of Rural Population Mobility', *China Information*, 10, 3–4 (1996), pp. 108–40.

——, 'Taking Grain as the Key Link: Population Registration and Development Discourse in China', in Luigi Tomba (ed.), *East Asian Capitalism: Conflict, Growth and Crisis* (Milan: Annali Fondazione Giangiacomo Feltrinelli, 2002).

Sulamith Heins Potter, 'The Position of Peasants in Modern China's Social Order', *Modern China*, 9, 4 (1983), pp. 465–99.

Research Group (Research Group on Organizational Characteristics of Rural Labour Mobility) 'Nongcun laodongli liudong de zuzhihua tezheng' (The Organizational Characteristics of Rural Labour Mobility), *Shehuixue Yanjiu*, 1 (1997), pp. 15–24.

James C. Scott, *Domination and the Arts of Resistance, Hidden Transcripts* (New Haven and London: Yale University Press, 1990).

——, *Seeing Like a State: How Certain Schemes to Improve the Human Condition Have Failed* (New Haven and London: Yale University Press, 1998).

Dorothy J. Solinger, *Contesting Citizenship in Urban China, Peasant Migrants, the State, and the Logic of the Market* (Berkeley: University of California Press, 1999).

Xiang Biao, 'Taobi, lianhe yu biaoda: "Zhejiangcu" de gushi' ('Escape, Alliance and Expression: The Story of 'Zhejiang Village'), *Chinese Social Sciences Quarterly* (Hong Kong), 22 (1998), pp. 91–111.

——, 'Zhejiang Village in Beijing: Creating a Visible Non-state Space Through Migration and Marketised Networks', in Frank N. Pieke and Hein Mallee (eds), *Internal and International Migration, Chinese Perspectives* (Richmond: Curzon, 1999).

Victor Yuan, 'Contract Worker Teams in Beijing', in Frank N. Pieke and Hein Mallee (eds), *Internal and International Migration, Chinese Perspectives*, Richmond: Curzon, 1999).

7 Gender, employment and women's resistance

Wang Zheng

This chapter examines the impact of social and economic transformation on women's lives by delineating changes in urban women's employment. Women's employment has been an intensely contested site that has not only reflected conflicting social interests and revealed gender assumptions, but has also shaped gender identities and class realignment. Women of diverse social groups have deployed differentiated strategies of resistance.

It is often asked 'Has reform improved the condition and status of women, or has it set it back?' Departing from simplistic assumptions concerning the existence of a monolithic Chinese womanhood, and a singular gender relationship, this chapter highlights multiple contradictory social realities experienced by contemporary women positioned differentially across hierarchies of age, urban/rural residence, education and class. Gender relationships are differentially affected depending on one's position in these and other power-laden hierarchies. Women's resistance, accordingly, takes different forms, employs variegated resources and aims at diverse goals.

This chapter examines the impact of social and economic transformation on women's lives by delineating changes in urban women's employment. The rapid diversification of the rural economy, the development of the market, the rise of industry at the township level as well as of household enterprises, and the opening of urban labour markets have also brought tremendous changes in rural women's employment. Here I focus on changes in employment in the urban setting, including the employment of women living in cities which the state classifies as 'rural'. Beginning with a brief review of Maoist policy on urban women's employment, this chapter explores changing patterns of urban women's employment and women's resistance and negotiation in the rapidly changing social, cultural and political milieu of post-Mao urban China.

Urban employment, gender and inequality in the Mao era

In the socialist, planned economy, the state guaranteed urban employment while prohibiting labour influx from rural areas (see chapter 6). Local governments assigned each resident a permanent job either in a state or collectively owned enterprise. Once assigned, mobility was largely restricted to promotion within the work unit. A work unit was not only a production unit but also an all-encompassing welfare institution that covered employees' health care, accident insurance and maternity leave. Some large work units offered housing and child-care as well. Employee benefits varied in different industries and state-run enterprises provided better packages than collective enterprises. But within the same work unit, men and women, old and young, generally received comparable benefits. Employment meant lifetime security.

Women's employment policy in the Mao era was framed within the Engelsian concept of women's liberation and gender equality: only through participation in social production would women achieve liberation. Employment meant socialist construction since the private sector virtually disappeared in the early 1950s. 'Housewife', by definition not a participant in social production, became a scorned urban social category and increasingly a historic relic. For urban women growing up in the Mao era, employment was taken for granted as an important component of a woman's life, even though far from all women experienced a sense of liberation by participating in social production. Women's employment enhanced their status at home since their income was vitally important to the family in the egalitarian low-income system of the Mao era.

Urban women in the Mao era enjoyed equal employment opportunities with men, and lifetime security and welfare benefits. This does not mean that they had achieved gender equality, as the Cultural Revolution slogan 'Women hold up half the sky' implied. A recent study investigating two state-owned factories in Guangzhou finds that, although the government issued equal employment guidelines from the early 1960s, specific job assignments invariably followed unstated gender lines. In an optical instrument factory, for example, of twenty-five categories of technical work, seven were seen as suitable for women and eighteen for men. In a machinery plant, fewer than twenty of 106 categories were seen as suitable for women. In both factories, service and auxiliary work was always 'female work'. This included maintenance of tools, cleaning, and operating day care centres, dining rooms and clinics. Men were overwhelmingly assigned to technical jobs and women to non-technical, auxiliary, and service jobs, regardless of educational level. This gendered employment hierarchy established women's subordinate position and shaped women's self-definition.[1]

While job assignment, promotion and allocation of resources such as housing in the workplace have reinforced both men's and women's identity, differential gendered social expectations also colour assessments of performance in the workplace. Women's family responsibilities and their tendency to focus expectations on their husbands' career development are major factors that render women workers less motivated than men to pursue promotion or join the party, a form of political capital and a means of networking critical for advancement and other benefits.

Another important factor kept women in subordinate positions. In Maoist egalitarianism, which reached a peak for the cohort entering the workplace during the Cultural Revolution, income differentials, including those based on skill, were relatively small in China's low-income, high-welfare, lifetime urban employment system. In line with the slogan that all jobs were equally important to the revolution, gendered job assignments were not perceived as discriminatory toward women.

Urban women employees enjoyed pay, benefits and security of which their rural sisters could only dream. Urban women's substantial gains in the Mao era, often cited by the state as proof of Chinese women's liberation, were inherent in privileging the urban working class over the peasantry. The huge gap in wages and benefits for working women (and men) in urban and rural areas continues in the post-Mao era, even when rural reform has rapidly improved rural people's living standard. A nationwide survey conducted by the Women's Federation in 1990 found that 82.6 per cent of urban women had pensions versus 5.6 per cent of rural women; 71 per cent of urban women had medical coverage versus 8 per cent of rural women; 79.9 per cent of urban women had paid sick leave versus 9.2 per cent of rural women; and 85.3 per cent of urban women had paid maternity leave versus 12.1 per cent of rural women.

The reform of the labour system in the 1980s has reduced, but hardly eliminated, the advantages enjoyed by urban workers. The state no longer guarantees urban employment (see chapter 3). Indeed, urban employment is no longer an exclusive privilege for urban dwellers. But throughout the 1980s, with rapid expansion of urban employment, workers with urban residence permits maintained their advantages in a two-tier employment structure that disadvantaged rural workers. Under pressure to reduce losses in the 1990s, however, state enterprises have laid off employees or turned to cheaper rural labour. With job creation slowed to a virtual halt, the influx of rural labour has reduced wages in many urban unskilled and service jobs to levels unacceptable to urban workers. Rural labour has thus undermined job prospects for urban workers. While the urban working-class experience in general involves prestige and security dwindling from levels enjoyed in the Mao era, the losses suffered by women workers have been greatest.

Moving from job assignment by government to a job market in which different ownership forms coexist and compete, freedom of mobility joins freedom of discrimination, and opportunities blend with insecurity. New employment patterns have broad social ramifications entailing realignment of social classes and gender position. This profoundly affects urban dwellers' relationships to the state and reshapes their identities. This is a gendered process in which urban men and women of diverse social positions engage in contestation at multiple levels.

Gendered layoffs: women workers bear the brunt of reform

Throughout the 1980s, China's high growth economy created millions of jobs annually, with women as well as men sharing in expanded and diversified employment opportunities. Since the 1980s, however, many women workers in the state sector have found themselves in the category of 'surplus labour'. Disproportionate numbers of women were among those laid off or forced to retire prior to the legal retirement age (for cadres and professionals, 60 years of age for men, 55 for women; and for workers, 55 years of age for men, 50 for women). Gendered layoffs reached new magnitudes in the late 1990s, coinciding with structural changes in China's industry and economic slowdown. At the heart of the employment crisis is China's manufacturing sector, which accounts for almost one-third of urban employees, as many state and collectively owned enterprises, now labelled as a drain on state resources, confront painful choices of technological change, merger, closure or bankruptcy. Official statistics reveal that by the end of 1997 there were 11.51 million laid-off workers (of which 7.87 million were from state-owned enterprises) in China's cities, with 3.5 million more projected for 1998. A survey by the State Statistical Bureau of 15,600 households in seventy-one cities across the country reveals that women constitute 62.8 per cent of the laid-off workers, while they account for less than 39 per cent of the total urban workforce.[2] Statistics from the *China Year Book* (2001) show that the number of urban female employees dropped from 58.89 million in 1995 to 44.11 million in 2000. The heaviest loss was concentrated in manufacturing, where the number of female employees dropped from 24.82 million in 1995 to 14.25 million in 2000. The proportion of total urban female employment decreased from 38.6 per cent in 1995 to 38 per cent in 2000. In other words, women have been singled out as special targets of the massive layoffs in state-owned and collective enterprises, and as a result, the gender gap in employment is widening rapidly.

More than any other issue, gendered layoffs reveal the disproportionate burden borne by women as a consequence of the reform. Women's journals and newspapers have paid much attention to the issue by publicizing individual laid-off women's miseries. Many surveys show that although work units are supposed to pay monthly subsidies to laid off workers (from 150 to over 300 yuan), many laid-off workers receive little or nothing. In order to boost the morale of laid-off women, an editorial in *Women of China* presented a touching analogy.

> The whole society is like a woman in delivery who is enduring the pain of contractions … The piercing pain shaking you is only one step away from the birth of a new life … Sisters, hang on a little bit longer. You will find your own path in your future choice.[3]

The pain of contractions may be an apt analogy to the pain that laid-off women are experiencing, but few women suffering the pain of layoffs can expect a joyful new life at the end of 'contractions'. Many have been forced to endure suffering in the form of humiliation and poverty. Many women workers protested:

> Before it was said that we workers were the masters. How come now we are so casually thrown out the door? Why are our contributions to the state-run enterprises no longer mentioned? The current state of the enterprises

was not caused by women workers. Why should we be told to swallow the bitter fruit?[4]

Why has the weight of urban reform in the form of unemployment impinged so heavily, and disproportionately, on women workers? Since the majority of laid-off women are in their thirties and forties with a high-school education or lower, many studies emphasize these women's reproductive role, domestic role and low education level as key factors disadvantaging them in the labour market. But the gender disparity in layoffs suggests that something deeper is involved.

The discriminatory structure of the socialist workplace disprivileges women workers in a market economy. As noted previously, most women lack the bargaining power that skilled male labourers and technicians have both inside their factories and outside in the job market. A 1998 survey from Chongqing indicates that women comprised 65 per cent of all those laid off and that more than 80 per cent of these women held non-technical and service jobs.[5] When state-owned enterprises are being transformed from all-encompassing 'work units' to profit-seeking entities, auxiliary and service components are the first to be cast off. Structural readjustment is profoundly gendered in its implications, if not its goals. Disproportionate numbers of women have been driven out of state industry and into low-prestige, low-pay collective- or private-service-sector jobs with few benefits. In short, gendered training and job assignment in the socialist planned economy provided the foundations for widening gender disparities in the reform era.

Although none of the reform policies specifies or rationalizes policies addressing gender, the explicit prioritization of profitability and sheer disregard of gendered consequences are indicative of the state's withdrawal from its previously proclaimed, if weakly implemented, commitment to gender equality. Abandoning women workers who have long been disadvantaged by gendered practices at workplaces, the state is creating an urban underclass whose predicament is aggravated by widespread gender discrimination.

With the end of state commitment to women's equality, 'freedom' of gender discrimination has become rampant. Where gender stereotypes previously structured job assignments, they now provide the rationale for layoffs. Indeed, there is abundant evidence that in addition to factors such as women's predominance in expendable service positions, gendered stereotyping by overwhelmingly male managers is at the heart of women's disproportionate unemployment. Asked why so many more women than men were laid off, a factory manager replied without hesitation, 'If you lay off men, they will get drunk and make trouble. But if you lay off women, they will just go home and take it quietly by themselves.'[6] This remark may be taken as representative of the mindset of many in power who would put women workers in jeopardy in order to achieve profitability or stability. From the perspective of the state, layoffs which leave most families with one job intact produce a result that is far less explosive than if many families were without even one income earner. From job assignment to layoffs, gender is a critical dimension in labour management and development strategies. But how have women reacted to this transformed social landscape? What resources have women deployed for negotiation or contestation?

Women's employment: a contested site

Long before gendered layoffs became a critical issue, women's employment was hotly debated. Since the early 1980s, intellectuals have crossed swords over the Maoist equal employment policy, relations between women's employment and 'modernity', patterns of women's employment in the market economy, and the predicament of laid-off women workers.[7] These debates reveal not only conflicting social and economic interests, but also different assumptions concerning gender. In the process of discursive contestation, new demands have emerged to shape policy-making processes, including those affecting employment and gender.

In the early 1980s, reformers criticized Maoist gendered employment policies for impeding economic growth. Rather than critiquing the skewed gender structure in the workplace, these critics simply pointed to urban women's high employment rate as a relic of Maoist egalitarianism and a source of inefficiency in enterprises. 'Women return home' was openly advocated in official journals and newspapers as urban reform began to confront unemployment problems compounded by more than ten million 'returned youth' from the countryside. Thus, even before the government issued any reform policies that threatened women's interests, a serious challenge to equal employment loomed in public discourse.

New theories rationalized sending women home. Women's liberation, it was said, outpaced the low level of productivity in China. According to this theory, China's economic development was still at a low level that was incompatible with full employment of women. Because women's physical characteristics made them less adaptable to various job requirements, excessive employment of women reduced enterprise efficiency. The goal of socialism, reformers asserted, is to increase productivity. To contribute to this goal, women should return home. This 'outpacing theory' (*chaoqian lun*) openly blamed women for the low productivity of the socialist planned economy. At a time when urban women activists were beginning to question the myth that 'Chinese women are liberated' and express their discontent with a masculinist Maoist 'gender equality' that taxed women with a double burden, advocates of the 'outpacing theory' claimed that Chinese women were too liberated, or liberated too early.[8]

Many urban educated men seized on the discussion of women's employment to express their long-held aversion toward gender equality. As one charged, 'In the name of equality between men and women, the role of men was suppressed in exchange for a relative increase in women's status.' Another complained, 'The helping that women took from the socialist "big rice pot" exceeded the value of the quantity and quality of their work.'[9] Some simply abandoned gender equality openly and called unabashedly for Chinese women to sacrifice themselves for the sake of national development. Japanese women's domesticity was cited as an example for Chinese women to emulate. Chinese women should like-wise return home and sacrifice themselves for the nation.

The anti-gender equality sentiment expressed in the debate over employment was not an isolated case in the 1980s. Throughout the 1980s, urban China was engulfed by a rising discourse of femininity that aimed at combating Maoist perspectives of gender equality and widening gender differences. Beginning as a critique of the ultra-left line of the Cultural Revolution, the discourse of femi-ninity evolved rapidly from condemning such Cultural Revolution era practices as identical clothing (see Emily Honig's chapter in Brownell and Wasserstrom 2002) and job assignments to a demand for new norms for women. The emerging market economy was quick to produce commodities to enhance femi-ninity. Gender differentiation in dress, social roles, behaviour and occupations became hallmarks of the decade. The challenge to women's equal employment was shaped by, and contributed to, the discourse of femininity.

Feminist voices and strategies

Amidst the rising discourse of femininity in the 1980s, few women or men contested such problematic proposals as 'women should choose feminine jobs'. Fewer disputed new norms of feminine appearance and feminine demeanour that were associated with the image of modernity. But when it came to defining women's social roles, sharply opposing views were expressed, often along gender lines. The debate on women's employment and the attack on gender equality in the form of the proposal that 'women return home', alarmed women activists. The defence of women's equal employment rights became a priority of the Women's Federation as well as of academics engaged in research on women's issues.

The Women's Federation played the most prominent role in blocking the proposal that 'women return home' in the 1980s, drawing on Maoist gender ideology to counterattack. When the suggestion to send women home first appeared in an article in 1980, the Shanghai Women's Federation quickly rejected the proposal as a solution to mitigate Shanghai employment problems.[10] They counterattacked, using unambiguous language of Maoist gender ideology drawn from Engels:

> Women's employment must be linked with women's liberation. Economics is the foundation. Without participation in social production, women would have no economic status. This would in turn undermine the equality between men and women in politics, society and family.[11]

They condemned the proposal that women return home as retrogressive. The 'retrogression' argument was widely repeated and disseminated by Women's Federation representatives throughout the country and by the mainstream media. Women's conscious appeal to 'the Marxist line of women's liberation' in defending employment rights reveals the continuing power of Maoist gender ideology as a source of resistance.

In the reform era, when the party's priority of developing a market economy conflicted with policies upholding gender equality, how could Maoist gender ideology be sustained? To answer this intriguing question, we need to understand that the roots of this discursive power lie deep in China's modern history. From the early twentieth century, especially since the rise of May Fourth feminism in 1919, women's liberation has been linked with the modernity project in nationalist discourse (see Wang 1999). The Communist Party built its legitimacy in part on its self-proclaimed role as liberator of Chinese women. In other words, maintaining the image of the liberator of women has been a pillar in maintaining the legitimacy of party rule. Just as the party could not openly abandon Marxism, it was hardly free to abandon the powerful signifier of modernity and socialism – gender equality. Indeed, in the half-century history of the People's Republic, equality between men and women is one major constitutional principle that has remained unchanged through social turmoil, constitutional revision and economic reform. At the same time, while the party has loudly proclaimed equality, deeply entrenched patterns of gender inequality in social institutions and law have been neglected (see Margaret Woo's chapter in Goldman and Perry 2002). As one contemporary Chinese scholar observed, 'Constitutional "equality between men and women" seems to be an untouchable cultural taboo.'[12] Contemporary attempts explicitly to detach gender equality from the goal of modernization could be seen as illegitimate in this dominant discourse.

Moreover, as the institutional centrepiece of gender discourse, the Women's Federation has continued to serve as both spokesperson for and symbol of gender equality in the reform era. A new term, 'the Marxist theory of women', was created in this period to suggest detachment from a stigmatized political era and to confirm a strong affinity to the party's continued claim to uphold Marxism. Although this stance was awkward in a political era in which upholding Marxism was seen by the public as a project of die-hard conservatives, promotion of the Marxist theory of women served both to remind the party of its commitment to gender equality and to consolidate the power of the official women's organization. Using the Marxist theory of women as leverage, the Women's Federation, and other women in the state apparatus, skilfully negotiated with the party on behalf of women.

Women in and outside the state system have sought with some success to influence public policy, law and discourse in order to protect women's equal employment rights. A series of policies and laws have been issued countering gender discrimination in the reform era. These include forbidding setting enrolment or recruitment requirements higher for women than for men; stipulating the same retirement age (60) for both male and female senior-level professionals; and forbidding laying off women during pregnancy, labour or breastfeeding.[13] In 1992, the Law on the Protection of Rights and Interests of Women was passed, which reiterated women's comprehensive equal rights in all aspects of social, economic, political and domestic life. Again, the 1994 Labour Law specified women's equal employment rights. However, these gender equality laws and policies lack legal power and are difficult to enforce in a market economy in the absence of a sound legal system. Violations of gender equality laws or policies have often been reported in journals and newspapers run by the Women's Federation system and the All-China Federation of Trade Unions, but few perpetrators have been punished. Not only does the private sector evade the laws with impunity, even government branches sometimes ignore them. Finding ways to enforce gender equality laws, rather than pushing for their passage, is among the most challenging tasks confronting women cadres and activists inside and outside government.

One significant development in this respect is that Women's Federations at different locations are playing an increasingly prominent role in supporting individual women to use the legal system to fight against the violation of their equal rights. The Departments of Protecting Women's Rights at different levels of Women's Federations have helped set up legal services for women, and have been directly involved in lawsuits initiated by women. In an interview in 2002, the director of the Department of Protecting Women's Rights of the Shanghai Women's Federation proudly told me many cases in which the department had helped individual women to win lawsuits. Of these lawsuits, a few were related to labour issues and initiated by pregnant women who lost their jobs because of their pregnancy. 'Without the women's organization's help, individual women would have little power to win lawsuits', the director emphasized.[14] These legal success stories may easily be eclipsed by numerous cases of violating women's rights. However, the director's firm pro-women position calls our attention to the potential of the official women's organization as an institutional resource for disadvantaged women.

Unable to stem the tide of layoffs in the late 1990s, the Women's Federation and the Women Workers Department of the Trade Union have devoted much effort to retraining, referral and reemployment. Vocational training centres and job referral services were established by the two organizations at local levels. A report in 2002 by the Women Workers Department of the Shanghai Trade Union indicates that since 1995 the Shanghai Trade Union has helped 250,000 laid-off workers to find new jobs, of whom over 60 per cent are women.[15] Many surveys and reports on laid-off workers have been published by the two organizations to call public attention to the plight of laid-off women, to press for government action to guarantee women's employment rights, and to establish social security and unemployment benefits to buffer the impact of institutional and industrial transformations.

After the Fourth UN Conference on Women held in Beijing in 1995, activists and researchers on women's issues found both reinforced legitimacy and new analytical frameworks to fight for gender equity. Since the Chinese government sponsored the conference and signed the UN documents pledging gender equality, official women's organizations and women activists have sought to hold the government accountable. On 8 March 1996, *The China Women's News* reprinted Jiang Zemin's welcome speech at the Fourth UN Conference on Women. One sentence from Jiang's speech was selected as the title, 'Equality

Between Men and Women is the Fundamental State Policy in Promoting Social Development in Our Country'. Following this reprint, presented as a new official document from the top leadership, newspaper reporters interviewed officials around the country asking what concrete measures they had taken to implement the 'fundamental state policy'.[16] The Women's Federation also campaigned to popularize the *Platform for Action*. Feminist scholars in academia utilized the congenial atmosphere to circulate through the official media feminist issues and concepts. In all these discursive manoeuvres, the central strategy has been to consolidate the connection between gender equality and modernity. The principles in the feminist documents passed by the UN Conference are presented as standard practice in 'modern civilizations' that China must adopt in the process of modernization.

Preparing and hosting the UN Conference enabled frequent interaction and communication between Chinese women activists and global feminists. A direct consequence of all these activities is that the feminist concept 'gender' (*shehui xingbie*), a term unfamiliar just a few years ago, has been adopted by many Chinese feminists in their analyses of the contemporary situation. The new conceptual tool borrowed from global feminism helped Chinese feminists to break out of their previous dilemma. Pursuing gender justice in the framework of Maoist gender ideology had not only limited their analytical power, but also made them look 'conservative' in the social context of deconstructing Maoism. In the 1980s, with the discourse of femininity on the rise, few women opposed the suggestion of gender differentiation in occupations because it sounded 'progressive' in its attempt to reverse Maoist 'unnatural' gender sameness. In the late 1990s, women researchers began gender critiques of the fad to 'feminize' women and encouraged women to cross gender boundaries to compete for high-tech, managerial and entrepreneurial jobs. Using gender together with other newly learned concepts such as 'sustainable development' and 'human-centred development', Chinese feminists are calling for a development agenda that prioritizes social justice and gender equity.

Activists in and outside the Women's Federation and scholars from academia have organized many training sessions and workshops to promote gender consciousness. Many of these workshops aim at changing consciousness of decision makers and power holders in different administrative positions, and actively intervening in the process of reform. In recent years, a growing number of women scholars have been engaging in establishing women's studies curricula in higher education. Funded by international donors, programmes training faculty members to create new courses and teaching material have been offered nationwide by feminist scholars. The official Guideline of Chinese Women's Development issued in 2001 also includes establishing women's studies programmes as a goal in the next decade. We may expect to see women's studies programmes being set up as feminist institutional bases in the near future. Never openly confrontational to the state, but ever ready to stretch boundaries in their own innovative ways, Chinese feminists have become a significant social force in China's transformation. In contrast with many other

critical voices in contemporary China, this feminist voice has gained some legitimacy in the dominant political discourse. This allows many feminists
legitimately to participate in the institutional changes of the reform era.

A further case to illustrate this point is the passage of reproductive security
policy in many cities. Since the early 1980s, feminists in and outside the state
system have been using Western feminist theory on the value of women's reproductive work to argue for public compensation. Efforts to establish public policies
to acknowledge the value of reproduction began in the early 1980s by Women's
Federations in some small cities, and the first Guideline of Chinese Women's
Development aimed at setting up reproductive security policy in all the cities was
issued by the end of 2000. In 2001, the Shanghai Municipal government, a late-
comer but the largest urban administrative unit that has a public policy for
women's reproductive work, issued a 'Method for Reproductive Security in
Shanghai City and Towns'. According to the method, 0.8 per cent is deducted
from the social security fund of each enterprise to set up a Reproductive Security
Fund (RSF). The RSF is managed by the municipal government. Women whose
work units pay for social security, and who abide by the birth control policy, can
apply for the fund. The fund covers women's maternity leave (three months' pay
for normal birth, six weeks' pay for miscarriage between three to seven months'
pregnancy, and one month's pay for miscarriage under three months' pregnancy), and covers medical expenses up to 2,500 yuan for normal birth, 400
yuan for miscarriage between three to seven months' pregnancy, and 200 yuan
for miscarriage under three months' pregnancy. The Method states clearly that
its goal is to promote women's employment. There are no statistics to show to
what extent this policy has improved women's chances of getting a job. But
certainly reproductive costs can no longer be an excuse for depriving women of
their job opportunities.[17]

As illustrated in this section, women activists within and outside the state
system have devoted much attention and energy to negotiation with the state.
However, the rapidly growing market economy has rendered the state impotent
in many realms and has generated its own discursive space. Rampant discriminatory practices in the job market and commercially popularized sexism are
powerful forces competing with the discourse of gender equality. This new social
environment has prepared fertile soil for the growth of feminism in China, as
well as presented serious obstacles to women activists.

Women's employment and 'modernity'

Despite the decline in the percentage of women's gainful employment, two
decades of economic reform involving privatization, commodification and
expansion of the service sector have created a large number and wide range of
jobs in cities as well as in dynamic rural regions. Many new occupations emerged
with a distinctive gender label and an image of 'modernity'. The new job market
is even more highly gendered than its predecessor, with women channelled
primarily to the service sector and secretarial jobs while men are recruited for

technical and managerial positions. However, gender dynamics intersecting with other social forces have led to certain unexpected consequences.

Changes in employment in the reform era are not limited to industrial restructuring. They reflect the rise of new industries and trades, and diversification of ownership forms. While state enterprise workers face mounting insecurity, numerous others have long been immersed in the volatile and risky private sector. According to 1998 statistics from the State Industry and Commerce Bureau, 18.35 million registered private enterprise owners are female, constituting 40.16 per cent of the total. Clearly many women have opted to become their own bosses.

The Women's Federation has appealed to the Women Entrepreneurs Association (*Nüqiyejia lianyihui*) for assistance for laid-off women workers from state enterprises. The Women's Federation proposed a slogan to span different forms of ownership, 'Hand in hand, sisters walk together on the road of career building'. The Women Entrepreneurs Association responded by calling on entrepreneurs 'actively [to] share the worries of the state'. It called on its members to absorb laid-off workers or help retrain them. Enterprises were also encouraged 'actively [to] participate in state enterprise reform, through purchase, merger, and lease to help state enterprises out of their predicament'.[18] The proposal could be interpreted as a discursive manoeuvre by women entrepreneurs to enhance their social status.

The confidence expressed by women entrepreneurs in this proposal is unmistakable. They are in a position to help the state, rather than to be dominated by the state. A close look at some of their achievements may clarify the source of their confidence. Zhai Meiqing, 34, vice-president of the Women Entrepreneurs Association, is the chief executive officer (CEO) of the multi-billion-yuan Xiangjiang Gold Seahorse Conglomerate in Guangdong province. Its 100-plus enterprises with over 10,000 employees include furniture, real estate and finance. Zhai has been credited with donating 60 million yuan to public welfare, helping 9,000 laid-off workers with subsidies and re-employing over 1,000 laid-off workers. Liu Yufen, 46, CEO of the East Xingtai Conglomerate in Hebei, has twenty-six enterprises with 230 million yuan in assets. She hired 740 laid-off workers and donated 860,000 yuan to build a school for orphans. These entrepreneurs are hailed as models by the Women's Federation and the government for both their business success and their social contributions.[19]

In contrast with women entrepreneurs who have risen in status through their business acumen and public profile, another group of women has achieved upward mobility drawing on human capital, specifically their youth and beauty. Replacing the 'iron rice bowl' of job security in urban China in the 1990s is the craze of creating the 'rice bowl of youth' (*qingchunfan*). Everywhere attractive young women have been sought to represent the shining image of 'modernity'. Booming service, commercial and entertainment industries post numerous age-, gender- and, often, height-specific advertisements seeking women under the age of 25 and above 165 centimetres in height. Stylish, elegant, or sexy, young 'Misses' (*xiaojie*) are displayed in remodelled or newly built 'modern' hotels, restaurants, department stores, travel services, night clubs, dance halls and so on. As older state industries lay off women workers over 35, these 'modern' young Misses, many with no particular education or technical skills, are entering the rising industries (mostly in the private sector, some with foreign investment) where their youth and beauty provide a ticket to incomes several times higher than those of their older sisters. Rather than clinging to a stable job, competitive young women in the fast lane often 'fire' their bosses in search of rapid upward mobility with their time-limited human capital.

In a sophisticated study of the 'rice bowl of youth' phenomenon, Zhang Zhen delves deeply into its social psychology and cultural meaning. 'The aura of their youth and beauty, coupled with a trained mellow voice which air-pumps the value of any plain object, magically touches the product and turns it into a commodity.' Zhang points out that:

> The vivacious image of young female eaters of the 'rice bowl of youth' has served in the fast-moving transition to a market economy as a novel energetic labor force, a model of social mobility, and above all, consumption as endorsed by the current official ideology, which intentionally promotes a form of 'democracy of consumption.'[20]

But there is more beneath the dazzling urban scene accentuated with commodified feminine beauty. Seeing the issue as 'a product or, in fact, a symptomatic form, of an urban mass culture that is imbued with sexual and commodity desires', Zhang finds 'an underlying structural anxiety of historical consciousness in which feminine youth and ephemeral beauty are paradoxically refashioned as a "timeless" object of male desire and as a rhetorical trope in modernist discourse'.[21]

The creation of the 'rice bowl of youth' is a 'joint venture' of consumerism and sexism that commodifies and objectifies women. Its contradictory aspects should not, however, be overlooked. Many a Miss Public Relations, Miss Shopping-guide and Miss Travel-guide is far from being a passively constructed 'decorative' object for the fulfilment of her bosses' utility needs and their male clients' sexual fantasies. Rather, many are active players in the melodrama of 'modernity', who consciously maximize their 'profits' by a range of strategies, including frequent job changes to advance their position, and investing in various adult education programmes to acquire new qualifications and skills. Seizing the 'rice bowl of youth', many young women catapult themselves into lasting careers. The inherent 'modern' values in this position, such as assertiveness and competitiveness, have been expressed prominently in young Misses' pursuit of career development in a competitive job market. This gendered employment pattern with its inherent contradictions, in short, provides opportunities for young women's social and economic advancement, even as it blocks employment access of older laid-off women workers, and reinforces gender stereotypes.

At one end of the 'rice bowl of youth', and far from the lowest paid, is the controversial occupation *sanpeinü* – literally, 'tri-service escorting girls'. These escorts, many working without a boss, accompany their clients in drinking, dancing and singing, and may provide other services that fall in the murky area that attracts both male clients and public security personnel. A report from Jinan alleges that 70 per cent of the arrested prostitutes in that city were *sanpeinü*. But while prostitution, though widespread, remains illegal in China, escorting has increasingly become a legitimate occupation. In recent years, some local governments have begun to levy income taxes on these 'temporary service personnel in the entertainment industry'. The trade has become a target of local revenue bureaux because of its high income and its large size. It is estimated that a *sanpeinü* in booming Shenyang may earn at least 4,000 yuan a month, and that 80 per cent of the 20,000 'temporary service personnel' in the city are female. Most *sanpeinü* are migrants, either from other cities or rural areas, as few would like their families to know the nature of their high-paid jobs.

Unlike other glittering Misses who have become symbols of modernity, *sanpeinü*, though sometimes indistinguishable from other Misses, are for many the symbol of moral degeneration. Public moral condemnation has mixed messages. Many accuse young women of being 'decadent and hedonistic'. Others are indignant at male clients' decadence and corruption. The prosperous entertainment industry, including escort services, is partly sustained by public funds, as many male clients are cadres who can easily get their entertainment expenses reimbursed by their work units. By matching wealthy or powerful male customers with young women 'temporary service personnel' – migrants of few means – escorting presents the starkest image of gender disparity in Chinese society. Many young women in this borderline trade earn a high income that they could never make in other occupations. Success stories in the popular literature tell of young women who launched private businesses after a few years of work in the trade. Cautionary tales, however, emphasize violence and abuse encountered by *sanpeinü*. Because of the ambiguous nature of the trade, few *sanpainü* seek protection from the state. Rather, evading state interference and taxation is as much a part of their business as skilful handling of their male clients. 'Resistance' may be a common experience in their daily life, but it involves very different strategies from those adopted by feminist activists.

In metropolises where foreign investment has underwritten acres of new high-rise buildings, another new social group is emerging along with the changed urban landscape. Young college-educated women have found clerical and managerial positions in foreign and joint-venture companies. Many from inland cities have secured jobs in foreign companies by migrating to the Special Economic Zone in the south. 'Miss Office' or 'White Collar Beauty' (*bailing liren*), terms associated with this group of professional women, share an affinity with the term 'rice bowl of youth' by accentuating their subjects' femininity. However, distinct from the 'rice bowl of youth', these terms connote a much higher status which is typically bought by a college degree and, more importantly, a high salary, often in a foreign company or joint venture. Most began with a clerical job, considered appealingly 'feminine' and suitable for young women. By the late 1990s, many of these educated young women had moved up to management, which is an 'unfeminine' sphere in popular discourse. A report in 1998 found that almost half of the personnel departments in foreign enterprises in Shanghai were run by women, and women constituted 63 per cent of the employees sent to foreign companies in Shanghai by the Shanghai Foreign Service Company. Of about 7,000 women employees, over 2,000 were at the senior managerial level in these foreign companies. One-third of the representatives, the top position for Chinese in foreign companies in Shanghai, were women. Within a decade the number of women in this position has increased dramatically from a few to over a hundred.[22]

White collar and managerial positions in foreign companies combined with occupations associated with the 'rice bowl of youth' have given rise to the emergence of an urban young female group with high income earnings. While most studies (by sampling married couples' income) show that the development of market economy raises living standards generally, as well as enlarging gender disparity in income in many cities, some researchers in Shanghai have found that the income of unmarried young women exceeds that of unmarried young men. Reportedly, a major reason for the reversed gender disparity in earning, besides the 'rice bowl of youth', is that more young women than men are white collar workers in foreign companies and joint ventures.[23] Although the reliability of this finding needs to be tested with more systematic and larger-scale research, it shows that the job market not only practices gender, but also age, discrimination. It thus calls our attention to other variables that affect women's employment opportunity.

The young urban professional women in foreign companies are a new elite group that has emerged in the reform era and is concentrated in a few large cities with mostly foreign investments. Ironically, certain gender norms unexpectedly work in favour of women. If we look for factors that contribute to the high percentage of women in foreign companies at a time when even the Chinese government discriminates against female college graduates, gender difference in specialities appears significant. The first requirement for working in foreign companies is a good command of a foreign language, particularly English. Foreign-language departments in universities have historically been among the few with more female than male students because foreign-language mastery has long been portrayed as an innate female strength. When both male and female foreign-language graduates enter the job market, more women than men seek 'feminine' clerical jobs in the private sector, jobs portrayed as glamorous, feminine and modern. The gender term 'White Collar Beauty' shapes young women's career choices. In the late 1990s, the term acquired new connotations of ability, high income and high consumption.

My interviews with young urban professional couples in Shanghai in the late 1990s revealed a common pattern in which the wife works in a foreign company and the husband in a government or academic job with less income but (until recently) higher prestige and lifetime security. A young male English professor whose wife works in a foreign company commented, 'It seems that women are more daring in entering the private sector. Or rather, they have fewer qualms.' If women with a college degree had fewer qualms about entering the private sector in the 1990s, they confront a more competitive job market in the twenty-first century. Shanghai is now attracting job applicants from all over the world. Many foreign companies are turning to applicants from their own countries who have studied Chinese. Chinese women professionals in foreign companies or joint ventures have begun to complain about a glass ceiling with both a racial and a gender tint.

The rise of young urban women in the 1990s is also a demographic phenomenon. The state has strictly controlled births since the late 1970s. However, many one-child families emerged in urban areas, especially metropolises, well before state enforcement of the one-child policy. With reduced family size and improved living standards, and with education heavily subsidized (until the 1990s), even two-child urban families often invested in the education of both sons and daughters. The percentage of women students in colleges has steadily increased from 24.2 in 1978 to 36.4 in 1996, and the number of women college students more than quadrupled in these years from 207,000 to 1.1 million.[24] Women students have also gained recognition for academic excellence. In recent years, the top candidates in the national college entrance exams have consistently been women. The phenomenon has caused a panic in a culture anxious to sustain the male sense of superiority. The media swiftly popularized an authoritative interpretation: female candidates' high performance is the product of the poor design of examination questions which fit in well with rigid female minds but fail to test the capacity of flexible male minds. So far no one has suggested that different socialization of a whole generation of only daughters may be the major reason for the rise of confident, assertive and competitive young women.

The arrival in the 1990s of a cohort of well-educated and strong-willed only daughters on the job market will give rise to new dynamics in gender discourse. Having been brought up with high expectations from their families, many female college graduates will experience frustrations once they try to locate a job that meets their standards. Top female graduates find that male classmates with inferior academic records are recruited for good jobs that are denied them. Gender discrimination is not subtle. Many advertisements of desirable jobs state clearly that only men need apply. A young professional woman related her sad experience: 'In college, I was always admired for my outstanding academic performance. I never experienced gender discrimination. But once I graduated, I was denied the job I sought simply because I was a woman.' Her superb academic record counted for naught. The painful experience strengthened her determination to fight for gender equality. Facing persistent and pervasive gender discrimination in employment, many young women begin to adopt an individual strategy, that is acquiring higher degrees to compete with men. Women applicants to graduate programmes have increased rapidly in recent years. How successful this strategy will be remains to be seen, though the ramifications of a large proportion of female higher degree holders in Chinese society will be significant. At least, the huge gap between young women graduates' expectations and social reality can be expected to give rise to growing feminist activism at a time when a feminist discourse is gaining increasing influence. This cohort of women may pose serious challenges to gender boundaries in employment and society.

Women and unemployment

In the 1990s, the magnitude of laid-off workers threatened social stability, prompting action by central and local governments. (See chapter 3.) In 1994, the Labour Department began the pilot 'Re-employment Project' in thirty selected cities and in 1995 it was taken nationwide. The 'Re-employment Project' mobilizes public resources to provide reemployment for laid-off workers with government support and facilities. At best, it is a stopgap measure that mitigates laid-off workers' deep resentment at being abandoned by the state. It does not change the reality that the state has discarded them after many years of service.

The state policy stipulates that laid-off workers retain a relationship with their work units unless they officially terminate it and take a job with another enterprise. Laid-off workers retain entitlement to medical coverage, pensions and housing unless their work units go bankrupt. Even in rare cases in which laid-off workers succeed in finding a higher-paid job, most experience downward mobility. Leaving state enterprises is still seen by many state workers as involving a loss of status. Re-employment, especially for older workers, involves reconstituting one's identity from a previously positively defined state worker to various ambiguous, uncertain or demeaning categories.

Re-employment options for laid-off women are generally limited and nearly all point to sharp downward mobility both in status and income.[25] In many big cities, laid-off state-sector women workers are being encouraged to work in community services. Shanghai, with large numbers of laid-off women textile workers, has pioneered this structural readjustment by providing low-paid neighbourhood jobs caring for the old, the young and the sick as domestic helpers, or encouraging private or collective-service businesses such as laundries, tailors, hairdressers, cleaning and food services. None of these jobs provides benefits or prestige comparable to that enjoyed by a state worker. Aware of the downward mobility in this re-employment, official women's organizations sought both to provide training and to upgrade the social status of domestic and service workers. The Shanghai Women's Federation and the Women Workers Committee in the Trade Union Federation have run training sessions in 'home economics' for laid-off women and issued certificates to graduates. They changed the name 'Maids Referral' to 'Home Economics Referral'. Equipping laid-off women with a certificate in home economics, official women's organizations tried to replace the scornful image of 'maids', long associated with rural women, with a respectable niche in urban 'modernity'. They also worked to secure state recognition of this 'new' occupation. In 1995, the Labour Department classified 'family service personnel' in the category of technical jobs. Although the state classification does not entail better pay and benefits in the private sector, some women have since officially obtained this credential as a technical worker in the hope that it may help them secure a job. Shanghai's experience has been propagandized nationally as a model.

This gendered re-employment solution promoted by official women's organizations has the negative implication of reinforcing a gender division of labour. However, the propaganda portraying home and community as the arena for women can also be interpreted as women's strategy to meet immediate practical needs, even survival needs, at a time of rampant unemployment. The majority of laid-off women are middle aged with few resources to compete in the new job market. Laid-off women with scant special skills and a family to support have limited choices. Community service provides many new and useful jobs that require minimal training.

Some widely circulated success stories herald achievements of laid-off women in creating new businesses in community services. A famous 'Mama Zhuang Vegetable Service' was created by a laid-off woman in Shanghai named Zhuang Weihong. She and her husband were both laid off in 1992, when she was in her mid-twenties. In 1996 she got an idea from a re-employment training school. Renting a room with borrowed money, she began a vegetable cleaning service with her family members. They shopped for vegetables, picked, cleaned and prepared them for cooking, then delivered them to clients' homes with a 10 per cent surcharge for processing. In eight months, their clients grew from their six neighbours to 300 families. Zhuang hired 140 employees (120 were laid-off workers) and installed a computer to track customer orders. Asked why a young woman would name the business 'Mama Zhuang' (which suggests an image of a woman at least over 50), Zhuang explained: 'Mama is the warmest person. Mama will never cheat you. Using this name means we will succeed with high quality of service and credentials.'[26] Here woman's role as mother is deployed skilfully and positively by a woman innovator tapping a market that had not previously existed while building on maternal images of service. The strength of 'female' roles and 'female' qualities in the service sector is a theme in many of the success stories about laid-off women's re-employment.

The mounting crisis of unemployment and various 'upgrading' efforts, including propaganda, seem, at least in Shanghai, to have changed the attitudes towards such re-employment of many laid-off women from resistance to acceptance. In 1997 alone, Shanghai trained 3,000 laid-off women in a 'family services' training programme. More than 90 per cent of them found jobs. By 2002, the term 'Shanghai maid' (*Shanghai baomu*) had entered public discourse. However, we should note that the feasibility of sending laid-off women workers to family service is also a function of the economic boom and the rise of a wealthy class in Shanghai. In other industrial cities plagued by the failure of state owned enterprises, laid-off women would not have many job openings in domestic service even if they were willing to take whatever is available.

The increasing supply of laid-off women as domestic helpers is shown clearly in the drastic change in the nature of 'Maids Referral' services run by neighbourhood residents' committees. Until recently, they referred rural women seeking a job in Shanghai to families seeking domestic help. But since early 1998, jobs for rural women are drying up as many of these jobs are being taken by laid-off women. A State Statistical Bureau survey in 1998 showed that in seven large cities, over 90 per cent of urban residents preferred local to rural women for domestic and community service. The employers do not have to provide room and board for local employees. They share the same dialect and have 'more harmonious interaction'. Moreover, middle-aged laid-off women come with rich experience in housework and childcare, and 'modern' training in home economics. Urban employment restructuring, therefore, directly affects employment opportunities of migrating rural young women.

'Peasant workers' in the city

Two decades of rapid industrialization and urbanization have resulted in a growing 'rural population' in urban areas. Millions of people with rural residence certificates who now work in cities are called 'peasants' or 'peasant workers' (*nongmingong*) and are subject to discriminatory state and business practices. Policies such as the requirement that families lacking urban residence permits have to pay for their children's education in public schools not only deter rural migrant workers from settling in cities, they also delineate second-class citizenship. The urban/rural divide follows migrants who settle in the urban areas, as chapter 6 in this volume shows.

Most rural workers have low-paid, low-skilled, low-status and frequently insecure jobs, many of which are, or at least were until recently, scorned by urban dwellers. Domestic service has long been the entry job for rural women coming to large cities. A 1988 study estimated that 40,000 rural women sought domestic work that year in Beijing alone. 'Little maid' (*xiao baomu*) became a trade associated with rural young women. Many rural women since the 1980s have also secured employment as waitresses and shop assistants. Some state and collective enterprises recruit rural women as contract workers to lower labour and benefit costs.

The majority of rural women work in the private sector where state labour protection and worker benefits are difficult to enforce. Long hours, low pay and hazardous work environments are common phenomena among private enterprises that employ young rural women. Ching Kwan Lee's study of management strategies in private industry in the booming southern city of Shenzhen, near Hong Kong, finds a pattern of gendered localistic authority that disguises class domination. Young rural women are introduced to factories by male relatives or acquaintances from their home towns. These male locals exercise paternalistic authority over women on the shop floors. As Lee points out, 'Localism and genderism not only organize the labor market and channel labor from all over China to Shenzhen, they are also incorporated into the factory to facilitate and legitimate managerial control.'[27]

Gender is also embodied in young women's praxis as migrant workers. In a study based on 109 letters between young women migrant workers and their families, Tan Shen notes that while many send money home to help their poor families, some young women specifically shoulder the responsibility of paying for their brothers' college education. Sometimes two sisters labour to support one brother. Tan tells a tragic story in which two Sichuan sisters worked extremely hard in a Shenzhen sweatshop for several years to put their older brother through college. Four months after his graduation, both sisters died in a fire caused by managerial violation of labour safety. Tan's study forcefully demonstrates that in such instances migration is not taken as a route for personal advance.[28]

The widely circulated new term 'maiden workers' (*dagong mei*) for young rural women workers connotes the lowest rank of the urban workforce. Being young and female in the context of Chinese traditional generation and gender hierarchy automatically places them in a subordinate position to senior males. Being 'rural', seen in urbanites' eyes in the context of urban craving for 'modernity', not only means that they lack a permanent urban residence, but also suggests their distance from the 'modern'. The social and cultural meanings of this element in their identity are new to many women who had never left their villages. The worst pain experienced by many is bearing the stigma of being 'rural'. At a meeting in Beijing organized by a women's journal, *Rural Women Knowing All*, to hear about migrant workers' experiences, some 'maiden workers' from Xiamen were invited to speak about their success stories. These 'maiden workers' had recently obtained Xiamen residence because of their excellent performance at work and also because the Women's Federation in Xiamen struggled hard to obtain a quota of twenty urban residences for 'maiden workers'. Contrary to the expectations of the meeting organizers, however, what they heard was a litany of sweat and tears. One after another these model 'maiden workers' recounted painful experiences of prejudice and discrimination based on their rural identity. In work, love, marriage, children's education, housing and all other aspects of their lives, they encountered adversity – constantly reminding them that they are the 'other' to urbanites.[29]

Despite discrimination, rural women workers generally regard working in cities as an opportunity. Many young unmarried women use migration as an effective means to resist undesirable arranged marriages. Freedom of mobility, in fact, also enables them to quit and change jobs frequently, the most common form of their resistance to abusive bosses and intolerable working conditions. In order to leave options open for a better job, Tan Shen finds that many young women workers opt not to sign a contract. Many young women from families that do not rely on their income come to big cities with a dream of personal development. Metropolises provide them with educational facilities and opportunities, and many have enrolled in secondary vocational schools or even colleges. As one 20-year-old woman from Shaanxi said, 'The best thing in Beijing is that there are so many schools. You can learn whatever you want to. You can also go to evening college. Our hometown does not have these. There is nothing there.' Arriving in Beijing with 800 yuan in savings from her family, she paid 400 yuan to enrol in a hairdressing school. Her dream is to open the first hairdressing salon in her home town after five years of work and study in Beijing.[30] The freedom to migrate has enabled this young woman to make a career choice likely to lead to upward mobility.

The deepening crisis of urban unemployment threatens such opportunities for rural as well as urban women. Since the mid-1990s, many big cities have restricted employment of rural workers. Many of the most desirable jobs always required urban residence. But now even many humble jobs are reserved for laid-off workers. For example, a 1996 Shanghai government document stipulated that any enterprise with 10 per cent laid-off workers cannot hire outside labour freely, and commercial and service enterprises must hire 50 per cent laid-off workers in their new recruitment of non-technical workers. Although some intellectuals criticize state regulations for blocking the free flow of labour and restricting competition, the state can be expected to adopt measures to limit the influx of rural migrants in order to maintain urban social stability.

Conclusion

A widely circulated cliché in contemporary Chinese society is that 'reform presents women with both opportunities and challenges'. Sounding inclusive, it glosses over tremendous differences among women, ranging from those who have ample opportunities and resources to those who face monumental challenges. This chapter highlights processes of differentiation and diversification among women in the reform era. 'Women' as a social category has to be complicated and concretized if it is to provide explanatory utility. Age, education, geographic location, residence (rural or urban), enterprise ownership form, type of industry, skills, capital and network resources are all important variables that intersect with gender in differentiating women in the turbulent social and economic transformations that are reshaping China.

Differentiation and diversification among women, however, do not reduce the salience of gender. Rather, the reform era has brought accelerated gender discrimination and gender conflicts. Conflicting gender interests are prominently expressed over women's employment. Gendered layoffs expose women's disadvantaged and subordinate status. Masculinist usage of young women as a trope for 'modernity', both in jobs and in advertisements, demonstrates not only men's dominance in economic enterprises but also their dominance in reproducing gendered cultural norms. Yet we have also noted the ability of women to seize diverse opportunities to rise in important sectors of the economy. In all of these contradictory sites 'women' retains its usefulness as a collective category. In contesting and manipulating gendered categories, we see multiple strategies of resistance ranging from those pursued by the Women's Federation and women's labour organizations to the individual strategies pursued by women of older and younger generations and different levels of education.

As a collective category, women occupy a unique discursive space in contemporary China. In the very period when the state has delegitimized 'class' as an analytical category while pursuing accelerated privatization and other strategies that contribute to class polarization, women activists and cadres have successfully made gender a legitimate category in public discourse. The fact that they have been able openly to demand and redefine gender equality testifies in part to the effectiveness of their resistance strategies. Resistance does not always require a confrontational or overtly oppositional stance, especially when the lines between conflicting interests are shifting and unstable. Standing between the state and the market, women have utilized the political and legal power of the state to combat socioeconomic practices detrimental to their interests, many of them practices that originate in state reform policies. Holding the state accountable for its rhetorical commitment to gender equality, consolidating the connection between gender equality and modernity, quietly expanding functions and influences of official and non-official women's organizations, women activists in and outside government strive to 'implement the fundamental state policy of gender equality'. Women's constant negotiations and manoeuvres are daily resistant practices behind the scene, taking place at various levels and diverse sites, contesting and stretching the boundaries without alarming the authorities, and reshaping the processes of reform with their strong sense of entitlement to hold up 'half the sky'.

The diverse implications of contemporary Chinese women's activities are far-reaching. Efforts by feminists to establish women's studies in higher education have the potential to develop a critical intellectual force in the male-dominated academy that has been paralysed by political pressures and the corrupt lures of both state power and the market. Critical scrutiny of gender inequality can be extended to other forms of hierarchy and injustice, thus making women's studies an avant-garde of intellectual resistance to political, economic and cultural domination. Outside the academy, women activists have engaged in political, social and cultural realms. While quietly exploring innovative ways to redefine women's relationship with the state, women's organizations may act more like interest groups that function with legitimacy in a political culture they have helped to shape. Busy consolidating the territory and legitimacy they have worked hard to gain, however, women activists in and outside the government have little incentive to jeopardize their own accomplishments by venturing into areas marked as politically taboo by the state. Even as feminist academics investigate how gender intersects with class, ethnicity, sexuality and other forms of domination, many women activists may consciously disassociate themselves from resistance strategies that clash directly with state power.

The transformation of official women's organizations has been a major factor in the changing landscape of Chinese women's activism. Challenged by women activists outside the government, consciously exploring their new identities, official women's organizations have assumed more functions as interest groups on behalf of women. Located in the state bureaucratic system, official women's organizations have limited but valuable accesses to state power and resources, which has enabled them to attract women activists and scholars to collaborate with them on many research projects. In the past two decades, official women's organizations have formed wide-ranging connections with women activists and scholars from all over the country. The newly formed (1999) Chinese Women's Research Association (*zhongguo funü yanjiuhui*) by the All-China Women's Federation, which includes on its executive committee scholars and senior administrators of universities nationwide, demonstrates the intention to form a wide coalition and to extend their influence to women of all walks of life. This is the only 'mass organization' that has paid state employees working from the top All-China Women's Federation down to each urban neighbourhood and rural town. The changing function of the Women's Federation is profoundly signifi-cant not only because a powerful women's interest group is emerging, but also because this interest group is still located in the state system. The contradictory functions and murky boundaries involved in the transformation of Fulian defy any existing theory on democratization.[31] What is clear is that because of the transformation of this largest women's organization, women have formed a different relationship with the state than other disadvantaged groups in China. Women have been able to negotiate with the state both inside and outside the state, though they can only negotiate as *women*. Chinese women have certainly come a long way from the days when class was the only legitimate social and political category.

Notes

1 Ping Ping, 'Guoyou qiye guanlide xingbie celue yu nügong de qiye yilai' (Gender Strategy in the Management of State Enterprises and Women Workers' Dependency on Enterprises), *Shehuixue yanjiu* (Sociology Studies), 1 (1998), pp. 55–62.

2 *Zhongguo funübao* (China Women's News), 12 June 1998. There are various statistics in regard to the total number of laid-off workers cited in journals and newspapers in China. But the percentage of women laid-off workers has been consistently over 60 per cent.

3 *Zhongfuo funü* (Women of China), 5 (1998), p. 7.

4 Fang Hong, 'Xiagang shiye nüzhigong de kunjing' (Laid-off and Unemployed Women in Predicament), *Zhongguo gongren* (Workers of China), 3 (1998), pp. 10–11.

5 *Zhongguo funübao* (China Women's News), 3 June 1998.

6 Many surveys, however, reveal situations contrary to this stereotype. They report 'extreme actions' taken by some laid-off women workers. 'Extreme actions' include destroying public property and factory equipment, and stealing enterprise property.

7 Liu Bohong, 'Guanyu nüxing jiuye wenti zongshu' (A Summary of Issues in Women's Employment), *Zhongguo funü lilun yanjiu shinian* (Women's Theoretical Research in China: 1981–1990) (Beijing: Zhongguo funü chubanshe, 199), p. 325.

8 The CCP myth of liberated Chinese women was most heartily embraced by these male advocates even when many cases of violence and discrimination against women were widely reported. For a discussion of Chinese women's critique of Maoist gender equality, see Wang Zheng, 'Research on Women in Contemporary China', in Gail Hershatter, Emily Honig, Lisa Rofel and Susan Mann (eds), *Guide to Women's Studies in China* (Berkeley: Center for East Asian Studies, 1998).

9 Chang Leren, 'Youhua peizhi he zuijia fenpei' (Optimization and Best Distribution), *Zhongguo funübao* (China Women's News), 11 July 1988.

10 The Shanghai-based journal *Shehui* (Society) set up a column for this debate. See issues 1–4 1984.

11 Zang Jian, 'Funü zhiye jiaose chongtu de lishi huigu' (A Historical Review of Conflicts over Women's Career Roles), in *Beijing daxue funü wenti dierjie guoji yantaohui*

lunwen ji (A Collection of Papers from the Second International Conference on Women's Issues by Beijing University) (Beijing: Women's Studies Centre, Beijing University, 1993), p. 114.

12 Li Dun, 'Guanyu xingbie: pingdeng, fazhan yu heping' (About Gender: Equality, Development and Peace), *Dongfang* (Orient), 4 (1995), pp. 17–21.

13 The adjustment of female senior professionals' retirement age is made in five documents issued by the Ministry of Personnel in 1990, entitled 'Guanyu gaoji zhuanjia tui (li)xiu youguan wenti de tongzhi' (On Issues Related to Senior Experts' Retirement).

14 The citation is from my interview with Cai Lanzhen on18 July 2002.

15 Zhang Lu, 'Weile zhenzheng yiyishang de pingdeng' (For Equality in a Real Sense), *Laodong bao* (Labor News), 17 June 2002.

16 The discursive manoeuvre can be discerned from *The China Women's News* in April 1996, when many interviews of high officials were printed. Behind the scenes, women cadres of Fulian have been talking about this accomplishment with pride and amusement.

17 In her talks to women cadres in Hunan while visiting there in August 2002, Peng Peiyun, the chair of the All-China Women's Federation, emphasized the importance of reproductive security policy to women's employment, and also indicated that the development of this policy was not even across the country. Apparently, the goal of setting up the policy in the cities nationwide by the end of 2000 has not yet been achieved. Peng's talks were publicized at the website of Hunan Women's Federation.

18 *Zhongguo funübao* (China Women's News), 1 June 1998.

19 *Jingji ribao* (Economy Daily), 8 July 1998.

20 Zhang Zhen, 'Mediating Time: The "Rice Bowl of Youth" in *Fin-de-siècle* Urban China', *Public Culture*, 12, 1 (Winter 2000), pp. 93–113.

21 *Ibid.*

22 Liu Jian, 'Bailing liren de ganga' (The Dilemma of the White Collar Beauties), *Zhongguo funübao* (China Women's News), 25 June 1998.

23 Hou Xiaofu, 'Shilun xiandaihua yu Zhongguo funü jingji diwei de bianqian' (On Modernity and the Transformation of Chinese Women's Economic Status), *Dongyue Luncong* (East Mountains Journal), Jinan (March 1997), pp. 49–53.

24 *China Statistical Yearbook* (Beijing: China Statistical Information and Consultancy Service Centre, 1997), p. 647.

25 Some surveys reveal, however, that in Special Economic Zones in Guangdong laid-off women have more opportunities to go into the private sector using family resources. They are less inclined to insist on a job in state-owned enterprises, as a longer history of privatization has reduced the prestige of such jobs and increased the desirability of working in the private sector.

26 *Zhongwai nüxing yanjiu xinxi* (Information on Women's Studies in China and Abroad) (April 1997), p. 6. This is an internal journal published by the China Women's College in Beijing.

27 Ching Kwan Lee, *Gender and the South China Miracle* (Berkeley: University of California Press, 1998), p. 135.

28 Tan Shen, 'Dagongmei neibu huati' (Internal Topics of Maiden Workers), *Shehuixue yanjiu* (Sociological Studies), 6 (1998), pp. 63–73.

29 Li Tao, 'Chongpo chengxiang zhijie' (Breaking the Boundary of Urban and Rural), *Nongjianü baishitong* (Rural Women Knowing All), 12 (1997), pp. 14–16.

30 *Zhongguo funübao* (China Women's News), 28 May 1996.

31 Two books published in 2002 (see Judd and Wesoky) examine the contemporary Chinese women's movement from different points of focus. Ellen R. Judd (2002) critiques Fulian's role in promoting rural women's participation in the market economy, while Sharon Wesoky (2002) suggests a symbiotic relationship between the

non-governmental women's organizations and the state. Neither pays adequate attention to the transformation of Fulian at different levels.

Suggested reading

Chinese Sociology and Anthropology, 29, 3 (Spring 1997) and (Spring 1998).

Susan Brownell and Jeffrey N. Wasserstrom (eds), *Chinese Femininities and Chinese Masculinities: A Reader* (Berkeley: University of California Press, 1998).

Merle Goldman and Elizabeth J. Perry (eds), *Changing Meanings of Citizenship in Modern China* (Cambridge, MA: Harvard University Press, 2002).

Gail Hershatter, Emily Honig, Lisa Rofel and Susan Mann (eds), *Guide to Women's Studies in China* (Berkeley: Center for East Asian Studies, 1998).

Emily Honig and Gail Hershatter, *Personal Voices: Chinese Women in the 1980s* (Stanford: Stanford University Press, 1988).

Tamara Jacka, *Women's Work in Rural China: Change and Opportunity in an Era of Reform* (Cambridge: Cambridge University Press, 1997).

Ellen R. Judd, *The Chinese Women's Movement Between State and Market* (Stanford: Stanford University Press, 2002)

Ching Kwan Lee, *Gender and the South China Miracle. Two Worlds of Factory Women* (Berkeley: University of California Press, 1998a).

——, 'The Labor Politics of Market Socialism', *Modern China*, 24, 1 (January 1998b).

Ping-Chun Hsiung, Maria Jaschok, Cecilia Milwertz (eds), *Chinese Women Organizing* (London: Berg, 2002)

Lisa Rofel, *Other Modernities: Gendered Yearnings in China after Socialism* (Berkeley: University of California Press, 1998).

Wang Zheng, *Women in the Chinese Enlightenment: Oral and Textual Histories* (Berkeley: University of California Press, 1999).

Sharon Wesoky, *Chinese Feminism Faces Globalization* (New York and London: Routledge, 2002).

8 Domination, resistance and accommodation in China's one-child campaign

Tyrene White

In 1949, as the Chinese Communist Party was poised to establish its new regime, China's population numbered nearly half a billion, a staggering figure that many believed would prove an unbearable drag on attempts to develop. It was two decades, however, before China began to make population control a state priority. In the early 1970s, birth limits were set at two or three children. By 1979, however, China's post-Mao leaders had become so concerned about the likely impact of population growth on their new development plans that they took the extreme step of launching a one-child-per-couple policy – the most extensive, aggressive and effective attempt ever made to subject child-bearing to direct state control and regulation.

Looking back, China's leaders and demographers argue that the two-decade delay after 1949 was a fateful mistake. By the time the state began to encourage fertility control, a huge new generation of young people had already been born and were approaching their child-bearing years. As a result, even with declining fertility levels (i.e., the average number of children born to a woman during her reproductive years), demographic momentum meant continued growth of total population size. In 1979, China's population hit the one billion mark, and by the century's end it had risen to nearly 1.27 billion despite aggressive enforcement of birth limits. The goal for 2010 is to contain population size at 1.4 billion, on the way to a predicted peak of about 1.6 billion somewhere around the middle of the twenty-first century. This expansion will continue to occur even though China's demographic transition from a high-fertility, high-mortality society to a low-fertility, low-mortality society is largely complete.[1]

No demographic transition can be explained by a single variable, and China's transition is no exception. The sudden and rapid decline in fertility which occurred after 1970 in both urban and rural areas suggests the strong influence of population control policies enacted at that time. Other factors were also at work, however. By the 1970s, improvements in levels of socioeconomic development, education and communication networks meant that more people were aware of the option of birth control. Moreover, infant mortality had declined, while the cost of child-rearing had gone up. In urban areas, living space was cramped and scarce, and the 'iron rice bowl' of state employment meant secure, if modest, retirement pensions and health benefits. For the first time, young urban couples were released from the prospect that a secure old age depended on producing male children. A growing proportion of women worked full-time, only to pull a second shift of housework, cooking and child care at home. Although data on this period remain very scarce, there can be little doubt that these changes, particularly in urban areas, began to affect individual calculations about how many children were desirable. As demographers have seen elsewhere, once the idea of smaller family size begins to take hold, it can spread very rapidly within a particular cultural and social context.

With 80 per cent of the population living in the countryside, however, it took more than socioeconomic development and attitudinal changes to bring fertility rates down so rapidly. After 1970, six forms of state intervention were used: 1) free access to contraceptives, abortion and sterilization; 2) promulgation and enforcement of late marriage guidelines, raising the average age at marriage from 22 in 1970 to 25 by 1979 (Banister 1987); 3) use of material incentives and penalties to encourage compliance with birth limits; 4) a mass campaign to promote smaller families and enforce birth limits; 5) the creation of a large family planning bureaucracy to implement birth control guidelines; and 6) the inclusion of population targets in the national economic planning process.

Making population targets a part of the central planning process in 1971 marked the culmination of a long internal political battle over how to view China's large and growing population. In 1949, Mao Zedong viewed population as an asset. Like Marx, he believed that the exploitative class systems of feudalism and imperialism, not overpopulation, were the causes of poverty, disease and unemployment. By the mid-1950s, however, the shock of China's first census results, combined with lagging levels of agricultural output, led other Chinese Communist Party (CCP) leaders (including Zhou Enlai and Deng Xiaoping) to urge the abandonment of China's pro-natalist policy and the promotion of voluntary birth control. Just as a public birth control campaign got under way, however, the programme was swept aside by the Great Leap Forward (1958–60), a radical campaign that promised prosperity but produced instead a devastating famine and an estimated fifteen to thirty million excess deaths.

Paradoxically, it was during this period of mobilization prior to the Great Leap that the core idea behind China's approach to population control took shape. Though Mao remained suspicious of the arguments for birth control and had a direct hand in pre-empting the fledgling campaign, it was he who suggested in 1957 that China should attempt to plan reproduction in the same way it aspired to plan material production (White 1994). At the time, birth planning (*jihua shengyu*), i.e. the attempt to regulate population growth so as to keep it in balance with levels of economic production and growth, was only a goal to be reached at some more advanced stage of socialist development. As China's population continued to grow, however, key leaders such as Premier Zhou Enlai came to believe that birth planning could not be postponed. In the early 1960s, after the disastrous Great Leap Forward, Liu Shaoqi and Zhou Enlai attempted to revive the birth control campaign, and in 1965 Zhou proposed the first national population control target – reducing the annual rate of population growth to 1 per cent by the end of the century. This second campaign, like the first, was aborted by the Cultural Revolution, but Zhou revived it with new urgency in the early 1970s, creating an extensive family planning bureaucracy to oversee implementation, providing free access to contraceptives, abortions and sterilizations, and introducing specific population targets into the annual and five-year economic plans. Socialist planning thus came to embrace human reproduction in much the same way that it embraced agricultural and industrial production. Local officials who were responsible for meeting grain and steel production quotas now began to receive quotas for babies.

In the early and mid-1970s, the campaign focus was 'later, longer, fewer', i.e. promoting later marriage, longer spacing between births (three to five years), and fewer births (a two-child ideal and a three-child limit). By mid-decade, the child-bearing norm began to tighten; the new slogan was 'one is not too few, two is enough, three is too many'. Even that policy was judged too lenient by the new Deng Xiaoping regime which came to power in 1978. In 1979, China's top demographers and scientists announced that if China were to achieve its economic goals by the year 2000, population had to be contained within 1.2 billion. To achieve that goal, the official birth limit was lowered to one child per couple (with some exceptions for special circumstances), and all child-bearing age couples, urban and rural, had to receive official birth permits from the state in order to give birth legally. Provinces drafted regulations offering economic incentives to encourage policy compliance and imposing stiff sanctions on policy violators.

In China's cities and towns, growing acceptance of the small-family norm, reinforced by the late-marriage policy and tight administrative control in workplaces and neighbourhoods, had brought the urban total fertility rate down from 3.3 in 1970 to about 1.5 by 1978, a remarkably low level for a developing country. With a large cohort of women about to enter their peak child-bearing years, however, the state deemed even this low level inadequate. To further suppress fertility and prevent more second births, state monitoring intensified in workplaces and neighbourhoods. Monthly gynaecological examinations for child-bearing age women, plus a system of marriage and birth permits provided by the work unit, ensured that anyone attempting to have a second child was caught in a tight surveillance net. Those who escaped the net faced severe penalties, including fines, loss of employment and perhaps even their coveted urban household registration.

If changing child-bearing preferences and state control worked together to induce compliance with the one-child policy in urban China, rural China posed a far more difficult challenge. Like rural populations in other places and times, life in the countryside encouraged higher levels of fertility. Agricultural work requires household labour, and unlike their urban counterparts, even very young rural children can be put to work in the service of family income. Moreover, while urban retirees could depend on a state pension for retirement support, rural families had no such welfare structure. Children were the only guarantee of old-age support, and the most destitute villagers were inevitably those who were alone and childless. Only a son could assure a couple that they would be spared such a fate. Daughters usually married out of the village, transportation links were often poor, and upon marriage a daughter's first obligation transferred to her husband's family. Even the most devoted daughter could not be counted on to provide either income or assistance. In urban areas, in contrast, nearby residency and convenient transportation allowed married daughters to be valuable assets to ageing parents.

In addition to these practical considerations, the traditional emphasis on bearing sons to carry on the ancestral line remained deeply entrenched in the countryside. As a result, although rural fertility levels were cut in half between 1971 and 1979 (declining from approximately six to three), much of rural China remained hostile to a two- or one-child limit, including the rural cadres who would have to enforce the policy.[2] When the rural reforms implemented after 1978 began to relax the state's administrative grip on the peasantry just as the one-child policy was launched, therefore, it set the stage for a prolonged and intense struggle over the control of child-bearing.

A substantial scholarship on China's birth planning programme has examined the process of policy evolution and implementation at the national and local levels, and the means by which the state has succeeded in meeting its fertility goals and overriding resistance (Greenhalgh, 1990, 1994; Greenhalgh, Zhu and Li, 1994; Li, 1995; White, 1990, 1991, 1994). Societal resistance, though pervasive and widespread, especially in the countryside, has received less systematic attention.[3] Still less attention has been given to the question of whether, and to what degree, societal resistance has shaped or influenced the evolution of policy.

Given the scale of grassroots resistance to China's population policy, this lacuna in the literature is odd. After all, rarely has there been a case in which the evidence of resistance is so manifest and easy to measure. Though violations of the birth plan are by no means the only form of resistance, the tens of millions of such births that have occurred over the past two decades are a living testament to just how widespread and sustained the resistance has been. By the mid-1990s, the state had nevertheless succeeded in pushing the total fertility rate down to the remarkably low level of 1.8. The case of birth planning in China thus confronts us with the apparent paradox of what appears to be a strong state *and* a strong society.

How can that be? Early models of state–society relations generally assumed that the distribution of power between state and society was zero sum; as the state gained in power, society lost, and vice versa. More recent formulations question this model, however, and emphasize instead the vague and overlapping boundaries between 'state' and 'society', and the internal conflicts that can weaken state authority.[4] In this case, tight fertility control applied to all child-bearing age couples, whether they were state officials in Beijing or poor peasants in a remote village. Party members, family planning officials and rural cadres were asked to set an example by taking the lead in embracing the one-child limit. Those past their child-bearing years were pressed to see that their children and relatives complied. The significance of this fact – that no one was left untouched by the policy – cannot be overstated. It meant that the state was at least as vulnerable to resistance from within its own ranks as it was to societal resistance. The struggle over child-bearing, then, has been more than a struggle by the state to dominate society's child-bearing. It has also been a prolonged struggle to contain and eliminate resistance at every level of state administration, particularly at the local level.

The limitations of a zero-sum, state-society model of power relations are also revealed by the pattern of resistance that has emerged. Not only has resistance ranged from open confrontation to more disguised forms of evasion, it has also taken the form of accommodation, with profound consequences. Caught between state demands to limit child-bearing to only one or two children, and cultural and social pressures to have a son, many couples have attempted to resolve the conflict by resorting to female infanticide, or more commonly, female infant abandonment and sex-selective abortion. Do strategies of accommodation such as these, poignant and tragic as they are, constitute a form of resistance? I will argue here that they do, that it is precisely such responses that bring us to the heart and extremity of the struggle. Though strategies of accommodation reveal the extent of state domination and power, they also reveal vividly the extent to which the right to engineer fertility remains contested political terrain.

Patterns of resistance

However successful the state's birth control policy may appear to be in the aggregate, success has been achieved in the face of widespread resistance that has taken three basic forms: confrontation, evasion and accommodation. Changing socioeconomic and political conditions in the quarter century since 1979 have created opportunities for new elaborations on existing approaches and techniques, but the three basic strategies have persisted.

Before exploring each pattern of resistance, it is important to recognize that the one-child limit has been strictly and consistently enforced only in China's cities and towns, and only among ethnically Han Chinese. In the countryside, where the policy was met with hostility and widespread resistance, intense pressures to comply in the early years of the campaign gave way in 1984 to a 'one-son or two-child policy'. In other words, those whose first child was a daughter were allowed to try again – for a son – after a four- or five-year wait between pregnancies. In the mid- and late-1980s, some provinces and regions relaxed the policy even more, allowing peasants to have two children, if properly spaced. Officially, these two-child provisions were usually limited to peasants living in poor, remote or mountainous areas, but the relaxation sometimes spilled over into more prosperous areas. For rural China, then, the one-child limit has been more of a goal than a reality, but this should not imply a lesser degree of state surveillance and regulation. Villagers, like city residents, had to have official permission to have a child, even their first, and many were forced to abort pregnancies that were 'extra-plan', or unauthorized, simply because they occurred too soon (i.e., before official permission to give birth had been received). Local officials had strict birth planning targets to meet, and harsh campaigns periodically brought new crackdowns on policy offenders. The reproductive process was blanketed by state regulation and control, forcing villagers to make hard choices between the claims of the state and their own child-bearing preferences.

Strategies of confrontation

The determination of the state after 1979 to prevent any 'unplanned' birth, but especially third or higher parity births (*duotai*), by pressing hard for abortion, sterilization or IUD insertion, confronted millions of households with the reality of state intrusion into the heart of family life. Families who saw child-bearing as their best long-term guarantee of strength, dignity and stature in the village (and their best defence against weakness, bullying and abuse by powerful families or clans), understood that birth limits profoundly threatened their future security. Little wonder, then, that attempts to round up pregnant women could provoke direct and often violent confrontation.

Violence and the threat of violence against birth planning officials escalated in the early 1980s, as pressures to limit childbirth increased dramatically. Irate husbands attacked birth planning officials who pressured their wives or relatives to have abortions. Others were assaulted out of anger over botched abortions, sterilizations or IUD insertions, and the failure of local officials to provide sufficient follow-up health care. The attacks were often directed against female cadres or doctors, who were frequently on the front-lines of implementation. In some cases, they were attacked and killed by bereaved family members. In one case, reported in *Hubei Daily* in April 1982, a doctor who reported a woman with a third pregnancy to the commune authorities was attacked by the woman's husband after he was fired from his job. Eight family members joined him in the beating, one of whom was the brigade party secretary.[5]

In the second half of the 1980s and the 1990s, as reform loosened the chokehold of rural cadres on peasant livelihood, rural conflict soared. In Suining county of Jiangsu province, for example, there were a reported 381 'incidents of revenge' between January 1987 and May 1988, one-third of them directly related to birth planning.[6] All of these incidents involved physical attacks on cadres by angry peasants, but there were also numerous attacks on property. Since cadres sometimes seized or destroyed peasant property in order to deter or punish birth planning offences, peasants retaliated in kind, destroying crops on cadres' land, killing their chickens or pigs, and damaging their homes and furnishings. These attacks became so frequent that one Henan county passed a law explicitly banning such acts of retaliation.[7] Such measures were hardly effective, however. As the number of strikes, protests and demonstrations by peasants escalated in the 1990s, ruthless enforcement of the birth control policy ranked high on the list of villagers' complaints. When local officials were pressed by their superiors to tighten implementation and crack down on 'unplanned' births, villagers sometimes struck back by attacking township authorities *en masse*.[8]

By the late 1990s, this type of direct confrontation was overlaid by a second type of confrontational resistance. As villagers became more aware of state laws protecting their rights, and more emboldened to act in defence of those rights, they began to appeal to the law and the courts to protect them from abusive enforcement practices, or to punish those who had perpetrated them (see chapters 4 and 5). This type of resistance, which Kevin O'Brien has termed 'rightful' or rights-based resistance, became an option for villagers in the late 1990s as a direct by-product of state efforts to ease cadre–peasant tensions over tax collection and to improve rural governance.[9] Unable to force peasants to pay the fees and taxes that padded local coffers, cadres frequently resorted to the same kinds of methods that they used to enforce birth limits or punish offenders, seizing or destroying property and using intimidation and violence to gain compliance. As tensions mounted in the 1990s, the state repeatedly issued regulations that outlawed such methods of tax collection and held cadres accountable for violations. This provoked a similar ban by the State Family Planning Commission.

Meanwhile, the implementation of village-level elections in many areas in the 1990s led to growing consciousness among villagers of laws regarding village self-management, and some began to seize on the law and their legal rights as morally grounded means of redress against abusive officials.[10] This led some to seek legal redress against family planning enforcers, even in cases where the complainants were in violation of the policy. In one widely reported case, for example, a couple in suburban Harbin with three boys submitted under pressure to a late-term abortion, only to have the baby survive the procedure. Hospital and family planning officials kept the baby from the parents and reportedly ordered that the baby be left to die. Irate nurses and staff members refused to cooperate, however, and journalists reported the story. The parents were eventually reunited with the baby and a group of hospital staff filed an official police report. The hospital director was investigated on charges of intent to murder and removed from her post, but vowed to sue two journalists for 'untruthful reporting'. Although media attention was critical in exposing this case, what is noteworthy is the extent to which the rural couple applied the rights-based logic of the journalists. Offered hush money by local officials to cover the excess-birth fine and to move away from the village, the baby's father refused, saying 'we didn't trust them. We trust the journalists who told us the hospital violated our rights. If necessary, we'll go to court to be witnesses … we want justice.'[11] This rights-based defence will not protect those who wilfully violate the policy and refuse to comply with birth limits, but it may give pause to officials who enforce those limits or punish violators after the fact.

Strategies of evasion

The most common strategy employed in resisting the one-child policy was that of avoiding the detection of an 'extra-plan' pregnancy until the child has been born. Within this category, there were two further subtypes – the independent evader, and the dependent one. Independent evaders attempted to circumvent the birth limits without relying on the silent acquiescence or active assistance of local officials. Dependent evaders, in contrast, relied on cadre collusion in order to succeed.

The simplest approach to avoiding detection was the attempt to time a pregnancy for the autumn. As women bundled themselves in several layers of clothing, or padded jackets, to protect against the winter cold, they were able to hide the pregnancy for several months. Assuming no-one in the village betrayed their secret, they might succeed in avoiding detection until very late in the term or even until childbirth. Keeping the secret was difficult, however, and women's leaders counted on village gossip to help with their work. Pregnant women usually told at least one person about the pregnancy, often their mother-in-law. Once she knew, however, she could not resist telling a friend. As the word began to spread, the women's leader discovered the pregnancy very quickly. How much pressure was brought to bear upon the pregnant woman, however, depended on how quickly the women's leader reported the problem to higher-level authorities. A small delay could mean the difference between getting caught or getting away, i.e. leaving the village until it was safe to return, or until the baby was born.

In other cases, women evaded detection by leaving the village altogether until after the child was born. In the 1970s and early 1980s, this strategy generally depended on having a relative or acquaintance outside one's village or town (ideally in a large county town or a city) with whom one could board for the duration of the pregnancy. By the mid-1980s, however, relaxations on travel and population movement led to the emergence of a burgeoning army of temporary migrants that came to be known as the 'floating population'. Estimated at 100 million by the late 1990s, this migrant population defied even the best efforts of birth control officials to keep track of their child-bearing. Those who were determined to have another child, therefore, often joined the ranks of the migrants and became part of the 'guerilla birth corps'. The sound logic behind this strategy was spelled out by a Yunnan villager:

> Since I am from another locality and my residence is not registered here, nobody here will interfere with how many children I am going to have … [When I go home] I will simply say that I have picked up and adopted an abandoned child here. Even if the residence of the child is not allowed to be registered, it will not matter because the child will then already be two or three years old. Somehow he will be recognized as my son.[12]

Notice that for this plan to work, the story does not have to be believed. It is sufficient that village cadres will eventually accept the presence of this additional child, since they will not be held directly responsible for births outside their own village or township. This villager was also counting on the failure of state efforts to crack down on migrant offenders, efforts that grew more aggressive over the course of the 1990s, particularly in major cities. Central and local regulations were promulgated requiring birth permits as a condition of employment, and obliging employers to monitor migrants to be sure they were in compliance with family planning rules. Though periodic campaigns and crackdowns could have temporary effect, migrants were by definition mobile, and able to seek refuge in flight or from fellow migrants.

A third strategy was to bribe medical personnel to remove intrauterine devices, normally implanted after the first birth. Some doctors began to provide such services on a regular basis, while others faked the quarterly or monthly gynaecological examination results, allowing 'illegally' pregnant women to go undetected. Still others could be paid to tie only one fallopian tube during sterilization, or to provide false certification of having undergone sterilization (normally required after a second birth). In 1994, a former vice-president of a county hospital in Hunan was executed for taking nearly 200,000 yuan in bribes between 1986 and 1991 in exchange for falsifying 448 sterilization certificates.[13] Medical personnel were also implicated in phoney certification schemes. A couple was permitted to have a second child if the first was born with physical or mental disabilities that would prevent the child from being a full-time labourer as an adult. This gave doctors another opportunity for fraud, since they could certify a healthy child as a defective one.[14] Similarly, official birth permits were controlled and issued by birth planning cadres. Peasants who could not find other ways around the birth limit sometimes discovered that local officials were willing to sell the permits. In 1988, officials in some localities were charging 1,600 yuan for a permit.[15]

Another evasive strategy was to marry or cohabit unofficially, without receiving an official marriage permit or registering with the civil affairs bureau. This was a strategy frequently employed by rural families anxious to arrange marriages before their children had reached the legal ages of 20 for women and 22 for men. Since family planning officials concentrated their efforts on married women, those who were secretly married and sheltered by their families were often able to become pregnant and give birth without detection. Nationwide, 6.1 million people had married under the legal age by 1988. That figure translated into about 15 per cent of all marriages, and those marriages contributed about 10 per cent of all births annually.[16] By 1994, under-age marriages numbered 1.6 million annually, representing 16 per cent of all marriages.[17] This large number of illegal marriages could not occur without the help and collusion of local officials. Villagers paid hefty bribes to acquire false certifications of age from village cadres or marriage certificates from township officials.

One of the most pervasive strategies used by cadres to cope with enforcement pressures from above and resistance from below was the cover-up – engaging in statistical fraud to hide excess births. Women known to have given birth, but who did so outside the village, were left off local birth rolls. Even those who gave birth in the village were sometimes omitted, and the omission was covered up by refusing to issue a household registration for the infant. Sending township officials into a village did not necessarily increase the likelihood of full disclosure. One former township cadre complained that village leaders did everything they could to obstruct the work of such teams. Village leaders warned peasants about the impending visit by the team, giving offending couples a chance to flee or hide. Village leaders sometimes hid themselves so as to avoid a confrontation. Other cadres welcomed the team and accompanied it into the village, but their 'assistance' was actually resistance, their actions designed to minimize the team's access to accurate data and move it quickly out of the village. These tactics were so effective that one former township official concluded that it was impossible for outsiders to know the true state of affairs in a village.[18]

Township officials did not always want to know the truth, however, since exceeding the local birth quota would have a negative impact on the leaders' work evaluations, salaries and bonuses. Family planning officials learned quickly that the local party secretary did not want to receive reports that would reflect badly on the township or threaten its privileged standing as an 'advanced unit'. And zealous cadres who sought out fraud learned that they would not be rewarded for 'rectifying' a fraudulent statistical report. As one former township cadre put it, an honest report would only destroy one's own career, since higher-level political leaders would be embarrassed and angered by the revelation.[19] He admitted that he had knowingly submitted false reports rather than face the censure that would come with accurate accounting.

Another form of cadre–peasant collusion was to levy fines for unplanned births rather than expend extra effort to prevent them. If grassroots women's leaders were unsuccessful in persuading a couple to abort an unauthorized pregnancy, village leaders sometimes did little or nothing to reinforce their efforts. This strategy allowed cadres to fulfil the letter of the law without provoking major confrontations with villagers. They could make it clear that heavy penalties would be levied after the child was born, but if that threat was not a sufficient deterrent, no further efforts were made. Leaders in some localities went further, implementing fines that were lower than those authorized by county or township regulations.

Cadres were particularly lenient with 'single-daughter households' (*dunühu*), or couples with two or more daughters but no sons. Sympathetic to their plight, village cadres often made no effort at enforcement, even refusing to impose fines if they gave birth to another girl. If couples violated the policy and had a son, however, payment of fines was transformed into a near-ritual performance. Cadres sent to collect the fines were received happily, and couples paid the fine as a part of the celebration over the birth. As one brigade women's leader said: 'They [rural couples] want to have a son. What can we do?'[20]

The same pattern prevailed with respect to sterilization. Pressed to meet sterilization quotas for couples with two or more children, cadres made every effort to avoid couples who had no sons. Even during major mobilizations like that of 1983, cadres worked to shield couples with no sons from the campaign. Because of the extreme pressures to meet sterilization quotas, they were not always successful in this effort, but during less intense periods they had no difficulty bypassing them. In Xinyu City of Jiangxi province, for example, more than 82 per cent of *duotai* births in 1985 were to couples with two or more daughters, including those with six or seven daughters. These births occurred despite a major sterilization mobilization during 1983 and 1984, because cadres had been unwilling to impose permanent birth control measures on couples without a son. Rather than resent the exceptions, other couples, even those with sons who had been mobilized for sterilization, tended to be sympathetic with this discriminating use of power.[21] So severe was the problem of official collusion that provinces and localities drafted administrative regulations laying out punishments for various kinds of policy violations. In 1998, for example, Hainan province drafted provisions for punishing eight specific forms of collusion to violate the birth planning rules, including all of those discussed above, and other provinces followed suit. These local efforts were subsequently reinforced by similar provisions in the national Population and Family Planning Law, which took effect in September 2002.[22]

Strategies of accommodation

Situated between the confrontational (public) and evasive (hidden or disguised) forms of resistance was a third pattern of response. Those desperate to have a son sometimes resorted to female infanticide, female infant abandonment, or, as the technology became available, sex-selective abortion. In one sense, this pattern of accommodating state controls on child-bearing may seem to be the ultimate evidence of state domination, an indicator of defeat and subordination rather than resistance. As James Scott argues, however, material domination – in this case, control over the number of children one has – is only one form of state domination. Transformative states also seek ideological and status domination, or control over the realm of legitimate ideas and the distribution of status and prestige within society.[23] Despite the CCP's massive and prolonged effort to justify its claim to control child-bearing by emphasizing the public and social costs of child-rearing and insisting that population growth is an impediment to modernization, it has been unable to overcome the influence of patriarchal culture. This competing world view, which continues to hold sway across rural China, places family loyalty and filial obligation, not socialist ethics, at the centre of the child-bearing calculus. The duty to produce a son and male heir supersedes any duty to the motherland, a conviction reinforced by the realignment of status and power since 1979. In the new rural world of money, markets, corruption and clans, the weak can be bullied and preyed upon by the strong. Having a son can help a family avoid the miserable fate of being among the weak.

Ironically, and tragically, the state's own policy has helped further to inscribe and reproduce this traditional world view (Greenhalgh and Li, 1995; Anagnost, 1995). After the extreme and ill-advised sterilization campaign in 1983, and in the wake of growing evidence of female infanticide, the state responded by simply reversing itself on the crucial issue of the value of female offspring. In the early 1980s, the thrust of the education campaign had been on repudiating the feudal idea that males (traditionally called a 'big happiness') were superior to females (a 'little happiness'), and insisting on the equal value of a boy or girl. In 1984, however, it effectively conceded the issue by modifying rural policy to allow single-daughter couples to try again – for a boy. Though the state did not condone the cultural preference for males, it did concede the economic and social realities that made sons more valuable. With the abandonment of collective agriculture and welfare, and with men privileged in the process of distributing collective goods (e.g., land, contracts, equipment), the importance of a son for prosperity and security was only reinforced. Rather than challenge that reality and risk further rural unrest, the state chose to concede the issue. Single-daughter households were given special dispensation to have a second child – to try again for a son.

Although the intent of the 1984 policy change was merely to legitimize what was already the *de facto* rural policy in many areas, its effect was to split the state's ideological hegemony into two conflicting spheres – one sphere that applied to all urban residents, state cadres and administrative personnel, and another that applied to the peasantry. Rural women were thus left in the tragic situation of being caught in the crosshairs of two mutually exclusive modes of discourse. With no means of escaping this dual subjugation, many chose, or were forced by family members to choose, a strategy of accommodation that guaranteed the birth of a son. Those who could not achieve this result were vulnerable to a life-time of pity, social ridicule and self-blame.[24]

In the early 1980s, when collective life, limited cash income, and restrictions on travel severely constrained the options of rural families, some took the desperate course of female infanticide to preserve the chance to have a son. As the 1980s progressed, however, two alternative strategies of accommodation became very common. The first was infant abandonment, which increased in the late 1980s and 1990s in response to a tightening of the birth control policies (Johnson *et al.* 1998). Civil affairs officials, who have primary responsibility for the system of social welfare institutes that care for abandoned and orphaned children, offered no reliable estimates of the size of the problem by the 1990s, though some reports suggested that as many as 160,000 were abandoned annually, the vast majority of them female. As Kay Johnson has argued, however, this figure likely underestimates the size of the problem, since many abandoned girls may never enter state institutions such as those managed by the civil affairs bureaucracy (Johnson 1996; Johnson *et al.* 1998). Instead, birth parents often try to identify likely prospects for adopting the child, e.g. couples with a son but without a daughter.

Even more disturbing is the escalating incidence of sex-selective abortion and its impact on China's sex ratio. In 1979, China produced its first ultrasound B machine, designed for a variety of diagnostic purposes, including pregnancy monitoring. By 1982, mass production of ultrasound equipment had begun, and imports added to the number in use. Thirteen thousand ultrasound machines were in use in hospitals and clinics by 1987, or roughly six machines for each county. By the early 1990s, all county hospitals and clinics, and most township clinics and family planning stations had ultrasound equipment capable of fetal sex determination.[25] Henan Province, for example, spent four million yuan during the 1991–5 plan period to equip its 2300-plus township technical service centres with ultrasound scanners.[26] Private clinics also flourished, as technicians took advantage of an emergent market.

Despite attempts by the state to outlaw the use of ultrasound technology to determine the sex of a fetus, easy access to the technology, combined with the lure of lucrative bribes and consultation fees, made ultrasound use vastly popular. This was especially true in many county towns and rural townships, where prosperity and proximity facilitated ultrasound diagnosis, but where modest degrees of upward mobility had done nothing to undermine the cultural prejudice and practical logic that favoured male offspring. Young couples raised in a village but now employed in township factories and living in the township seat may have been far more willing than their peers a decade earlier to have only two children. If the first were a girl, however, it remained vital to many that the second be a boy (Chu 2001). They may have been modern in their preference for a small family in order to hold on to their new-found prosperity, but when it came to desiring a son, tradition and contemporary social realities conspired. Because township and village cadres tacitly agreed with them, they could count on them to look the other way when they made their pay-off to the medical technician. The cadres, after all, would much prefer to see couples resort to induced abortion of females to guarantee having a son, rather than have a second daughter and be tempted to try again, as many two-daughter households did. If the couple kept trying for a son, the local birth plan was threatened. If the couple used available technology to guarantee the birth of a son, the cadres' problem was solved.[27]

The impact of sex-selective abortion on China's sex ratio became increasingly clear in the 1990s. In 1982, the Chinese sex ratio at birth, 107.2 males for every 100 females, was already slightly in excess of the world norm of 105–106 males for every 100 females. Though this figure raised questions about female infanticide and 'missing girls', those questions were dismissed by Chinese spokesmen, who argued that the sex ratio was well within normal bounds and in keeping with China's own population history. Over the next two decades, however, the sex ratio at birth rose dramatically, to 111.2 in 1985, 113.8 in 1989, 116 in 1992 and 117.4 in 1995. It remained at this high level over the next five years, and was confirmed by data from the 2000 census. Some of this increase was evident in first births, but much more of it was reflected in second and higher-order births. In 1990, the figures for second and third or higher-order births were 121 and 127, respectively. By 2000, they had skyrocketed to 151.9 and 159.4.[28]

Some of this gap can be accounted for by the underreporting of female births. Underreporting is suggested both by surveys of rural areas that reveal 'hidden' births not reported in official statistical reports, and by the lessening of the sex ratio imbalance for school-age children. In the 1992 sample survey, the sex ratio for the age 0–4 cohort was a very skewed 113.9. For the age 5–9 cohort, however, the ratio dropped to 107.81. This decline is what would be expected if previously unreported females were registered for school and then placed on local population rolls. Such children might never have appeared in vital statistics on births and deaths, sparing local officials the embarrassment of exceeding their local birth targets. Once older, however, they may be registered as migrants or adoptees, and the degree of male bias in the sex ratio declines accordingly.

In the early 1990s, Chinese demographer Zeng Yi, along with several colleagues, argued that such underreporting accounted for anywhere from 43 to 75 per cent of the skew in the sex ratio at birth (Zeng *et al.* 1993). However, since incentives and pressures to undercount all unplanned births have been relatively constant over the past decade, underreporting alone cannot explain the steady rise in the sex ratio at birth. Moreover, the results of a 1995 sample survey revealed that urban areas were also experiencing skewed sex ratios. Beijing, for example, registered an overall sex ratio at birth of 122.6, and 148.8 for second and higher-parity births. This high sex ratio at birth placed Beijing on a par with such provinces as Jiangsu (125.1), Fujian (126.2), Jiangxi (129.1), Henan (128.0), Hubei (134.6), Guangdong (125.2) and Shaanxi (125.4). Tianjin also came in high, with an overall sex ratio at birth of 110.6 and a rate of 142.9 for second and higher-parity births. And while Shanghai's overall rate was within a normal range, the rate for second and higher-parity births was an exceptionally high 175.0 (Gao *et al.* 1997).

Although the one-child policy is no doubt a contributing factor in producing these alarming figures, they are consistent with trends elsewhere in East Asia where son preference remains strong. South Korea, Taiwan and India all registered increases in the male to female sex ratio as ultrasound technology became widely available (Park and Cho 1995; Das Gupta and Bhat 1997; Eberstadt 1998). Outside China, the problem is most severe in South Korea, where the sex ratio at birth in 1993 was 116. This figure, which is roughly equivalent to the Chinese case, demonstrates clearly that the problem is not limited to China, nor is it merely the result of the one-child policy. Rather, it is a cultural and structural problem, one that cannot be explained away (as the CCP has sought to do) as the product of rural backwardness.

Still, the Chinese case, which pits state control over child-bearing against deeply imbedded cultural prejudices and child-bearing preferences, remains unique. China's relentless emphasis over the past thirty years on sheer numbers of births – on targets, quotas and per capita accounting – combined with its neglect of women's issues and its gendered politics of reproduction, has opened up the space within which an accommodative style of resistance can grow. Just as new birth control technologies and surgical advances facilitated the state's move to engineer child-bearing, so too has technology become the medium through which couples struggle to engineer the sex composition of their offspring. They may accommodate the state's birth limitation policy, but they seek to do it on their own terms, rejecting in the process the state's claim of ideological hegemony.

Resistance and the prospects for policy change

The struggle for dominion over child-bearing in China has led to paradox, tragedy and irony. The paradox we are confronted with in China's experience of the one-child policy is the simultaneous existence of massive evidence demonstrating the state's capacity to engineer child-bearing, *and* massive evidence of resistance, including successful resistance. The tragedy of the policy is that it has forced a large portion of the population to choose between two types of hegemonic discourse – a socialist and developmental one that emphasizes duty to the collective society, and a patriarchal one that emphasizes duty to family and ancestors – both of which have been legitimated by the state, though the latter was intended to be subordinate to the former.

The sad irony of this case is that if major policy reforms are eventually enacted, they may be due as much to countless acts of accommodation as to more traditional acts of resistance. The ultrasound technology that allows couples to discover the sex of the fetus, combined with the prosperity that has led to its widespread distribution, has made it possible for those caught between the state's discourse linking modernization and prosperity to birth planning and a secondary, state-complicit, cultural discourse linking status and dignity to male offspring to attempt to accommodate both. The consequences, however, have been alarming enough to produce a type of 'voice' that is increasingly urgent in content, but corporate in structure and non-confrontational in tone.[29] The core constituencies behind this 'voice' are demographers, family planning officials and Women's Federation officials who are alarmed about the implications of current trends with sex ratios and rapid population ageing. The skewed sex ratios mean an impending shortage of wives for as many as thirty to fifty million men, which the Women's Federation rightly describes as an 'army of bachelors'. Since the marriage market places poor men at the greatest disadvantage in competing for a wife, this shortfall of brides could have explosive social consequences. And rapid fertility decline, coupled with increasing life expectancy, means that over the next several decades China's population will age almost as rapidly as the populations of Western Europe, North America and Japan. In these countries, which enjoy wealth and stable systems of welfare, anxieties about rapid population ageing are already monopolizing leadership attention. China will face similar levels of elderly dependence without either of those advantages, and with the disadvantage of a demographic structure in which a shrinking proportion of the population will have to support a very large population of both old and young.

Some of those who are stressing these negative side-effects of the one-child policy have advocated a modified and less coercive approach to population control since the early 1980s. As insiders within the system of population institutes, think-tanks and academic departments, they have had to be very cautious in how, and to what degree, they challenge the reigning orthodoxy (Greenhalgh 2001). By 1998, however, they had succeeded in getting the post-Deng leadership to launch an experiment in several counties implementing what was described as a genuinely voluntary family planning programme, one that stressed positive incentives to limit childbirth rather than mandatory control. This project, supported by the United Nations Fund for Population Activities (UNFPA) and subsequently expanded to thirty-two counties, is a hopeful sign that reform-minded insiders might be having an impact, and that China might finally be starting to shed its crude and mechanical approach to population control. Although residents in the project areas were limited to two children, a constraint that makes it impossible to describe the approach as truly voluntary, birth permits and quotas were eliminated, and couples were given more freedom of choice on when to give birth and what type of contraceptive to use.[30]

Progress remains slow, however, as reports of new local campaigns make clear. In 2001, for example, family planning officials in Guangdong's Huaiji county were given a target of 20,000 abortions or sterilizations by year's end, a campaign goal triggered by the 2000 census, which revealed their failure to meet local population control targets. After local complaints and media reports surfaced, local officials were ordered to stop the campaign and undergo re-education on how properly to implement the family planning policy. The impulse to rely on such strong-arm tactics will remain strong, however, so long as local officials are held accountable for achieving specific population targets in a limited period of time.[31]

Modest though the changes have been thus far, advocates of policy reform have been aided in recent years by conditions that were not present when the one-child policy was adopted in 1979. First, those born after 1978 and now entering their child-bearing years have grown up against the backdrop of rapid development, increased prosperity and the one-child policy. Their hopes and dreams often centre on leaving the village, or alternatively, on leaving agricultural work. The images brought to them from the vastly expanded communications networks and opportunities for travel reinforce the idea of the urban, one-child family as the symbol of modernity. As a result, many of today's young rural couples may simply take for granted the message that had to be drilled into the generation before them – that their lives will be more prosperous and secure if they choose to have fewer children (Chu 2001). If this proves to be true, if the new world they have grown up in has instilled a genuine desire for a one- or two-child family, then moving towards a more voluntary approach to birth planning without risking a significant fertility rebound should be feasible.

A second and more important factor that has encouraged advocates of reform is a shift in the global discourse on population growth and women's rights. When China began to implement its one-child policy in 1979, it was widely lauded by those in the international family planning community who subscribed to the dominant theory that population growth was a primary, if not *the* primary, impediment to economic growth. For them, China's acceptance of this position, and its determination to place tight curbs on population growth, was so important that the very disturbing methods by which China sought to achieve its aims were often overlooked. By the mid-1990s, another school of thought began to dominate the discourse on population and development. This alternative approach, which was crystallized in Cairo at the 1994 United Nations International Conference on Population and Development, emphasizes the importance of alleviating poverty, improving the status of women and protecting women's rights (including reproductive rights) as the more just and effective approach to population issues.

Those in China in a position to argue persuasively for a change in China's methods and goals were aided by this shift in the global discourse and agenda. In the early 1970s, China's leaders quietly but radically embraced the dominant Western demographic theory of the time – that reducing population growth was a prerequisite for socioeconomic development, and that the overpopulated nations of the developing world could not afford to wait for a development-induced demographic transition like that which occurred in Europe. In the post-Mao era, this theory has legitimated the regime's insistence that population control is the linchpin of the modernization strategy, even as it has come under increased international criticism.

The new language of Cairo – protecting women's rights and taking a more holistic approach to achieving demographic goals – emerged at a time when the State Family Planning Commission (SFPC) was growing more concerned about the consequences of using coercion and harsh sanctions to achieve China's population targets (Greenhalgh 2001). The failure to achieve those targets during the Eighth Five-Year Plan (1986–90), a failure that was carefully documented by the 1990 census, led to a new crackdown in the early 1990s that got quick results, but it left in its wake new concerns about excessive coercion, rising sex ratios at birth and overly rapid population ageing. The Cairo agenda gave Chinese officials a framework through which to articulate these concerns, and provided institutional contacts and resources they could use to experiment with a softer approach to enforcement. The UN's Fourth World Conference on Women in Beijing in 1995 reinforced the Cairo message, provoked a new wave of feminist thinking and action, and further encouraged SFPC officials to consider a more client-centred approach that gave greater consideration to women's needs and their reproductive health (Greenhalgh 2001).

Still, the road to reform has been slow and rife with controversy. After some internal debate, China officially reavowed its one-child policy in 2000, and in 2001 passed a long-debated Population and Family Planning Law that upheld the existing policy and gave compliance the force of law. Although the law included provisions that echoed the Cairo and Beijing conference agendas, calling for an 'informed choice of safe, effective, and appropriate contraceptive methods', and one prohibiting officials from infringing on 'personal rights, property rights, or other legitimate rights and interests', it reaffirmed China's basic approach to population control. Nevertheless, the chorus for reform appears to be growing louder, even if the pace of change remains very slow.

Let us hope that the pace of change will pick up soon, remedying the most appalling side-effects of the one-child policy and releasing China's child-bearing age couples from the hard choices and temptations that now confront them. It is the state that has taught the population that the social engineering of child-bearing is a legitimate and virtuous course. Now that individual couples have a modern, efficient and hi-tech method by which to engineer the sex composition of their own households, the dangers that have always been inherent in such a course are revealing themselves. Ideological exhortation alone will not solve this contradiction. To overcome it, the state will also have to alter the structural conditions and policies that encourage the continued cultural and social subordination of women.

Notes

1 Even in the absence of China's one-child policy, surveys suggest that most couples would prefer no more than two or three children, while many would continue to choose to have only one, particularly in urban areas. This suggests that, while China's demographic transition may not yet be fully complete in the countryside, its overall fertility level would remain relatively low even if couples were left to exercise their individual choice.

2 The total fertility rate refers to the average number of children that would be born to a woman during her lifetime if she conformed to the actual fertility rates of women at all ages during a specific year. In other words, this figure is reached by adding up all of the age-specific fertility rates for a given year (e.g., the number of births per 1,000 women at age 15, 16, 17...48, 49, and so on until child-bearing ceases).

3 Two exceptions are Wasserstrom (1984), and Greenhalgh and Li (1995).

4 See Elizabeth J. Perry, 'Trends in the Study of Chinese Politics: State-Society Relations', *China Quarterly* (1994), pp. 704–13; and Joel S. Migdal, *State in Society: Studying How States and Societies Transform and Constitute One Another* (Cambridge: Cambridge University Press, 2001).

5 Wan Simei, 'Ouda jihua shengyu gongzuo renyuan faji burong' (Beating Birth Planning Work Personnel in Violation of Law and Discipline Will Not be Tolerated), *Hubei ribao*, 12 (April 1982), p. 2.

6 Su Suining, 'There are Many Causes of Strained Relations Between Cadres and Masses in the Rural Areas', *Nongmin Ribao*, 26 September 1988, p. 1, in *FBIS-China*, 7 October 1988, p. 13.

7 'Zhizhi silei pohuai jihua shengyu gongzuode xingwei' (Stop Four Kinds of Behaviour that Wreck Birth Planning Work), *Jiankang bao, jihua shengyu ban* (Health Gazette, Birth Planning Edition), 1 March 1985.

8 See, for example, the report of a riot in Caojiang township, Guangdong province, after officials tried to impose severe fines on offending couples. Daniel Kwan, 'Caojiang Official Denies Riot Over Family Planning Policy', *South China Morning Post*, 8 September 1997, p. 8.

9 Kevin J. O'Brien, 'Rightful Resistance', *World Politics*, 49 (October 1996), pp. 31–55.

10 Kevin J. O'Brien, 'Rightful Resistance'; Lianjiang Li and Kevin J. O'Brien, 'Villagers and Popular Resistance in Contemporary China', *Modern China*, 22, 1 (January 1996), pp. 28–61.

11 Calum Macleod, 'A Fight for China's Miracle Baby', *United Press International*, 3 September 2001.

12 Xu Yaping, 'Plug Up a Loophole in Planned Parenthood Work', *Renmin ribao*, 4 June 1985, translated in *FBIS-China*, 5 June 1985, p. K3.

13 Du Xin and Yu Changhong, 'Zhongguo nongcunde shengyu dachao' (The Great Tide of Rural Child-bearing in China), *Liaowang choukan haiwaiban* (Outlook Weekly Magazine, Overseas Edition), 43 (23 October 1989), p. 19; *Xinhua*, 'Henan Province Executes Hospital Official', in *FBIS-China*, 24 October 1994, p. 79.

14 Henan Province Rural Survey Team, Rural Economy Bureau, 'Yao duju chao jihua shengyude loudong' (Loopholes for Extra-plan Births Must Be Stopped Up), *Nongcun gongzuo tongxun*, 5 (1988), p. 46.

15 Zhong Cheng 'Delegates and Members Show Concern for Birth Planning', *Zhongguo xinwen she*, 11 April 1988, in *FBIS-China*, 13 April 1988, p. 33.

16 *China Daily*, 9 January 1988, p. 1; Zhu Baoxia, 'Birth Control Planned for Transient Population', *China Daily*, 27 February 1991, in *FBIS-China*, 27 February 1991, p. 35.

17 *Xinhua*, 'Government to Curb Illegal Marriages', *FBIS-China*, 1 March 1994, p. 23.

18 Interview File 900307.

19 Interview File 900722.

20 Interview Files 821012 and 900307.

21 Wang Peishu, 'Wanshan shengyu zhengce, kaihao "xiao kouzi"de guanjian shi duzhu "da kouzi"' (The Key to Perfecting Birth Policy and 'Opening a Small Hole' is Stopping Up the 'Big Hole'), *Xibei renkou*, 3 (1987), pp. 20–1.

22 For Hainan, see *Hainan Ribao*, 20 December 1997, p. 5, in *FBIS-China*, 14 January 1998. An unofficial English translation of China's Population and Family Planning Law can be found at <http://www.unescap.org/pop/database/law_china/ ch_record052.htm>. This website, sponsored by the UN's Economic and Social Commission for Asia and the Pacific (UNESCAP), also provides English translations of other laws, regulations and speeches relevant to China's family planning programme. For a complete list, see <http://www.unescap.org/pop/database/ law_china/chtitle.htm>.

23 James C. Scott, *Domination and the Arts of Resistance: Hidden Transcripts* (New Haven: Yale University Press, 1990); Joel S. Migdal, *State in Society*.

24 The agony of being caught in this double bind is rendered very poignantly in Mo Yan's short story, 'Explosions'. Mo Yan, *Explosions and Other Stories* (Hong Kong: Renditions Paperbacks, 1991).

25 Zeng Yi, Tu Ping, Gu Baochang, Xu Yi, Li Bohua and Li Yongping, 'Causes and Implications of the Recent Increase in the Reported Sex Ratio at Birth in China', *Population and Development Review*, 19 (June 1993), p. 291; Su Ping, 'Wo guo chusheng yinger xingbie wenti tanlun' (Investigation Into the Question of Our Country's Birth and Infant Sex Ratio), *Renkou Yanjiu*, 1 (1993); Mu Guangsong, 'Jinnian lai zhongguo chusheng xingbie bi shanggao pian gao xianxiangde lilun jieshi' (A Theoretical Explanation of the Elevation and Deviation in Recent Years of the Sex Ratio at Birth), *Renkou yu jingji*, 88, 1 (1995), pp. 48–51.

26 Henan Provincial Family Planning Commission, 'Strengthen Leadership, Put and End to the Backward State in Family Planning Work', *Nongmin Ribao*, 27 March 1996, p. 2, in *FBIS-China*, 27 March 1996.

27 For confirmation of this line of thinking among child-bearing age women and rural officials, see the important study by Chu Junhong, 'Prenatal Sex Determination and Sex-Selective Abortion in Rural Central China', *Population and Development Review* (2001), pp. 259–82.

28 'China Sees a High Gender Ratio of Newborns', 1 August 2002, at <http://www.cpirc.org.cn/enews20020514.htm>. This is the website for the China Population Information Research Center.

29 The concept of 'voice' as a type of response to institutional pressures is drawn from Albert Hirschman, *Exit, Voice, and Loyalty: Responses to Decline in Firms, Organizations, and States*, (Cambridge, MA: Harvard University Press, 1970).

30 This project became the centre of controversy in the USA in 2001–2002 as conservatives successfully pressed the Bush administration to cut off funding for UNFPA on grounds that the organization helped China maintain 'a program of coercive abortion'. This decision was made despite a State Department investigation that concluded, as did the European Union, that the UNFPA programme was a positive step towards reform in China's programme. For one of many media reports on this controversy, see Philip P. Pan, 'China's One-Child Policy Now a Double Standard: Limits and Penalties Applied Unevenly', *The Washington Post*, 20 August 2002.

31 Additional evidence of just how difficult the campaign habit is to break comes from Kay Johnson, who found in 2001 that several Anhui counties, responding to the

problem of rising sex ratios at birth, were cracking down on voluntary abortions, which were assumed to be for the purposes of sex selection. Anyone caught aborting a second pregnancy automatically forfeited the right eventually to have an in-quota second child. Personal correspondence from Kay Johnson.

Suggested reading

On resistance to the one-child policy

Susan Greenhalgh and Jiali Li, 'Engendering Reproductive Policy and Practice in Peasant China: For a Feminist Demography of Reproduction', *Signs: Journal of Women in Culture and Society*, 20 (Spring 1995), pp. 601–41.

Jeffrey Wasserstrom, 'Resistance to the One-Child Family, *Modern China*, 10 (July 1984), pp. 345–74.

On policy evolution and implementation

Judith Banister, *China's Changing Population* (Stanford: Stanford University Press, 1987).

Susan Greenhalgh, 'The Evolution of the One-child Policy in Shaanxi', *The China Quarterly*, 122 (June 1990), pp. 191–229.

——,'Controlling Births and Bodies in Village China', *American Ethnologist*, 21 (1994), pp. 3–30.

Susan Greenhalgh, Zhu Chuzhu and Li Nan, 'Restraining Population Growth in Three Chinese Villages', *Population and Development Review*, 20 (June 1994), pp. 365–93.

Jiali Li, 'China's One-child Policy: A Case Study of Hebei Province, 1979–1988', *Population and Development Review*, 21 (September 1995), pp. 563–85.

Tyrene White, 'Postrevolutionary Mobilization in China: The One-child Policy Revisited', *World Politics*, 43 (October 1990), pp. 53–76.

——, 'Birth Planning Between Plan and Market: The Impact of Reform on China's One-child Policy', in *China's Economic Dilemmas in the 1990s: The Problems of Reform, Modernization, and Interdependence* (US Congress, Joint Economic Committee, 1991), vol. 1, pp. 252–69.

——, 'The Origins of China's Birth Planning Policy', in Christina K. Gilmartin, Gail Hershatter, Lisa Rofel and Tyrene White (eds), *Engendering China: Women, Culture, and the State* (Cambridge and London: Harvard University Press, 1994), pp. 250–78.

On gender and birth control in China

Ann Anagnost, 'A Surfeit of Bodies: Population and the Rationality of the State in Post-Mao China', in Faye D. Ginsberg and Rayna Rapp (eds), *Conceiving the New World Order: The Global Politics of Reproduction* (Berkeley: University of California Press, 1995), pp. 22–41.

Susan Greenhalgh and Jiali Li, 'Engendering Reproductive Policy and Practice in Peasant China: For a Feminist Demography of Reproduction', *Signs: Journal of Women in Culture and Society*, 20 (Spring 1995), pp. 601–41.

On infant abandonment

Kay Johnson, 'The Politics of the Revival of Infant Abandonment in China, with Special Reference to Hunan', *Population and Development Review*, 22 (March 1996), 77–98.

Kay Johnson, Huang Banghan and Wang Liyao, 'Infant Abandonment and Adoption in China', *Population and Development Review*, 24 (September 1998), pp. 469–510.

On the sex ratio of the Chinese population

Chu Junhong, 'Prenatal Sex Determination and Sex-selective Abortion in Rural Central China', *Population and Development Review* (2001), pp. 259–82.
Gao Lin, Liu Xiaolan and Xia Ping, 'Beijing shi renkou chusheng xingbiebi fenxi' (An Analysis of the Sex Ratio at Birth in Beijing), *Renkou yanjiu* (Population Research), 21 (September 1997), pp. 25–33.
Zeng Yi, Tu Ping, Gu Baochang, Xu Yi, Li Bohua and Li Yongping, 'Causes and Implications of the Recent Increase in the Reported Sex Ratio at Birth in China', *Population and Development Review*, 19 (June 1993), pp. 283–302.

On skewed sex ratios elsewhere in Asia

Monica Das Gupta and P.N. Mari Bhat, 'Fertility Decline and Increased Manifestation of Sex Bias in India', *Population Studies*, 51 (1997), pp. 307–15.
Nicholas Eberstadt, 'Asia Tomorrow, Gray and Male', *The National Interest*, 53 (Fall 1998), pp. 56–65.
Chai Bin Park and Nam-Hoon Cho, 'Consequences of Son Preference in a Low-fertility Society: Imbalance of the Sex Ratio at Birth in Korea, *Population and Development Review*, 21 (March 1995), pp. 59–84.

On feminism and the prospects for policy reform

Susan Greenhalgh, 'Fresh Winds in Beijing: Chinese Feminists Speak Out on the One-child Policy and Women's Lives', *Signs: Journal of Women in Culture and Society*, 26, 3 (Spring 2001), pp. 847–88.

On the general dynamics of population growth and the relationship between population and development

Joel Cohen, *How Many People Can the Earth Support?* (London: W.W. Norton, 1995).
Laurie Ann Mazur (ed.), *Beyond the Numbers: A Reader on Population, Consumption, and the Environment* (New York: Island Press, 1994).
Joseph A. McFalls Jr, 'Population: A Lively Introduction', *Population Bulletin* (September 1998), available online at the Population Reference Bureau website, <http://www.prb.org>.

9 Environmental protests in rural China[1]

Jun Jing

The problems of air pollution, soil erosion and fouled water in China have become so grave that they are reported in the Chinese press practically every day, often accompanied by announcements of government plans to combat one ecological failing after another. What the Chinese news media rarely mention, however, is how ordinary people are reacting to the country's deepening environmental crisis. This question is addressed here by looking at environmental protests in rural China, focusing on two specific cases. Environmental protests in the People's Republic are a relatively recent phenomenon. The promulgation of China's first environmental law, in 1979, has not only provided a legal basis for environmental protection but also enhanced the public's sense of basic rights in favour of justifying forceful, sometimes even violent, environmental protests. Such protests embody a rich, culturally informed repertoire of social movements with roots in Chinese history. Specifically, kinship, popular religion, moral concerns and ancient tales of justice serve as important institutional and symbolic resources in the mobilization of protesters at the grassroots level. The interplay of these issues informs the social and cultural context in which rural environmental protests take place and are organized, usually with an emphasis on ecological improvements essential for people's well-being rather than on trying to save the natural environment for its own sake.

A brief explication: why rural China?

More than 70 per cent of China's people live in rural areas, mostly on land that has been intensively farmed for centuries. Over the past fifty years, the precarious ecology of soil and water, already pushed to its limits to sustain a large population, has come under even greater strain with the drive toward industrialization and rapid economic development. Ambitious development projects of the Maoist era and the post-Mao economic reforms have in many ways improved general living standards. But they have also inflicted immense environmental damage in a countryside that could ill afford it. One result has been mounting protests against industrial polluters and ill-conceived projects that jeopardize the livelihood of rural residents. I have chosen to focus on rural-based environmental protests because these have been a rarely studied aspect of rural

life in China and also because so much of the environmental movement literature elsewhere has focused on urban activists.

In preparation for this chapter, I reviewed official records of 278 environmental disputes dating from the mid-1970s to the early 1990s.[2] A total of
forty-seven of these disputes involved forceful popular protests in rural China,
which ranged from collective lawsuits and petition movements to sabotage and
even riots. These official records reveal how a severe conflict between unbridled
development and ecological balance has placed many villagers on the front-lines
of environmentally related political action in China, both in identifying problems and in seeking to solve them, by influencing government policies, the
behaviour of enterprises and even court decisions. To make better sense of the
rise of environmental protests in the Chinese countryside, I focus my discussion
on two specific cases. Both were encountered in the course of my field research,
enabling me to interview the protest organizers. Central to this discussion is an
analysis of what can be characterized as a 'cultural and symbolic life-world'. I
use this phrase to call attention to the ways by which environmental protests are
influenced by and connected to kinship ideology, popular religion and customary
practices within the settings of everyday life in village China.

Background information

After the most devastating floods in more than forty years hit the Yangtze River
valley in the summer of 1998, Chinese officials acknowledged the contribution
of human activity, even public policy, to the devastation. Human settlements in
flood plains had eliminated areas of water absorption for the river to expand
safely, while excessive logging had removed forests that once helped check the
rain's flow into the Yangtze. In 1950, about 25 per cent of the river's middle
section was forested. Since then, more than half of the forests have been eliminated.

Deforestation, in fact a nationwide problem, leads to soil erosion and the
consequent loss of arable land. But other forces are at play as well. From 1979 to
1986, about 19 million acres of arable land were lost under the combined assault
of soil erosion, urbanization and industrialization. Since then, another 4 million
acres have been lost each year. Industrial projects alone claimed 1.5 million acres
a year. The degradation of water and air quality is even more disturbing. A 1988
survey of 532 rivers found 436 badly polluted; 80 per cent of the waste water
discharged into these rivers was untreated. In 1993, roughly 8 per cent of farm-
lands received river water so polluted that it could not be used for irrigation,
leading to an estimated loss in grain production of 1 million tons. In major cities
today, levels of total suspended particulates and sulphur dioxide are two to five
times the World Health Organization's guidelines. Fouled air is responsible for
178,000 deaths a year, mostly in cities. Rural residents are also affected by air
pollution, particularly since sulphur dioxide and nitrous oxide emissions react
with atmospheric water and oxygen to form acid rain, damaging forests, crops
and human health.[3]

China's central leadership was first awakened to the hazards of environmental degradation in 1972, when Dalian Bay in the far north-east turned black with untreated industrial waste. In the same year, state authorities read the startling report that fish in a Beijing reservoir had been poisoned by heavy metal discharged from neighbouring factories. But it was not until 1979 that China's first Environmental Protection Law was promulgated, on a trial basis. By 1989, it was revised for full implementation. During that intervening decade, the central government put unprecedented effort into environmental protection, adopting more laws, imposing heavier penalties for violations, and applying advanced technology to control pollution. One result of this effort was the establishment of the National Environmental Protection Agency in 1979, whose network of 70,000 employees has since been extended to every county. More recently, a few non-governmental organizations have emerged in the larger Chinese cities. Of these, the best known are Friends of Nature and Global Village of Beijing, founded in 1994 and 1995, respectively. The priority of these citizens' organizations, usually led by intellectuals, is to raise public awareness of environmental issues through exhibitions, organized tree-planting trips and tours of wildlife areas.

It was precisely during the experimental phase of China's Environmental Protection Law that environmental protests swept both urban and rural areas. Before this period, environmental protests were relatively rare, and they were often quickly suppressed by the government. Leaders of the few documented environmental protests prior to 1979 were treated harshly by local officials, and some of them were even thrown in jail and charged with 'counter-revolutionary' crimes. Although this charge was later removed from Chinese law, it was once used with devastating effect against organizers of different kinds of social protests. With the enactment of the 1979 Environmental Protection Law, the government has become more tolerant of environmental protests, so long as they are not too disruptive. Most have been small-scale actions by people immediately affected by a local polluter or engineering project. These victim interest groups have almost always engaged in direct protests in the form of petitions, lawsuits and even sabotage. Typical goals are compensation for damages, the installation of pollution-control technologies, and occasionally the relocation of serious offenders. The victim interest groups are the focal point in my discussion of the two rural cases of environmental protest.

A village's struggle for clean water

The first case involves Dachuan, a village in Gansu province, northwest China, in a decades-long protest movement against a fertilizer factory. The village and the factory are separated by only a paved road and a railroad. Most of Dachuan's 3,600 residents earn their living from agriculture. The factory is run by the provincial government and produces urea. None of its 3,000 salaried employees is from Dachuan. Since it began operations in 1971, the factory has been discharging its waste water into a stream that runs through Dachuan's fields before entering the Yellow River. This section of the river, until 1981 the village's only source of drinking water, became severely contaminated.

Through repeated protests, the village persuaded the factory to build a pipeline to deliver clean water to six of the village's eight production teams in 1981 and to a seventh team in 1992. The remaining team was left without clean water as late as 1998. By then, the factory claimed that it had invested 16 million yuan in pollution control. That the river remained contaminated, the factory said, was caused by technical problems that it was doing its best to fix. No legal action was taken by the local county government's environmental protection agency, partly because the factory is a provincial-level enterprise over which the local county government had no jurisdiction. County and township officials also discouraged Dachuan from filing a civil lawsuit, fearing that it would cost too much money and that Dachuan still might not win against a major enterprise, whose powerful connections extended from the provincial government to the court system.

With legal avenues barred, Dachuan's villagers turned to protest. I witnessed one action taken by the villagers against the fertilizer factory in 1996. A flash flood had swept down the 2-kilometre-long stream that runs from the factory to the Yellow River, destroying a bridge linking Dachuan to the local township seat. Dachuan's village head and a fish merchant led 200 local residents to the factory, blocked its entrance and demanded that the factory rebuild the bridge. They insisted that the factory had the obligation to build a new bridge because, although the stream had once been only 20 metres wide, the factory's daily discharge of 360 cubic metres of waste water had widened it to 60 metres, weakening the foundation of the old bridge. Any new bridge over the much widened and heavily contaminated stream would be considerably longer.

As in previous protests, the villagers cited the factory's contamination of the water and its unfulfilled obligations to Dachuan. The protesters asked the factory's security guards to tell factory officials to come out with their wives and children to drink up ten plastic bottles of water the villagers had brought from the contaminated stream. They promised never to come back to demonstrate again if the factory's Communist Party secretary, general manager and their families came out and drank the foul water in front of the crowd. Similar demands had been made during previous protests, usually accompanied by accusing questions: if factory employees and their families dare not drink from the stream, how can management not expect local villagers to demand safe drinking water? Aren't the rural people as human as the factory workers? Are the lives of the village's children worth less than those of factory children? On this occasion in 1996, the factory's party secretary and general manager, in keeping with past practice, refused to come out to talk with the agitated villagers. So a group of young people from Dachuan drove ten tractors up to the factory, each carrying a full load of contaminated water from the stream. Using rubber pipes, they shot the water over the factory wall. After ten days of bombardment by demonstrators, the factory agreed to provide Dachuan with 150,000 yuan to build a new bridge and repair a pump to provide tap-water to more than 600 people in the village's seventh production team who were still drinking from the polluted river.

The village's initial appeals to the factory had not been antagonistic. They only evolved into fierce protests as the local people came to appreciate the threat that the polluted water posed to human health and agricultural production, while the factory's corrective measures always fell short of the village's expectations. Dachuan's protests went through four stages. At first, the villagers were not fully aware of how harmful the contamination was, although the factory's discharge of incompletely burned fuel was already leaving patches of carbon black on the water's surface. They would wait for the carbon black to float downstream before drawing water for drinking and cooking. It was not until the mid-1970s, when a horse and thirty sheep went blind, that the villagers began to realize that drinking from the river could be hazardous to human health too. Dachuan's village cadres went to the factory to complain. As a gesture of compensation, one that did not solve the problem of water pollution, the factory agreed to hire some villagers on a temporary basis and give the village discounts on fertilizer.

The second phase of Dachuan's protest movement coincided with the break-up of agricultural communes in 1980–81, when farmland was distributed to individual households to manage. A stretch of cultivated fields along the polluted stream was turned over to households whose members numbered more than 100 people. But the stream was so contaminated that the crops along the banks were damaged from excess ammonia. When villagers working these fields demanded action to solve the problem, Dachuan's cadres led the villagers in a blockade of the factory gate, preventing the factory's trucks from making deliveries. This initial blockade lasted only one day, but then other villagers joined to demand the factory solve the drinking water problem. After three more days of demonstrations, the factory agreed to supply tap-water to the central part of Dachuan.

The third phase of the village's protests began in the mid-1980s, within the context of China's birth control policy. (See chapter 8.) The county government restricted rural couples from having more than two children and imposed a three-year interval between the first and second births. As violations of the policy resulted in forced abortions, human reproduction became a dominant subject of anxious conversation among the villages. This anxiety was reflected in the growing number of worshippers drawn to a fertility temple in Dachuan. Meanwhile, speculation about the causes of stillbirths and birth defects in the village increasingly focused on the factory, prompting the village to resume its protests.

The liberalization of the Chinese economy also had a direct impact on Dachuan's protests, as seen in the fourth phase of the village's struggle against the factory, from the mid-1980s to the mid-1990s. Every year in this period saw demonstrations against the factory, with protests ranging from small rallies to major blockades. In addition to anger over the factory's threat to people's health, there was growing concern about the village's fish ponds. As part of the effort under the economic reforms to develop new lines of commercial production, these ponds had multiplied from a handful in the early 1980s to more than 300 by the early 1990s, mostly for raising Yellow River carp. The fish ponds depended on water drawn from the Yellow River, which remained polluted.

The four phases of Dachuan's protests represent a 'cognitive revolution'. By that I mean a process whereby the villagers' understanding of water pollution advanced at several critical points, as when dozens of domesticated animals went blind, when special health problems were highlighted by the state's population policy, and when the village's economic development was put at risk. The cumulative effect of this process was a comprehensive awareness of the damaging consequences of water pollution, rather than just a single aspect of the problem, as in the past. Human health, however, remained the most contentious issue in each phase of the village's struggle against the factory. This issue will be explored more fully later.

Petitions for a liveable environment

The second case is a protest movement against local officials in charge of population resettlement for the Three Gorges Dam project on the Yangtze River. The petition movement began in 1997 among more than 10,000 rural residents in Gaoyang Township, Yunyang county, now part of Chongqing municipality. The Gaoyang petition movement began with accusations against local officials on three points. First, the petitioners blamed county officials for not distributing the full financial compensation that the central government already allocated for local people either to resettle on higher ground nearby or to move to other counties. Second, township officials were accused of embezzling resettlement funds. Third, the petitioners claimed that corruption among township officials and village cadres was responsible for a failed land reclamation project, which had been funded by the central government for local resettlers to move into a liveable environment. The third accusation, dealing with the environmental aspects of the Gaoyang petition movement, is our primary concern here. The relevant information is selected from three petition letters, ten government documents, published studies of the Three Gorges Dam project, interviews I conducted with the petition movement organizers during field research in Yunyang in 1998, and follow-up interviews in 2000 and 2001 with officials and scholars who were familiar with this case.

The Three Gorges Dam project is unprecedented in terms of physical size and the number of people slated for relocation. The project, whose construction began in 1994, cost at least $25 billion, for capital construction and population resettlement. The government plan calls for the dam to be 185 metres high and 2,000 metres wide, holding back a reservoir extending 640 kilometres upstream. The dam's generating capacity of nearly 18,000 megawatts would be 50 per cent greater than the world's current largest hydroelectric station, Itaipu in Paraguay. The first group of generators in the dam is to begin operating in the year 2003, requiring the reservoir water to rise to 135 metres above sea level. The entire project, scheduled for completion by 2009, requires the relocation of at least 1.3

million people. More than half of the resettlers, living in 1,352 villages, need new farmland to restart their lives.[4] An experiment for transferring some of the rural resettlers into factories to ease the pressures on land was dropped completely in 1997, as unemployment in the Three Gorges area rose to 20 per cent of the industrial workforce, a problem that also afflicted other parts of China in the aftermath of a government decision to restructure the state-owned industrial sector.

In Gaoyang, where the petition movement took place, the only way to create extra farmland is by building terraces on higher ground. But even the most successful land reclamation would fall far short of providing enough arable land. Already Gaoyang has 25,118 rural residents and only 16,950 *mu*, or about 2,825 acres, of arable land. This comes to just 0.6 *mu*, or about a tenth of an acre, of arable land per person, already an extremely low figure to sustain a livelihood from farming. Once the Three Gorges project is complete, 40 per cent of Gaoyang's farmland will be inundated and 60 per cent of its rural residents will have to move. Since many of these people wanted to stay in the vicinity to be close to relatives and fellow villagers, they desperately looked to the land reclamation project as a way to rebuild the foundation of their livelihood.

The state provided land reclamation funds to township officials to manage, and for village cadres to distribute as payment for labour. By 1995, the reclamation project was supposed to provide at least some of the relocating villagers with access to new land. But one village after another discovered that many of the so-called terraced lands were not level, had little topsoil, and were too scattered to farm. Local officials, however, had reported to higher authorities that these were usable fields. Furthermore, village cadres and township officials were found to have falsely included in their reclamation reports already cultivated farmland and even some fields that did not exist at all. In total, the petition movement organizers told the central government, nearly 1,000 *mu* of the allegedly reclaimed land were unusable or non-existent. They charged that much of the land reclamation funds, amounting to 3 million yuan, had been embezzled by local officials.

The petitioners spelled out in their first letter to the central government what they thought would happen in Gaoyang if wrongdoing among local officials were not checked:

> In the future, when desperate resettlers rush to government compounds begging for food, what then? And, what if these impoverished throngs decide to rush onto the streets of our cities and large urban areas to stage demonstrations to protest the embezzlement of compensation funds by local officials and to demand restitution of these monies? … If the central government takes no action until conflicts break out, the lessons to be learned will be learned too late.

To send this warning, the petitioners organized a village-by-village investigation into the so-called reclaimed lands that in fact had been never reclaimed or did not exist at all. They then wrote in the petition letter:

According to our investigation, such false claims cover the following villages: 275 *mu* by Liutou, 285 *mu* by Hongmiao, 20 *mu* by Pailou, 25 *mu* by Lishu, 128 *mu* by Gaoyang, 70 *mu* by Tuanbao, 125 *mu* by Zouma, 130 *mu* by Mingchong, 25 *mu* by Tongxi, and 10 *mu* by Tianzhuang. Together, these add up to 993 *mu* of land that was falsely claimed as reclaimed and arable land.

After the first letter from Gaoyang reached Beijing by mail, officials in (the city of) Chongqing were told to investigate. Chongqing had been recently separated from the jurisdiction of Sichuan province and granted a special municipality status – joining Beijing, Tianjin and Shanghai – under the direct supervision of the central government. This move allowed Chongqing to incorporate smaller cities and rural counties in the upper part of the Three Gorges that had been part of Sichuan. All these cities and counties will be partially flooded once the dam is built. In fact, 80 per cent of the people slated for resettlement live in these cities and counties. The remaining 20 per cent are in the downstream province of Hubei.

The initial investigation by Chongqing authorities only scratched the surface of Gaoyang's problems. But it led to more investigations. Meanwhile, a second petition letter was sent to Beijing. By the summer of 1998, the party secretary and five top officials of Gaoyang Township were fired from their positions. The party secretary and one of these officials were imprisoned. However, these officials were brought down not on charges related to land reclamation but because they were found to have taken bribes in the construction of Gaoyang's new township seat, which is relatively small and can accommodate only a few hundred resettlers. The failed land reclamation, by contrast, is politically explosive. It affects thousands of rural residents and raises questions as to whether the Three Gorges Dam project can deal effectively with the many problems of rural resettlement in an already bleak ecological environment.

With the reclamation problem still unsolved, local officials moved against the two leading petitioners. An internal county government document accused them of having been troublemakers during the Cultural Revolution (1966–76), adding that the police should deal sternly with them if they engaged in any action that might constitute a criminal offence. To eliminate support for the petitioners at the village level, in August 1998, the county government launched a 'laws and village security campaign', and villagers were told to dissociate themselves from the petition movement. Fearing retaliation from local officials, the two men leading the movement hurried to Beijing to submit the third petition. There, they hand-delivered it to the Offices for Receiving People's Letters and Visits under the State Council, the Central Committee of the Chinese Communist Party, and the Three Gorges Construction Committee.

The Gaoyang case shows that the petitioners were keenly aware that their accusations of official wrongdoing must be framed in terms acceptable to the central government, because they raised serious questions about the feasibility of the politically glorified Three Gorges project. This case also demonstrates the petitioners' strong consciousness of political and civil rights. As the two leading petitioners told a sociology student who helped them type and print their third petition letter, their visit to Beijing was aimed at establishing an official record of their constitutionally protected right to write letters to national leaders to expose abuses by local officials.

Chinese culture and the nature of environmental protest

At the beginning of this chapter, I said that the two protest movements under discussion operated within a 'cultural and symbolic life-world'. To explain this, I first suggest that an overtly political protest may achieve an immediate success but be incapable of further elaboration. I further argue that a protest is most effective when it resonates with a society's value system and its symbolic manifestations. Among the most important of these are death rituals, cosmological beliefs or the telling and retelling of morality tales from history. To elaborate this point, I will analyse the Dachuan case of a descent group and the local worship of fertility goddesses. For Gaoyang, my analysis is concerned with funeral symbolism and its meaning for the petition movement. For both cases, I will underscore the relevance of Chinese culture to environmental protests.

Kinship and fertility goddesses: the Dachuan case

At first glance, it would seem that Dachuan's protests against the fertilizer factory were led by the village committee in cooperation with the leaders of the village's eight production teams. A closer look, however, reveals the indelible influence of a dominant lineage in the village's organized struggle for safe drinking water. More than 85 per cent of Dachuan's households are surnamed Kong and trace their ancestry to Confucius (Kong Fuzi in Chinese).[5] Until the early 1950s, the Kongs were organized as a formal lineage. They maintained an ancestral hall, held an annual ceremony of ancestor worship, and used the incomes from more than 200 *mu* of land to finance rituals, local defence and a primary school. Institutionally speaking, the Kong lineage collapsed in the Maoist era but made a partial recovery later, as embodied in the reconstruction of the Kong ancestor hall in 1991. The Kongs also dominated Dachuan politically. From 1958 to 1998, the village chief, the local Communist Party boss, and the accountant general were all individuals surnamed Kong.[6]

So, given the lineage-grounded framework of Dachuan's organizational structure, it is no surprise that the village cadres tapped into the collective identity of the Kongs to mobilize protests against the factory. Above all, they emphasized the factory's threat to the ability of the Kongs to have healthy babies. This concern was a major catalyst for the reconstruction of four temples on a mountain behind the main residential area of Dachuan. Levelled by government decree during the Cultural Revolution, these temples were fully rebuilt in the mid-1980s. Six goddesses and one male deity (a water-control god) were enshrined, in the form of elaborately painted clay statues of varying sizes. Each goddess is believed to possess the ability to help women give birth, protect young children and cure life-threatening diseases.

The new enshrinement of the six goddesses merged together two types of anxiety-ridden experience: the effect of the Chinese government's population policy and the increasing awareness in Dachuan of the fertilizer factory's threat to people's health, especially the physical well-being of women and children. In Yongjing county, where Dachuan is located, a central government policy for birth control was implemented locally through much of the 1970s. Partly because of this policy, Yongjing county's birth rate of 40 newborns per 1,000 in 1968 declined to 18 newborns per 1,000 in 1978. By 1982, the annual birth rate declined to 13 births per 1,000. To further reduce population growth, the county government adopted a stricter quota of two births for a rural couple and imposed a requirement of a three-year interval between the first and second births. A second child was allowed even if the first was a boy. To quell resistance to the birth quota, the county government organized officials, doctors and policemen into special task forces to enforce the birth quota and the spacing of births. Dachuan became the target of one of these task forces, because government officials believed that Dachuan had too many *hei haizi*, or 'black babies'. That is to say, women in Dachuan found different ways to disguise their pregnancies and hide their unregistered newborns.

The implementation of the population policy was two-pronged. On one side, forcible means were adopted. Using intrauterine devices was compulsory, routinely checked by sent-down doctors. Tubal ligations of young women who had given birth to two or more children were performed at local clinics, by force when resistance was encountered. On the other side, persuasion was utilized. Blackboards were erected at a major intersection in Dachuan and a loudspeaker system was used by village cadres to publicize official recommendations for public health. These recommendations, in line with national campaigns, promoted what was described as 'scientific child care' (*kexue yu er*). Through radio and television, simplified questions and answers were provided to why having fewer children is important to the rural family and the well-being of the next generation of young people. Specific recommendations covered pregnancy tests, breastfeeding, weaning and nutrition.

The impact of this combination of education and coercion was deeply felt in Dachuan. In interviews with six upper middle-aged women who went from door to door to raise money to have deity statues made, they said that local women did not associate miscarriages and stillbirths with the fertilizer factory's discharge of waste water until the government embarked on the education drive to promote scientific child care. Moreover, they said that concerns for women and children's health were stimulated by an experimental programme to immunize rural children against infectious diseases. This government-funded programme brought a team of doctors from a county hospital to Dachuan every year. Local children stood in lines to be vaccinated while their mothers talked with the doctors and nurses. This was a perfect opportunity for village women to obtain free advice about their own and their children's health.

Repeatedly, the doctors told the women that it was dangerous to drink from the polluted Yellow River. They said it could cause miscarriages and stillbirths as well as mental retardation and stunted growth in children. The doctors' warning was made more alarming by the televised reports of environmental problems elsewhere in China. One report was about water pollution in south China and its effect on pregnant women. Among those who paid special attention to this report was the village's party boss, who was the most powerful man in Dachuan but had no biological children of his own. His wife had suffered several miscarriages, after which the couple decided to adopt a little girl. No boys were available for adoption in Dachuan or in nearby villages. Convinced that his wife's miscarriages were caused by the fouled water, the party boss played a leading role in the village's protests against the factory. His adopted daughter later married a Mr Xi, a junior township official. Instead of leaving Dachuan, the bride stayed put and the groom came to live with her. If they had two sons, the newlyweds promised at a witnessed ceremony, one would bear the surname Kong, after his mother's adoptive father, to maintain his patrilineal line of descent.

Although Dachuan's party boss stated in public that he did not condone the worship of fertility goddesses, he was once seen taking a portion of the food offerings from a goddess temple to bring home after most visitors had left following a midnight ceremony. The food offerings are considered blessed by the enshrined goddesses and are expected to enhance the health of children and adults alike. This expectation is based on the popular belief that people and deities enjoy a reciprocal relationship. Temple rituals suggest that deities depend on regular worship and offerings, which make them strong and powerful. So when food offerings to deities are ample and regular, supplicants can hope for something in return, which includes the blessed foods to take home. There are many expressions of this belief. For example, new temple-goers in Dachuan were often told by regular visitors that they should let their children eat some of the food offerings to 'ensure peace and safety' (*bao ping an*).

Dachuan's most popular goddesses are known as *sanxiao niangniang*, or 'Three Heavenly Mothers'. Their half-life-sized statues in a temple called *bai zi gong* (the Palace of One Hundred Sons) are adorned with silk attire. Attached to their clothes, necks and arms are homemade embroideries. Many of these depict fish, lotus flowers or half-open pomegranates. Because fish produce a multitude of eggs at one time and a pomegranate or a lotus flower contains many seeds they are fertility symbols. Other embroideries have little boys sitting atop a fish, playing with a lotus flower, or climbing out of a pomegranate. These religious artworks are constantly replaced by new ones from villagers hoping for babies. After a simple rite of offering money and incense, a piece of temple embroidery may be taken home. It is usually kept in a couple's bed in the hope that a boy will be born in timely fashion.

It appears that the new enshrinement of fertility goddesses represented an urgency to have babies quickly and safely, constituting a religiously grounded manifestation of the village's concerns over the polluted water. It is hence by no means an accident that one of the major demands in Dachuan's protests against the factory was framed in terms of the continuity of the family line and the health of village women and children. More specifically, the village cadres vowed to end the protests only if at least one of two conditions were met. First, the whole village must have safe drinking water. Second, the factory's top leaders, their wives, children and grandchildren must each drink one small bottle of water fetched from the contaminated stream leading to the Yellow River. Considering that safe drinking water had been available to the families of the factory's own employees since the factory was founded, Dachuan's second condition for ending its protests was an especially stirring one. It was a demand that the factory leaders do for the villagers precisely what they had done for the protection of their own families.

Funeral symbolism and internal trust: the Gaoyang case

Organized protests in China and elsewhere in the world often embrace culturally meaningful symbols and a politically adept language. In the Gaoyang case, this tendency was embodied in three petition letters, secret meetings to select the petition movement's leaders, and an emphasis on loyalty. In the three petition letters, the central government's resettlement policies were praised but described as being jeopardized by local officials. These letters included diplomatically phrased statements to win over central authorities by saying that the petitioners fully endorsed the goal of constructing a world-class dam to provide electricity for national development, and understood that even though the project required local villagers to make considerable sacrifices, the state had designed sound compensatory measures in return. According to these letters, corrupt local officials had sabotaged central policies and had to be investigated by the state. In other words, the articulation of grievances in these letters echoed the rhetorical themes of popular protests throughout China's dynastic history: The emperor is just and kind but his benevolence is being thwarted by evil local officials.

By contrast, the manner in which local participants were mobilized to join the petition movement could be quite threatening to the state. In launching the petition movement, village meetings were held without the knowledge of township officials, and these secret meetings resulted in the selection of forty representatives from all of the fourteen affected villages in Gaoyang to form a unified petition team. By secret ballot, this team chose three leaders, who then took an oath pledging to represent fairly the participating villages. One of the three leaders was Gaoyang's retired Communist Party head. He later quit the petition movement under government pressure exerted through his family and former colleagues.

The petition movement leaders' oath also bound them never to betray their comrades and supporters even in the face of official persecution. Emblematic of this resolve and as part of the plan to deliver the first letter to Beijing, the forty-member team decided to make 100 white gowns inscribed with three slogans written in black characters: 'Resettlers Want a Meeting with Higher Authorities';

'Resettlers Want to Express Their Grievances'; and 'Resettlers Want to Live'. The planned trip to Beijing was immediately exposed by an informer, and local officials responded quickly. The petitioners who had been selected to go to Beijing were ordered not to leave Gaoyang and were told to surrender their petition letter to county officials. Angry officials at the township level warned a rural businessman that if he paid to have the white gowns made, as he had promised at a secret meeting, he would forfeit his business licence.

It is easy to understand why the officials did not want the letter to be delivered. But why were they enraged by the white gowns? Was it simply because they would display three protest slogans? To address these questions, it should be remembered that white is the traditional Chinese colour of death and mourning. It is the colour of funeral trappings such as wreaths, paper flowers, poetic couplets and attire, including caps, gowns and shoes.[7] The transfer of funeral symbolism to social protests actually is an important feature of China's political culture. In Beijing, popular demonstrations at Tiananmen Square in 1976 and 1989 usurped the official mourning for a national leader, turning it into a forum to express anger with the political regime.[8] In New York City, Chinese restaurant workers paraded white wreaths in a 1996 strike against an exploitative employer. In Taiwan, demonstrations against a nuclear plant engaged in what the local newspapers called a 'battle of the coffins', when protesters carried four coffins to the plant and set up a spirit altar.[9] Whatever the specific symbols of death and funeral used in these situations, the ultimate statement being made was that a serious crime had been committed.

The messages intended by such funeral trappings can vary, and the Gaoyang petitioners' plan to wear white gowns for delivering their first letter to the central government was meant not only to express grievances but also to convey their readiness to die for their cause. So high were the risks they were taking when they accused local officials, and so unpredictable the consequences of their taking on the Three Gorges Dam project, that the Gaoyang petitioners feared imprisonment and even execution. The white gowns thus symbolized their preparation for martyrdom. In fact, as soon as she heard about the white gowns, the frightened wife of one of the petition leaders asked him for a divorce, as a way of protecting herself and her children in case her husband were arrested or executed as a criminal.

The informer's disclosure of the plan to secretly visit Beijing and the withdrawal of one petition leader under pressure heightened the movement organizers' appreciation of the dangers of betrayal. While speaking of their determination to go as far as dying for the petition movement, they tried hard to build internal trust by emphasizing the righteousness of their cause and the unspeakable nature of disloyalty. In so doing, they repeatedly made references to the unfortunate example of Song Jiang in *Outlaws of the Marshes*, an epic story about rebellions in the twelfth century that evolved from a written narrative from 1400 to an extended edition in 1641.

Largely a work of literary imagination based on the slightest historical evidence, the story features 108 bandit heroes led by Song Jiang, a petty official who had numerous unpleasant encounters with the law but maintained a sense of loyalty to the throne. Even as a bandit chieftain who coined the popular slogan of 'Doing Justice in the Name of Heaven', Song Jiang sought and received an imperial pardon; his decision to surrender his forces to the state and to lead them in government campaigns against other rebels was only grudgingly approved by his followers and set the stage for wrenching conflicts of loyalty. Song Jiang's respect for the throne rivalled his devotion to his sworn brother rebels, who followed his lead only to meet tragic ends.

References to Song Jiang in Gaoyang's petition movement needed no elaboration; his legend had been recounted over the centuries by storytellers, portrayed in local operas, and more recently turned into television dramas. Every petitioner appreciated the irony of Song Jiang's death at the hands of corrupt officials who had him poisoned in the emperor's name. Every petitioner also knew that Song Jiang's surrender to the throne did not benefit his followers but instead led them to deadly situations from which they did not return alive.

It would be misleading to suggest, however, that the Gaoyang petitioners cited Song Jiang as a negative example while favouring other rebels in the novel who had little respect for state authorities. The petitioners wanted their grievances to be heard by the central government, which remained in their eyes the ultimate institution that might offer them real help. Like the symbolism of white gowns in confirming their willingness to die, reference to Song Jiang was an evocation of the petition movement's unpredictable consequences. In 2000, officials of the local county accused the leaders of the Gaoyang petition movement of having violated laws regarding public order. The two leaders of this movement were imprisoned subsequently. As a result of this setback, public demonstrations and organization petitions associated with the earlier phases of this movement in Gaoyang came to a stop, but unhappy resettlers continued to send anonymous letters to the provincial government to voice their complaints and their demands for justice.

Conclusion: environmental crisis and local protests

To situate the Dachuan and Gaoyang cases in the broader context of similar protests, it is important to recognize that China's environmental problems evolved into a severe crisis in the 1980s and that that crisis persisted into the 1990s. Two major transformations of Chinese society under the rule of the Communist Party were responsible for this environmental crisis. From the 1950s through much of the 1970s, the Chinese government, under the leadership of Mao Zedong, pursued variants of the Soviet model of development so as to transform a largely agrarian country into an industrial society. Mao's economic programme resulted in a basic infrastructure for development in favour of heavy, military and chemical industries. The introduction of rural reforms in the late 1970s and the initiation of urban reforms in the mid-1980s started off the country's transformation away from a command economy to a market-oriented one. Official statistics show that between 1978 and 1995 China's per capita GDP growth averaged 8 per cent a year; other statistics suggest a growth rate of 6–7 per cent. Still, whatever the precise figure, China's economic growth in these years was almost unprecedented. Only South Korea and Taiwan had similar rates.

The development strategy under Mao that laid down China's industrial infrastructure and the rapid economic growth of the post-Mao era that lifted at least 100 million people out of absolute poverty have turned out to be extremely damaging to China's environment. In 1996 in Guangdong province, for example, the provincial government shut down 739 factories to cut back on the waste water and emissions that had dangerously polluted rivers and air.[10] And in 1997, the central government dispatched official delegations to Henan, Jiangsu, Shandong, and Anhui provinces to investigate and discipline 1,562 factories for turning the Huai River, the third largest waterway in China, into a belt of blackened water too polluted for consumption or irrigation.[11]

Although many studies and news reports on China's environmental problems are available, few scholarly or government surveys have been conducted on environmental protests. One source of information on such protests is the official publication of what are known as 'selected cases of environmental disputes'. Chosen for models for study in environmental law enforcement, these documents reveal that the leading forms of environmental protests in rural China are petitioning government agencies, filing lawsuits and staging demonstrations. Environmental protests take place in cities also. In fact, urbanites may be quicker than rural residents to engage in blockades, sabotage and even collective violence, which government and court officials identify as 'extreme action in environmental disputes'. Of eighty-eight environmental disputes in urban and suburban Shanghai recorded in a publication released by the Shanghai Municipal Agency of Environmental Protection, forty-four of these predominantly urban disputes involved 'extreme action' and only five resorted to the judicial system.[12] Compare this with forty-seven disputes in rural areas recorded in two publications of the Chinese Environmental Science Press. Only eleven of these rural disputes involved 'extreme action', whereas twenty-five were handled by the court, with verdicts returned mostly in favour of the rural litigants.[13] Since these were selected cases rather than survey findings, the relevant court rulings should not be readily taken as evidence of the effectiveness of China's legal system in protecting the rural population against environmental damage. But they are indicative of the growing trend of taking environmental issues to court.

The reasons behind the documented urban and rural differences with regard to the use of 'extreme action' – which often has involved collective violence – are complex and may have to do with a stronger sense of entitlement among urban Shanghai residents. Nonetheless, the use of violent means to retaliate against industrial polluters is still a significant form of protest in the rural disputes and a quarter of the recorded rural cases led to violence such as scuffles, sabotage, harassment and forceful detention of factory leaders.[14] The greater resort to the judicial system in the countryside, on the other hand, can be traced to the limited power of local, especially county-level, governments in imposing administrative penalties against violators of China's environmental laws. By these laws, a county-level government can punish only those enterprises operating under its administrative jurisdiction. These include county, township, village and private enterprises. A county government, however, cannot resort to administrative penalties, such as imposing fines or shutting down facilities, to punish industrial polluters if they are beyond its administrative jurisdiction. In these situations, the power of administrative punishment, as written in environmental laws, is rendered useless.

An alternative is to ask the victims to file a civil lawsuit to be handled by the court system. That this has been done frequently explains why over half of the rural disputes I mentioned above resulted in lawsuits. But even if a provincial-level enterprise is sued and held responsible by a county court, it would appeal and bring the lawsuit to a higher court where it expects to be judged more favourably than in the county court. This is certainly why in the Dachuan case I have discussed, the village cadres did not go to court, following the advice of township and county officials who claimed to have a better knowledge of how the judicial system would handle a lawsuit against the nearby fertilizer factory, which is a provincial-level enterprise.

In other environmentally related protests, such as the Gaoyang case, China's environmental laws can hardly be applied at all for political reasons or due to special government decisions. It is widely accepted, for example, that the construction of the Three Gorges Dam will further damage an already fragile ecological system along the Yangtze River, especially the middle and lower reaches. But since this is a state-sponsored construction project of unusual political importance, its devastating environmental impact is not subject to the possible scrutiny of the country's environmental laws.

The rise of environmental protests in China in the past twenty years is emblematic of the growing consciousness of community and individual rights among ordinary citizens as well as the cumulative effect of newly promulgated laws. In rural areas particularly, the inauguration of drastic economic and administrative changes in the 1980s and 1990s has led to a readjustment of state–society relations. Economic liberalization included agricultural decollectivization, marketization, and the legitimization of geographical mobility and the private sector. Administrative reforms were typified by the promulgation of the Organic Law of Villagers' Committees and the Administration Litigation Law, in 1987 and 1990, respectively.

These changes altered the power relations in village China, sometimes weakening the political base of rural cadres and leading to incidents in which ordinary villagers took upon themselves the task of organizing the local people to defend their community and individual rights. The Gaoyang case is an example of this trend, whereas the Dachuan case demonstrates the close cooperation of village cadres and local residents in a community struggle for clean water. Both cases show that Chinese villagers can become instant political activists when their livelihood is threatened. Of course, the specific means of organizing themselves to engage in protests are dependent on other factors such as government policies, bureaucratic reactions and state laws.[15]

On the basis of my study of the Dachuan and Gaoyang cases and my examination of forty-seven similar rural cases (as documented in the two official publications mentioned earlier), I suggest that environmentally related protests in the Chinese countryside display four characteristics that merit emphasis. First, cultural factors play a central role in the mobilization of participants. This often takes place through appeals to kinship ties, village unity, popular religion and the security of the rural family. Second, economic grievances, health claims or legal demands are accompanied by distinctly moral judgements and a remarkable sense of entitlement for a society with a poor record of human rights. Third, protest organizers not only appear highly aware of the country's environmental laws, they also know the importance of taking advantage of fissures within the government to find allies or at least sympathizers among the leadership. And finally, people in rural China who do not necessarily regard themselves as the state's adversaries are capable of launching well-organized and forceful protests against environmental abuses. But the ways in which they go about organizing their protests reflect the centrality of particular social values and moral concerns. These protests are not meant to save an endangered environment for its own sake, independent of its relevance to people. Rather, they are aimed at seeking social justice to protect the ecological basis of human existence.

Notes

1   Research for this chapter benefited from the provision of a travel grant by the Research Foundation of the City University of New York. The current and revised chapter benefits from the provision of a research grant by the Wenner-Gren Foundation for Anthropological Research in the 2000–2001 academic year. I give my heartfelt thanks to both institutions for supporting my field research in the Three Gorges area.

2   These official records are found in the following sources: Shanghai Municipal Environmental Agency Protection, *Environmental Pollution, Conflict between Factories and Masses, and Conflict Resolution (Huanjing wuran changqun maodun yu chuli duice)*, (Shanghai: Huangdong Politics and Law College Press, 1994); Xie Zhenhua (ed.), *Typical Cases of Environmental Violations and Guidelines of Environmental Law Enforcement in China (Zhongguo huanjing dianxing anli yu zhifa tiyao)* (Beijing: China Environmental Science Press, 1994); Zhao Yongkang (ed.), *Selected Cases of Environmental Disputes (Huanjing jiufen anli)* (Beijing: China Environmental Science Press, 1989).

3   For more information on China's environmental crisis, see He Baochang, *China On the Edge: The Crisis of Ecology and Development* (San Francisco: China Books & Periodicals, 1991); Vaclav Smil, *China's Environmental Crisis: An Inquiry into the Limits of National Development* (Armonk: M.E. Sharpe, 1993); World Bank, *Clear Water, Blue Skies: China's Environment in the New Century* (Washington, DC: The International Bank for Reconstruction and Development, 1997).

4   See Jing Jun, 'Population Resettlement: Past Lessons for the Three Gorges Dam Project', *The China Journal*, 38 (July 1997), pp. 65–92; Dai Qing (ed.), *The River Dragon Has Come: The Three Gorges Dam and the Fate of China's Yangtze River and Its People* (Armonk: M.E. Sharpe, 1998).

5 For a detailed social history of this Kong lineage, see Jing Jun, *The Temple of Memories: History, Power, and Morality in a Chinese Village* (Stanford: Stanford University Press, 1996).

6 For additional information on the overlapping of kinship ties and village administration in the Maoist and post-Mao eras, see Edward Friedman, Paul Pickowicz and Mark Selden, *Chinese Village, Socialist State* (New Haven: Yale University Press, 1991); Huang Shu-min, *The Spiral Road: Change in a Chinese Village through the Eyes of a Communist Party Leader* (Boulder: Westview Press, 1989); Jack Potter and Sulamith Potter, *China's Peasants: The Anthropology of a Revolution* (Cambridge: Cambridge University Press, 1990).

7 For a comprehensive analysis of Chinese funerals and mourning rites, see James Watson and Evelyn Rawski (eds), *Death Ritual in Late Imperial and Modern China* (Berkeley: University of California Press, 1996).

8 See Rubie Watson, 'Making Secret Histories: Memory and Mourning in Post-Mao China', in Rubie Watson (ed.), *Memory, History, and Opposition Under State Socialism* (Santa Fe: School of American Research Press, 1994), pp. 65–86; Joseph W. Esherick and Jeffrey N. Wasserstrom, 'Acting out Democracy: Political Theatre in Modern China', in Jeffrey N. Wasserstrom and Elizabeth J. Perry (eds), *Popular Protest and Political Culture in Modern China: Learning from 1989* (Boulder: Westview, 1992), pp. 28–66.

9 See Robert P. Weller and Hsin-Hung Michael Hsiao, 'Culture, Gender, and Community in Taiwan's Environmental Movement', in Arne Kalland and Gerald Persoon (eds), *Environmental Movements in Asia* (London: Curzon, 1998), pp. 83–108.

10 'Locals Long for the Return of Blue Skies to Guangzhou', *China Daily*, 5 June 1997, p. 3.

11 Cai Haili, 'Can Environmental Protection Work in China?', *Harvard China Review*, 1, 1 (1998), pp. 84–6.

12 Shanghai Municipal Agency of Environmental Protection, *Environmental Pollution*.

13 Xie Zhenhua (ed.), *Typical Cases*; Zhao Yongkang (ed.), *Selected Cases*.

14 On the causalities of different forms of collective violence in the contemporary Chinese countryside, see, e.g., Elizabeth J. Perry, 'Rural Collective Violence: the Fruits of Recent Reforms', in Elizabeth J. Perry and Christine Wong (eds), *The Political Economy of Reform in Post-Mao China* (Cambridge, MA: Harvard University Press, 1985), pp. 179–92.

15 See Kevin O'Brien and Lianjiang Li, 'The Politics of Lodging Complaints in Rural China', *China Quarterly*, 143 (September 1995), pp. 756–83; Minxin Pei, 'Citizens vs. Mandarins: Administrative Litigation in China', *China Quarterly*, 152 (December 1997), pp. 832–62.

Suggested reading

Cai Haili, 'Can Environmental Protection Work in China?' *Harvard China Review*, 1, 1 (1998), pp. 84–6.

Terry Cannon (ed.), *China's Economic Growth: The Impact on Regions, Migration and the Environment* (New York: St Martin's Press, 2000)

Dai Qing (ed.), *The River Dragon Has Come: The Three Gorges Dam and the Fate of China's Yangtze River and Its People* (Armonk: M.E. Sharpe, 1998).

Richard Louis Edmonds (ed.), *Managing the Chinese Environment* (New York and Oxford: Oxford University Press, 2000).

Mark Elvin and Ts'ui-jung Liu, *Sediments of Time: Environment and Society in Chinese History* (Cambridge: Cambridge University Press, 1998).

He Baochang, *China on the Edge: The Crisis of Ecology and Development* (San Francisco: China Books & Periodicals, 1991).

Jing Jun, 'Population Resettlement: Past Lessons for the Three Gorges Dam Project', *The China Journal*, Vol. 38, July 1997, pp. 65–92.

Kevin O'Brien and Lianjiang Li, 'The Politics of Lodging Complaints in Rural China', *China Quarterly*, 143 (September 1995), pp. 756–83.

Minxin Pei, 'Citizens vs. Mandarins: Administrative Litigation in China', *China Quarterly*, 152 (December 1997), pp. 832–62.

Elizabeth J. Perry, 'Rural Collective Violence: the Fruits of Recent Reforms', in Elizabeth J. Perry and Christine Wong (eds), *The Political Economy of Reform in Post-Mao China* (Cambridge, MA: Harvard University Press, 1985), pp. 179–92.

Judith Shapiro, *Mao's War against Nature: Politics and the Environment in Revolutionary China* (Cambridge: Cambridge University Press, 2001).

Vaclav Smil, *China's Environmental Crisis: An Inquiry into the Limits of National Development* (Armonk: M.E. Sharpe, 1993).

Robert P. Weller and Hsin-Hung Michael Hsiao, 'Culture, Gender, and Community in Taiwan's Environmental Movement', in Arne Kalland and Gerald Persoon (eds), *Environmental Movements in Asia* (London: Curzon, 1998), pp. 83–108.

World Bank, *Clear Water, Blue Skies: China's Environment in the New Century* (Washington, DC: The International Bank for Reconstruction and Development, 1997).

10 Alter/native Mongolian identity

From nationality to ethnic group

Uradyn E. Bulag

Introduction

Ethnic conflict and unrest are among the myriad social problems confronting China in the era of reform and opening. In recent years, Chinese leaders have warned of ethno-nationalist insurgencies in Tibet, Xinjiang and Inner Mongolia, and in the wake of 9–11 have branded dissident movements in these autonomous regions as terrorist. While launching ambitious affirmative action programmes, the Chinese state has not hesitated to deploy military and security forces to suppress minority resistance and unrest. The high international profile of the exiled Dalai Lama and the tension and military crackdown in Xinjiang have propelled ethnic issues, including questions of national self-determination, on to the world stage. Whereas questions of ethno-nationalism and human rights now occupy a central place in China's relations with neighbouring countries, as well as Europe and America, fluctuating Western discourse on ethnicity and nationalism, and particularly on terror, does not augur well for minorities in China and other regions of ethnic conflict.

The Chinese state has been quick to seize the opportunities opened up by 9–11 to change its terminology in framing ethnic activism: instead of the conventional term 'secessionism', or the more colorful 'splittism', the Chinese government now routinely labels ethnic protest as terrorism – with open US government support in the case of Xinjiang. The result has not simply been to delegitimize the East Turkestan civil rights and independence movements, but to set off minority resistance *per se* against 'humanity', thereby ignoring the specific historical conditions that brew ethnic dissent.

Behind this terminological rectification are changes in conceptualizing not only ethnic resistance, but also the place of ethnicity and ethno-nationalism in an age when new forms of governance other than national states are on the rise. Until recently, the dominant approach in the West has pitted ethnic nationalism against communist multinational states – the source of much of the celebration of ethnic resistance against 'Communism'. This approach is predicated on a 'denial of the coevalness'[1] of the histories of nationalism, as though ethno-nationalism in communist states were a primitive ancestor of Western nationalism, representing freedom, liberty, democracy and brotherhood, now directed against totalitarianism. But above all it essentializes ethnicity as the exclusive definition of identity for minority peoples, and it isolates ethnicity from the complex and fluid socio-economic and political contexts of ethnic relations, including intra-ethnic divisions and diverse aspirations of minority peoples. Small wonder that when ethno-nationalism triumphed against communism in the Soviet Union and Yugoslavia, and turned into bloody infighting among ethnic groups, we saw a hasty denunciation of ethno-nationalism, labelling it as ethnic cleansing, accompanied with a nostalgia for the good old empire, now wrapped up in new linguistic veneers such as multiculturalism. The consequence of such Manichean framing deprives humanity of the basic conceptual tools for a negotiated settlement of ethnic disputes. More importantly, throughout the world, regimes have taken advantage of this conceptual incoherence ruthlessly to crack down on minority resistance.

Anthropologists and sociologists have long highlighted the fluidity of ethnic identities and boundaries in China and elsewhere. Instead of positing an ineluctable conflict with the state's communist or modernist agenda, proponents of this perspective call attention to the fact that the officially registered minority populations have increased dramatically in the post-Mao era, thanks in part to affirmative action policies that have given certain material advantages to minorities, such as exemption from the policy of limiting each family to one child, greater political representation in their own titular autonomous units, and privileged access to higher education and official positions.[2] The result is both population growth rates exceeding those of the Han, and decisions by many to register their ethnicity as a minority. The role of the state in inventing and classifying ethnic minorities and the latter's response to the state have led Dru Gladney to argue for a dialogical interpretation of ethnicity in China. He notes that established ethnic groups and the state are engaged in ongoing processes of social and political negotiation mediated on the basis of relations of power and hierarchy. Ethnic resistance in this view is a product of the state's own making, yet one that it cannot completely control: 'the role of the state must not be over-privileged. Even the most totalitarian of regimes has its limits. Ethnicity has a power and resilience of its own that acts in dialectical fashion with the state apparatus.'[3]

There is much truth in this perspective. It must, however, be qualified in situations such as those of Inner Mongolia, Tibet and Xinjiang. What we see in Inner Mongolia is not an invention of the Mongolian nationality by the Chinese state – the modern Mongolian nationality developed in a wider context, in relation to Russians, Manchus, Tibetans, Japanese and Chinese – but the transformation of the Mongolian nationality in China from a 'society' into a social category. At the heart of the issue is the tension concerning whether to categorize the Mongols, Tibetans and Uyghurs in 'national' terms, or in 'ethnic' terms. Should one recognize them as 'nationalities' (*minzu*), as they do themselves, one would highlight history, state tradition and culture, as well as the process of 'incorporation' or 'colonization'. The 'national' approach presupposes that a nation or nationality exists as a society with a fully functional division of labour. The 'ethnic' approach treats minorities as a 'category', whose legitimacy lies in its 'relationship' to a dominant other, and whose analytical focus centres on the symbolic or discursive maintenance of 'boundaries', rather than the 'content' or nature of the group. One may say that 'Tibetan Studies' or 'Mongolian Studies' or 'Uyghur Studies' adopt the former approach, whereas anthropological studies of Chinese ethnicities tend to emphasize the latter perspective. While protagonists of either approach seldom communicate with each other, they sometimes accuse the other of either 'orientalism' or 'post-modernism'. I propose that contemporary ethnic or national minority conflicts and demands can be more fruitfully understood from a historically sensitive examination of the passage from nation or nationality to ethnic group, or from nationalism to ethnicity, not only in terminology, but also in substance.

This chapter examines the development and changing trajectory of the Mongolian nationality in the Inner Mongolia Autonomous Region. It highlights the discrepancy between the promised liberation and the abject reality, the conditions that shape Mongol complicity and resistance, and the changing nature of Chinese state policy towards minority nationalities. It does not provide a general ethnoscape for China. China is a multinational state whose one hundred million minority peoples constitute 8 per cent of the population and occupy approximately 60 per cent of the national territory, including its most sensitive border areas. The official recognition of fifty-five minorities indicates, however, that minority nationalities are fragmented and that each is numerically insignificant *vis-à-vis* the one-billion strong majority 'Han Chinese': the largest minority, the Zhuang, number just over fifteen million, while the smallest number only several thousand. There is no uniform pattern of minorities, as each has its distinct history, culture, language and territorial association. Nor are minority nationalities unified by any single religion. However, a study of the Mongols is warranted, for the Inner Mongolia Autonomous Region was the first instance of minority autonomy (instituted in May 1947), and it became a model that was subsequently applied to other non-Chinese peoples in the form of autonomous territorial institutions at the provincial level in Tibet, Xinjiang, Guangxi and Ningxia, and at lower levels within Chinese provinces. Likewise, many Tibetans and Uyghurs see in Inner Mongolia's fate important clues to their imminent future.

Remapping Inner Mongolia: from nationality to ethnic group

Has the last half-century fulfilled the promise of a reborn Mongolian nationality blossoming in its own 'autonomous' region? There has been an increase in the Mongol population, large numbers of Mongolian officials serve in all sectors throughout the autonomous region, and other positive signs point to a flourishing Mongolian nationality within the multinational People's Republic. Yet, how do we account for the discrepancy between Chinese government claims of gains achieved by the Mongols and other minorities, and the widely held

Mongolian perception that the autonomous region has provided the institutional framework under which the very survival of the Mongolian nationality has been undermined? There can be no easy answer to this question, and I believe the crux of the matter lies precisely in how it is conceptualized. The official perspective ignores the overriding fact that until 1900, for all their problems, Mongols enjoyed far greater autonomy under the Qing dynasty than anything conceivable a century later. In the thirteenth and fourteenth centuries, Mongols were world conquerors, building the largest land empire the world has seen. Although subjugated by the Manchus for over two and half centuries between the mid-seventeenth and early twentieth centuries, and divided into two administrative regions, Outer and Inner Mongolia, Mongols enjoyed higher status within the Qing empire than other groups, including the Chinese. Above all, Mongols were autonomous of the Chinese, with the Great Wall the boundary between Mongolia and China, and with migration of Chinese to Inner and Outer Mongolia tightly controlled. It was this territorial-material foundation that enabled Outer Mongolia to achieve nominal independence when the Qing collapsed in 1911 and the Chinese set up their own 'Republic of China'.

Inner Mongolian nationalism was principally galvanized by two contrasting events. One was the Outer Mongolian victory in defending their homeland and surviving as a nation at a time when Inner Mongolia was overrun by Chinese warlords and inundated with Chinese immigrants who confiscated pastureland for cultivation. Second was the erasure of the very name 'Inner Mongolia' from the map. In 1928, having conquered north China and set up central government rule under the Chinese Nationalist Party (Guomindang), Jiang Jieshi placed all frontier territories under newly created provinces, such as Rehe, Chahar, Suiyuan, Ningxia and Qinghai, a process that divided the historic Mongol homeland into several provinces, and deprived Mongols of political and military control. Of all the territories of the former Qing empire, only Outer Mongolia and central Tibet remained beyond Chinese control.

In 1949, the People's Republic of China proclaimed a multinational state, promising autonomy for minority nationalities. China's national autonomy system is as much a projection of the Chinese Communist Party's (CCP) ideological commitment to equality as it is a concession to Mongol and other non-Chinese demands to recognize difference and autonomy. The latter goals emerged as the product of strategic alliances linking minority nationalities and the CCP in order to defeat the Guomindang. One group that made particularly important contributions to the Chinese Communist victory, and consequently was able to bargain for some form of 'autonomy', were the Mongols of Inner Mongolia. The critical role played by Mongol communists in the consolidation of CCP power, and their strategic geographical location on the border of the independent Mongolian People's Republic (MPR) and the Soviet Union, as well as their ethnic affinity with the MPR, were central to this outcome. In this situation, Mongols sought to become a socialist 'nationality' within an autonomous territory, while recognizing China's sovereignty.

This autonomy and the socialist nationality-building process lie at the heart of nationality problems in contemporary Inner Mongolia. The Mongols' vision of the autonomous region as an ethnic safe haven in which they would develop their own culture and economy clashed with a Communist Party commitment to developing 'Chinese' socialism. Nationality autonomy was a temporary concession; the ultimate goal viewed from Beijing being full integration into China, rather than a commitment to equality and 'liberation'.

The national regional autonomy concept, providing no constitutional right to secession, violates the very principle of 'autonomy': minorities were not granted exclusive rights to territory but were blended with Chinese, the ostensible goal being the latter 'helping' the former, that is the 'advanced' showing the way to the 'backward'. The result was settlement of large numbers of Chinese in many so-called nationality 'autonomous areas'; indeed, in many cases, the Chinese came to outnumber the titular minority (*zhuti minzu*) by far. This gerrymandering leaves both sides deeply aggrieved: minorities blame the Chinese for colonization by settlers, repeating Guomindang practices, and Chinese settlers lash out at the minorities for enjoying excessive privileges, appealing to majoritarian democratic principles. A fruitful analysis of ethnicity in China should heed this dual perception and the conflict that it embodies.

The Inner Mongolia Autonomous Government, established in 1947 on Mongol territory previously incorporated in the Japanese puppet state Manchukuo, boldly called for return of all historic Mongol territory as Mao Zedong had promised in 1935. In soliciting Mongol help against Japanese invasion and the Guomindang shortly after the Long March, Mao promised:

> We maintain that the six leagues, twenty-four sections, and forty-nine banners of Inner Mongolia, Chahar, the two sections of Tumute as well as the whole area of the three special banners in Ningxia, whether they have changed their status into *xian* or have been designated as grassland, should be returned to the Inner Mongolian people as part of their territory. The titles of the three administrative provinces of Re[he], Cha[har], and Sui[yuan] and their de facto administrative offices should be abolished. Under no circumstances should other nationalities be allowed to occupy the land of the Inner Mongolian nation or expropriate it under various excuses.[4]

Mongols began their westward expansion from eastern Mongolia as soon as the People's Republic of China was proclaimed. In 1949, Jirim league of Liaobei province and Jo'uda league of Rehe province were incorporated into Inner Mongolia. Moving from Ulaanhot to Zhangjiakou, the capital of Chahar province in 1949, Inner Mongolian government personnel oversaw the incorporation of three ethnically mixed counties of Chahar province when the latter was abolished in 1952. In 1954, Suiyuan province was incorporated in Inner Mongolia, not however without compromising the autonomy of Inner Mongolia by mutual concessions in a scheme called opening 'two doors'. Under the terms of this incorporation, Suiyuan opened its door to Mongols, and Mongols allowed Chinese to remain in an enlarged Inner Mongolia. In 1956, the Inner Mongolia Autonomous Region took its current shape with some large chunks of former Mongol land that had been lost to neighbouring provinces reorganized as Mongolian autonomous counties.

This territorial expansion might be seen as a remarkable victory for the Mongols, especially compared to the fragmentation of Tibet into the Tibet Autonomous Region, the Kham region in Sichuan province, and the Amdo region in Qinghai and Gansu provinces, whose reunification as Tibet remains a priority of the Dalai Lama. However, the Mongol territorial victory was won at a huge cost, for it increased the already substantial demographic disparity between Mongols and Chinese, causing further problems for Mongols in terms of cultural survival. Ironically, the Mongol territorial ambition to 'recover' lost Inner Mongolian territory, leaving unsolved the demographic imbalance in favour of the Chinese within the recovered territory, resulted in ever deeper integration. Table 10.1 shows the population breakdowns by region and nationality in 1937 in the territories of historical Inner Mongolia:

By 1949, while there were 835,000 Mongols, a reduction of 10,000, the Chinese population of entire Inner Mongolia had shot up to 5,154,000, an increase of almost one and a half million, lowering the Mongol percentage to 13.7 per cent.[5] As is clear from Table 10.1, as early as 1937 Suiyuan province already had over two million Chinese. The incorporation of this number of Chinese into the Inner Mongolia Autonomous Region in 1954 severely reduced the overall population ratio which was 39.8 per cent in eastern Mongolia.

The territorial expansion of the Inner Mongolia Autonomous Region was accompanied by a severe reduction in autonomous rights as the party's national programme of land reform, agricultural collectivization and nationalization of industry proceeded throughout China including Inner Mongolia. Moreover, whatever the constitutional guarantees of minority rights, the central reality in Inner Mongolia was a massive influx of Chinese migrants, whose arrival coincided with land reform and collectivization, as well as the transfer of large and

Table 10.1   Population breakdowns by region and nationality in the territories of historical Inner Mongolia, 1937

Region	Chinese	Mongol	Total	Mongol (%)
Hinggan East	47,868	19,980	67,848	29.4
Hinggan South	303,573	314,447	618,020	50.8
Hinggan West	339,224	114,583	453,807	25.2
Hinggan North	24,032	28,176	52,208	53.9
Rehe	796,854	103,328	900,182	11.4
Suiyuan	2,064,565	195,435	2,260,000	8.6
Chahar	142,997	68,477	211,474	32.3
Total	3,719,113	844,429	4,563,542	18.5

Source: Adapted from Song Naigong (ed.), *Zhongguo Renkou: Nei Menggu Fence* (China's Population: Inner Mongolia) (Beijing: Zhongguo Caizheng Jingji Chubanshe, 1987), pp. 52, 54.

medium-sized factories from coastal and inland China. Between 1950 and 1957, 1,536,100 Chinese migrated into Inner Mongolia. An additional 1,926,600 Chinese moved in between 1958 and 1960 as famine refugees.[6] More pastures were reclaimed for agriculture during this period than in any previous time.

Faced with the Chinese influx, Mongol cadres and intellectuals began to call for implementation of autonomous rights guaranteeing equality and so on. After 1958, however, demands for autonomy were attacked as treasonous to China and as undermining Chinese national unity. Chinese officials accused Mongols, especially Mongol communist officials, of conspiring to create a pan-Mongolian state. As a result, more than 20,000 Mongols were killed and more than 300,000 injured during the turmoil in Inner Mongolia from 1967 to 1969, according to official party figures released in 1982.[7] This was by far the highest number of officially acknowledged casualties and deaths in any single province or autonomous region during the Cultural Revolution. In 1969, as Sino–Soviet tension escalated, the territory of the Inner Mongolia Autonomous Region was drastically reduced, with several leagues turned over for administrative purposes to Heilongjiang, Jilin, Liaoning and Gansu provinces, and Ningxia Hui Autonomous Region. As soon as the Cultural Revolution was over, Mongols mounted campaigns to reclaim their lost territories, and in 1979 they succeeded. However, this 1979 territorial unification, presented as both Mongol victory and the gift of a magnanimous party's great 'nationality policy', left unresolved the old issue of territory and population. Even a small-scale effort in 1979–80 to oust Chinese settlers who had moved in during the Cultural Revolution, and who had participated in brutally persecuting the Mongols, was halted by direct orders from the party centre, and the Mongol officials involved were punished.

Paradoxes of linguistic resistance

How did the Mongols develop their 'nationality' under these circumstances? Nationality or *minzu* was initially defined on the basis of Stalin's four criteria: common territory, common economy, common language and common psychological make-up. For Mongols, these four criteria occupy the central place in their national consciousness, and the success or failure to satisfy them has direct bearing on their perception of the Mongolian nationality as prospering or dying. I focus here on language and economy.

In the *minzu*-building project, the Chinese state went so far as to invent scripts for some minorities that had no written language, not primarily for the cultural reproduction of the *minzu* concerned, but to enable them better to absorb communist-cum-Chinese ideas. There was no need to invent the Mongol written language, which has long existed. However, language is one of the criteria that creates 'difference', thereby justifying 'autonomy', and it can produce a drama of linguistic resistance, an outcome discussed below in the context of the processes through which Mongols lost their 'society' and became an 'ethnic group'.

Towards the end of the Qing dynasty, as some Mongols settled down and took up farming, intermixed with growing numbers of Chinese settlers, they quickly lost their language, becoming Chinese speakers. Only those in the shrinking pastoral areas continued to speak Mongolian, a gift of the lack of Chinese penetration. Mongol language loss was thus concurrent with and a product in large part of Chinese colonization. Inner Mongolian nationalism in the early twentieth century developed precisely in response to both this cultural loss and colonization. It was those groups that had lost the language that became the most ardent nationalists or communists-cum-nationalists. For instance, the Harchin, a highly sinicized Mongol group scattered in today's Inner Mongolia and Liaoning province, founded and staffed the bulk of the Inner Mongolian People's Revolutionary Party, a party launched in 1925 and disbanded in 1928–9. And it was the sinicized Tumed Mongols in today's central Inner Mongolia who provided leadership to the Inner Mongolian communist movement. Ulanhu, a Tumed and the paramount communist leader of Inner Mongolia who founded and led the Autonomous Region, could not even speak Mongolian, although he studied in Moscow and was fluent in Russian. The Horchin Mongols, many of whom were pidgin Mongol speakers, whose intellectuals were more at home in Chinese than Mongolian, became ardent nationalists and nationalistic communists, aspiring to Mongolian independence/autonomy. They constitute the majority of contemporary Mongolian leaders and intellectuals.

In short, it was largely sinicized or half-sinicized Mongols who became nationalists and communists, and took up the historic task of liberating the Mongols from Chinese rule, or achieving autonomy from and equality with the Chinese. As nationalists, they aspired to revive and develop the Mongol language, perhaps precisely because they were themselves largely bereft of it, and this they attempted in the Inner Mongolia Autonomous Region as part of their *minzu*-building project.

Language became a major issue in 1952, as soon as the seat of government moved to Hohhot, originally a monastic town divided between Manchu (army), Chinese (merchants) and Mongol (monks and pilgrims) quarters, which quickly became overwhelmingly Chinese with the migration of tens of thousands of workers and officials from north China. Very soon, the children of Mongol cadres and intellectuals lost their language because of the combination of peer pressure from Chinese children and classroom instruction in Chinese rather than Mongol. The children of sinicized Mongol cadres and intellectuals, of course, had little chance of mastering Mongolian language in this new setting. This situation stirred strong resentment among Mongol officials and intellectuals, who voiced their criticism in the Hundred Flowers Movement in 1957. If, in old China, Mongols had lost their language because of the oppression of 'Great Han Chauvinists', they asked, what could account for the loss of Mongol language in the New China in which ethnic oppression was supposed to have been eliminated and all nationalities were equal? One month later, this officially sanctioned criticism was crushed as a veiled attack on the party and the Chinese nation. Language became an issue precisely when it became one of the defining principles of Mongol nationality.

The Chinese communist nationality policy has a built-in contradiction: its class approach impels it to take affirmative action towards minorities, but it simultaneously subscribes to an 'ideology of contempt' for minority languages and cultures. In a nationalizing communist regime such as China's, this 'ideology of contempt' has taken on a strong Chinese chauvinist colouring. Therefore, no sooner did the Mongols begin to enjoy some of their newly gained rights, including the right to use their language, than this aspiration was considered by the Chinese as contravening Chinese national interest and communist ideology. An in-built majoritarian morality of communism enabled the Chinese leadership to make the Chinese, by virtue of their numerical majority, the chosen 'people', and their language (*putonghua* or Mandarin, the officially recognized dialect of the Beijing area) the advanced language of destiny. Curiously, the very term *minzu* or nationality was reserved almost solely for minorities, while the Chinese (Han) came to be tacitly recognized as 'the people'. By this logic, minority nationalities have been defined as 'backward', meaning that their salvation lies in being assimilated by the Chinese 'people'. From this perspective, the initial promotion of minority languages, ostensibly presented to promote 'nationality equality', had, in effect, put them on the lower rung of the Chinese communist ideological hierarchy of languages. Thus persistent clinging to one's nationality language could be seen as 'reactionary', if not the deliberate sabotage of socialist 'construction'.

This association of political correctness and linguistic chauvinism posed a stark choice to Mongols: to remain politically and scientifically 'backward' (thereby inevitably subjecting themselves to the Chinese civilizing mission)[8] or to 'catch up', in the first instance by incorporating key loan words from Chinese but ultimately by abandoning the Mongol language in favour of Chinese. While a few Chinese-leaning Mongol linguists advocated taking in not only borrowed words from Chinese, but even sounds and grammatical components, most Mongol officials resisted this by forming a committee to borrow words from Cyrillic Mongolian used in the Mongolian People's Republic. They rejected the idea that Chinese was the only appropriate source of loan words. Their unique link to the MPR, where a Communist government was established in 1921, the very year that the Chinese Communist Party was founded, provided a proud alternative. Mongols then not only resisted in terms of cultural difference, but also from an ideological and political high ground. However, tensions between China and its neighbouring MPR and the Soviet Union mounted throughout the 1950s. Ever politically acute, in the late 1950s, Ulanhu said that the reason for Inner Mongolia to adopt MPR linguistic practices was to use Inner Mongolian newspapers and books to propagate Mao Zedong thought to the MPR, pandering to Mao's dream of recovering the lost 'Outer Mongolia'. For this reason, Inner Mongolia need not insist on retaining distinctive Inner Mongolian language practices, but would follow those of the MPR (Tumen and Zhu 1995: 135). This 'public transcript' conveniently disguised an Inner Mongolian aspiration for cultural unification with the MPR behind a façade of Chinese patriotism.

Mongol linguistic resistance was poignantly demonstrated in 1957 by Ulanhu, who delivered his speech in Mongolian on the tenth anniversary of the founding of the Inner Mongolia Autonomous Region. Many Mongols were moved to tears, and could not forget his act even after his death in 1988. Mongols interpreted his Mongol speech as defiance against a Chinese chauvinist onslaught against Mongol culture. It was sensational because Ulanhu could not speak Mongolian, since he belonged to the Tumed Mongol group which had lost Mongolian language a century ago. He read his speech from a text written in Cyrillic that was translated from his original Chinese.

The limited minority language right granted in the package of nationality autonomy had a hidden trap. The Chinese majority might tolerate the continued use of minority languages if this was seen as useful to enhance communist consciousness, or if conditions were not 'ripe', meaning not enough indigenous communists were trained, as in the case of Tibetans or Uyghurs. But how could Inner Mongolian communists promote their language in their autonomous region, especially at a time when Mongols had become a numerical minority in their own autonomous region? Mongol communists dominated the local political arena, but they were vastly outnumbered by Chinese communist cadres, some of them new arrivals. As early as 1953, Ulanhu reported that some Chinese cadres took offence at Mongols reading Mongolian: 'If you read only Mongolian, you still haven't overcome your narrow nationalist thought. Proletarians are not divided by nationality.' He cited another example. 'In the Ulanchab League, a public security officer spoke in Chinese. When some people suggested he speak in Mongolian, another cadre shouted a slogan against this suggestion: "Oppose narrow nationalism!" '9

Against seemingly insurmountable obstacles to Mongols using their own language in Inner Mongolia, they devised an ingenious approach. Since they were the titular nationality, and Mongolian was an official language along with Chinese in Inner Mongolia, they held that it was the duty of Mongolians to learn Chinese, and for Chinese cadres in Inner Mongolia to learn Mongolian. In 1962, the Inner Mongolian government launched a programme financially to reward government employees and party cadres who learned Mongolian and used it in their everyday work. This programme was applicable to Chinese and other nationalities in Inner Mongolia. If a Chinese demonstrated Mongolian ability, he or she would be rewarded. However, unlike in the province of Quebec in Canada where minority language French is legally enforced, in Inner Mongolia, this meagre material reward proved ineffective. Attempts by Mongol leaders to bribe Chinese to learn 'backward' Mongolian fell flat. Perhaps there were simply not enough funds to make it worthwhile for the 'advanced' to learn from the 'backward'.

In the event, such efforts to strengthen Mongol language use were crushed in 1966, when Chinese was vigorously promoted as the 'unified motherland language', and Mongolian was prohibited in many areas. Only a little more than a decade elapsed between inventing scripts for some minorities and banning minority languages. Such a contradictory course could not but provoke resistance.

Immediately after the Cultural Revolution formally ended in 1976, Mongols mounted strong resistance to learning Chinese. In 1981, Chuluun Bagan, a Mongol linguist, strongly argued in favour of preserving Mongolian, insisting that forcing Mongols to learn Chinese was assimilationism of the worst kind.[10] Shenamjil made more serious charges:

> Encouraging those children who didn't know Chinese to study Chinese directly resulted in a dismal situation in which they learned well neither Chinese nor their nationality language. This practice has wasted minority talents, adversely impacted the development of the intelligence of the people of minority nationalities, negatively influencing the development of the economy and culture of minority regions.[11]

This post Cultural Revolution reaction against the monopoly of the Chinese language spurred enthusiasm throughout Inner Mongolia to revive the use of Mongolian in public and in private. Even some sinicized Mongols set out to reclaim their linguistic heritage.

The Tumed are a Chinese-speaking Mongolian group in Inner Mongolia who enjoy political leverage over both Chinese and other Mongol groups, thanks largely to the high profile role played by Ulanhu and other Tumed communists. Their success depended on their mastery of Chinese, their association with communism, and an ethnic consciousness that enabled them to build ties to other Mongols. After 1949, their ethnic consciousness was shaped in part by the loss of Mongolian language by other Mongol groups. In the 1950s, they set up many *minzu* primary schools and middle schools that recruited only Mongol students. Where Mongol students were few, they made sure that a general school would have a 'Mongolian students class' (*mengshengban*), separate from Chinese students. One of the aims for such 'nationality' schools and classes was to facilitate the learning of Mongolian. But this was not quite successful. Mongol students were reluctant to learn Mongolian because of fears of social stigma in a predominantly Chinese social environment.

After 1976, with the end of the Cultural Revolution, however, Mongol officials who had been deposed and in many instances placed under house arrest or imprisoned, regained power across Inner Mongolia, and some even attained positions in Beijing. They then resumed and sought to expand Mongol education and cultural revival. The Mongol cultural sentiment of many of these Tumed officials surpassed that of many other Mongols, due to the fact that they suffered perhaps the fiercest attacks from the Chinese during the Cultural Revolution.

The new attempt to provide a Mongol education began in September 1979. The Tumed Banner Education Bureau then set up an experimental kindergarten at Nationality Primary School at Bagshi Commune, recruiting fifty-nine 6-year-olds who were taught everything from mathematics to history in Mongolian. Six Mongolian teachers were invited from the pastoral areas, so that the children could learn 'pure' standard Mongolian. In order to create a good language environment, the kindergarten was located in a closed compound, where both children and teachers lived. It was complete immersion, with orders issued that conversations in everyday life as well as in the classroom be conducted in Mongolian. The following year, fifty children from the kindergarten entered first grade to continue their education in Mongolian. Chinese students moved to a separate newly built school. On this foundation, the banner built a 'Mongolian Nationality Primary School' in October 1982 in the banner centre. Its eight classes divided into three grades and had 201 boarding pupils, all taught in Mongolian. What is interesting is that Chinese was taught only from the fifth grade, and then in the manner that a foreign language might be taught.[12] The students were not allowed to leave the compound without permission, and they returned home only on holidays. Lest they be contaminated by their Chinese-speaking parents and relatives or Chinese neighbours, during vacations they were sent to the grassland to learn directly from pure Mongol-speaking herders.

The Tumed Mongolizing project was admired by many Mongols. It was remarkable in their eyes that, having lost the Mongol language for over a century, the Tumed were determined to reclaim their cultural heritage. But the project was doomed from the start.

Note the practice of *fengbi shi jiaoyu* (closed-door education) as a means to create a small utopian community cut off from the polluting wider world. One might question the fundamental concept of such an educational method, resting as it did on a premise of seclusion that could only produce students unfamiliar with, and hence unable to cope with, a wider society. This Mongolizing educational enterprise turned out Mongol-speaking Tumed Mongols, who lacked the ability to succeed in the wider Inner Mongolian society increasingly dominated by Chinese in all sectors. The difficulty these students faced in obtaining employment contrasts sharply with that of their parents or grandparents, who were successful not only in the regional but also in the national political and economic arena in no small part because of their mastery of spoken and written Chinese. Understandably, local Mongols sharply criticized such schemes as crippling or wasting the talent of the younger generation of Tumed Mongols. Although these schools quickly lost students to Chinese schools, the project nevertheless continued to receive support from what Naran Bilik calls oldtimers, i.e. some Mongol intellectuals and cadres, 'who supported the establishment of the school and invested much emotional capital with political metaphors'.[13]

This case shows, at a different level, the role of minority cadres/intellectuals in their perception of the Mongol nationality. However, rather than simplistically criticizing the cultural nationalists, we need to grasp the social context that impelled some Tumed Mongol intellectuals to take such desperate measures.

This romantic resistance failed precisely because it could not solve the material condition for the reproduction of national culture. Mongols, as a minority, have been unable to create favourable conditions for the use of Mongolian to pursue a career, achieve social mobility and, above all, realize social values. The pursuit of the cultural value system by Mongol political and cultural leaders diverged significantly from lived material reality, i.e. the pervasive market economy dominated by a Chinese-speaking majority within and without Inner

Mongolia since the 1980s. In this situation, Mongols as a group have experienced the loss of formal positional power even as a small number of adept individuals with social capital have managed to achieve marginal success. Market economy demands the ability to translate dwindling Mongol social capital into economic capital, to use French sociologist Pierre Bourdieu's helpful terms. The cruel reality is that in cities and banner centres, there are hardly any work units in which Mongolian language is required or even useful. Since almost all jobs are controlled by Chinese, even university-level Mongolian knowledge is tantamount to illiteracy. It is such bitter personal experiences that now compel many parents to make sure that their tragedy will not be repeated by their children.

This experience sets in motion many processes. These include a unique 'voluntary' drive to shed ethnic identity, leading many Mongols to intensify efforts to learn Chinese in their determination not to be left behind. Those who have forgotten Mongolian are admired, since they seem equipped, at least linguistically and socially, to join directly in economic development. In a 1997 tour of a banner in western Inner Mongolia, which is predominantly pastoral, and where local people speak Mongol and have only stammering proficiency in Chinese, I noted that a Mongol cadre who was trained from primary school to university in Mongolian chose to explain technical matters and policies in Chinese to herders who could barely understand him. In a township-level middle school, 10 per cent of the Mongol students applied to join Chinese language class, hoping to secure a factory or commercial job. The party secretary of the township complained to me that he did not write Chinese well. Not only did this hamper promotion, he also understood that the reports that he and fellow leaders wrote in Mongolian were ignored at the higher levels. As a result, there was scant hope that much-needed financial support for alleviating poverty would ever be allocated to his village. His 'hidden transcript' did not however translate into insisting on using Mongolian. Instead, he quietly honed his Chinese and made sure that his children attended Chinese schools.

A telling example is provided by Mongol language researchers and professors in several elite universities in Hohhot, the capital of Inner Mongolia, who send their own children to Chinese-language schools. Ironically, these teachers instruct students to read and write Mongolian, yet make sure that their own children learn Chinese and specialize not in Mongolian studies but in science or computer courses taught exclusively in Chinese. Many of them now regret that they stayed on as teachers not because they loved it, but because they knew nothing else. They spoke as victims who had suddenly awoken from a bad dream. Through the combined weight of diverse institutions and social processes, people speaking non-Chinese languages are now induced, as Bourdieu puts it, 'to collaborate in the destruction of their instruments of expression'.[14]

But it is not inevitable that the Mongol language deprives its speakers of opportunities for advancement. This is the outcome of processes whereby the *minzu* project is subverted by chauvinism. Because of this subversion, Mongols have lost the political and linguistic capital they had long accumulated. Nor can hard work enable them to re-accumulate this capital. As Bourdieu advises, capital is related to *the* specific field or arena in which a form is utilized. Political capital and linguistic capital take their form from the arena within which they are utilized. Since the 'arena' has changed from socialist *minzu*-building to a capitalist market economy, in which *minzu* is more an obstacle than an advantage, and in which individualism is prioritized, it requires different forms of capital. The socialist Mongolian *minzu* subjects suddenly found themselves 'bankrupt' in this transition initiated by the reformist Chinese party-state.

Grassland identity as resistance symbol for Mongols?

In the cases of linguistic resistance examined above, pastoral areas were often imagined to be the ideal cultural setting for Mongols. Pastoralism, an economic and social practice adapted to the ecology of the grasslands and dating back to antiquity, has become the ultimate cultural symbol defining the core of Mongol identity. In the process of developing socialist Mongolian *minzu*, other economic activities, such as farming, although practised by a large proportion of the Mongol population, including some pastoralists, came to be associated with memories of Chinese colonization and thus were viewed by Mongols as alien to Mongolness.

For three and a half centuries pastoralism was preserved and farming spurned among Mongols in order to maintain a Mongol military prowess that could be used in the service of the Manchu rule of China. Mongols were unable, however, to cope with the avalanche of Chinese immigrants, agricultural expansion and cultural assimilation that resulted from the Qing dynasty's new immigration policy in 1902. Following the fall of the Qing in 1911, defending pasture against Chinese agricultural colonization became a battle cry that was the driving force behind Inner Mongolian nationalism. Numerous Mongol uprisings occurred between 1910 and the 1940s, including clashes with Mongol nobles for selling land, as well as resistance against Chinese land grabbing.

Agricultural expansion remained an extremely sensitive issue in Inner Mongolia after 1949. In 1958, in a major turn of policy towards ethnic minorities, the Chinese state began a massive colonization programme that turned a large part of Mongol pasture into military farms along the northern borders with the MPR and the Soviet Union. Military farming and civilian agricultural expansion were informed by Chinese disdain towards pastoralism, a perspective that denigrates pasture as wild land (*huangdi*), as well as by a socialist evolutionary hierarchy that conveniently ranks farming above pastoralism in a hierarchy of economic activities that slights the nature of the steppe terrain. Mongol herders were enjoined to abandon pastoral production in favour of farming under the slogan 'Herders should not eat grain with a guilty conscience' (*mumin bu chi kuixin liang*). In the frenzy of the Great Leap Forward, the Chinese exercised dominion over Mongols, attacking pastoralism and accelerating large-scale Chinese migration to the Mongol homeland.

The famine disaster of the Great Leap Forward and the Chinese admission of mistakes provided the first opportunity for Mongols to negotiate a settlement of the military farms directly with Beijing. By 1962, most of the military farms were returned to pasture. Chinese immigration was also temporarily halted. This move earned Ulanhu huge popularity among Mongol herders, and his feat remains legendary today when opening grassland for agricultural use can no longer be resisted effectively. The success of this resistance in the early 1960s was predicated on the counter-critique developed by Mongols who argued that expansive military farming at the expense of grassland violated the party's nationality policy and showed disrespect for nationality autonomy. Moreover, they argued that the policy turned valuable pasture land into desert.

It is possible that inter-ethnic confrontation between farming and herding in Inner Mongolia only strengthened ethnic polarization between these two modes of production in socialist China. The Mongol emotional tie linked to pastoralism may be described, following Fujitani, as a Mongolian 'mnemonic site', referring to a 'material vehicle of meaning that helped construct a memory ... or that served as a symbolic marker'.[15] Similarly, farming is a 'mnemonic site' of the Chinese. Each side struggles to invest positive meaning to its side, and negative meaning to the opposing side.

We should be cautious not to invest Mongol resistance with too much romanticism. The binary ethnic divide between farming and pastoralism ultimately shaped a socialist Mongol identity based on the image of the herder, and yet, as Almaz Khan has shown, this hegemonic herder symbolism marginalizes the majority of eastern Mongols who have long been farmers.[16] Since farming is excluded from the cultural repertoire used to construct a socialist Mongol nationality identity in China's Inner Mongolia, Mongol farmers become an unnameable category in the Mongol imagination.

Nor were there other possibilities for forging Mongol identity, in contrast, for example, with the identity of Tibetans, many of whom looked to Buddhism and its Lamas as a foundation for identity. Attempts were made in the 1950s to create modernist categories, such as the industrial working class, but these ultimately failed not only because the small number of Mongol workers were soon engulfed by the much larger Chinese migrant population, but above all because industry came to be appropriated by the Chinese, in both practice and image. It was not modernization *per se* that was responsible for this outcome but its concurrent sinicization that has exacted a heavy toll on Mongols. Urbanization and modernization have led to loss of Mongol language and culture, as urbanity is defined as Chinese because of the overwhelming Chinese predominance in the cities. For example, over 90 per cent of the residents of the capital, Hohhot, are Chinese. The image and the reality of a Mongolian industrial working class never developed.

Herders, grasslands and livestock thus became the primary markers of Mongol ethnicity during the socialist period. The grasslands represent more than a homeland; they stand for pure 'nature' (*baigal*), filled with fresh air and familiar smells, herds, yurts and mobility. This makes for the strongest possible contrast to Chinese culture, which is sedentary and agricultural with the predominance of grain, pig farming, commercial guile and dirt. The Mongol herder symbol is strategically boundary setting, and all its attributes can be summed up in a single factor: difference from the Chinese. It is an essentialist symbol, naturalized, ahistoricized and sanitized.

This grassland identity, whatever its romantic nationalist overtones, offers a paucity of other attributes to which modern Mongols individually aspire, i.e. productivity, progress, social mobility, creativity, technological skills and excitement. Because of this, upwardly mobile elements of the Mongol population continue to move to the cities, and few aspire to return 'home', that is to the grasslands. There is an extreme disjuncture of increasing urbanization and sinicization together with the increasing romanticization of the pastoral. Few bridges are available to connect the two, which remain separated by the state's household registration system (*hukou*). This only intensifies the rhetoric of Mongol 'intellectuals' claiming to defend their 'Mongol' identity in the grasslands. They sing songs, drink and cry, celebrating their pastoral identity. They also dream and yearn for power, re-imagining an 'underground' Mongol identity, based on military prowess and the moral qualities of the fighter symbolized by Chinggis Khan, the world conqueror.

In short, bereft of territorial autonomy, the *minzu*-building project necessarily delineates, strengthens and distorts ethnic consciousness. It also defines what constitutes a member of a nationality, often blithely disregarding contemporary social reality and aspirations that may be independent of, or at odds with, stereotypical *minzu* categories. A *minzu* is no longer a 'society' in its own right, but a location or positioning within the political economy of a nation-state.

When Chinese resist: rectifying the name of Inner Mongolia

I have so far discussed how China's dispensation of national autonomy in Inner Mongolia, while granting Mongols titular status, failed to provide for a material environment conducive to national reproduction of the Mongols. Putting the Mongols in a 'relational' context imbues them with characteristics of ethnicity, rather than a society with full integrity. This does not mean that the Mongols are the only people who feel victimized. The Chinese, by virtue of being the non-titular majority in Inner Mongolia, feel oppressed by their ostensibly second-class status, even as they rule the Chinese state and far outnumber Mongols in the autonomous region. For a long time, they have been represented by the state in Inner Mongolia as 'helpers' or 'guests', and while Mongols feel they have been colonized by these permanent migrants, the Chinese feel that their 'construction' of the frontier did not bring them appropriate material or spiritual benefit. They now fight for a rightful place in their host minority region, much as immigrants to Western countries who fight for equal rights. One important difference lies in the fact that whereas internationally there are laws and covenants as well as rights groups monitoring such matters, in China, an ethnic division of labour privileges the Chinese colonization as defending the motherland, and criminalizes minority opponents as 'splittists' or, since 9–11, as 'terrorists'.

The party-state long ago embarked on a process systematically to remove the foundations of minority autonomy by assertions of native status for Chinese everywhere, including in minority autonomous regions. Ever since the removal of Ulanhu from Inner Mongolia in 1966 at the start of the Cultural Revolution, the party secretary, the highest authority of Inner Mongolia, has been Chinese, a pattern found in all autonomous regions. Since 1994, in Inner Mongolia the top positions of both the People's Congress and the party have been held by Chinese, making an open mockery of claims of 'national autonomy'. A recent attempt to allay Mongol concerns resulted in a 1994 appointment to the post of party secretary of a Chinese from Shandong province with familial ties in Inner Mongolia, presenting him as a local 'Inner Mongolian' (*Neimeng ren*), a new identity that has no foundation in ethnicity.

Indeed, in the 1990s the Mongols would find their historic claim based on a history as the indigenous people of the region questioned. In 1994, a Chinese party leader delivered a lecture at the Inner Mongolia Party School, asserting that Chinese, not Mongols, were indigenous to the region. His extensive documentary sources and archaeological science were deployed to prove that Mongols settled in Inner Mongolia only 700 or 800 years ago, when they began to expand from their Siberian 'homeland', whereas the Chinese settled there before the Han dynasty 2,000 years ago.

This is not an isolated case peculiar to Inner Mongolia, but part of a concerted effort by local Chinese party leaders and academicians in minority regions. For instance, He Jihong, a Chinese scholar in Xinjiang, wrote that before the Han dynasty, only the Qang, Saizhong, Dayueshi, Wusong, Yilan and Han were indigenous (*tuzhu*) to Xinjiang. All of these except the Chinese subsequently disappeared without a trace. The Uyghurs, Mongols and other nationalities in Xinjiang, according to this view, only migrated there after the Chinese.[17] He further asserted that China would never suffer the same fate of dismemberment as the former Soviet Union, not only because the Chinese were indigenous in Xinjiang, but because Chinese and minorities in Xinjiang are bound by blood relations nurtured through centuries of intermarriage.[18] This claim to indigenous status is the basis for asserting Chinese contributions to the 'development' and 'prosperity' of the region.

Perhaps the most successful Chinese area of 'indigenization' was in changing native Mongolian administrative names while pushing for municipalization. Until 1976, the Inner Mongolia Autonomous Region had only two municipalities, Baotou and Hohhot. Now there are five additional municipalities: Wuhai established in 1976, Chifeng (formerly Jo'uda League) in 1981, Tongliao (formerly Jirim League) in 1999, Ordos (formerly Yekeju League) in 2001 and Hulunbuir (formerly Hulunbuir League) in 2002, outnumbering the prefecture-level leagues: Alasha, Bayannuur, Ulaanchab, Silingol and Hinggan. What is remarkable is that, except for Hulunbuir, none of the original league names has been retained.

The proliferation of cities or municipalities in Inner Mongolia is, among other things, also a reflection of this ethnic struggle, and a strategy of the

Chinese to expand their territorial space. Cities are not supposed to be ethnic, or autonomous, as we can glean from the absence of 'city' in the definition of autonomous areas in China's Law on Regional National Autonomy, and the fact that there are no autonomous cities in the People's Republic. I argue that although cities are also customarily associated with things 'Chinese', this legal lacuna and the obvious benefits to local officials of being honoured by the rise to city status trumps ethnic sensitivity.

This 'rectification of names' is of more than casual interest. Each change marked the brutal history of one nationality defeating the other, constituting in effect a regime change. Recall that Inner Mongolia disappeared from the Chinese map by 1928, and the founding of the Inner Mongolia Autonomous Government in 1947 led to the dismantling of Chinese provinces built on Mongol territories. Restoration of the Mongol administration along with their names, such as the change of Guisui (Return to Civilization and Pacify Barbarians City) to Hohhot (Blue City) in 1954, were presented to Mongols as the blessing of the party.

Less than thirty years later, in 1981, however, Jo'uda League was renamed Chifeng Municipality. At one stroke, a league with a Mongol name was turned into a city with a Chinese name. This did not go unchallenged. According to a senior Mongol official who participated in the meeting that discussed the choice of the name, the then party secretary Zhou Hui, a Chinese appointed by the CCP Central Committee, insisted on choosing Chifeng as the official name for the new municipality. A participant in the meeting suggested that even if the original Mongol name Jo'uda were not used, at least the Mongol word Ulaanhad for Chifeng be chosen, if only to show a token respect to the feelings of Mongols in this region. According to my informant, Zhou Hui shouted angrily at the speaker for exhibiting Mongol nationalist sentiment. The speaker happened to be a Chinese, but Zhou mistook him for a Mongol, whose mistake was to call for respecting the historical fact that Jo'uda League was a Mongol unit.

The change of Jirim League to Tongliao Municipality in October 1999 also replaces a Mongol name with a Chinese name meaning 'penetrating or opening up the Liao'. The historical reference is to the Liao dynasty (AD 916–1125) founded by non-Chinese Kitan people. As the party secretary and the mayor of Tongliao Municipality wrote in a glowing piece published in *People's Daily* on 6 October 1999,

> This is the result of deepening reform, expanding opening-up, and acceler-ating development undertaken by the people of Tongliao under the leadership of the Party ... By replacing league with municipality (*che meng she shi*), history once again gives Tongliao people a development opportunity that comes only once in a thousand years.[19]

One cannot but notice a forward outlook expressed in the above rhetoric, as though the advancement of the people of Tongliao had been until 1999 hampered by the Mongol administrative unit called Jirim League, and the renaming had at long last emancipated them.

In contrast to these dismal stories of 'rectification of names' at the expense of Mongol culture and autonomy, the change of Yekeju League to Ordos Municipality (E'erduosi Shi) appears encouraging, even gratifying, to Mongol sensibility. It is ostensibly the revival of the more authentic tribal name of the local Mongols, a name associated with the shrine of Chinggis Khan, replacing Yekeju, an administrative name imposed by the Qing dynasty and meaning 'Great Monastery'. Transformed into a municipality, Ordos appears to be both authentically Mongol and modern.

The territory of Yekeju League, surrounded by the Great Wall to the south, and encircled by the Yellow River to the west, north and east, is known as Ordos internationally as well as within China. The name Ordos derives from the local tradition of worshipping and safeguarding shrines of Chinggis Khan and other royal household members, a tradition instituted by Khubilai Khan.

It was not until the post-Mao period, after the thorough destruction of the Chinggis Khan shrine during the Cultural Revolution, that Mongols in the region began to take the initiative to promote a local 'Ordos culture' in relation to Chinggis Khan. Ordos songs, Ordos weddings and Ordos women's dresses have become the core of 'Inner Mongolian' culture, due not only to their natural appeal, but also to new folkloric aestheticization, and above all to the general identification with Chinggis Khan. Throughout the 1980s and 1990s, the so-called Chinggis Khan mausoleum was promoted not so much as a Mongol cultural tradition of ancestral worship but as the apotheosis of a great Chinese hero, 'the only Chinese who ever conquered the Europeans'. No doubt Mongols, as a minority, feel flattered by the Chinese state's renewed interest in Chinggis Khan. The mausoleum has been renovated and expanded, attracting millions of Chinese, Mongolian and overseas tourists every year to experience the glory of China's racial victory over the Whites.[20]

But these ethnocultural developments alone would not be sufficient to transform a league into a municipality, for urbanization has to do with industrialization. Until the 1970s, the league had been a rather poor region, with a dual economy of pastoralism and agriculture. In the 1980s, however, three major industries emerged: cashmere sweaters, coal mining and chemicals, all dominated by local Chinese. They were so successful that within the decade they became the three most successful industries in all Inner Mongolia. They were also the first three Inner Mongolian industries to be listed on the stock markets in Shanghai and Shenzhen in 1994. Between 1995 and 1997 the core companies of the Ordos Group Corporation, Yekeju League Chemical Industrial Group Corporation and the Yekeju Coal Group Corporation made up one-third of all the stocks of Inner Mongolian companies in Shanghai and Shenzhen stock markets, and they raised funds exceeding 2 billion yuan, constituting over 70 per cent of all the capital in Inner Mongolia raised in the stock market.[21] Today, these three industrial groups have become cross-regional and transnational companies.

The Ordos Group Corporation is particularly interesting. In the mid-1990s, Ordos brand cashmere sweaters became well known throughout China. Seductive advertisements with a one-line poem – 'Ordos Cashmere Sweater Warms the Entire World' – beam across TV screens in China, and Ordos cashmere sweater billboard posters are common sights in many urban centres. The Ordos, or rather its misspelled, though official, rendition 'Erdos', brand trade mark, was formally recognized as a 'Chinese famous trade mark' by the state Industrial and Commercial Administration Bureau of China on January 5, 1999. The brand value of 'Erdos' topped 3.4 billion yuan in 2000, by which time it had become the most lucrative brand in Inner Mongolia.[22]

Promoting the 'Erdos' brand name became a successful strategy to capitalize on the ethnopolitical significance of this region's tribal name associated with Chinggis Khan. Indeed, this industrially promoted, lyrically aestheticized brand name continues to accrue tremendous value for the company. Unfortunately, however, the 'Erdos' brand has neither promoted Mongol culture nor helped Mongols.

Local Mongols were initially encouraged to raise goats, but when this led to rapid desertification, the company looked to the Mongol herders in Mongolia to provide the cashmere. Their recent domination of the Mongolian cashmere market has 'aroused strong Mongolian nationalist feelings'.[23] Nonetheless, this exploitation of cashmere resources, both locally and internationally, has not stopped the Ordos group from imposing a corporate model on the Yekeju League. In a hagiographic book promoting the Ordos Group Corporation, two Chinese authors, Cheng Li and Wang Xun, write as though the Ordos Group Corporation were the real force for the Ordos renaissance: 'Ordos is like a golden steed, soaring up, galloping in front in the picture of the Inner Mongolia Autonomous Region's rapidly advancing economy …'.[24]

We are witnessing in China's peripheries a form of settler colonialism reminiscent of patterns found in the Commonwealth nations. The 'indigenized' Chinese settlers are now able 'legitimately' to enter areas previously reserved for 'autonomous' minorities, not only as the defenders of the nation, but as co-developers or even as original developers of the frontier. Secure and comfortable in their new homeland, they now appropriate minority cultural elements, some of them central resistance symbols, such as Chinggis Khan and pastoralism in the form of goats, not only as signs of civility and a taste for the exotic, but above all as contributing to the great cause of 'multiculturalism' (*duoyuan wenhua*).

Farewell nationality!

Nationality (*minzu*) highlights central contradictions of the Chinese socialist nationality-ethnicity continuum. The socialist nationality of the *minzu* is to be constructed for the ultimate purpose of its destruction. Having made its contribution to national unity and economic development, its mission is complete.

As a substitute for minority political, linguistic and economic autonomy, a multiculturalism has recently been promoted, celebrating the colourful and diverse cultures of the Chinese nation. Minority cultures and arts, symbols precisely of their inferiority in an era of modernization, have been invested with intrinsic value in this multiculturalism. Minorities and their cultures, in this new multicultural discourse, do not exist in their own right, but as part of the Chinese nation. They now occupy prominent positions in specialized theme parks concocted for national and international consumption in Beijing, Shenzhen and Florida, among others. Besides being displayed in these human zoos, minorities become the antithesis of the Chinese, serving to unite the Chinese, as reflected in the denunciation and suppression of minority secessionism or, to use a more fashionable term, 'terrorism'. In this new alternating celebratory and denunciatory mode of multiculturalism, history and ethnopolitics are conveniently forgotten.

History repeats itself. The Chinese Communists-now-turned-ultra-nationalists evoke a concept of 'Chinese nation' which they repudiated in the name of national equality when they were battling the Guomindang. As early as the 1920s, the Guomindang, then ruling China, began to develop misgivings about the foundational pact of the original Republic, that is one of a China that consisted of five *minzu*: Chinese (Han), Mongol, Manchu, Tibetan and Muslim. They proceeded to promote the idea of the Chinese nation (*Zhonghua Minzu*) based on the Chinese *minzu*, and designated the four other *minzu* as the *buzu* or subordinate 'branches' of the 'nation', a vision that culminated in Jiang Jieshi's *China's Destiny*, a Mein Kampfian blueprint for China's future. It was this redesignation that legitimated Republican China's agenda to assimilate all minority nationalities into the Chinese nation, by means of military conquest and massive Chinese migration into non-Chinese areas. For its part, the CCP, then a minority party seeking to survive in the hinterlands by carving out revolutionary bases, criticized the Guomindang's chauvinism and, in a bid for support, called for autonomy/national self-determination for non-Chinese minorities, including Mongols. A combination of various factors, viz. minority struggle against Chinese territorial annexation, the communist principle of class-national equality, the CCP use of minorities against the Guomindang and the moral obligation to fulfil promises, as well as the wider communist world dominated by the Soviet Union, resulted in the massive state project of identifying nationalities and granting them autonomous territorial units.

In the aftermath of the Soviet and Yugoslavian collapse along ethnic lines in the early 1990s, there has been a subtle movement within Chinese political and academic circles to redefine the minorities not as nationalities, but rather as 'ethnic groups'. Since nationality autonomy, the central promise of the Chinese state through which minorities have been organized, is in disarray, a more effective vehicle for understanding ethnic processes is thought to lie in the study of 'inter-ethnic relations' rather than 'nationality questions'. In 1995, the English name of China's flagship propaganda journal *Minzu Tuanjie* was changed from *Nationality Unity* to *Ethnic Unity*. Chinese laws have all been retranslated into English, replacing 'nationality' with 'ethnic group'. Although officially the government continues to use *minzu* to refer to both nationalities and nation, in

Chinese, within scholarly circles, there already is a clear terminological distinction, using *zuqun* to translate 'ethnic group', and reserving *minzu* and/or *guozu* for nation. Behind the name change are questions of reconceptualizing the entire arena of China's nationality issues, from the legal position of the nationalities to territorial and other rights associated with autonomy.

This chapter has documented important elements of the unique historically grounded processes whereby Inner Mongols have been transformed from a nationality to an ethnic group. The story of the conflicts surrounding Mongolian language revival and loss clearly indicates one of the important processes resulting in the disappearance of Mongols' *minzu* characteristics en route to becoming an ethnic group. As Mongols become urbanized, their homeland penetrated by Chinese settlers, they lose the vital conditions for developing as a fully fledged nationality that was once rooted in a pastoral life. They are now losing the very administrative names that were once the hallmark of their 'liberation' and 'rebirth'. Ironically, although socialism and autonomy both promised to deliver national salvation, they became the very tomb to bury aspirations for developing as a nationality. Before we drop the use of 'nationality' or *minzu* in favour of 'ethnic group' or *zuqun* in a utopian multicultural China, or before we jump on the international bandwagon denouncing any ethno-nationalist movement as 'terrorist', it is necessary to examine the political economy of *minzu*-building and its demise in China's peripheries.

Acknowledgements

I thank Mark Selden and Elizabeth Perry for insightful comments and advice. Mistakes are mine alone.

Notes

1 Cf. Johannes Fabian, *Time and the Other: How Anthropology Makes Its Object* (New York: Columbia University Press, 1983).
2 Cf. Barry Sautman, 'Is Xinjiang an Internal Colony?', *Inner Asia*, 2, 2 (2000), pp. 239–71.
3 Dru C. Gladney, *Muslim Chinese: Ethnic Nationalism in the People's Republic* (Cambridge, MA: Council on East Asian Studies, Harvard University, 1991), p. 332.
4 Stuart Schram (trans.), *Mao's Road to Power: Revolutionary Writings 1912–1949: Toward the Second United Front January 1935–July 1937* (Armonk: M.E. Sharpe, 1999), p. 71.
5 Song Naigong (ed.), *Zhongguo Renkou: Nei Menggu Fence* (Beijing: Zhongguo Caizheng Jingji Chubanshe, 1987), p. 349.
6 *Ibid.*, pp. 66–7.
7 *Crackdown in Inner Mongolia. An Asia Watch Report* (USA Human Rights Watch, 1991).
8 Stevan Harrell, 'Civilizing Projects and Reactions to Them', in S. Harrell (ed.), *Cultural Encounters on China's Ethnic Frontiers* (Seattle: University of Washington Press, 1995), pp. 3–36.
9 Ulanhu, 'Wulanfu Zhuxi zai Menggu Yuwen Gongzuo Huiyi shang de Baogao' (Chairman Ulanhu's Report at the Conference on Mongolian Language Work), 16 May 1953 (handwritten manuscript).

10 Chuluun Bagan, 'Jianchi Minzu Yuyan Wenzi de Pingdeng Diwei' (Uphold the Equal Position of the Nationality Languages and Scripts), in *Neimenggu Zizhiqu minzu yanjiu xuehui shoujie nianhui lunwen xuanji* (Selected Articles from the First Annual Meeting of the Nationality Research Association of the Inner Mongolia Autonomous Region) (Huhehaote: compiled by Neimenggu Zizhiqu minzu yanjiu xuehui, unofficial publication, 1981), pp. 122–3.

11 Shenamjil, *Yuyan yu Zhili Kaifa* (Language and the Development of Intelligence) (Huhehaote: Nei Menggu Renmin Chubanshe, 1990), p. 54.

12 Tumote (Tumote Zuoqi 'Tumote Zhi' Biancuan Weiyuanhui), *Tumote Zhi* (Records of the Tumed) (Huhehaote: Nei Menggu Renmin Chubanshe, 1987), pp. 634–59.

13 Naran Bilik, 'The Mongol-Han Relations in a New Configuration of Social Revolution', *Central Asian Survey*, 17, 1 (1998), p. 72.

14 Pierre Bourdieu, *Language and Symbolic Power* (Cambridge, MA: Harvard University Press, 1991), p. 7.

15 Takashi Fujitani, 'Inventing, Forgetting, Remembering: Toward a Historical Ethnography of the Nation-State', in Harumi Befu (ed.), *Cultural Nationalism in East Asia: Representation and Identity* (Berkeley: Institute of East Asian Studies, University of California, 1993), p. 89.

16 Almaz Khan, 'Who are the Mongols? State, Ethnicity, and the Politics of Representation in the PRC', in Melissa J. Brown (ed.), *Negotiating Ethnicities in China and Taiwan* (Berkeley: Institute of East Asian Studies, University of California, 1996), pp.125–59.

17 He Jihong, *Xiyu Lungao* (Treatise on the Western Territory) (Urumqi: Xinjiang Renmin Chubanshe, 1996), pp. 14–26.

18 *Ibid.*, pp. 53–63. But for a critical study of the inter-ethnic marriage (*heqin*) system and practice in China and Inner Asia, see Uradyn E. Bulag, *The Mongols at China's Edge: History and the Politics of National Unity* (Lanham: Rowman and Littlefield, 2002), chap. 3.

19 Zhu Guangkai and Zhao Shuanglian, 'Xushi erfa, Zaichuang Jiaji' (Saving up Propensity to Create Splendour Again), *Renmin Ribao*, 6 October 1999, p. 4.

20 According to a recent Xinhua report ('Genghis Khan's Tomb Tourism Zone to Be Upgraded', Hohhot, 10 December 2001), Inner Mongolia plans to invest 200 million yuan to build the area of Chinggis Khan's Mausoleum into 'a world-class tourist destination'. The two-year project will cover 80 sq. km.

21 Cheng Li and Wang Xun, *Zhongxibu de Shuguang; E'erduosi Xianxiang Touxi* (The Dawn of Central and Western China: An Analysis of the Ordos Phenomenon) (Huhehaote: Nei Menggu Jiaoyu Chubanshe, 1998), p. 173.

22 See the corporation's website: <http://www.chinaerdos.com/english/news/index.html>.

23 Morris Rossabi, 'A New Mongolia in a New World', *Proceedings of the Conference 'Mongolian Political and Economic Development During the Past Ten Years and Future Prospect'* (Taipei: Mongolian and Tibetan Affairs Commission, 2000), pp. 42–85.

24 Cheng Li and Wang Xun, *Zhongxibu de Shuguang: E'erduosi Xianxiang Touxi*, p. 210.

Suggested reading

Uradyn E. Bulag, *The Mongols at China's Edge: History and the Politics of National Unity* (Lanham: Rowman and Littlefield, 2002).

Dru C. Gladney, *Muslim Chinese: Ethnic Nationalism in the People's Republic* (Cambridge, MA: Harvard University Press, Council on East Asian Studies, 1996).

Stevan Harrell, *Ways of Being Ethnic in Southwest China* (Seattle: University of Washington Press, 2001).

Ralph A. Litzinger, *Other Chinas: The Yao and the Politics of National Belonging* (Durham, NC: Duke University Press, 2000).

Erik Mueggler, *The Age of Wild Ghosts: Memory, Violence, and Place in Southwest China* (Berkeley: University of California Press, 2001).

Louisa Schein, *Minority Rules: The Miao and the Feminine in China's Cultural Politics* (Durham, NC: Duke University Press, 2000).

Tumen and Zhu Dongli, *Kang Sheng yü Neirendang Yuan'an* (Kang Sheng and the Unjust Case of the Inner Mongolia People's Revolutionary Party) (Beijing: Zhonggong Zhongyang Dangxiao Chubanshe, 1995).

11 The new cybersects

Resistance and repression in the reform era

Patricia M. Thornton

One unforeseen consequence of the Deng Xiaoping reform agenda has been the resurgence of popular interest in religious traditions and spiritual practices. Like the erosion of institutional structures that presaged the fall of dynasties in imperial times, the dismantling of Mao-era organizations, the relaxation of centralized control over local decision making, and the opening of Chinese markets to international exchanges have created conditions favourable to the proliferation of heterodox sects and popular quasi-religious practices. Syncretic sects, both new and old, have emerged in large numbers during the reform era, some springing back to life and taking root in their native soil several decades after communist officials supposedly eradicated them in the early 1950s. The widespread revival of shrine building, temple fairs, geomancy and rituals of exorcism have all been noted by visitors to the Chinese countryside since 1978. Nor is this trend a purely rural phenomenon: by many accounts, church attendance and recruitment are generally on the rise again in China's cities as well.

The revival of popular interest in spiritual matters has hardly gone unnoticed by party and state officials, who have seen their moral and ideological credibility eroded over the course of the post-Mao era. Central and local rulers have been repeatedly vexed by the emergence of heterodox groups throughout Chinese history, and the current Chinese leadership is no exception. Even before the full impact of the initial Dengist reform programme could be evaluated, alarms were sounded about the return of odious 'superstitious practices' and 'feudal organizations' in the countryside. From 1980–2, campaigns to eliminate fortune-telling, witchcraft and other 'feudal superstitious activities' were carried out in Shaanxi, Hainan and Anhui, all areas rife with such activities according to local officials. In 1985, one Ministry of Public Security report lamented that the explosion of 'reactionary sects and societies' during the period of reform 'formed the largest source of counter-revolution in the struggle against us' and furthermore predicted that the effort to suppress such groups would surely be 'a long-term and protracted one'.[1] Over the course of the next decade, 'anti-superstition campaigns' and movements to suppress and criticize 'pseudo-scientific thinking' were launched in several provinces to stem the flow of such practices in rural areas. Even more recently, the crackdown against so-called 'illegal heretical sects' that began in July of 1999 has resulted in tens of thousands of arrests, detentions and seizures across the country. Yet these repeated repressive measures have neither managed to eradicate fully such groups nor to prevent their adherents from engaging in a wide variety of acts of resistance against the regime.

The resilience of syncretic sects in contemporary China owes much to the larger sociological context of reform. As the post-Mao leadership has continued to open to international economic forces, the domestic population as a whole has grown increasingly mobile and technologically savvy. The widespread availability of cellular phones, fax machines and computers with access to the Internet has increased both the quality and quantity of information and media sources accessible to many Chinese citizens. It is therefore not surprising that in the face of the current ban against such groups, a number of contemporary syncretic sects have come to incorporate these new technologies not only in their quests for survival, but also in their struggles with local and central authorities. While contemporary syncretic sects certainly share the religious heritage of their predecessors in imperial and republican times, they lay claim to a host of new resources, and use these to attract both domestic and international support.

The rebirth (or reinvention) of syncretic religious traditions and practices in China, alongside the country's rapidly modernizing information and communications systems, has produced a unique hybrid form of politico-religious mobilization that I refer to as cyber-sectarianism.[2] Scholars of religion have long noted that it is not merely the content of doctrines that shapes particular religious organizations and practices, but also the form and method of their transmission that channel their development.[3] The best-equipped syncretic sects operating in greater China today combine extensive web-based strategies of text distribution, recruitment and information sharing with international media campaigns that draw on human rights discourses for legitimation. Funded at least in part by overseas Chinese communities in which they operate more openly, some reform-era sects have also joined forces with other dissident groups abroad and lobbied international authorities for support. The technological resources at the disposal of these groups facilitate the development of a particular organizational form: highly dispersed small groups of practitioners that may remain largely anonymous within the larger social context and operate in relative secrecy, while still linked remotely to a larger network of believers who share a set of practices and texts, and often a common devotion to a particular leader. Overseas supporters provide funding and support; domestic practitioners distribute tracts, participate in acts of resistance, and share information on the internal situation with outsiders. Collectively, members and practitioners of such sects construct virtual communities of faith, exchanging personal testimonies and engaging in collective study via email, on-line chat rooms and web-based message boards.

The elusive organizational characteristics of such new groups have proved formidable obstacles to the mainland leaders who seek to suppress them.[4] Whereas many have likened the current heavy-handed crackdown against 'heretical sects' to the methods used to suppress 'counter-revolutionary' religious groups in the early 1950s, or to the mass campaigns of the Mao era,[5] the organizational strategies of these new sects are decidedly high-tech, extremely mobile and multifaceted, leading one noted authority to liken the current contest between mainland authorities and syncretic sects to a 'giant fighting a ghost'.[6]

This chapter details the emergence of cyber-sectarianism in contemporary China by tracing the evolution of two quasi-religious *qigong* groups established in the late 1980s and early 1990s into nationally and internationally recognized movements. Broadly syncretic, both *Falun Gong* (Practice of the Dharma Wheel) and *Zhonghua Yansheng Yizhi Gong* (Practice of Life Preservation and Wisdom Accretion, hereafter *Zhong Gong*) interweave traditional Chinese religious themes with meditation, breathing and body cultivation techniques designed to preserve physical health and promote spiritual development. Both achieved national prominence during the so-called '*qigong* fever' (*qigong re*) that gripped China during the Deng era, a popular fascination that was initially not only tolerated, but even encouraged, by political leaders. Part and parcel of the broader public fascination with supernatural and spiritual matters that erupted during the post-Mao period, the *qigong* craze mushroomed after 1989, despite a few early attempts to curb the trend. At the forefront of the movement was a handful of nationally-recognized *qigong* masters who claimed hundreds of thousands of loyal followers, including a significant number of party and government cadres. Relying at least in part on their adherents within the power structure, several of these sects began to mobilize, both overtly and covertly, against state attempts to curtail their influence and activities during the 1990s. Alarmed by the increasingly political orientation of such groups and the potential of their leaders to challenge party authority, the Beijing leadership initiated a forceful crackdown against all so-called 'heretical sects' in 1999, which has indeed been successful in severely curtailing their efforts to recruit and retain members within the country. Yet by establishing bases overseas and transferring much of their work to the realm of virtual reality, these new cybersects have managed to hang on in defiance of the current ban, and continue to deploy high-tech strategics of organization, protest and resistance both on the Chinese mainland as well as abroad.

The sociological context of spiritual revival

Research on syncretic sects in Chinese history has linked the sporadic growth and spread of heterodox religious practices to periods of heightened economic dislocation, social turmoil and increased commercialization. Weak or inefficient institutions during the imperial era were periodically unable to absorb the challenges wrought by large-scale socioeconomic change, and popular religious sects offered appealing ideological and organizational alternatives, particularly among newly disenfranchised groups. Recent research has demonstrated that syncretic sects, while operating outside the realm of state-recognized orthodoxy, were by no means uniformly anti-dynastic or politically subversive in intent.[7] Nonetheless, imperial and Republican-era authorities in general took a dim view of such groups and periodically moved to repress and eliminate them; occasionally, the very act of suppression drove such sects into open confrontation with authorities.[8]

In the early years of its existence, the Communist Party made repeated attempts to reach out to certain syncretic sects, recognizing in them a rebellious or even quasi-revolutionary potential it hoped to tap.[9] Yet such alliances generally proved to be neither particularly fruitful for the Communists nor long-lived, as most sectarian groups embraced both a set of practices and a religious agenda that the early revolutionaries found objectionable. Shortly after the Communist victory on the mainland, all religious and quasi-religious sects not recognized as one of the five state-defined orthodox belief systems (Buddhism, Daoism, Islam, Protestantism and Catholicism) were targeted for elimination as part of the movement to suppress counter-revolutionaries. Those who survived this and subsequent campaigns to eradicate 'feudal beliefs' were driven either to renounce their affiliations or to continue their religious observances in secrecy; however, it is by no means clear how effective such methods were at eliminating popular religious practices in post-revolution China. Fairly frequent reports of sporadic sectarian activity surfaced throughout the Mao era, and the repeated local and national campaigns to eradicate traditional cultural and superstitious practices strongly suggest that while most such groups lost the ability to function openly and publicly, some succeeded in surviving underground.[10]

Deng's denunciation of Maoist ultra-leftism on the heels of the cataclysmic Cultural Revolution, combined with agricultural decollectivization and the introduction of free market reforms, created a sociological context not altogether unlike the ideological and institutional erosion that allowed syncretic sects to flourish in late imperial China. The dismantling of the commune system and the privatization of state-owned enterprises seriously compromised the access of many reform-era citizens to reliable health care and other services; newly relaxed restrictions on rural–urban migration produced a new underclass in many Chinese cities; and the widespread political dislocation caused by the Cultural Revolution, as well as the subsequent influx of foreign goods and ideas, all served to gradually undermine the orthodox foundations of state and party power. Not surprisingly, new variants of organizational forms and practices widespread in pre-revolutionary times – clans, blood feuds, temple associations and geomancy, to name a few – began to reappear in the countryside to fill the institutional vacuum left in the wake of the reforms.

Against the dramatic backdrop of these larger institutional and ideological transformations, in March of 1979, the *Sichuan Daily News* (*Sichuan Ribao*) reported the story of a 12-year-old schoolboy from Dazu county who could read with his ear. According to the account, Tang Yu discovered this ability one day when his ear brushed against a classmate's clothing and he was able to 'read' the brand of cigarettes his friend was carrying in his pocket. Two months later, his abilities were demonstrated before a local cadre, who soon discovered that the boy could read any number of characters written on a piece of paper and then crumpled into a small ball when the paper was held up to the boy's ear. Word of the boy's wondrous ability quickly became a national sensation, picked up by media outlets across the county. Weeks later, Tang was investigated by a team of provincial-level researchers interested in discovering the extent and full nature of his talents, as well as a group from the prestigious Chinese Academy of Science. The case was exposed as a hoax and a report of their findings published in the *People's Daily* within months of the original article. However, this revelation did not prevent a rash of similar stories from appearing in newspapers across the country. Media outlets in Beijing, Hunan, Hubei, Anhui, Hebei and Liaoning all reported similar cases of people who were discovered to be able to read characters with their noses, hands, feet and other body parts, triggering an intense public interest in paranormal abilities.[11]

Arguing in defence of Tang Yu and his alleged abilities was the popular Shanghai-based magazine *Nature* (*Ziran zazhi*). Two months after the *People's Daily* article exposed Tang as a hoax, *Nature* countered with a piece entitled 'Reading with the Ear may not be Preposterous' (*Yier renzi weibi huangmiu*); over the course of the next two years, *Nature* published no fewer than fifty-three articles on the scientifically documented 'extraordinary abilities' of a wide variety of people in China, and hosted a large-scale conference on paranormal phenomena in Shanghai that involved more than eighty experts from eight provinces and major cities. The meeting attracted the attention of the National Science Committee (*Guojia kewei*), which set up its own organization to investigate and research claims of paranormal abilities. With this organizational structure in place and funding from the National Science Committee in hand, the Liaison to Investigate Human Paranormal Abilities began to solicit letters and reports of potential cases for investigation in 1981.[12]

It was not long before the Liaison and the teams of researchers associated with it stumbled across the case of Yan Xin, a graduate of the Chengdu Academy of Chinese Medicine. Yan asserted that he could project his vital life force, or *qi*, outside of his body in order to cure a variety of illnesses in others, including cancer. By the mid-1980s, a proliferation of new print media had appeared in China's largest cities, all eagerly competing for the attention of the reading public, and stories about Yan Xin and others like him appeared in the press with increasing frequency. In 1987, when the *Guangming Daily* reported that Yan Xin's extraordinary psychokinetic and healing abilities had been certified by a team of researchers from Qinghua University, Yan Xin became a national sensation. Months after the Qinghua study, Liaoning officials battling the worst forest fire there in modern history urgently appealed to Yan, requesting that he use his abilities to help to control the blaze; when the fire was successfully contained shortly thereafter, Yan claimed credit for ameliorating a national disaster and his popularity soared even further. His '*qi*-empowered' lectures[13] routinely drew crowds numbering over a thousand people, and a partially fictionalized account of his life and teachings, *A Great Qigong Master*, became a runaway best-seller in late 1989.[14] Yan Xin was quickly followed by a succession of other self-proclaimed *qigong* masters 'coming out of the mountains' eager to demonstrate their paranormal abilities and spread their teachings to a receptive public audience.

Qigong sects: breathing new life into old traditions

While rooted in ancient beliefs and practices, the category of *qigong* as a set of methods for physical and spiritual cultivation is a relatively recent invention. Various techniques for manipulating the breath and redirecting bodily energy are described in ancient Daoist texts, and contemporary body cultivation practices are clearly informed by the quietistic meditative traditions associated with Daoism. Meditative postures and movements have also been associated with Chan Buddhism, which dates back to the sixth century in China, and were practised to attain the dharma body. These early body cultivation techniques constituted one branch of esoteric religious practices, generally taught by monks or adepts to small numbers of students, and as part of a larger canon of religious beliefs.[15]

The term *qigong* was introduced into popular parlance in 1953, when Liu Guizhen published The Practice of *Qigong* Therapy (*Qigong liaofa shijian*). Liu, a minor party official, claimed he had cured himself of a life-threatening illness by using a set of special breathing exercises he learned from a peasant. Liu coined the term *qigong* (*qi*, often translated as 'breath', 'spirit' or 'vital energy'; and *gong* meaning 'practice', 'skill' or 'ability') to describe these practices, and opened clinics in Tangshan and Beidaihe to experiment with and adapt the curative exercises for clinical use. President Liu Shaoqi invited him to continue his research in Beijing, where he counted among his patients several high-ranking cadres. While temporarily out of favour during the Cultural Revolution, Liu Guizhen's *qigong* practices were recognized as a specialized subfield of traditional Chinese medicine by the end of the 1970s. Occasional reports of remarkable *qigong* cures made their way into the public domain, as when the well-known Beijing actress Guo Lin published a 1980 account describing a type of *qigong* she developed that had miraculously cured her of cancer. Yet *qigong* was considered little more than a subfield of medical practice and a subject of clinical research until shortly before Liu's death in 1983, when the elderly Liu announced that he had in fact discovered that *qi* could be projected out of the body of one individual and into other human and animal subjects, as well as material objects.[16]

Liu's stunning announcement of his discovery of 'external qi' (*waiqi*) presaged the emergence of Yan Xin by only a few years. As public fascination with Yan Xin spread, a procession of adepts who had mastered the art of manipulating 'external qi' emerged to share the spotlight with him. The most famous of these included Zhang Baosheng, who demonstrated his command of external *qi* by removing pills from a sealed medicine bottle and transporting them around a locked room, and Zhang Weixiang, who claimed the ability to speak with higher life-forms and to cure illnesses using rays of light. Others claimed the ability to fly through the air at speeds exceeding those of commercial airliners, or to use a sort of 'x-ray *gong*' to see through the earth itself.[17]

The central leadership appears to have been equally susceptible to the explosion of popular interest in *qigong* during this era. With Liu Shaoqi's short-lived sponsorship of Liu Guizhen in the early 1960s serving as a historical precedent, the ageing state and party elite began turning to *qigong* masters for treatment of various ills on a regular basis. One Hong Kong periodical claimed that each one of the so-called 'Eight Elders' of the Party's Central Committee during the late 1980s (including Deng Xiaoping, Chen Yun, Yang Shangkun and Li Xiannian) personally retained four to five *qigong* masters for regular specialized treatments and, in some cases, soothsaying sessions; over two hundred *qigong* adepts were purportedly on the payroll at the Zhongnanhai leadership compound by the summer of 1990.[18] Ironically, Jiang Zemin himself purportedly received personalized treatments for arthritis and neck pain from *qigong* master Zhang Hongbao, the founder of the Zhonggong movement, whose extradition from the USA he later demanded due to an outstanding arrest warrant.[19]

Generally speaking, over the course of the late 1980s and early 1990s, the character of the '*qigong* fever' that gripped (mostly) urban China[20] gradually became increasingly spiritual in its focus, incorporating religious themes and texts. Whereas Yan Xin and the earliest wave of *qigong* teachers had some background training in Chinese traditional medicine and focused primarily on the goals of physical healing and health improvement, by the late 1980s, newer adepts were claiming connections to the early esoteric roots of Daoist and Buddhist schools, and advocated spiritual and social transformation. These new leaders and the schools they established were broadly synthetic, drawing on a variety of religious and philosophical traditions, as their pre-revolutionary counterparts had decades earlier. However, they were also the distinct products of Mao-era socialist society, and incorporated themes and elements from the state socialist canon into their teaching. As such, the syncretic *qigong* sects of the second decade of the reforms represented a new post-revolutionary variant in the modern history of quasi-religious mobilization in China.

Post-revolutionary sectarianism

Syncretic sectarianism in pre-revolutionary China involved the incorporation of specific elements of various belief systems in new ways, producing doctrines or practices that radically differentiated one group from other rival associations or outsiders.[21] The rapid proliferation of *qigong* masters in the mid- to late 1980s encouraged just this type of organizational competition, with each new master seeking to distinguish him- or herself from the crowd not only in terms of ability, but also in terms of doctrine. A staggering array of syncretic *gongs* appeared, including Nature-centred Gong (*Daziran zhongxin gong*), Taiji Gong (*Taiji qigong*), Eight Trigrams *qigong* (*Bagua qigong*), National Gong (*Guo Gong*) and Fragrant Gong (*Xiang Gong*). Many of these clearly drew upon either remembered or reconstructed traditional religious practices for their inspiration, but the fact that all were coterminous with the discourses of both scientism and post-revolutionary socialism shaped the nature of their syncretism in specific ways.

By far the best known and most popular of the highly syncretic *qigong* sects that emerged during the second decade of reform was *Falun Gong*, which at its height claimed seventy million adherents in mainland China, and *Zhong Gong*, which claimed thirty-eight million.[22] The founders of both movements, Li Hongzhi and Zhang Hongbao, and the cultivation systems they developed, owe much to Daoist, Buddhist and folk religious themes. However, the syncretism of both movements extends to post-revolutionary concepts and practices as well. Li and Zhang both came of age during the Cultural Revolution, and refer frequently to it in their writings and addresses. Zhang Hongbao maintains that the Cultural Revolution inspired his personal spiritual quest; by contrast, Li Hongzhi, recalls the Cultural Revolution as a harrowing backdrop to his own more traditional religious training, and as a period characterized by moral stringency. Yet despite these differences, both find inspiration, as well as the source of the ills plaguing the contemporary Chinese body politic, in the politics of the Maoist era.

Zhong Gong founder Zhang Hongbao made his way into the public spotlight not long after Yan Xin's discovery by the Chinese media. Born in Harbin on 5 January 1954, Zhang was just entering his teenage years at the onset of the Cultural Revolution. As the class monitor in his junior high, he purportedly became active in the Red Guard movement, undertaking a rigorous study of 'Marxism–Leninism–Mao Zedong Thought' that culminated in a pilgrimage to Beijing, alongside many other Red Guards. At the age of fourteen, Zhang was 'sent down' to the countryside, where he spent ten years working on Shanhe Commune in rural Heilongjiang.[23]

During his decade in the countryside, Zhang successfully applied for membership in the Communist Youth League; he attended the Beian Prefectural Party School in 1973, and underwent training at the Heilongjiang Provincial Farm Bureau Cadre School in 1974. Labouring successively as a platoon leader, tractor driver, cook, commander of the local militia and head of the Theory Study Section of the Propaganda Department of the commune, Zhang was singled out for honours as a 'model labourer' (*laodong mofan*). When he left the commune after ten years to attend Harbin Metallurgy Technical School, he served as a student member of the school's party committee, and became a party member in 1979, subsequently holding a succession of local-level party posts.

In 1985, Zhang accepted a fellowship from the Beijing Science and Technology University (BSTU) to study economic management (*jingji guanli*). While enrolled at BSTU, he took courses in law at People's University, and *qigong*, Chinese and Western medicine at the Advanced *Qigong* Study Institute in Beijing. Zhang appears to have sustained little interest in the study of either law or management, but focused instead on his other interests, serving, for example, as the president of the university's *Qigong* Science Research Society. His thesis, entitled 'The Declaration of a Destined Leader', apparently had little to do with economic management, and therefore did not meet with the approval of his advisory committee, but did serve as a rough blueprint for his future endeavours.[24] In 1987, Zhang established the Haidian *Qigong* Science Research

Institute and became its director. The following year, Zhang founded a Chinese-American joint venture enterprise, the 'Beijing International *Qigong* Service Company, Ltd.' (*Beijing guoji qigong fuwu youxian gongsi*), and began publicly to promote what he called *Zhonghua Yangsheng Yizhi Gong* (*Zhong Gong*), or the Practice of Life Preservation and Wisdom Accretion.

Zhang Hongbao's *qigong* practices are but a part of a larger highly structured philosophical system that takes the mythical *qilin* (sometimes translated as 'Chinese unicorn') as its symbol. The essential syncretism of Zhang's vision is represented by the *qilin* itself, whose form is a composite of several different animals.[25] Similarly, Zhang's ideological framework represents a synthesis of traditional philosophical and religious concepts, interwoven with scientific jargon and post-revolutionary themes. He credits his years of intensive study of Marxism–Leninism–Mao Zedong Thought as a 'sent-down' youth during the Cultural Revolution for transforming him from 'an ignorant youngster who would admire "an educated youth" from Beijing simply for his ability to memorize the Communist Manifesto, to an expert tutoring people in their study of Marxist classics'.[26] His Cultural Revolution experiences led him to conclude that Marxism–Leninism–Mao Zedong thought was inherently riddled with contradictions and could not therefore be considered 'scientific' because the underlying assumption of dialectical materialism – namely, the separation of material reality from the realm of ideas – is 'utterly flat and lacking in power' (*cangbai wuli*) in the face of the miraculous powers of the *qigong* master. What Marx and Engels failed to appreciate was the fact that 'thought and matter have a dialectical, and not a master–slave, relationship', with thought and spirit actually existing as forms of *yin* matter, a realm governed by motion that occurs beyond the speed of light. Zhang's own breakthrough discovery (*tupo kou*) that 'the power of thought' (*yinianli*) has a measurable material existence in the *yin* realm, became the 'golden key' (*jin yaoshi*) that unlocked for him the mysteries of the universe.[27] Practitioners of Zhang Hongbao's *qigong* exercises seek to transform themselves into superhuman masters able to exert hidden *yin* forces on common *yang* matter in order to heal diseases, develop powers of extrasensory perception and perform supernatural wonders. The practices themselves are borrowed from Daoist meditative exercises, but incorporate Buddhist techniques as well.[28] Underlying this set of physical practices is a sixteen-point moral code known as the 'Eight Virtues and Eight Admonitions', general tenets that urge self-control and self-restraint in everyday social life.[29]

Despite the assimilative nature of Zhang Hongbao's highly syncretic approach, the *Zhong Gong* organization in mainland China displayed markedly sectarian characteristics early on, including quasi-religious rituals not unlike those common among Chinese secret societies. Novices enrolling in *Zhong Gong* academies or study centres participated in a simple initiation ritual that involved standing collectively to offer the *heshi*, a traditional Buddhist greeting, before a portrait of Master Zhang, followed by a solemn recitation of the 'Eight Virtues and Eight Admonitions'. Senior disciples routinely engaged in more elaborate ritual observances, with many purportedly signing a written oath to remain forever loyal to Master Zhang: '*Zhong Gong* followers in life, *Zhong Gong* ghosts in death'.[30]

Falun Gong manifests a similar combination of syncretic and sectarian elements, interweaving Buddhist, Daoist and post-revolutionary themes and practices.[31] The syncretism of Li Hongzhi's message is reflected in his account of his past, in which he credits a succession of teachers from different traditions for training him.[32] Between 1960 and 1969, he completed his primary education in Changchun, and graduated from junior high school at the age of eighteen. Li maintains that he was being extensively trained during this period, first by a Buddhist master, and then by a Daoist. Former schoolmates and teachers recall him as an ordinary child who did not earn exceptional grades in school. Like Zhang Hongbao, at the height of the Cultural Revolution Li also applied to join the Communist Youth League.[33]

After graduating from junior high school, Li Hongzhi served as a trumpet player on an army stud farm and later at the Jilin Provincial Forest Police head-quarters. In 1982, following his discharge from a decade of military service, he took up a position at the Changchun Cereals and Oil Company, where his highly syncretic training continued; *Falun Gong* sources note that 'In the ten or more years that followed, he would change masters practically every time he reached a new level; some were Buddhist masters, others Daoist masters.'[34] Fellow employees in Changchun recall that Li began practising 'Chanmi Gong' in 1988, taking part in two training courses, then going on to study 'Jingongbagua Gong'.[35] In 1991, Li retired from his company job, 'retaining his position but not his salary [*tingxin liuzhi*], in order to begin practising *qigong*', and in May of the following year, both official and *Falun Gong* accounts agree that Li began teaching his own system of *qigong* to the general public.

Li's message involves an apocalyptic vision of a society in an advanced state of moral degeneration. In the current period of decline, the material world is overrun with bad karma, which Li envisions as a black sticky substance that inheres in material objects as well as the bodies of living beings. Its antithesis, virtue (*de*), is a white matter that enters the body each time one does a good deed or falls victim to the evil and destructive acts of others. The five basic postures or exercises observed daily by *Falun Gong* practitioners assist them in the removal of bad karma, but much of this work is also done by a small rotating dharma wheel which Li implants in the lower abdomens of his followers. To further assist them in the process of cultivation, Li dispatches dharma bodies (*fashen*) to protect them during their sufferings and heal them from illnesses during the current period of turmoil. Li predicts that the world is now poised on the cusp of a violent and catastrophic denouement during which only a select few will be saved. Those who wish to practice *Falun Gong* seriously must strictly maintain the purity of their devotion to the practice, and not only cease other forms of spiritual disci-pline, but avoid reading or even thinking about them, lest such thoughts deform the rotating dharma wheel Li has implanted within them. Thus, while *Falun Gong* and Li's own spiritual training are highly synthetic, incorporating elements and ideas from several traditions (most notably Buddhism and Daoism), it is also markedly sectarian, forbidding practitioners from engaging in other practices and reading other religious texts.[36]

Falun Gong practices are equally syncretic, incorporating elements of quietistic Daoist meditation with postures and hand gestures inspired by Buddhist and Tantric traditions.[37] Adherents have combined these with ritual elements associated with Chinese folk religious practices, such as the burning of incense, the consecrating of food and kowtowing before portraits of Li. In collective practice, groups in Changchun were praised by Li for convening exercise sessions in which they would recite or hand-copy *Falun Gong* texts in turn, pausing to discuss particular passages and reflect upon how such principles might be applied in their daily lives.[38] Some practitioners have found the style of these small group study sessions uncomfortably reminiscent of the small group political study sessions popularized under Mao.[39] Li's style of moral self-improvement certainly owes much to the structure of the emulation campaigns of the Mao era, and he often draws parallels between the moral rectitude of his practitioners and that of Maoist moral exemplar Lei Feng, or 'model workers and heroes' of previous decades. Li urged his followers not to take credit for their good deeds, a practice he felt certain would cause 'some to wonder how at this time "Lei Feng" would emerge' again in an era in which self-aggrandizement and boastful behaviour had become the norm.[40]

Yet Li by no means regards the developments of the Mao era as uniformly positive. The political upheaval of the Cultural Revolution occupies a central place in Li's diagnosis of the Chinese body politic, and he attributes the social maladies he diagnoses in the contemporary period directly to its lingering effects. For example, during one 1999 address in New York, Li reflected:

> Prior to the Cultural Revolution, China was known throughout the world as 'the land of ceremony and propriety' [*liyi zhi bang*], no matter which aspect civilization, cleanliness or appearances – all were extremely refined. The national civilizations [*guojia wenming*] of the countries surrounding China were all brought over to them by Chinese people, all emulated China [audience applauds]. But you know what happened? After the Cultural Revolution took this [civilization] as the 'Four Olds' and destroyed it, [our] exquisite [civilization] took a roll in the mud, rubbed its hands until they became callused and grew lice [on its body] that we call 'revolutionary parasites' [*geming chong*]. People regarded filth as beauty. This kind of perspective has continued on, and although the living conditions of people today are better, and comparatively speaking a bit more refined, yet this perspective left over from the Cultural Revolution has still not been eradicated.[41]

Elsewhere Li claims that the Cultural Revolution delivered 'an unforgettable blow to (Chinese) souls';[42] that it represented a period of unprecedented evil;[43] and that the ideology of 'radical egalitarianism' it fostered resulted in an epidemic of 'Oriental jealousy' during the reform era that his cultivation practice aspires to cure.[44] The Cultural Revolution therefore represents a watershed in modern Chinese history, a radical break with the traditions of the past that failed to provide any meaningful alternative moral vision.

The loss of the party's ideological mandate during the post-Mao era, along with the steady erosion of institutional structures providing key social goods such as health care and education, provided a context within which the syncretic *qigong* sects of the 1980s and 1990s flourished. *Zhong Gong* and *Falun Gong* offered ethical systems that successfully conjoined contemporary post-socialist themes to pre-revolutionary religious traditions, as well as educational and basic health care services to large numbers of Chinese citizens whose access to such services has been attenuated since Mao's death. Not surprisingly, one unpublished survey of *Falun Gong* practitioners early on in the crackdown revealed that the average follower was a woman over the age of 40 in the lowest income bracket within her community.[45] Yet as such groups multiplied in power and strength during the reform era, the central leadership grew increasingly wary. Following the 4 June 1989 crackdown against the student movement, stringent new regulations were imposed upon all social organizations, which resulted in much higher levels of government surveillance over popular *qigong* sects. New regulations required local governments to establish administrative offices to ensure compliance. In early December 1990, the celebrated *qigong* master Zhang Xiangyu, who had skyrocketed to fame for her ability to speak 'the language of the cosmos', effect miracle cures and project her *qi* out to tens of thousands of audience participants at a single gathering, was arrested. The charges against her ranged from practising *qigong* therapy without the proper authority to do so to having organized a large public gathering without the prior approval of the Beijing police. Unofficially, it was rumored that Zhang was arrested because she had criticized then-President Yang Shangkun, during a private treatment, for sending in the army to put down the student demonstrations in Tiananmen Square.[46] Whatever the reason for her arrest, Zhang Xiangyu's incarceration and the closing down of her Nature *Qigong* schools had a dampening effect on the surge in *qigong*'s popularity during the early 1990s, sending several noted *qigong* masters back to the mountains whence they came.

From syncretic sects to cybersects

The arrest of Zhang Xiangyu marked a turning point in the media coverage of the *qigong* boom, as articles critical of 'pseudo-scientific' and 'superstitious' *qigong* practices began appearing more frequently in the press. The prestigious Chinese Academy of Science (CAS) and well-known members of the Chinese traditional medicine establishment in Beijing voiced concerns over some of the more extreme claims put forth by some popular *qigong* masters. In a highly publicized August 1990 appearance in Beijing, Sima Nan performed what he referred to as his own 'special extraordinary magic *qigong*', an exhibition designed to expose the 'secret techniques and tricks' employed by *qigong* masters to make it appear as though they had supernormal powers. He subsequently embarked upon a career in debunking those he referred to as 'hucksters' in the *qigong* business.[47]

Under this considerably less friendly climate in early 1990s, *Zhong Gong* founder Zhang Hongbao retreated to a remote base area he established near Sichuan's Qingchengshan, an area long regarded as the centre for religious Daoism. Surrounded by a team of legal advisers, Zhang cultivated close relationships with local government officials in the area of Qilin City (*Qilin cheng*), and reorganized his followers as employees of a sprawling web of private enterprises owned by his parent firm, the Qilin Group (*Qilin jituan*). When the *Beijing Daily* (*Beijing Ribao*) pre-emptively reported in 1994 that his Beijing-based International *Qigong* Service Enterprise had been shut down pending an investigation into possible criminal wrongdoing, Zhang hired the defence team of the Gang of Four trial to defend him, and managed to extract a public apology from the paper. He followed this lawsuit with a string of unsuccessful legal actions against the government that lasted five years, during which he nonetheless managed to evade arrest. In 2000, when Chongqing authorities ordered Zhang Hongbao's Chongqing International Life Technology University to close its doors, school employees resisted the order; one elderly disciple purportedly committed suicide in protest.[48]

Falun Gong practitioners also grew increasingly defiant as state and party officials turned a critical eye towards the *Falun Gong* movement. In 1996, not long after Li Hongzhi left China and began promoting his *qigong* practices abroad, the quasi-governmental Chinese Society of *Qigong* Science suspended the registration of Li's flagship organization, the Research Society of Falun Dafa, for 'advocating superstition'. A few months later, shortly after a *Guangming Daily* article entitled 'Forever Sound the Alarm' made similar accusations against the group, Li Hongzhi's books were banned by the Press and Publications Administration, as well as by some local governments.[49] *Falun Gong* practitioners responded by staging mass protests around the offices of media outlets that published or broadcast reports critical of the group or its leader; such sit-in demonstrations frequently involved more than a thousand participants per gathering, with many of them practising *Falun Gong* exercises during the protest, playing *Falun Gong* music and distributing leaflets to passers-by. Some reporters and government officials complained of being harassed by phone calls from defiant practitioners; a few claimed that similar tactics targeted their residences.[50]

The tension escalated precipitously in April 1999, when a popular science magazine affiliated with Tianjin Normal University published an article written by a CAS scientist entitled 'I Do Not Approve of Teenagers Practising *Qigong*', in which he criticized *Falun Gong* as 'sham *qigong*'. In the week that followed, thousands of practitioners descended upon the offices both of the magazine and the Tianjin municipal government, leading to a spate of arrests. With several Tianjin practitioners still in police custody, more than ten thousand *Falun Gong* activists gathered before Zhongnanhai, the gated residential compound of the top party and state elite near the centre of Beijing. Their silent protest began in the early morning hours of 25 April, almost ten years to the day that the *People's Daily* had published an editorial condemning the Tiananmen student protestors as 'hooligans', and was the largest such public

gathering since the 4 June crackdown. The demonstration continued for thirteen hours and appeared to take cadres both inside and outside the compound
by surprise.[51]

For his part, Li Hongzhi claimed no prior knowledge of the protest; however,
Chinese customs officials were quick to point out that Li, a US resident since
1996, flew back to Beijing on 22 April for a stay lasting nearly two full days. Li is
alleged to have met with practitioners several times to monitor the situation in
Tianjin, as well as to organize the Beijing protest. During the event itself, Li is
furthermore accused of having logged some twenty telephone calls to the participants.[52] When later questioned by Australian reporters about his role in the
incident, Li alluded somewhat cryptically to the convenience of the Internet in
facilitating long-distance communication, and remarked that practitioners
frequently learn of such events on the worldwide web.[53]

The 25 April sit-in marked a critical juncture for the *Falun Gong* movement,
representing its first public protest directed towards the central authorities. The
central leadership officially banned *Falun Gong* less than two months later,
launching a major political offensive that ultimately extended not only to other
quasi-religious *qigong* groups such as *Zhong Gong*, but to all organizations deemed
to be 'heretical sects' (*xiejiao*). In the brutal crackdown that ensued, *Falun Gong*
and *Zhong Gong* offices, schools and other facilities were forced to close down,
their assets confiscated and their key personnel detained or arrested. Zhang
Hongbao responded with the so-called 'Action 99–8' campaign, encouraging all
Zhong Gong supporters to fax, post and distribute as widely as possible two letters
supposedly penned by public security personnel who were also supporters of
Zhong Gong. The two documents, 'Do not Exercise Dictatorship against the
People' and 'A Letter from a Young Police Officer', were purportedly distributed
to a hundred thousand local police substations in early August 1999, along with
over two thousand county police offices, three hundred municipal public security
bureaux, thirty-one provincial public security departments and ten thousand
departments in the judiciary as well. The letters accused Jiang Zemin of
pursuing his policy of 'stability of paramount importance' to the end of perpet-
uating his own reign at all costs, wantonly violating the Chinese constitution and
attacking traditional Chinese culture in the consolidation of his own power.
Accusing communist rule for 'not allowing people to lead a single day of peace
and subjecting the country to perpetual chaos', the authors furthermore named
Jiang Zemin as an 'unrepentant reactionary', who, by initiating a crackdown
against so-called 'heretical sects', had launched a second 'Cultural Revolution'.[54]
Shortly thereafter, Zhang Hongbao and a close associate managed to make their
way first to Thailand, and then to Guam, where both applied for political
asylum in the USA. Chinese officials demanded Zhang's return to the People's
Republic to stand trial for allegedly raping two female adherents back in 1994,
incidents which were only investigated once the crackdown against *Zhong Gong*
was already well under way.[55]

With both leaders residing abroad, the *Zhong Gong* and *Falun Gong* movements
gradually shifted the brunt of their organizational work to virtual reality. The

Foreign Liaison Group of the Falun Dafa Research Society established a protocol for monitoring *Falun Gong's* presence on the web as early as 1995;[56] the main *Zhong Gong* group site was established some five years later, in April 2000. Both groups have managed to convey a good deal of information to interested parties through the Internet, including texts of lectures and speeches by Zhang Hongbao and Li Hongzhi both in the original Chinese as well as translated into foreign languages, photographic images of leaders and practitioners, and information about the situation of practitioners still within mainland China. The *Falun Gong* movement in particular has developed a series of highly elaborate websites, some with electronic bulletin boards and email distribution lists that provide interested parties with newsletters and updated news information, all of which are capable of linking overseas practitioners to those still residing in mainland China. As the crackdown against mainland practitioners intensified in the autumn of 1999, the structure of the movement bifurcated: while *Falun Gong* activists abroad pursued high-profile activities such as lobbying foreign governments, mainland Chinese groups adopted a cell-like structure similar to those of other underground organizations (including the Chinese Communist Party in decades past) and shifted primarily to web-based communication strategies. Despite the attempts of the mainland authorities to block public access to certain websites, practitioners managed to evade controls by using untraceable web-based email accounts accessed in Internet cafes, erecting firewalls that detect signals from computers attempting to identify particular users, and logging on to banned websites via proxy servers. More technologically savvy practitioners deploy encryption programs and switch Internet accounts, operating systems, hard-disk drives and telephone lines frequently in order to conceal their identities.[57] Several *Falun Gong* websites provide instructions on how to evade official surveillance by using proxy servers to log on to view or download banned information; practitioners in China continue to use the Internet to upload information on the on-going crackdown to those abroad.

Chinese authorities initially responded to *Falun Gong's* leap into cyberspace by creating a ring of anti-*Falun Gong* websites to broadcast the state's official view of the group, and by attempting to increase surveillance over Internet use. Ministry of State Security agents routinely visit the offices of Internet service providers to install updated monitoring devices that track individual email accounts and filter access to specific websites. The list of banned sites continues to grow and now even includes some search engines that permit users to view 'cached' versions of documents without linking directly to specific sites. The Ministry of Public Security has also played an intermittently more proactive role in suppressing cyberactivism: within days of the July 1999 decision to ban the movement, *Falun Gong* website operators abroad complained that they were being overwhelmed with electronic requests that blocked normal computer traffic, a tactic known as a 'denial of service' attack. Several were also repeatedly victimized by hackers, with at least one attempt apparently originating from the Beijing offices of the Public Security Ministry's Internet Monitoring Bureau.[58] Ministry officials responded to such charges by accusing *Falun Gong* practitioners of having illegally obtained and leaked classified state documents pertaining to the handling of *Falun Gong*.[59] Both *Falun Gong* and *Zhong Gong* websites do make classified police or public security documents available for general viewing, and the *Falun Gong* sites carry regularly updated information on the conditions in the labour reform camps to which practitioners have been sent. *Falun Gong* sources continue to maintain that Chinese officials penetrate movement bulletin boards to engage in cyber-espionage and to spread harmful rumours.

The early stages of the cyberwar between the outlawed *qigong* sects and mainland authorities apparently did little to curtail more protest within Chinese borders. The period between the 25 April 1999 sit-down and the 22 July decision to ban the group saw over three hundred demonstrations by *Falun Gong* practitioners at various locations around the country.[60] These continued over the ensuing months: according to official statistics, by the year's end, over 35,000 practitioners had been arrested in Beijing alone for participating in public demonstrations. During the following year, waves of *Falun Gong* adherents staged demonstrations in Beijing to mark the Chinese New Year, the first anniversary of the 25 April protest, Li Hongzhi's birthday and the National Day celebration in Tiananmen Square. On 1 January 2001, as the new millennium dawned, an estimated seven hundred pro-*Falun Gong* demonstrators were arrested in Tiananmen Square. Despite the impressive size of the New Year protest, it was quickly overshadowed by the dramatic self-immolation of five people purporting to be *Falun Gong* adherents on 23 January, the eve of the Spring Festival. Two of those involved in the incident died of their injuries, one of them a 13-year-old girl who had accompanied her mother to the square. This protest and the ensuing news coverage appeared to mark a shift in public opinion within the People's Republic, and while adherents abroad claim that the self-immolators were not true practitioners, the government's propaganda campaign against the movement seemed to make significant inroads in the months that followed.[61]

Driven even further underground, mainland adherents have resorted to more technologically elaborate means of subverting the state's ban. In February of 2002, *Falun Gong* activists hacked into the television cables serving the northeastern city of Anshan, and managed to broadcast their own views for several minutes; a few weeks later, activists in Changchun apparently hacked into that city's cable network and broadcast nearly twenty minutes of video footage while an anonymous narrator extolled Master Li's 'outstanding contributions'. Other more surreptitious acts of resistance have been recorded as well: night-time leafleting raids on housing projects have been reported in various urban neighbourhoods, and painted slogans have suddenly appeared on walls and lamp-posts.[62] Some of these acts of resistance have been quite high profile: on 24 January 2000, sixteen *Falung Gong* activists succeeded in unfurling a giant portrait of Li Honghzhi directly above the famed portrait of Mao Zedong in Tiananmen Square, obscuring Mao's image;[63] a year later, a *Falun Gong* banner flew for nearly an hour atop the headquarters of the People's Armed Police in Beijing's Haidian district, and slogans were found painted on walls within the tightly guarded headquarters of the air force located nearby.[64]

Falun Gong adherents abroad have continued to wage an impressive multi-front campaign focusing on Chinese human rights violations, using tactics similar to those deployed by some of the pro-democracy dissidents described in Minxin Pei's contribution to this volume. Like their fellow practitioners in mainland China, *Falun Gong* activists abroad also make extensive use of the Internet in order to maintain a high level of pressure on mainland Chinese authorities. Aside from engaging in vigorous lobbying efforts, letter-writing and email campaigns directed at local and national governments and international organizations, *Falun Gong* activists have persuaded numerous state and municipal officials to declare particular dates local 'Falun Dafa' or 'Li Hongzhi' days, have participated in local community events by marching or leafleting, and continue to organize information and exercise sessions in public parks abroad. Other recent efforts have included a bid to nominate Li Hongzhi for the Nobel Peace Prize, and the filing of formal lawsuits against various Chinese officials for their brutal handling of the crackdown against the movement in the People's Republic.

The *Zhong Gong* movement has been considerably less successful in extending its reach and popularity abroad, as well as in developing a viable web-based community of practitioners. Zhang Hongbao, while apparently still offering occasional *qigong* classes in North America, seems to have more or less shed his role as venerated *qigong* master for that of the political dissident in exile. While detained in Guam, when Zhang began a hunger strike to press for his release, an array of overseas Chinese dissident organizations – including the Free China Movement, the Chinese Democracy Party and the Joint Conference of Chinese Overseas Democracy Movement – rallied to his cause, organizing a press conference to draw attention to his plight.[65] Shortly after winning his bid for political asylum in the USA, Zhang returned the favour by joining forces with the outlawed Chinese Democracy Freedom Party, and by establishing an organization designed to push for the release of political dissidents from mainland Chinese jails.[66] *Zhong Gong* organizers in China have been arrested as recently as September 2001 for attempting to organize resistance to the government's continuing seizure of *Zhong Gong* property,[67] but do not appear to have been targeted as vigorously by mainland authorities as have *Falun Gong* practitioners.[68] Nonetheless, the virtual links between *Zhong Gong* and other overseas organizations, most notably Liu Siqing's Hong Kong based Information Centre for Democracy and Human Rights, remain close.[69]

Conclusion: the rise of Chinese cybersects

The speed and accessibility of web-based communications have fundamentally altered the manner in which some contemporary syncretic sects operate in greater China. With the broad reach afforded them by the web, many such groups have undertaken ambitious international recruitment campaigns, circulating key texts in several languages and even adopting news-like formats to broadcast their views on web-based television. The ease with which activists can now make contact with one another, media representatives and transnational human rights organizations, has greatly facilitated the ability of such organizations to circumvent Chinese state authorities. It has also made it much easier for such groups to cement alliances and collaborate in times of need. In recent years the web-based organizational strategies of the contemporary *qigong* movements have been adopted with varying degrees of success by more traditional quasi-religious groups, most notably the Yiguandao, which has established an impressive 'web ring' of interlinked sites with news and information pertaining to Yiguandao organizations throughout East and South-east Asia. Exiled Tibetan Buddhist groups and representatives of other religious sects are also following suit, and, as chapter 12 demonstrates, some Chinese Christian sects are building up their presence on the web as well. With financial and personnel resources held in reserve in societies in which they are permitted to operate more openly, many such groups may once again eye their traditional home soil on the Chinese mainland with both increased interest and capability.

However, as the cases of *Falun Gong* and *Zhong Gong* suggest, not all such sects are capable of making a successful transition from traditional syncretic sect to virtual community of faith. *Zhong Gong*, perhaps in part because it has not suffered the type of brutal repression to which *Falun Gong* has been subjected, has largely receded from international public attention along with its enigmatic leader. *Falun Gong* has lost considerable organizational strength as well: with Li Hongzhi residing abroad and maintaining a low profile throughout most of 2000, at least one local chapter began to seek spiritual inspiration elsewhere. Some underground *Falun Gong* cells in mainland China have purportedly been overtaken by charismatic 'tutors' or 'facilitators' to whom practitioners can more readily relate, or now follow scriptures not penned by Li.[70] Some thirty-odd members of *Falun Gong*'s Hong Kong chapter experienced a collective revelation on Buddha's birthday that a 37-year-old activist in their midst was in fact the 'Lord of Buddhas'. A former owner of a trading company, Belinda Pang in Hong Kong, announced that all of Li Hongzhi's most recent revelations must be false because he had already clearly left to 'quietly watch the practitioners and people in the world' perched atop a cliff somewhere in the USA, presumably leaving her in control.[71] While Li's supremacy within the movement has been challenged before,[72] such issues seem destined to revisit the group in the future, particularly as adherents across the globe are encouraged to post and share their personal revelations, visions and experiences on movement websites alongside those of Master Li.

Yet, as others have noted, the supposedly anonymous and egalitarian nature of web-based exchanges is illusory. The Internet may indeed invite broad-based participation by dissolving formidable boundaries, but it erects others that are no less imposing. The unequal distribution of technological expertise allows alternative hierarchies to emerge, creating a condition some have referred to as crypto-anarchy.[73] Within newly emerging cybersects, technical and media wizards could easily play a much greater role in defining the movement. Just a few weeks before Belinda Pang emerged, one astute observer noted that *Falun*

Gong had undergone 'a dark evolution' that involved the emergence of' 'a hard core of radicalized followers' who were no longer dependent upon Li's guidance for the movement to grow.[74] The high level of technological and public relations expertise required to keep such a group in working order demands considerable organizational skill that may well be in short supply among charismatic mystics, and the marriage between technological expertise and spiritual vision may not always be a harmonious one.

Acknowledgements

I wish to thank Kevin O'Brien, Elizabeth Perry, Mark Selden and Thomas Thornton for their comments and suggestions.

Notes

1   Gonganbu, *Fandong Hui-Dao-Men jianjie (Neibu faxing)* (An Introduction to Reactionary Sects and Secret Societies – restricted publication) (Beijing: Qunzhong chubanshe, 1985), chap. 2, as translated by Robin Munro, 'Syncretic Sects and Secret Societies: Revival in the 1980s', *Chinese Sociology and Anthropology*, 21, 4 (Summer 1989), pp. 49–84.
2   Some organizational and strategic elements of these new cybersects parallel those found in, for example, Shining Path in Peru and the Heaven's Gate cult in the USA; however, what sets these contemporary Chinese cybersects apart from such groups is the degree of their reliance on the web to maintain their existence in the face of severe government repression. In this manner contemporary cybersects also bear strong similarities to other covert networks associated with underground terrorist cells and collusive criminal gangs. The anonymity provided by the web permits such groups to maintain a very high level of secrecy without hampering the effectiveness of intragroup communication.
3   See, for example, Barend ter Haar, *Ritual & Mythology of the Chinese Triads : Creating an Identity* (Leiden: Brill, 1999).
4   On the institutional adaptations of *Falun Gong* organizations in the first decade of its existence, see James Tong, 'An Organizational Analysis of the Falun Gong: Structure, Communications, Financing', *The China Quarterly*, 171 (September 2002), pp. 636–60.
5   For an analysis of the crackdown against *Falun Gong* that likens it to attempts to suppress syncretic sects in earlier periods, see Elizabeth J. Perry, 'Challenging the Mandate of Heaven: Popular Protest in Modern China', *Critical Asian Studies*, 33, 2 (2001), pp. 163–80.
6   Lu Xiaobo of Barnard College, quoted by Elizabeth Rosenthal in 'Beijing in Battle With Sect: "A Giant Fighting a Ghost" ', *New York Times*, 26 January 2001, p. 1.
7   On imperial-era syncretic sects, see Susan Naquin, *Millenarian Rebellion in China: The Eight Trigrams Uprising of 1813* (New Haven: Yale University Press, 1976), as well as her 'The Transmission of White Lotus Sectarianism in late Imperial China', in David Johnson, Andrew J. Nathan and Evelyn S. Rawski (eds), *Popular Culture in Late Imperial China* (Berkeley: University of California Press, 1985), pp. 255–91; Daniel L. Overmyer, *Folk Buddhist Religion: Dissenting Sects in Late Traditional China* (Cambridge, MA; Harvard University Press, 1976), as well as his 'Alternatives: Popular Religious Sects in China', *Modern China*, 7, 2 (1981), pp. 153–90; David Ownby, *Brotherhoods and Secret Societies in Early and Mid-Qing China* (Stanford: Stanford University Press, 1996); Dian Murray, 'Migration, Protection and Racketeering: The Spread of the Tiandihui in China', in David Ownby and Mary Somers (eds), *'Secret Societies' Reconsidered: Perspectives on the Social History of Modern South China and Southeast Asia* (Armonk: ME

Sharpe, 1993), pp. 177–89; and Barend ter Haar,*The White Lotus Society and White Lotus Teachings: Reality and Label* (Leiden: Brill, 1990).

8 For one such example, see Elizabeth J. Perry and Tom Chang, 'The Mystery of Yellow Cliff: A Controversial "Rebellion" in the late Qing', *Modern China*, 6, 2 (1980), pp. 123–60.

9 For example, see Elizabeth J. Perry, *Rebels and Revolutionaries in North China* (Stanford: Stanford University Press, 1980); Chen Yongfa, *Making Revolution: The Communist Movement in Eastern and Central China 1937–45* (Berkeley: University of California Press, 1986); Odoric Wou, *Mobilizing the Masses: Building Revolution in Henan* (Stanford: Stanford University Press, 1994).

10 Donald E. MacInnes, *Religion in China Today: Policy and Practice* (Maryknoll: Orbis, 1989).

11 Shen Zhenyu, Zeng Zhaogui and Xu Shengguo, *Zheng yü xie* (Orthodoxy and heteroxy) (Beijing: Qunzhong chubanshe, 2001), pp. 12–33; see also Zhu Xiaoyang, 'Spirit and Flesh: Sturm and Drang', *Shidai* (October 1989), trans. Paul Lam, and John Minford, Benjamin Penny and Zhu Xiaoyang (eds), 'The *Qigong* Boom', *Chinese Sociology and Anthropology*, 27, 1 (Fall 1994), pp. 35–6.

12 Shen Zhenyu, Zeng Zhaogui and Xu Shengguo, *Zheng yu xie*, pp. 56–9.

13 A translated transcript of one of Yan Xin's 'qi-empowered' lectures appears in Benjamin Penny and Zhu Xiaoyang (eds), 'The *Qigong* Boom', pp. 59–68.

14 Ke Yunlu, *Da Qigongshi* (Beijing: Renmin wenxue chubanshe, 1989); portions of the preface of the novel have been translated and appear in Penny and Zhu, and another excerpt describing one of the protaganists (named Yao Jiu) public addresses appears in Geremie Barmé and Linda Jaivin, *New Ghosts, Old Dreams* (New York, Times Books, 1992), pp. 377–80.

15 See Jian Xu, 'Body, Discourse and the Cultural Politics of Contemporary Chinese *Qigong*', *The Journal of Asian Studies*, 58, 4 (November 1999), p. 963.

16 Jian Xu, 'Body, Discourse and the Cultural Politics of Contemporary Chinese *Qigong*', pp. 963, 973; Marlowe Hood, 'Mystics, Ghosts and Faith Healers: Forces of China's Past Re-emerge in a New Occult Craze', *Los Angeles Times*, 19 April 1992.

17 Shen Zhenyu, Zeng Zhaogui and Xu Shengguo, *Zheng yü xie*, pp. 192–203; Zhu Xiaoyang, 'Spirit and Flesh: Sturm and Drang', p. 39.

18 Li Da, 'Zhonggong qingli "*qigong* dang" ', (Party Central Purges '*qigong* Party'), *Dangdai shishi zhoukan* (The Current Age Weekly), 25 August 1990, pp. 14–15.

19 Chen Zong, '*Zhong Gong* bei dacheng xiejiao canzhao pohuai' (*Zhong Gong* is Attacked as a Heretical Sect and Destroyed), *Qian Xiao* (Vanguard) (Hong Kong) (June 2000), p. 32; cf. Amnesty International, 'The Crackdown on *Falun Gong* and Other So-called "Heretical Organizations" ', 17 March 2000, p. 8; and Charles Hutzler, 'Another "Evil Cult": China Cracks Down on Meditation Sect', Associated Press report, 31 January 2000.

20 On the urban features of the movement, see Nancy N. Chen, 'Urban Spaces and the Experience of Qigong', in Deborah Davis, Richard Kraus, Barry Naughton and Elizabeth J. Perry (eds), *Urban Spaces in Contemporary China* (Washington, DC: Woodrow Wilson Center Press, 1995), pp. 347–61.

21 Stevan Harrell and Elizabeth J. Perry, 'Syncretic Sects in Chinese History: An Introduction', *Modern China*, 8, 3 (July 1982), pp. 286–7.

22 Craig S. Smith, 'Asylum Plea by Chinese Sect's leader Perplexes the US', *The New York Times*, 31 July 2000, p. 3.

23 The section that follows is a summary of the material in Zhang Hongbao, 'Wode jianli' (My Curriculum Vitae), found on the official *Zhong Gong* website, <http://www.zgzg.net>.

24 For these biographical details, see Qing Xin, 'Tantan Zhang Hongbao yu zhengzhi' (On Zhang Hongbao and Politics), on the official *Zhong Gong* website, <http://www.zgzg.net>.

25 See Zhang Hongbao, ' "Qilin wenhua jiianjie" zhaiyao' (Summary of 'Qinlin culture synopsis') (no date), formerly available on <http://members.tripodeasia.com.cn/akun99/004.html> and <http://go3.163.com/jmhh/new/qlwh/004.html>; cached versions may still be accessible.

26 Qing Xin, 'Tantan Zhang Hongbao yü zhengzhi' (On Zhang Hongbao and Politics), on the official *Zhong Gong* website, <http://www.zgzg.net>

27 Ji Yi, *Daqigong shi chushan* (A Great *qigong* Master Comes out of Retirement) (Beijing: Hualing chubanshe, 1990), pp. 105, 264; as cited by Wang Yunshui, *Dangdai Zhongguo xiejiao* (Heretical Sects in Contemporary China) (Lhasa: Xizang renmin chubanshe, 1998), pp. 141–4.

28 From the premier issue of *Qilin wenhua* (1992), a short-lived *Zhong Gong* periodical, cited in Zhong Kewen, ' "Falun gong" heyi chengshi (How could '*Falun Gong*' gain influence?) (Beijing: Dangdai Zhongguo chubanshe), pp. 373–79.

29 See '*Zhong Gong* daode quan' (*Zhong Gong*'s moral outlook), <http://www.zgzg.net>

30 Shen Zhenyu, Zeng Zhaogui and Xu Shengguo, *Zheng yu xie*, p. 227; on the worshipful attitude of *Zhong Gong* practitioners toward Master Zhang, and his distinctly imperial demeanor, see Marlowe Hood, 'Mystics, Ghosts and Faith Healers', p. 20.

31 Patricia M. Thornton', Framing Dissent in Contemporary China: Irony, Ambiguity and Metonymy', *The China Quarterly*, 171 (September 2002), pp. 661–81.

32 Research Office of the Ministry of Public Security, 'Li Hongzhi: The Man and His Deeds', *People's Daily* (Overseas edition), trans. Ming Xia and Shiping Hua, *Chinese Law and Government*, 32, 5 (September–October 1999), p. 56.

33 Li Hongzhi, 'Zhongguo *Falun Gong* chuangshiren, *Falun Gong* yanjiuhui huizhang Li Hongzhi Xiansheng xiaozhuan' (Brief Biography of Li Hongzhi, Founder of *Falun Gong* and President of the *Falun Gong* Research Society), trans. Ming Xia and Shiping Hua, *Chinese Law and Government*, 32, 6 (November–December 1999), p. 17.

34 *Ibid.*

35 Research Office of the Ministry of Public Security, 'Li Hongzhi: The Man and His Deeds', p. 58.

36 David Palmer offers an excellent summary of Li Hongzhi's main teachings in his 'The Doctrine of Li Hongzhi', *China Perspectives*, 35 (May–June 2001), pp. 14–23.

37 On *Falun Gong* hand positions, see 'The Hand Positions for Sending Forth Righteous Thoughts', in Li Hongzhi, *Essentials for Further Advancement II*, <http://www.falundafa.org/book/eng/jjz3.htm>; for discussions of Tantrism, see various sections of *Zhuan Falun* [Turn the Dharma Wheel] (Hong Kong: Falun fofa chubanshe, 1998); text also available in several languages at <http://www.falundafa.org>.

38 Li Hongzhi, 'Suggestions at Beijing Conference of Falun Dafa's Assistants', 17 December 1994, *Falun Dafa Explication* (hereafter, *FLDFE*), p. 62, <http://www.falun-canada.net/works/eng/yj/yj_eng2.html>.

39 These practices are discussed in the question and answer session in Li Hongzhi, 'Falun Buddha Fa: Lecture at the First Conference in North America', 29–30 March 1998, New York; Li has, however, spoken against the practice of burning incense to honour him, warning that this might harm his reputation, particularly if adherents focus on formal rituals to the exclusion of true spiritual cultivation. Li Hongzhi, *Zhuan Falun* (English edition), p. 90 (section on Guanding), available on-line at <http://www.falundafa.org/book/eng/lecture4.html#4>.

40 Li Hongzhi, 'Suggestions at Beijing Conference of Falun Dafa's Assistants', *FLDFE* (my trans.). For similar references, see pp. 39 and 55 of the English edition of the text.

41 Li Hongzhi, 'Zai Meiguo dongbu Fahuishang jianghua' (Speech at the East Coast (US) Fa Conference), 27–28 March 1999, New York.

42 Li Hongzhi, *Zailun mixin* (Further Comments on Superstition), 13 July 1999, <http://www.falundafa.org/book/chigb/jw_28.htm>.

43 Li Hongzhi, 'Teaching the Fa at the Washington, DC Fa Conference', 22 July 2002, Washington, DC.
44 Li Hongzhi, *Zhuan Falun*.
45 Beatrice Leung, 'China and Falun Gong: Party and Society Relations in the Modern Era', *The Journal of Contemporary China* (forthcoming).
46 Li Da, 'Zhonggong qingli "*qigong* dang"', p. 15. See also the *Beijing Wanbao* (Beijing Evening News) article by Zhang Minghui and Zhang Yang, trans. Zhu Xiaoyang and Benjamin Penny, 'The *Qigong* Boom', pp. 27–34.
47 At the time, Sima Nan maintained 'If I didn't expose the cheap tricks of these hucksters, and allowed *qigong* to be trampled upon by pretenders, I would not be fit to be called a *qigong* master.' Reports of Sima Nan's performances and his views were published in *Zhongguo kexuebao* (Chinese Science Report), *Zhongguo funü bao* (China Women's' Report), *Xinmin wanbao* (New People's Nightly), *Jiankang bao* (Health Report) and *Cankao xiaoxi* (Reference News). The reports of Zhang Hongbao's purported sexual liaisons, as alleged by his former wife and a babysitter, were published in *Qingchun* (Green Spring) and the June 1993 issue of *Shijie qigong lingbao* (*Qigong* World Headline News); see Wang Yunshui, *Dangdai Zhongguo xiejiao*, pp. 366–67.
48 Yin Xin, '"*Zhong Gong*" de fazhan he renxing fankang' (The Development and Tenacious Resistance of '*Zhong Gong*'), *Qian Xiao* (October 2000), pp. 35–6.
49 Ming Xia and Shiping Hua, 'Editor's Introduction: The Battle Between the Chinese Government and the *Falun Gong*', *Chinese Law and Government*, 32, 5 (September–October 1999), p. 8. However, this is apparently a point of contention: *Falun Gong* sources maintain that Li voluntarily withdrew from the society, claiming that he would no longer offer *Falun Gong* classes in China, and that his overseas teaching had also ceased. See 'The Truth about Whether *Falun Gong* has an Organization', trasn. Ming Xia and Shiping Hua, 'The *Falun Gong*: Qigong, Code of Ethics and Religion', *Chinese Law and Government*, 32, 6 (November–December 1999), pp. 63–4.
50 *People's Daily* commentary, 'The Political Motive Behind the More than Three Hundred Sieges', trans. Ming Xia and Shiping Hua in 'The *Falun Gong*: Qigong, Code of Ethics and Religion', pp. 87–90.
51 One radio news broadcast on 25 April 1999 quotes a protestor saying 'Premier Zhu Rongji agreed to meet some of Falungong's members this morning at 8.30am but he has not said what should be done yet' (see 'AFP: Largest Demonstration Since Tiananmen in Beijing', Foreign Broadcast Information Service (FBIS), FBIS-CHI-1999-0425). Other accounts of the incident indicate that Premier Zhu Rongji did emerge and speak briefly with the demonstrators during the event.
52 Xinhua News Agency, 'Li Hongzhi's Role in the Illegal Gathering' (12 August 1999), FBIS-CHI-1999-0812.
53 Transcript of Li Hongzhi's meeting members of the press in Sydney, Australia on 2 May 1999, at <http://www.falundafa.org/fldfbb/news990502.htm>.
54 Guan Kaicheng, '*Zhong Gong* "99–8" quanguo xingdong neimu baoguang' (Exposing *Zhong Gong*'s Behind-the-scenes National "99–8" Action), 2 February 2000, <http://www.zgzg.net>; see also Wei Zhen, '*Zhong Gong* "99.8" quanguo xingdong zhuandi de xin zhi yi', (The First Letter Transmitted by Followers to the Whole Country During Action '99.8') and Li Kejiang, '*Zhong Gong* "99.8" quanguo xingdong zhuandi de xin zhi er' (The Second Letter Transmitted by Followers to the Whole Country During Action '99.8'), and other relevant documents at <:http://www.zgzg.net>.
55 Erick Eckholm, 'Beijing Lists Charges Against Sect Leader Who Fled to Guam', *The New York Times*, 15 September 2000, p. 22. *Zhong Gong* denied the allegations and pointed out that manufactured charges of sexual impropriety have been used to jail

political dissidents before in the People's Republic. British Broadcasting Corporation, BBC Summary of World Broadcasts, '*Zhong Gong* Says Authorities Framed Leader', 22 September 2000.

56 The Foreign Liaison Group of the Falun Dafa Research Society, 'Falun Dafa's Transmission of Internet Notice', 15 June 1997, <http://www.falundafa.org/fldfbb/gonggao970615.htm>.

57 Craig S. Smith, 'A Movement in Hiding: Sect Clings to the Web in the Face of Beijing's Ban', *The New York Times*, 5 July 2001, p. 1; Oliver August, 'Revolution by Email in China', *The Australian Times*, 2 November 1999, p. C11.

58 Peter Svensson, 'China Sect Claims Sites Under Attack', Associated Press online report, 31 July 1999, available through LexisNexis.

59 Deutsche Presse-Agentur, 'Roundup: China Accuses *Falun Gong* Followers of Stealing State Secrets', 25 October 1999.

60 *People's Daily* (Overseas Edition), 'The Political Motive Behind the More than Three Hundred Sieges', 5 August 1999, trans. in Ming Xia and Shiping Hua, 'The Battle Between the Chinese Government and the *Falun Gong*', pp. 87–90.

61 Benoit Vermander, 'Looking at China Through the Mirror of *Falun Gong*', *China Perspectives* 35 (May–June 2001), pp. 4–6.

62 John Leicester, 'TV Hijackings, Email Attacks: China's Government, *Falun Gong* Battle for a Hazy Concept – Truth', The Associated Press Online, 13 April 2002, available through LexisNexis.

63 Associated Press report online, 'Police Stop Falun Gong Believers from Putting Guru's Portrait over Mao's', 29 January 2000, available through LexisNexis.

64 David Murphy, 'Losing Battle', *Far Eastern Economic Review*, 164, 6 (15 February 2001), pp. 24–25.

65 US Newswire, ' "Campaign to Free Master Zhang Hongbao" to Hold Press Conference Dec. 20', 19 December 2000.

66 The group established by Zhang Hongbao and Yan Qingxin, the colleague who secretly fled the mainland with him, is 'The Chinese Anti-Political Persecution Alliance' (*Zhongguo fanzhengzhi yapo tongmenghui*); for information on *Zhong Gong*'s involvement with the Chinese Democracy Freedom Party, see <http://www.zgzg.net>.

67 Associated Press report, 'China Sentences Two Organizers of Banned Exercise Group', 19 September 2001.

68 The crackdown against *Zhong Gong* appears to have targeted mostly those in leadership positions, but by the end of 2000, it was estimated that some six hundred *Zhong Gong* adherents had been arrested in the People's Republic. Kyodo News Service, 'Four Jailed Over Police Letters Criticizing Chinese President', *Japan Economic Newswire*, 29 December 2000.

69 The Information Centre was established by former Tiananmen Square student activist Liu Siping after he fled mainland China in 1989.

70 Craig S. Smith, 'A Movement in Hiding'.

71 Pang's description of the fate of Master Li is based upon a photograph of him in meditation that is still featured prominently on the main *Falun Gong* website. Craig S. Smith, 'Split Develops in Leadership of Sect', *The New York Times*, 3 August 2000, p. 10; Linda Yeung, 'A Buddha Called Belinda', *South China Morning Post*, 27 July 2000, p. 13.

72 See relevant sections of Li Hongzhi's *FLDFE*.

73 For examples, see several of the essays in Peter Ludlow (ed.), *Crypto Anarchy, Cyberstates and Pirate Utopias* (Cambridge, MA: The MIT Press, 2001).

74 Susan V. Lawrence, 'Faith and Fear', *Far Eastern Economic Review*, 20 April 2000, p. 16.

Suggested resources

Ming Xia and Shiping Hua, 'The Battle Between the Chinese Government and the *Falun Gong*', *Chinese Law and Government*, 32, 5 (September–October 1999).

Ming Xia and Shiping Hua, 'The *Falun Gong: Qigong*, Code of Ethics and Religion', *Chinese Law and Government*, 32, 6 (November–December 1999).

Robin Munro, 'Syncretic Sects and Secret Societies: Revival in the 1980s', *Chinese Sociology and Anthropology*, 21, 4 (Summer 1989).

David Palmer, 'The Doctrine of Li Hongzhi', *China Perspectives*, 35 (May–June 2001), pp. 14–23.

Elizabeth J. Perry, 'Challenging the Mandate of Heaven: Popular Protest in Modern China', *Critical Asian Studies*, 33, 2 (2001), pp. 163–80.

Patricia M.Thornton, 'Framing Dissent in Contemporary China: Irony, Ambiguity and Metonymy', *The China Quarterly*, 171 (September 2002), pp. 661–81.

James Tong, 'An Organizational Analysis of the Falun Gong: Structure, Communications, Financing', *The China Quarterly*, 171 (September 2002), pp. 636–60.

Jian Xu, 'Body, Discourse and the Cultural Politics of Contemporary Chinese *Qigong*,' *The Journal of Asian Studies*, 58, 4 (November 1999), pp. 961–91.

Websites
<http://www.falundafa.org> (English).
<http://www.clearwisdom.net> (English).
<http://www.faluninfo.net> (English).
<http://www.zgzg.net> (English).

In addition, Barend ter Haar at Leiden University maintains an excellent website with an annotated list of links and resources on *Falun Gong* and new religious groups in the People's Republic, including an extensive bibliography of sources, <http://www.let.leidenuniv.nl/bth/falun.htm> (English)

12 Chinese Christianity
Indigenization and conflict

Richard Madsen

An unforeseen consequence of the policies of the Reform era has been an enormous growth in religious belief. After being severely restricted in the first decade and a half of the Maoist era, virtually all forms of public religious practice were suppressed during the Cultural Revolution, and replaced by a quasi-religious cult of Mao, complete with sacred texts (the Little Red Book), rituals, and claims of miracles. But amid the chaos of the Cultural Revolution, the Mao cult imploded. After the death of Mao and the overthrow of his close associates, the Deng Xiaoping regime relaxed restrictions on religious practice – and the mobility and freedoms of an expanding market economy made many remaining restrictions easy to subvert. In this environment, hundreds and thousands of religious flowers began to bloom, some of them replications of pre-revolutionary religious forms, many others new mutations of the old. According to the government's own – almost certainly underestimated – figures, there are over 100 million religious believers in China today. If we consider 'religion' to include any form of evocation of supernatural powers – and therefore include traditional folk practices like burning incense to gods or ancestors at life-cycle rituals or at seasonal festivals – then according to Peter Ng, a religious studies scholar at the Chinese University of Hong Kong, as much as 95 per cent of the Chinese population might be considered religious to some degree.[1]

Along with other forms of religion in China, Christianity has seen a remarkable growth in the past two decades. The number of Catholics has grown from about three million in 1949 to over ten million today, of Protestants from fewer than one million to over twenty million.[2] As with other major religions in China, this growth represents not merely a revival of beliefs held and practices carried out before the establishment of the People's Republic, but also a re-creation and re-invention of traditions in the light of new political and social realities. In the process, both Catholicism and Protestantism have become deeply indigenized – Christianity with Chinese characteristics – a development that sometimes causes concern both among Western Christian leaders and Chinese government officials. The indigenization involves an adaptation to an enormously variegated Chinese culture and leads to great variations in the ways in which both Protestants and Catholics practise their faith. These differences generate much internal conflict, as well as varying patterns of cooperation and conflict with the wider Chinese society and with the government.

To understand these developments, let us first briefly review the history of Chinese Christianity.

Partial unity under foreign authority

Until recently, Christianity was considered a 'foreign religion' (*yangjiao*) in China, not simply because its doctrines and rituals were imported from the West, but because it was controlled by foreign authorities. The first missionaries to China in the early modern era were Catholics – Jesuits, Dominicans, Franciscans – who came in the early seventeenth century. The missionaries soon took to fighting among themselves over whether or not Confucian ritual practices could be incorporated into Catholicism. In 1693, the Kangxi emperor declared Catholicism – at least the accommodationist version promoted by the Jesuit missionaries – to be an 'orthodox teaching'. But at the beginning of the eighteenth century, the Pope ruled in favour of those who argued that Catholics had to make a clean break with Confucian rituals, and in 1724, the Yongzheng emperor declared Catholicism to be a 'heterodox teaching' (he used the same term, *xiejiao*, that the government now applies to groups such as the *Falun Gong*). This was not only because China's rulers disagreed with the substance of the Pope's reasoning about why Chinese Catholics could not practise certain Confucian rituals, but because they considered it simply unacceptable that the Pope would issue an order forbidding Chinese Catholics to do something that the emperor had declared to be correct. Government restrictions against Catholicism were only lifted in the nineteenth century, under pressure from Western imperialists. Under protection of the French government, foreign missionaries could promote forms of the Catholic faith that conformed to Vatican-approved doctrines (although the Vatican itself was concerned that missionaries in China were overly influenced by the French government). Protestant missionaries were also granted freedom of movement under the nineteenth-century Unequal Treaties. Although divided by denomination and not as centrally organized as the Catholics, Protestant communities were usually under the control of various mission boards, on whom they depended for funds as well as for a steady supply of foreign pastors.[3]

For both Catholics and Protestants, local religious practice was by no means entirely shaped by foreign authorities. Indeed, local Catholic and Protestant communities were constantly coming up with creative interpretations of the faith, sometimes to the consternation of foreign authorities. In the twentieth century some Protestants developed organizations that were almost entirely independent of foreign authority. Such independent groups tended to grow more dynamically than those under the control of foreign missionaries.[4] A prime example was the 'Little Flock' of Ni Tuosheng ('Watchman Nee'), who stressed such Pentecostal themes as prophesy and healing through personal contact with the Holy Spirit and who was often antagonistic towards missions and foreign

Christians.[5] Yet the various forms of foreign control provided an overall order and regularity to Chinese Christian life, and gave Christianity its pronounced foreign flavour.

After the establishment of the People's Republic of China (PRC), the new government aggressively moved to cut all Christian communities off from foreign authority. All foreign missionaries were quickly expelled. New forms of organization were devised to place all Christian communities firmly under the control of the state. For the Protestants, the agency of control was called the 'Three Autonomies Movement', and it was supposed to ensure that Protestant communities would be autonomous in governance, financial support and methods of propagating the Gospel. But the Three Autonomies Movement was really a 'mass organization' that acted as a transmission belt from Communist Party and state authorities to local communities. Chinese government control replaced foreign control. Those Protestant communities that were seen as most dangerous to the Three Autonomies programme and were most harshly attacked were actually those, such as Watchman Nee's Little Flock, that were most completely indigenized and most thoroughly autonomous.[6] Rather than being brought into the Three Autonomies Movement, the Little Flock and similar groups such as the True Jesus Church and the Jesus Family were suppressed and their leaders jailed as counter-revolutionaries. Watchman Nee died in prison in 1972.[7]

On the other hand, the whole Catholic Church was seen as dangerous, because it was relatively well unified under papal authority – and with a Pope in the 1950s (Pius XII) who was resolutely anti-communist. The mass organization established for Catholics was called the 'Catholic Patriotic Association'. To be a member of this organization, one had to renounce allegiance to the Vatican. The Vatican forbade Chinese Catholics to join the Catholic Patriotic Association, under pain of excommunication. The Chinese government, on the other hand, imprisoned prominent church leaders who refused to join. The conflict between the government and the Vatican reached a high point in 1957, when, in the overall context of the anti-rightist campaign, five bishops under the Catholic Patriotic Association consecrated a number of new bishops without Vatican approval. There is still debate among some Catholics about whether that part of the church that accepts the authority of the Catholic Patriotic Association is in a state of 'schism' from Rome. (Representatives of the Vatican have recently affirmed that it is not.)[8] In any case, most Chinese Catholics did not accept the moral authority of those bishops who collaborated with the Catholic Patriotic Association and they were forced to carry on their faith in secret, without the benefit of bishops and priests who could function publicly.[9]

For both Protestants and Catholics, government control went hand in hand with a range of efforts to discourage religious practice. Although from the beginning the PRC constitution guaranteed freedom of religious belief, it did not guarantee freedom of religious association. Gathering together for public worship was only permissible under the auspices of the Three Autonomies Movement or the Catholic Patriotic Association. Under the direction of the government's Religious Affairs Bureau and the party's United Front Department, moreover, the Protestant and Catholic mass organizations restricted venues for worship and subjected worshippers to surveillance. Finally, during the Cultural Revolution, even the officially approved religious associations were shut down, many of their cadres imprisoned, and all religious practice denounced.[10]

After the Third Plenum of the Eleventh Party Congress in late 1978, the Deng Xiaoping regime began to implement more relaxed policies on religion. The primary framework for these policies, Central Committee Document 19, was promulgated in 1982. This document rejected 'ultra-leftist' attempts to destroy religion, acknowledged that religious belief and practice would be around for a long time, and admitted that religion could serve constructive social purposes, even though such belief was fundamentally erroneous.[11] The policy gave both Protestant and Catholic church leaders (organized for Protestants in the Chinese Christian Council and for Catholics in the Catholic Bishops' Association) greater autonomy over matters of theology and liturgy, but still specified that they had to submit to the overall direction and supervision of the reconstituted Three Autonomies Movement and Catholic Patriotic Association. The government had replaced a policy of suppression with one of cooptation and control.

But the state has had difficulty achieving either cooptation or control. Many religious believers reject the government-approved venues for worship and gather together in houses or illegally constructed church buildings. There are a variety of reasons for this rejection. Some Christians are opposed in principle to worshipping in any group that is supervised by an atheistic Communist Party. But most stay away from government-approved venues for more pragmatic reasons. Many Protestants join 'house churches' simply because the government has not allowed the construction of an officially approved church near to them. Others may stay away from an officially approved congregation because they do not like the pastor or do not have good personal relations with the congregants. Others simply prefer the informality of small congregations to the stiffness of formally organized churches. Often participation in a 'house church' or an 'official' church is due to a mixture of principled and pragmatic motives.[12]

The choices for Catholics are more conflicted. Alongside the officially approved Catholic Church there is a vigorous 'underground church'. The two parts of the Catholic Church are organized by parallel hierarchies. The constitution of an underground hierarchy was facilitated by a set of secret Vatican instructions issued in 1978. Similar to instructions issued to Catholics in Eastern Europe, the Vatican allowed underground bishops to choose and to consecrate successor bishops without getting the standard bureaucratic approval from the Roman Curia. The purpose was to allow ageing underground bishops to choose successors even though they could not communicate regularly with the Vatican. Under these circumstances, some underground bishops consecrated many new bishops who had only minimal theological training or who lacked other qualifications that the Vatican might have desired. Patron–client relations could easily develop between a senior bishop and those whom he had consecrated. Perhaps partly to make up for weak formal qualifications, some of these underground bishops (and the priests they ordained) seemed eager to emphasize their willingness to provoke government authorities and to accept martyrdom as proof of their qualifications for church leadership.[13]

Meanwhile, in the officially approved open church, there has developed a hierarchy that is by no means out of communion with the Vatican. The bishops who are at the head of the Catholic Patriotic Association are regarded with suspicion by many Catholics. But many bishops who preside over the open church have actually been quietly approved by the Vatican. By the beginning of the twenty-first century, over two-thirds had in fact received such 'apostolic mandates'. There is no longer a stark division between an underground church whose primary religious loyalty is to the Pope and an official church whose primary loyalty is to the Chinese government. However, because the Vatican has no diplomatic relations with the PRC, it cannot establish direct, open, formal ties with China's Catholics, and lack of such ties creates ambiguities. In many places underground and official Catholics get along well. Sometimes underground and official bishops even live in the same residence and celebrate religious rituals together. (These arrangements work best in places where the church has sufficiently cajoled or bribed local officials to gain a relatively free space for religious activities.) But other times, the divisions between underground and official hierarchies give rise to harsh factional rivalries, which have even culminated in violence.[14]

Diversity within an authority vacuum

In the Reform era, therefore, the government, despite considerable effort to the contrary, has started to lose effective control over Chinese Protestants and Catholics. But this does not mean that foreign authorities have regained control that was broken by the Chinese revolution. Some foreign church leaders, such as those in the Vatican, are trying to reassert their authority, but they have only partly succeeded. Others, such as evangelical Christian missionaries from the USA, are actively pouring in money and personnel to convert China to their form of Christianity, but the decentralized nature of the fastest growing new Christian groups makes it very difficult to maintain external control. The result is that despite explosive growth of Christian communities in the past twenty years, there are no coherent structures of authority to give shape to them.

To an unprecedented degree, then, the nature of Chinese Christianity is now being determined by local communities drawing on the resources of local culture. Before 1949, the less than one million Chinese Protestants were predominantly urban, and in theology, liturgy, music and styles of preaching their congregations replicated the American and British congregations from which their missionaries had come. Indigenous churches such as Watchman Nee's Little Flock, with strong roots in the countryside, were a minority, albeit a dynamically growing one. Now the pattern is reversed.

The spectacular growth of Chinese Protestantism in the past two decades has come mainly in the countryside, and it is driven by local evangelists preaching a spirit-filled gospel similar to, and in important cases in direct continuity with, groups such as the Little Flock. As Daniel Bays puts it, many of these rural Chinese Protestants 'have only minimal knowledge of the Christian doctrines and ritual behavior that would be familiar to most urban Christians'.[15] The anti-intellectualism of fundamentalist Protestantism is perhaps an important asset. This kind of Christianity does not have to build specialized institutions to provide extensive theological education either for its leaders or followers, and it does not need a complicated authority structure to enforce doctrinal discipline. It can readily take root in local communities because its adherents easily blend the expression of their faith with local folk culture. It travels widely because it travels light. Drawing on popular culture, such local communities in China often place great stress on miraculous faith healing, shamanistic communication with spirits and charismatic leadership. According to Ryan Dunch, the religious culture of such communities stresses

> direct personal experience of God, centered on literal reading of the Bible, spread by itinerant preachers with little in the way of formal education (theological or otherwise), but a great deal of dedication and enthusiasm. Suspicions of the state, and of the [Three Autonomies Association] for its ties to the state, are characteristic, as is an otherworldly and often eschato-logical orientation.[16]

Meanwhile, churches under the Three Autonomies Movement – which in theory was supposed to break the Protestant faith from Western control – mimic many of the forms of organization and worship of slightly old-fashioned, middle-class Western congregations. As Daniel Bays puts it,

> Many Western visitors to [Three Autonomies] churches today, seeing the robed choir, hearing familiar western hymns sung in Chinese and an evan-gelical sermon they might have heard in the US or UK, wonder aloud how indigenous the Chinese church really is.[17]

But the Three Autonomies churches are relatively stagnant.

Some of the rapidly growing Christian groups are deeply antagonistic both to established church leaders and to the Communist government. As Daniel Bays describes them, such groups

> often have a charismatic leader that proclaims himself to be Christ or otherwise divine, and who creates new sacred instructions or scriptures. They typically denounce orthodox Christian congregations, perform alleged spectacular miracles, promise deliverance from an imminent apoc-alypse, and demand obedience and resources from their followers. In some respects they are similar to various sectarian movements of late imperial

China, such as the White Lotus groups or even the Taipings of the nineteenth century.[18]

An example would be the 'Shouters Sect', the object of a recent suppression campaign. The group was founded by Li Changshou ('Witness Lee'), a disciple of Watchman Nee who fled to Taiwan in the 1950s and eventually to California. According to a recent Ministry of Public Security document, the Shouters 'infiltrated into China in 1979' and by 1983 had spread to '360 counties, cities in 20 provinces and autonomous regions, with up to 200,000 deceived believers'.[19] The Shouters produced a number of offshoots with names such as the 'Lord God Sect', the 'Practical God' and 'Eastern Lightning', the latter taking its name from a phrase in Gospel of Matthew: 'As the lightning comes out of the east and shines even to the west, so also shall the coming of the Son of Man be' (Matthew 24:27).

But these groups are by no means part of a unified charismatic evangelical Christianity. For example, Shouters – and their supporters among American evangelical Christians – call the Eastern Lightning a 'cult from the nest of Satan'.[20] (The Three Autonomies Movement has also denounced the Eastern Lightning.)[21] They claim that the Eastern Lightning (which was founded by a former Shouter and features a belief in a female reincarnation of Christ) uses lies, bribery, sexual seduction and outright coercion to steal evangelical Christians away from the true faith. One feature that Eastern Lightning does share with the Shouters, however, is a vehement hostility to the government. In response, the Public Security Ministry defines the Shouters and its progeny as illegal organizations that have 'sprung up in China under the banner of religion', and it has moved to eradicate them by arresting their leaders and forbidding their members to assemble.[22] The crackdowns have intensified since 1999 – as part of a general crackdown against illegal religious organizations that began with the campaign against the *Falun Gong*. (See chapter 11.) The Eastern Lightning is seen as especially dangerous and, according to a document from the Shijiazhuang Public Security Bureau, is second in priority only to *Falun Gong* as a target of suppression.[23]

Similar developments are taking place among the Catholics. Especially in rural areas – and since the eighteenth century, most Catholic conversions have taken place in the countryside – Catholicism is today as much a folk religion as a world religion. There is a long history to this development. In the eighteenth century, when Catholicism was cut off from an intellectual elite, deprived of the ministry of foreign missionaries, and labelled a heterodoxy, rural Catholics took on many of the features of heterodox folk sects, to the point that local officials sometimes confused them with groups such as the White Lotus.[24]

To be sure, Catholics would have denied any connection between their faith and folk Buddhism. Yet like folk Buddhist sects (and unlike those converts whom the Jesuits originally made among the Confucian elite), they harboured beliefs that the world was corrupt and could only be saved by the coming of a millennial saviour. In continuity with European Catholic piety of their time, they laid great stress on Marian devotion, but their imagining of the Virgin Mary bore interesting similarities to the White Lotus fascination with a salvific 'Eternal Mother'. In the absence of priests, Catholic communities developed their own local lay leadership, like the folk Buddhist leaders of other rural communities. (There was often considerable tension between these lay Catholic leaders and missionary priests after the missionaries were finally able to return to China in the mid-nineteenth century.)[25]

This folk religious legacy continued through the twentieth century, though it was mostly forced underground in the Maoist era. It is now more publicly visible and, if anything, seems to have become amplified in the past two decades. There is a great enthusiasm about purported visions of the Virgin Mary, who is seen not just as a loving mother, but, in her role as Our Lady Queen of China, as a defender of the faithful against the forces of evil. In North China, villagers pass on stories about how Holy Mary appeared in their village during the Boxer rebellion and helped them drive out the evil Boxers – an oral tradition that is in sharp contrast to the official line, enshrined in local government museums, about the Boxers' heroic contribution to anti-imperialism.[26]

Marian apparitions inspired a number of mass movements of Catholics during the 1950s. At least one of these, near Taiyuan in Shanxi province, was crushed by the military. Donglu, a small village near Baoding in Hebei province that was the site of one of the most spectacular of the Boxer-era Marian apparitions and an important pilgrimage destination throughout the first half of the twentieth century, became a major site of conflict and resistance during the Reform era. Its church was destroyed during the Cultural Revolution, but in the 1980s, after it became possible to worship in public, local Catholics put up an image of Our Lady Queen of China on the place where the church had stood, and as many as twenty thousand pilgrims came each year to worship in front of the picture. In the late 1980s, the local Catholics began to build a huge cathedral, which can now hold several thousand persons. Many apparitions are reported there and tens of thousands of Catholics visit every year. Fearful of the potential for unrest, the People's Liberation Army occupied the village in 1999, shut down the church, took away its revered image of Mary and arrested the local underground bishop and many of the clergy. Despite this – or probably because of it – Mary continues to appear.[27]

As is the case in most other parts of the world, neither ecclesiastical nor government authorities are particularly welcoming of Mary's apparitions – unless and until they can coopt them. Like the great majority of Chinese Catholics, the officially approved bishops promote a strong Marian devotion, but they seem somewhat cooler to visions and miracles than the underground – which enhances the underground's populist credibility. Meanwhile, the Chinese government is particularly ill equipped to coopt Marian apparitions (which, as in most of the world, have had a strong anti-Communist flavour). Marian apparitions and other such charismatic events bring unpredictability into both the internal life of the church and relations between the church and the state.[28]

One issue on which the interests of the Vatican and the PRC government coincide is in establishing more order over the devotional practices of grassroots Catholics. It was this coincidence of interests that led to some significant progress toward the normalization of Sino–Vatican relations in 1999 – until the government started applying to the underground church pressure similar to the pressure it was applying to the *Falun Gong*.[29]

Although the greatest growth of Protestantism and the staunchest support of Catholicism are found in the poorer sectors of rural China, it should not be assumed that Christianity has no attraction to the upper classes. Both Protestant and Catholic forms of Christianity are flourishing in the prosperous entrepreneurial city of Wenzhou. And there has been a significant movement toward Christianity on the part of intellectuals.

But even among these strata, the most dynamic growth is beyond the control of church authorities or political authorities. Wenzhou, for example, is a city with the most open entrepreneurial market economy in China. Residents are little dependent on government support, many are widely travelled as petty merchants, and they have the discretionary income to build a great variety of churches, most of them not connected with the Three Autonomies Association or with the Catholic Patriotic Association.[30]

Among prominent intellectuals there is also a growing number of 'culture Christians', university scholars in such fields as history, literature and philosophy who have been drawn to Christianity through study of its role in the ascendancy of the West.[31] The writing of some of these seems to be not simply an expression of detached scholarship but of personal faith. But, as Daniel Bays, writes,

> Whereas sometimes Chinese Christian intellectuals outside of China are willing to participate in conferences and publications revealing their identity as Christian believers, intellectuals in China who study Christianity, including those who may be believers, have very little or no connection with the organized church ...[32]

Here too, then, Christian growth is driven by indigenous social and cultural forces that are not under the control of religious or secular authorities.

The consequence of these patterns of growth is that Chinese Christianity has become enormously diverse. There are different forms of Christianity to fit with the culture of different social strata, regional circumstances and historical legacies. It is this very diversity that has allowed Christianity to grow so quickly during the Reform era. But the diversity leads to division. Different Protestant sects bitterly denounce one another for heresy. Different Catholic groups dispute with one another about who is properly loyal to the Pope. In some cases, such disputes lead to intra-religious violence. Evangelical Christians claim that their members have been beaten and abducted by members of the Eastern Lightning.[33] Underground Catholics have physically attacked leaders in the official church. For example, on Good Friday of 2001, an underground Catholic in

Harbin cut off the ear of a priest who was the local head of the local Catholic Patriotic Association – presumably in imitation of Saint Peter's cutting off the ear of the high priest's servant who came to arrest Jesus in the Garden of Gethsemene.[34]

One government response is to use divide and rule tactics to pit various Christian factions against one another. In the late 1990s, religious affairs officials became worried when many official and underground factions within the Catholic Church had begun informally to resolve their differences, but on terms other than those laid out by official spokespersons for the Catholic Patriotic Association. The response was an attempt to recruit 'additional politically reliable persons to become involved with the leadership group of the Patriotic Association at the provincial level', and to use this leadership core to 'convert the majority and isolate the minority'.[35] Predictably, the result was an increase in polarization within the Catholic Church. Besides giving special favours to factions that denounce more radical co-religionists, the government – according to the suspicions of some local Christians I have interviewed – may have used *agents provocateurs* to encourage outrageous behaviour that discredits some independent groups.

The fomenting of such divisions, however, can get out of hand, further undermining political stability. For the government, there is no easy way out of this dilemma. It is very difficult to control religious movements with the standard tools of statecraft. Widely perceived as corrupt, the Chinese government has little capacity to exert credible moral authority and has to rely even more heavily than most governments on material rewards and punishments. As applied to Christians, this involves government patronage – salaries for reliable church leaders, funds for rebuilding church buildings. But in the eyes of some independent Christian communities, receipt of such patronage is itself a sign of lack of fidelity to Christ. To control such recalcitrant Christians, the government resorts to harsh sanctions – fines and prison for unauthorized church leaders and destruction of unauthorized church buildings. For instance, hundreds of unauthorized church buildings in Fujian and in the Wenzhou area of Zhejiang – many built with remittances from local Christians who now work in sweatshops in the USA – were dynamited or bulldozed in 1999.[36] Such aggression, however, only deepens the determination of Christians imbued with a cult of martyrdom, or who are convinced of the coming of a new millennium.

For their part, many church leaders would like to establish more unity among Christians. But they too lack tools to do this. One way for religious leaders to assert authority would be to provide more trained pastors for local communities. But many of the new rural sects downplay intellectual doctrines and look to an immediate, emotional connection with God, characteristics that suggest quite a different route for the selection of clergy. And, as some Catholic seminarians have discovered, advanced theological training itself, especially when it is carried out in an urban setting, serves only to alienate them from the rural grassroots of the church.[37]

Infrastructures of belief

Any attempt to introduce more order and unity into fragmented Christian communities would have to contend not only with diversity of belief and styles of worship, but with diversity in what might be called the infrastructure of belief, the specific kinds of social relationships within which a Christian identity is embedded. In some places, Christian identity is intimately connected with ethnicity, in other places with family and kinship relations. In such places the primary locus of Christian community is the village or region. In still other places, Christianity takes the form of voluntary associations that bring together a diverse array of individuals seeking salvation. In such places, the locus is the sectarian organization, whose local branches are networked with others throughout the society. Finally, in some places, Christianity may be the heritage of certain class fractions, like the old professional middle classes who gained their visions of modernity from Christian colleges and the YMCA before 1949. These different social infrastructures produce different motives for accepting and maintaining a Christian identity.

Christianity as ethnicity is seen most clearly among certain national minorities in the southwest. In parts of Yunnan and Guizhou, missionaries in the early twentieth century (both Catholics and Protestants, but more often Protestant) managed to convert whole ethnic groups and indeed to deepen their sense of ethnic identity by creating writing systems for their languages.

Christianity as the expression of family and kin relations is especially characteristic of many Catholic villages. In the nineteenth and early twentieth centuries, Catholic missionaries aimed to convert not individuals but families and lineages. They attempted to create replicas of Catholic villages in countries such as France, where all of social life was intertwined with the church. In many parts of China, whole villages, or whole lineages (people with the same surname who claim descent from a single ancestor) within villages are Catholic. Marriages to non-Catholics are discouraged, and children are automatically baptized into the faith. In such communities, even 'lax Catholics', who profess little personal belief, nonetheless have to retain a minimal Catholic identity. At the very least, they will have to be buried as a Catholic, because there is no other way that they can be connected with their ancestors. The Chinese government's policies of household registration, which give everyone a state-imposed identity and restrict movement from countryside to city, make it much more difficult than it would be in the USA for rural Chinese to leave behind ethnic or family ties.

In places such as Hebei province, where whole counties (such as Xian county) are composed of such Catholic villages, Catholic identity takes on some of the characteristics of an ethnicity – an identity that one cannot shed even if one wanted to and which is therefore intensified rather than weakened by social and political discrimination against Catholicism. When Christianity becomes either a component of ethnicity or an essential expression of family relationships, it acquires enormous staying power. Persecution may even intensify Christian commitment. The only force that dissolves it is mobility away from one's rural roots into an anonymous urban environment where one's place of origin is of little consequence.[38]

As in imperial China, rural people with limited opportunities for geographical mobility can nonetheless transcend family and lineage by joining sectarian organizations. In pre-modern China, such organizations were usually decentralized networks of local, voluntary associations. Many of the rapidly growing Protestant or 'quasi-Christian' sects fit this pattern – which is also the pattern of Buddhist and Daoist groups such as the *Falun Gong* and the Unity Way (*Yiguandao*). Historically, such organizations have usually been divided into a dedicated core group and a large fluid periphery. Growth in membership is driven by personal quests for salvation, which multiply as society becomes more unstable and prospects of happiness more precarious. Grafted onto traditional methods of constructing social networks, modern communications technologies – cell phones, Internet, video discs – may make such organizations extraordinarily flexible and effective. (See chapter 11.) Membership may be unstable, however, as people on the periphery come and go in response to changing life conditions. Since such groups usually do not have highly codified belief systems, the content of belief can fluctuate widely over space and time.[39]

The stable urban congregations associated with the Three Autonomies Movement are perhaps examples of Christianity as the heritage of a class fraction. Most of these Protestant congregants seem not to be new converts but the descendants of those mainly middle-class Chinese who passed through Christian colleges or participated in associations such as the YMCA in the early twentieth century. Besides carrying on the ritual traditions of the denominations (Episcopalian, Presbyterian, Methodist, etc.) that evangelized their parents and grandparents (even though the Chinese Protestant Church is officially supposed to be 'post-denominational'), members of these congregations often still affirm the virtues of moral discipline and social service that constituted the ideals of a professional calling in the early twentieth century.

These infrastructures of Chinese Christian faith are not completely exclusive and they do not rigidly determine the varieties of Christian faith. But they do suggest the complexity of the causes behind the development of Christianity in China, and they suggest that different kinds of Christianity are likely to follow very different patterns of growth. The disunity of Chinese Christianity is at least in part a reflection of the underlying disunity of the society as a whole. Chinese Christianity is being indigenized into all of the contradictions and all of the uneven development of contemporary Chinese culture and society.

Globalization

Emphasizing the indigenization of Chinese Christianity does not imply imperviousness to the influences of global religious currents on China. There is in fact an enormous amount of communication between Christians around the world and counterparts in China, and significant amounts of money and other resources flow into China from the outside. (Eastern Lightning, for one example, has an American-based website: <:http://www.godword.org>.) Interconnection with global Christianity certainly adds a level of complexity to Chinese Christianity. But the sources of global support at times work at such cross purposes, and their recipients in China are so varied, that foreign church members have no way of predicting the effects of their interventions. Globalization produces an abundance of unintended and not always beneficial consequences, but subordination of Christianity to outside authorities is not among them.

Take, for example, the international connections of the Catholic Church. Although the Vatican does not have diplomatic relations with China, it communicates with Chinese church leaders through a diplomat based in Hong Kong, and on the basis of this communication determines which Chinese bishops ought to get 'apostolic mandates'. Many Catholics, both in underground and official church factions, are avid listeners to Vatican Radio and the Jesuit-run Radio Veritas. But the Vatican does not necessarily communicate with one voice. The Congregation for Evangelization of Peoples (usually known by its old Latin name, *Propaganda Fidei*) tends to take a more assertive position against the Catholic Patriotic Association than the Vatican Secretariat of State, which on occasion sends its own unofficial diplomats to China. Meanwhile various Asian prelates, such as the cardinals of Manila and of Tokyo, have paid their own visits to China. Many other lower ranking Chinese Catholic church workers from Hong Kong, Taiwan, and the Philippines are constantly circulating in and out of China, providing religious training, organizational assistance, or just moral support to various factions of the church. Some of these workers are in excellent communication with members of the official church, others have better ties with the underground church. They sometimes advocate the positions of these different factions outside China.

The situation is further complicated by connections with Europe, North America and Australia. Many church groups, often based in different religious orders (such as the Jesuits, Maryknoll, etc.) have 'China Programmes' that often cooperate but sometimes work at cross purposes. The different foreign approaches often reflect wider divisions within the worldwide Catholic church. In the USA, for example, traditionalist, politically conservative Catholics dominate the Cardinal Kung Foundation, which publicizes the plight of the underground church and channels money and other forms of aid into it. More liberal Catholics tend to work through the US Catholic China Bureau, which cooperates more with the officially approved portion of the church. Catholics in China receive many mixed messages, and different factions can use one or another source of foreign support to their advantage.[40] Even though many foreign Catholic leaders sincerely work to help bring about reconciliation among contending Chinese factions, it seems that the net effect of increased global communication overall is to raise the intensity of local factional conflict.

The same is true for Protestants. Mainline American Protestants have worked constructively with the Three Autonomies Movement to help establish the Amity Foundation, which provides a variety of church-based charitable and educational services. The Amity Foundation also runs a large printing press in Nanjing which has supplied millions of bibles to the Chinese Church. Evangelical Protestants, on the other hand, run training programmes for missionaries, who often enter China under the guise of English teachers. These illegal missionaries are denounced by the leaders of the Three Autonomies Movement, and are sometimes apprehended and expelled by Chinese authorities. American Evangelical churches also run extensive programmes to smuggle bibles into China. (The government limits the distribution of bibles to authorized Christian communities.) Televangelists operate broadcasting stations that beam Christian programmes into China. Entrepreneurial religious groups in China can therefore draw on a wide variety of outside resources and can often turn them to purposes not intended by their donors. The availability of these resources has certainly helped increase the number of Christians, but it has also increased the level of conflict within Christianity.[41]

The variety of international contacts with Chinese Christians also produces a variety of positions in the international debates about what, if anything, should be done to promote religious freedom in China. These different positions of advocacy in international forums also inspire different factions among Chinese Christians to pursue different strategies of cooperation and conflict with the Chinese government. In the absence of any unified, one-directional pressure from the international community, the balance of power between religious communities and the Chinese government will ultimately depend on domestic forces.

Conclusion: indigenization and conflict

The growth of Christianity in China over the past two decades should be seen as part of a more general efflorescence of indigenous religion in contemporary Chinese culture, an efflorescence that includes Islam, Tibetan Buddhism, Mahayana Buddhism, Daoism, shamanism, worship of all sorts of local deities, ancestor worship and many 'new religions', such as *Falun Gong*, that often draw upon elements from many of the above.[42] Some of these religious developments, such as Islam and Tibetan Buddhism, are closely bound up with ethnicity; others, such as the worship of ancestors and local gods, are intimately tied to family and kinship; still others, such as many of the new religions, are the result of quests for personal meaning. Chinese Christianity, in different contexts, is all of the above. What is remarkable about it is its ability to take on the hues of all of the different parts of the Chinese cultural landscape.

This is not to deny that Christianity is a global religion and that its recent development has been made possible by China's openness to transnational communication. Such openness has allowed Chinese Christians to import not only ideas, but also methods of organization from abroad, not to mention the money that helps in the construction of church buildings, provision of bibles and other educational material, and support for religious personnel. Yet, under the present circumstances, it is mainly the Chinese themselves who control the terms on which these foreign resources are used – thus the ambivalence in the normative assessments by foreign Christian leaders of the state of Chinese Christianity.

But the Chinese who control the terms of Christianity's import are not part of some unified society. They have many different reasons for acquiring or maintaining a Christian identity, and they shape Christianity to their own ends. The sinification of Christianity is an indigenization into many different fragments of China. While many at the grassroots see in the fragmentation exciting opportunities for religious entrepreneurship, their political and religious authorities see such fragmentation as problematic. Thus, there are ongoing conflicts between local Christian groups trying to gain some practical autonomy over their interpretation of the faith as well as, on the one hand, government authorities trying to limit such autonomy through coercion and, on the other hand, transnational religious authorities trying to limit such autonomy through moral appeals. For the time being the forces of fragmentation seem to be winning.

The forces creating the fragmentation, of course, long pre-date the establishment of the PRC. As we have seen, there were conflicts among various Catholic factions almost from the beginning of the Catholic missionary enterprise in the seventeenth century, and these conflicts led to patterns of tension with different parts of Chinese society and with the state. The influx of Protestant missionaries in the nineteenth century was accompanied by infighting among Protestants themselves, and with complex patterns of both alliance and conflict with Chinese society and state. Some of the most important consequences of Christian influence, such as the Taiping Rebellion, whose leader claimed to be the younger brother of Jesus, were unintended and disowned by most Christian missionaries. Resentment at the special privileges enjoyed by Christians because of their association with Western imperialism helped bring on the anti-Christian violence of the Boxer movement at the beginning of the twentieth century. The suffering endured by Christians helped deepen a cult of martyrdom and a belief in miraculous help delivered through the Virgin Mary (for Catholics) and the Holy Spirit (for Protestants). Amalgamated with local culture, these beliefs have helped to nurture a bewildering variety of grassroots, populist, sometimes millenarian folk Christian practices – practices which have led to bitter conflicts among Christians and with the state.

As part of its effort to overcome the general fragmentation of Chinese society, the Maoist regime tried both to weaken Christian religious practice and to establish tight control over Christian communities. With the collapse of the Maoist project, Chinese society in general – and Christian communities in particular – have returned to early twentieth-century fragmentation. So far as Christian communities are concerned, it is a return with a vengeance. Hardened by the persecutions of the Cultural Revolution, intensified by powerful global flows of money and information, and sharpened by increasing economic polarization in Chinese society, Christian communities are stronger, more entrepreneurial and sometimes more militant than ever. Neither coercion nor cooptation seems effective in bringing this turbulent Christianity under state control.

Although the recent growth of Chinese Christianity is impressive, it is hardly what Protestant missionaries at the beginning of the twentieth century hoped would be the 'Christian conquest of China'. Christian expansion is part of an expansion of all forms of religiosity. What is significant is that Christianity has become thoroughly at home in a syncretistic Chinese culture. Traditional Chinese temples often display statues of deities from many different religious temples – Bodhisattvas, Daoist immortals, and in some places recently even statues of Mao Zedong. (Not long ago I saw a pendant purchased in Nanjing with an image of Guanyin on one side and Mao on the other!) One will never, as far as I know, find a statue of Jesus in such temples. But the Christ, in many different guises, now has a home in Chinese culture along with the whole untidy pantheon of coexisting deities. Throughout its history as a missionary religion, Christianity has been committed to domination or at least incorporation rather than such coexistence. But the configuration of Chinese society makes such Christian religious hegemony unrealistic. Perhaps, indeed, it makes the hegemony of any single unifying force unrealistic. The interplay of religious, cultural and social evolution will transform China in ways that are for now inherently unpredictable.

Notes

1   Peter Tze Ming Ng, 'Religious Situations in China Today: Secularization Theory Revisited', Paper presented at the Association for the Sociology of Religion Meetings (Chicago, 14–16 August 2002). Part of the debate over numbers hinges on one's definition of religion. Officially approved Chinese theorists distinguish between 'religion' (some variant of the major institutionalized world religions), 'evil cults' (offshoots of world religion, such as the *Falun Gong*, which the government deems illegitimate and subversive), and 'feudal superstition' (the customary rituals, myths and moral practices that Western scholars would commonly classify as 'folk religion'). The government's estimate of 100 people practising 'religion' does not include the many people who practise Buddhism, Christianity, etc., in the 'underground', outside the official framework established by the government to regulate religious practice. And if we broaden the definition of religion to include 'evil cults' and 'feudal superstition', the numbers of people who have at least occasionally engaged in some form of religious practice becomes very high indeed.
2   There is controversy over the numbers. The Chinese government's official statistics are considerably lower, but take no account of unregistered or 'underground' Christians. I have based my estimates on the statistics provided by reputable outside experts, presenting their more conservative estimates. See Richard Madsen, 'Catholic Revival during the Reform Era'; and Daniel H. Bays, 'Chinese Protestant Christianity Today' in *China Quarterly* (June 2003), special issue on religion in China.
3   George Minamiki, SJ, *The Chinese Rites Controversy: From its Beginnings to Modern Times* (Chicago: Loyola University Press, 1985); D.E. Mungello (ed.), *The Chinese Rites Controversy: Its History and Meaning* (Sankt Augustin, Germany: Monumenta Serica, 1994); Paul A. Cohen, *China and Christianity: The Missionary Movement and the Growth of Chinese Anti-foreignism, 1860–1870* (Ann Arbor: University of Michigan Press, 1963).
4   Daniel H. Bays, 'The Growth of Independent Christianity in China, 1900–1937', in Daniel H. Bays (ed.), *Christianity in China: From the Eighteenth Century to the Present* (Stanford: Stanford University Press, 1996), pp. 307–16.
5   *Ibid.*, pp. 311–12.

6 See Daniel H. Bays, 'Chinese Protestant Christianity Today'.

7 Daniel H. Bays, 'The Growth of Independent Christianity in China', p. 312.

8 See the bitter disagreement of the Cardinal Kung Foundation, which advocates support for the underground church, with a statement by Cardinal Josef Tomko, the head of the Vatican's Congregation for Evangelization of Peoples, that the underground and official Catholic communities are 'one Church', and not in schism. Cardinal Kung Foundation Online Newsletter 2001, <http://www.cardinalkungfoundation.org>.

9 Kim-kwong Chan, *Struggling for Survival: The Catholic Church in China from 1949–1970* (Hong Kong: Christian Study Centre on Religion and Culture, 1992).

10 *Ibid.*

11 A translation of this document can be found in *Chinese Law and Government*, 33, 2 (May–June 2000). For discussion of policy towards religion, see Pitman Potter, 'Belief in Control: Policy and Law on Religion in the People's Republic of China', *China Quarterly* (June 2003), special issue on Religion in China.

12 Jason Kindopp, 'Fragmented and Defiant: China's Protestants Today', in Jason Kindopp and Carol Lee Hamrin (eds), *God and Caesar in China: Church–State Tensions in Chinese Politics and U.S.–China Relations* (Washington, DC: Brookings University Press).

13 Richard Madsen, *China's Catholics: Tragedy and Hope in an Emerging Civil Society* (Berkeley: University of California Press, 1998), pp. 41–45.

14 Richard Madsen, 'Catholic Revival during the Reform Era'; and Richard Madsen, *China's Catholics*, pp. 41–9.

15 Daniel H. Bays, 'Chinese Protestant Christianity Today'.

16 Ryan Dunch, 'Protestant Christianity in China Today: Fragile, Fragmented, Flourishing', in Stephen Uhalley, Jr and Xiaoxin Wu (eds), *China and Christianity: Burdened Past, Hopeful Future* (Armonk: M.E. Sharpe, 2001), p. 201.

17 Daniel H. Bays, 'Chinese Protestant Christianity Today'.

18 *Ibid.*

19 Ministry of Public Security of the PRC, 'Notice on Various Issues Regarding Identifying and Banning of Cultic Organizations', 30 April 2000, in Shixiong Li and Xiqiu (Bob) Fu (eds), *Religion and National Security in China: Secret Documents from China's Security Sector, Feb. 11, 2002*, <:http://www.religiousfreedomforchina.org>.

20 'Testimony given by a Brother from Shandong', trans. and pub. K.H. Pang, Chinese Christian Church of Saipan, 'China's Cult of Satan – Lightning of the East' (Saipan, Guam, September 2000). Paul Hattaway, Director of Asia Harvest, 'When China's Christians Wish They Were in Prison: An Examination of the Eastern Lightning Cult in China', <http://www.asiaharvest.org>. For an Eastern Lightning point of view, see: <http://www.godword.org>.

21 'Malicious Eastern Lightning', *Tianfeng*, 1997.

22 Ministry of Public Security, 'Notice on Various Issues Regarding Identifying and Banning of Cultic Organizations'.

23 Shijiazhuang Ministry of Public Security Document, 14 September 2000, in *Religion and National Security in China*, <:http://www.religiousfreedomforchina.org>, p. 76.

24 Richard Madsen, 'Catholicism as Chinese Folk Religion', in Stephen Uhalley, Jr and Xiaoxin Wu (eds), *China and Christianity*, pp. 233–49.

25 *Ibid.*, p. 240–45.

26 Richard Madsen, *China's Catholics*, p. 91.

27 *Ibid.*, pp. 91–93.

28 For a historical perspective on Marian apparitions, see David Blackbourne, *Marpingen: Apparitions of the Virgin Mary in 19th Century Germany* (New York: Knopf, 1994).

29 Richard Madsen, 'Saints and the State: Religious Evolution and Problems of Governance in China', *Asian Perspective*, 25, 4 (2001), pp. 187–211.

30 Mayfair Mei-hui Yang, 'Spatial Struggles: State Disenchantment and Popular Re-appropriation of Space in Rural Southeast China', *Journal of Asian Studies* (forthcoming 2003).

31 Zhou Xinping, 'Discussion on "Culture Christians" in China', in Stephen Uhalley, Jr and Xiaoxin Wu (eds), *China and Christianity*, pp. 283–300.

32 Daniel H. Bays, 'Chinese Protestant Christianity Today'.

33 'Testimony of a Brother from Shandong'.

34 UCAN News, 23 April 2001 and 30 May 2001.

35 Central Party Secretariat, 'Document 26 Regarding the Strengthening of Catholic Church Work in the New Circumstances', trans. in *Tripod* (Holy Spirit Study Centre, Hong Kong), 20, 116 (2000), pp. 35–6.

36 Frank Langfitt, 'Faith, Power Collide in a Changing China', *Baltimore Sun*, 27 August 2000.

37 Yü Min, 'The Church in China: On-going Concerns and Challenges', trans. Norman Walling, SJ, *Tripod*, 20, 117 (May–June 2000), pp. 27–8.

38 Richard Madsen, *China's Catholics*, pp. 107–25.

39 Fan Lizhu, 'Spiritual Changes among Chinese Youth: Faith as Meaning Making', Paper presented at Association for the Sociology of Religion meetings (Chicago, 14–16, August 2002).

40 Richard Madsen, 'Catholic Revival during the Reform Era'.

41 Daniel H. Bays, 'Chinese Protestant Christianity Today'.

42 See essays by Daniel Overmyer, Dru Gladney, Raoul Birnbaum, Lai Chi Tim, Kenneth Dean, Fan Lizhu and Nancy Chen in *China Quarterly* (June 2003), special issue on Chinese religion.

13 Suicide as resistance in Chinese society[1]

Sing Lee and Arthur Kleinman

For Gentlemen of purpose and men of benevolence, while it is inconceivable that they should seek to stay alive at the expense of benevolence, it may happen that they have to accept death in order to have benevolence accomplished.

(*Analects*, Book XV.9)[2]

Mao recognized that the reason why people respect martyrs through suicide is not because they respect suicide as such, but rather because they stand in awe of the fearless spirit of 'resisting' tyranny.

(Witke 1973: 21)

In the West we ask of a suicide, 'Why?' In China the question is more commonly 'Who? Who drove her to this? Who is responsible' ... for a woman it is the most damning public accusation she can make of her mother-in-law, her husband, or her son.

(Wolf 1975: 112)

Introduction

Suicide is a universal phenomenon of humankind that has been shown to have different causes and consequences. When 33-year-old Kevin Carter, a celebrated South African photojournalist, killed himself only several months after winning the highly prestigious Pulitzer Prize for photographing a starving toddler in the Southern Sudan, who had, in one of the Sudan's civil war-created famines, fallen down alone in a stubble field with a huge vulture nearby, an icon of African misery, his suicide could be attributed to a number of different things: remorse over letting the child die and appropriating the image of her death for fame and fortune to begin with, but also substance abuse, break-up of his marriage and separation from his own small daughter, as well as to be sure his manic-depressive disorder.

Depending on the observer's disciplinary bias and discursive context, the life of a suicide examined microscopically can support different causal interpretations – thick craniums or excess phosphorus in the brain for physicians in the nineteenth century (Farberow 1975), depression and/or borderline personality disorder for a modern psychiatrist, negative cognition for a psychologist, anomie for a sociologist, patriarchy for a feminist, or change of local meanings for an anthropologist. The death certificate, however, does not have space or authorization for the complex account of a life, rather a local term or at most a phrase is assigned to indicate the cause of death. In addition, political and economic factors may affect how readily a death is ascribed to suicide, and hence the rate and pattern of suicide to be reported. For example, authoritarian regimes have suppressed the reporting of deaths as suicide and prohibited the disclosure of suicide statistics because of concern that such data will be used to critique the state. Thus, until the late 1980s, data on suicide was embargoed in China. In market economies, the need to seek compensation from insurance companies, in addition to the subsequent shame and guilt that exist among family members, may make the suicide's family prefer a disguise of accidental death.

At the collective level of social statistics, nonetheless, it has been repeatedly shown that suicide rates can serve as an index of societal problems, such as economic downturn, political violence, social chaos, and the current phase of disorganized global capitalism. Emile Durkheim (1897), the great French sociologist and anthropologist who was active at the end of the nineteenth and in the early twentieth centuries, described kinds of suicide that represented, he surmised, responses to anomic tensions of social breakdown and others that responded to socially approved opportunities for altruistic action. Mao Zedong too, in his early writing on women who killed themselves in order to defy forced marriages, saw such suicides as being the consequence of a number of societal ills. He further attributed the causes of these deaths to active personal struggle against the evils of society, such as the sexual double standard of chastity, lack of the freedom of love, and other aspects of patriarchalism that disempowered women in pre-Communist China. Thus, he emphasized that 'suicide is a most emphatic way of seeking life', and that 'The more society causes people to lose their hopes, then the more people in society will commit suicide' (Witke, 1973: 20). In this regard, Mao provided a sense of the complexity of suicide by effectively linking the subjective psychological state of hopelessness within an individual to broad social forces that the suicidal person both confronted and succumbed to.

Suicide rates differ widely across the countries in the world. The suicide rate in the USA is about 10/100,000 and has been on a decade-long decline. Nonetheless, for every two homicides there are three suicides in the USA (Goldsmith *et al.* 2002). Following the dismantling of socialism, some Eastern European countries now demonstrate the highest suicide rates in the world, especially those that were part of the former Soviet Union prior to 1990.[3] Austria, Finland and other Northern European countries have long had high suicide rates. The rates in Western Europe are lower, and those in Southern Europe such as Greece and Malta are among the lowest globally. Reliable official rates are not yet available in some Asian countries such as India and Indonesia, but those on hand indicate substantial spatial and temporal variability (Schmidtke *et al.* 1999). The suicide rate in Japan remains higher than those of the other two high-income Asian societies of Singapore and Hong Kong, but it does not reach the level of rural China (Phillips *et al.* 2002). Nonetheless, there has been a worrying increase in suicide among middle-aged Japanese men in the last few years that seems related to Japan's economic and business crisis (Saywell and McManus 2001).

The rate of suicide also varies with gender. It is two to six times more common in men in Europe, North America, Africa and Latin America. This gender ratio is less pronounced in Asian countries, being, for example, about 1.3 in Hong Kong and Singapore, 1.7 in Japan, and 1.1 in India respectively (Adityanjee 1986; Murray and Lopez 1996). The ratio between youth and elderly suicide varies by society (Desjarlais *et al.* 1995). And, even if two societies have the same suicide rates, the local causes, meanings and impacts of suicide can still be quite different (Baechler 1979). As a social index, suicide may therefore be indexing different things across different communities.

Suicide in Chinese history

For complex historical, political and social reasons, suicide in China has not gone through a period of critical social science enquiry as in the West. Nonetheless, there is ample evidence that suicide has a long history and ancient provenance in Chinese culture. In a scholarly dissertation on suicide in pre-modern China, Lin (1990: 7) has even suggested that 'suicide is a hallmark of Chinese culture'. Suicide was connected, for example, with defeated generals and princes during the changing of dynasties (*gai chao huan dai*), with wars, corrupt emperors and inauspicious family situations. It was variously described as an act of ardent loyalty towards an emperor (*zhong chen bu shi er zhu*), as a moral protest, and as a strategy for dealing with exploitative and oppressive social relations (Da 1993; He 1996). Mass suicide, involving at times hundreds and even thousands of people, and affirming moral commitment to a leader, was part of the record of Chinese history (He 1996: 187). This moral grounding of suicide is salient for social analysis because it illuminates the downside of society that some suicides may be criticizing.

When transposed into the female life world, suicide was available to women as a way of defending their loyalty and chastity (*zhen jie*). More commonly, it was an ultimate means of escape (*jie tuo*) from life situations they found to be more unbearable than death (*sheng bu ru si*), such as forced (re-)marriage, brutal bondage as a kind of slave and producer of sons in miserably oppressive family situations, accusations of adultery or incest, marriage to abusive husbands who squandered the family fortune, took concubines and other wives, abuse by in-laws and the like (Wolf 1975; Witke, 1973).

Its cultural intelligibility notwithstanding, suicide is not simply authorized in the Chinese tradition. As an unnatural death it was to be avoided and the *felo-de-se* was in some texts not to be mourned. Suicide was polluted and polluting. It also entails economic loss by diminishing productive and/or reproductive power. Whatever the individual motives involved, suicide is often seen to be a rejection of everything in society on the level of cultural production, and compels the members of society to doubt its core values. Confucian teachings too, do not simply encourage suicide as a way of fulfilling virtue (*sha shen cheng ren*) or choosing righteousness (*she sheng qu yi*). There is, for example, the filial notion that 'Our bodies, in every hair and bit of skin, are acquired from our parents, and must not be injured or damaged' (*shen ti fa fu shou zhi fu mu, bu ke wei shang*). Suicide notes left by dead persons typically convey a deep sense of apology and of unfulfilled filial responsibility towards their parents or other family members (Liu and Li 1990: 41). To die and become a solitary spirit with no one to depend on (*gu hun wu yi*) is, in fact, against the Confucian emphasis on family solidarity.

Unlike the Christian churches' explicit anti-suicide stance (Farberow 1975), the Chinese cultural tradition generally and Confucian doctrine more narrowly are somewhat ambiguous, and can be used either to support suicide as prosocial, or discourage it as antisocial. This is not surprising as Chinese have been shown to appropriate the Confucian past both as a moral ideal and for solving practical problems in daily life (Lin 1990). When these uses are not in agreement, then the tension between them allows for creative ambiguity as well as the difficulties of normlessness and hypocrisy. At turbulent times when it was necessary to choose between loyalty to the country (*zhong*), the husband (*zhen*) and the father (*xiao*), women who killed themselves emulated and defied Confucian teachings at the same time. For this reason, the larger community, the clan and the family might react to their death differently.

Suicide in modern China

Suicide rates in Hong Kong and Taiwan have been relatively stable and comparable to the global average, being 10.6 per 100,000 and 10.0 per 100,000 per year (1981–94), respectively (Yip 1996). Following the onset of the Asian economic crisis, the rate has gone up to about 13 per 100,000 per year in Hong Kong, which is still not high by global standards. This may suggest that Chinese people are not particularly prone to suicide.[4] But data made available in China since the early 1990s have suggested a very different picture. These data have come from a variety of sources: the Chinese Ministry of Health, the World Health Organization (WHO, based on figures from the Chinese Academy of Preventive Medicine's county level reporting system) and the World Bank, as well as Chinese investigators and others.

According to the World Bank's Global Burden of Disease study (Murray and Lopez 1996), there were 343,000 suicides in China in 1990, about three times the global average, making suicide the fifth most important health problem in the country. Among women it is a greater source of lost workdays than common diseases such as diabetes, heart disease or cancer. This study also found that although China has 21 per cent of the world's population, it accounts for 44 per cent of all reported suicides worldwide and for an astounding 56 per cent of all female suicides worldwide.[5] Young rural females are at particularly high risk: for those between 15 and 35 years of age, suicide accounts for more than 20 per cent of all deaths (Phillips *et al.* 2002). Using data from the thirty-nine countries that provide suicide statistics to the WHO, we and other colleagues at Harvard Medical School compiled the *World Mental Health* report (Desjarlais *et al.* 1995). This found that China has the second highest suicide rate amongst young adults aged 15 to 24 (after Sri Lanka), and the third highest rate amongst the elderly (after Hungary and Sri Lanka). Moreover, China is one of the very few countries in the world that report higher rates of completed suicide in women than in men. Although Chinese researchers' estimates are invariably, and perhaps rightly, lower than those made by Western researchers (e.g., Da 1993: 22.8 per 100,000; He 1996: 17.1 per 100,000; Phillips *et al.* 2002: 23 per 100,000),[6] it is almost certain that China still has the world's largest number of reported suicides by virtue of its 1.26 billion population – at least 600 people are killing themselves each day.

Data on suicide in China have challenged a number of entrenched facts and theories in the West, such as male dominance in suicide, lower rate of suicide in rural than urban areas, and the inevitability of clinical depression among those who kill themselves.

In most Western countries, male suicides outnumber female suicides by 3–5 times. This gendered pattern has promoted views of womanhood that we do not endorse. For example, Jean Baechler has written that

> women endure misfortune better than do men. Their social roles require them to face unbearable problems less frequently ... As daughters, wives, and mistresses, and conforming to the dependency which nature and culture encourage, women have a greater tendency to reach their ends by the *threat* [our emphasis] of trying to kill themselves ... Dangerous and aggressive behavior generally is not characteristic of women.
>
> (Baechler 1979: 291)

In more recent years, some psychiatrists have trivialized female suicidal behaviour as 'manipulative', 'hysterical' or 'pseudocidal'.

Suicide in China also casts doubt on the notion that social isolation, crowding and laxness of social control lead to more suicides in urban than rural areas. For example, Halbwacks (1930, cited in Taylor 1988: 16) suggested that 'suicide was relatively higher in urban areas because the urban way of life was more transitory and impersonal, and left increasing numbers of individuals socially isolated from their fellows and hence vulnerable to suicide'. But the rural idyll is a myth in China (as well as certain Western countries such as the USA, where suicide among rural young men is a growing problem). Although suicides may be less likely to be reported in rural than urban regions, the rural rates of suicide are threefold the urban rates (Phillips *et al.* 2002). Finally, we know very little about suicide among the 100 million members of the migrant population who are floating and suffering from an ambiguous mode of social positioning in China. (See also chapter 6.) Being legally rural, they are subjected to official harassment as well as substantial discrimination vis-à-vis employment, welfare, courtship, legal rights and access to health care that may adversely affect their mental health status (Lu *et al.* 1999). Yet, some migrants have no doubt been both creative in coping and economically successful. At present, research evidence is lacking to show that they are more susceptible to suicide than rural people who do not migrate. Research is clearly needed. Nonetheless, it should be noted that deaths among these migrants are officially registered as rural deaths. As urban–rural borders become more fluid, even while the state upholds *hukou* differences, the sharp demarcation of youth suicide as a predominantly rural phenomenon may be blurring.

Suicide in China disputes Western assumptions in yet another way, namely that it is predominantly a result of psychiatric disease, especially depression. What we do know is that even though the rates of depression and substance abuse are going up in China, they are much lower than in the West including the USA (Lee 1999).[7] Yet, the rate of suicide is about three times higher in China than the USA (Murray and Lopez 1996). Thus, unless new research were to show that our current epidemiological and clinical data are completely wrong, it is hard to imagine that depression is largely responsible for China's suicides. In a recent research study based on standardized instruments that generated diagnoses according to those recommended by the American Psychiatric Association, only 38 per cent of attempted suicides in China were found to be associated with any kind of psychiatric disorder (Li *et al.* 2001). Rather, family and interpersonal problems featured prominently among suicides and attempted suicides (Ji 2000). A recent psychological autopsy study, using standardized diagnostic instruments that have been used in the West, indicated that about 60 per cent of completed suicides in China were connected with mental disorders (Phillips *et al.* in press). That is still lower than rates found in Western studies of mental disorders in suicide.

Suicide is also notable in our time because the rates are going up in many developing societies, together with rates of alcohol abuse, illicit substance abuse, violence, sexually transmitted diseases, and depression and anxiety disorders, as what we and our colleagues have called 'the downside of capitalism' and the traumatic social health consequences of global social change (Desjarlais *et al.* 1995). Although all these rates have been going up in China too, we cannot be entirely sure over the long term if the suicide rate in China is going up or coming down, because the only valid data are from the last fifteen years. Tellingly, He (1996) cited one study which estimated that the annual suicide rate among the faculty at 'one well-known university' in China was 87.4 per 100,000 during the Cultural Revolution (1966–76), and as high as 532 per 100,000 for the year 1970. The cause of suicide was reported to be political in 95.2 per cent of cases (He 1996: 191 and 292). Such a political situation clearly does not apply to contemporary rural China.

Given this estimate and other anecdotal information from the Cultural Revolution, there is reason to suspect that the rate during that chaotic and destructive time may well have been even greater than it is at the present period of relative political stability and economic prosperity, although the subgroups of people most affected could be different in the two periods.[8]

Psychiatric epidemiologists speak of baseline rates, but this idea is of dubious validity from the standpoint of anthropology. They assume a societal state of changeless equilibrium that is contradicted by the experience of Chinese in the twentieth century, which has been one of near constant but variegated societal change.

Suicide as resistance

Unlike Durkheim's classic theory of suicide, which has been criticized for leaving out individual motives and their relationship with social values (Baechler 1979; La Fontaine 1975), recent anthropological theory emphasizes that human experience is *inter-subjective*: people live in close relation to others in local worlds (villages, clans, neighbourhoods, networks, work units, families), and what is at stake in those worlds affects what is at stake for individuals (Kleinman and Kleinman 1997). Large-scale economic, political and cultural transformations – such as the global changes of our era – can alter or threaten what is at stake. People's actions are influenced not only by what individuals think and feel, but by the values and practices that characterize the local worlds in which they live, struggle and die. Indeed, what people feel and what they value is so closely linked that moral processes and emotional processes interfuse. That is to say, collective delegitimation experiences are associated with subjective states of demoralization; relegitimation at the social level realizes remoralization at the level of individuals.

Seen in this anthropological way, suicide can be understood as a means of resisting social power and thereby as a strategy in the inter-subjective struggles of everyday social experience. The phenomenologist Max Scheler ([1928] 1971) argued that resistance is a part of ordinary existence. The social and natural worlds resist our purposes and plans, and we in turn resist the imposition of authority, especially when it threatens what is most at stake for individuals in their local worlds. Thus, for example, the political scientist James Scott, in several publications (e.g., 1990), has shown how villagers – who are responding to a change in the moral economy in which they live, that alters what they have learned to expect from others and what is expected from them – may resort to foot-dragging, rumour, non-compliance and even sabotage to indicate their unwillingness to go along with changes in everyday life conditions that they now regard as unacceptable, and to resist the power of those who coerce them. Likewise, Lucien Bianco (1978) has demonstrated a range of peasant resistance in Republican China, from tax protest to rent strikes to crowd violence and revolt. He cautions, however, that such anti-fiscal riots were usually non-coordinated and presented no major threat to the authorities. Albeit common, they did not depict the claims of the most disadvantaged layers in the rural population. Bianco then notes that 'one of the most popular ways to take revenge upon a pitiless creditor is to commit suicide before his door' (1978: 280). Even though this is 'a roundabout way of expressing aggression towards the exploiter' (301), it could serve to make the landlord lose face.[9]

The question we want to examine is under what conditions do ordinary Chinese men and women in particular embody (or strategically employ) suicide as a form of social resistance? What kind of resistance is it? What consequences, if any, does it have? How should we respond to it?

Suicide as social resistance or moral transcendence has been recorded in different Asian societies. The classical examples cited are *seppuku* in Japan and *suttee* in India. The tradition of moral deaths via suicide in Japan is found in the nobility of failure – a Confucian tradition of a specifically Japanese kind – as Ivan Morris (1975) described in his historical account of 'tragic heroes'. A more recent example is suicide among youth who resist the 'examination hell' that arises from the Japanese educational system's high emphasis on achievement and competition (Prewitt 1988). Likewise, in response to high rates of bullying (*ijime*) and collective exclusion, young Japanese school students were reported to seek refuge in suicide that also constituted 'revenge on the tormentors' (Tanaka 2001).

Although China is often left out of such interpretations, there are, in fact, various historical examples of suicide as resistance in the Chinese tradition. Of course this is only one of many different kinds of suicide among the Chinese (Lin 1990). Thus, the suicide of Qü Yuan (340–278 BC), as told in *Li Sao*, may be a quintessentially Chinese example of the right of a scholar-bureaucrat to criticize the policies of a government by taking his life. Compared to the adversarial style of fault finding, by drowning himself in the Miluo River (on 5 May, lunar calendar), Qü Yuan was engaging in a mode of criticism that did not upset the rules of social harmony and hierarchy so much underscored in Chinese culture.

But his suicide needs also to be seen as an active moral act inasmuch as it is meant to show that even death is preferable to living under unacceptable political conditions. For just this reason, Qü Yuan's example has traditionally been valued by Chinese, who persevere in the rituals of dragon boat racing, and of throwing glutinous rice in lotus leaves into the river/sea, symbolically preventing his body from being eaten by hungry fish, and feeding his hungry ghost. Thereby they celebrate, remember and reaffirm resistance as a part of their cultural identity. In other words, the scholar-bureaucrat in the Chinese tradition was expected to be an independent source of moral authority who had the right to criticize and respond to the times he lived in. Suicide for Qü Yuan could be interpreted as both a criticism and an act of resistance. In this way, it has the paradoxical effect of 'living by killing' – living not at the physical level but in the moral and cultural plane (*jing shen bu si*).

Chinese history also has many examples of scholar-bureaucrats who withdrew from public life, with excuses such as age, sickness, madness and eccentricity because they did not want to serve a particular emperor or his regime. These acts could be considered social resistance as well, and might even become examples of 'dying to achieve virtue' (*sha shen cheng ren*), as when officials of the last Ming emperor refused to serve the new Qing dynasty. Mao himself, as Witke (1973: 21) recorded, recognized that the reason why people respect martyrs through suicide is not because they respect suicide as such, but rather because they stand in awe of the fearless spirit of 'resisting' tyranny. But the concept of social resistance does not have to involve the political domain alone. It can occur inside an institution and, perhaps most commonly, in the family. For example, Chinese history contains innumerable accounts of women who committed suicide to resist intra-familial oppression and exploitation. Some did so to avoid forced marriages that they found unacceptable.[10] Others were resisting the overbearing brutality of husbands and in-laws. Yet others were responding to miscarriage, involuntary female infanticide, polygamy and forced prostitution. In these pernicious patriarchal contexts, suicide provides both subjective escape and, intended or not, a means of social resistance. Etymologically, the word 'resist' was borrowed from Old French *resister* and directly from Latin *resistere*, meaning to 'stand still' or 'stand against' (Barnhart 1995: 657). Hanging (*shangdiao*), the most common method of suicide in traditional Chinese society and in contemporary Japan, was the final, but unequivocal, way of standing still against and above oppressive authorities, often with the suicide ceremonially dressed prior to the ultimate act.

In these cases suicide created social consequences that could make it a powerful action, even though a desperate and final one for the dead person. For example, daughters-in-law who rebelled against degrading oppression in highly authoritarian families by committing suicide caused the family to lose the social production and reproduction of an important member. They also menaced the family's prosperity with the inauspiciousness of the death, and with the threatening presence of a hungry ghost, which could attack family members, causing illness or misfortune (Wolf 1975). There are texts that show that the *hun* of the person who committed suicide by hanging polluted the ground under the body, and the dirt had to be removed as another example of the dire consequences for the family of this sociomoral form of death.

Case studies in contemporary China

Can the concept of social resistance help us to understand the distinct pattern suicide takes in China nowadays? Though no substitute for detailed ethnography, some reports of suicide from contemporary China provide, in a modest way, stories that do sound like social resistance. During the implementation of the Marriage Law in the early 1950s, suicide or the threat of it was often used by Chinese women to resolve divorce negotiations. These acts constituted resistance against abusive in-laws and other forms of patriarchal authority during a period when women were far from being truly liberated in China (Diamant 2000). There were also many anecdotal accounts of intellectuals who committed suicide during the Cultural Revolution as an ultimate act of defiance against political brutality and betrayal by the state (Wu 1991). In more recent times, there have been newspaper reports of group suicides of Chinese farmers in Hunan to protest enforcement of a law preventing burials of family members in ancestral lands that the local state now regards as too valuable for agricultural purposes. Other suicides have protested corruption, injustice and the laying off of hundreds of thousands of workers at moribund state-owned enterprises.

Liu and Li (1990) described a number of cases which, fragmented as they are, suggest that suicide may constitute resistance against the exploitative components of traditional culture and the downside of China's economic reforms (He 1998). A young rural woman, Chen, had a three-year relationship with young man, Li. They had sex several times, resulting in pregnancy. When Li demanded separation, Chen pleaded many times in vain. Feeling hopeless and too ashamed to face people (*wu lian jian ren*), she swallowed a large amount of pesticide. She then walked to the court and died there (He 1998: 91). This should not be understood only as an impulsive act by an individual that followed broken love, or a woman's way of freeing herself from the terrible shame of pre-marital pregnancy in rural China. It can also be interpreted as a premeditated act based in the inter-subjectivity of social experiences that constituted a moral accusation against Li's irresponsibility and resistance against the double sexual standard that still prevailed in rural China. While compelling evidence for either interpretation is not presently available, the confluence of other stories and sources of data makes the issue of resistance at least as salient as the clichéd common-sense intuition of impulsiveness.

In contrast with ancient times, for example, young rural women nowadays are aware that choice in marriage is possible, especially in urban China. Yet the custom that 'matches are to be arranged by parents' order and on the match-worker's word' (*fu mu zhi ming, mei shuo zhi yan*) remains influential. The anomic gap between expectation and actuality then intensifies young women's frustration over arranged (and often mercenary) marriage. The latter is typically of low quality and high stability, and causes fatalism that has been considered a psychological antecedent to suicide (Durkheim 1966). Liu and Li described cases of group suicide among young rural women in Fujian, where they literally formed a suicidal 'alliance' (*tong meng*) to protest against arranged marriage. The story of three such girls, all with the surname of Chen, is instructive:

> Chen[1] was 18 years old. Under her parents' arrangement, she was engaged when she was only twelve. Although she was supposed to have been 'in love' with this man for six years, the two of them never spoke. Their relationship consisted only of 'casting a sidelong glance' at each other occasionally. Chen[2] was engaged even earlier, at the innocent age of ten. On growing up, she became very dissatisfied with the prospect of a loveless marriage. Chen[3] was a lively girl who was good at singing and dancing. She was engaged at an early age, but fell in love instead with a young male actor from the village's theatrical troupe. Although she wanted to break off the engagement, her parents were insistent that she should comply. Being similarly afflicted and feeling much pity for one another, the three girls decided to mimic a scene in a play by choosing to die together in protest against the arranged marriage. It was two days after they died that people discovered their bodies at a secluded hillside.
>
> (Liu and Li 1990: 112)

Similar incidents have been reported from other rural provinces such as Jiangxi, where fifteen young women dressed themselves in choice clothes and threw themselves into a lake together. Some of them were reported to believe that after they died they might return to live better lives as urban girls (*South China Morning Post*, 15 October 1988, cited in Philips *et al.* 1999). In more traditional times and in other rural areas, these girls might have prayed for spiritual release and heavenly happiness.[11] Their longing for urban status tallies with the widely demonstrated fact and the everyday perception among Chinese that urban and rural lives are now as unequal as heaven and hell (*tian yuan zhi bie*). Of course, many more women, who would comply with their parents' arrangement for fear of incurring gossip (*ren yan ke wei*) and chastisement, merely put up with a lifetime of 'sharing the same bed but dreaming different dreams' (*tong chuang yi meng*).

Suicide may, of course, occur after marriage. Zhou's parents arranged for her to marry a man she did not love. Despite her resentment, she was forced to accept the marriage. Afterwards, she tried hard to develop feelings for him, and did everything she could to be a good wife. However, her husband was a habitual gambler who scolded and quarrelled with her all the time. Feeling utterly helpless, she chose an alternative way of escape and protest that was suicide (Liu and Li 1990: 93). This case demonstrates that suicide may be the last strategy used by disempowered women in oppressive marriage situations.

Workplace harassment, though not necessarily recognized as such, also occurred. For example, after being raped and then continually tormented by her supervisor, a 17-year-old temporary worker at a supply and marketing agency left home to kill herself. Before she died, she left her parents the following note:

Dear Dad and Mom:

Forgive me for doing this. I hate myself! Why am I a woman?! Why is the world so unfair to me?! Although I am only 17, I find my life not worth living any more. Instead of having beautiful dreams, I am suffering … I am tormented by a wolf disguised as human. He scares me, but I dare not complain as he is so powerful. I cannot lose my dignity as a woman but if I don't comply, I will lose my job. Then neither you nor society will sympathize with me – I cannot stand such contempt (*bai yan*). You may not believe it, the person who makes me take this path is my supervisor – Wang X.X. Mom, after I am gone, please redress the injustice and seek revenge for me and have him punished … This is the only way I can reduce my mental pain. Forgive your non-filial daughter. Mom, don't come and find me, and don't cry for me. Take care, Dad and Mom. Let me repay all your love and care from childhood in my next life!

Your daughter's last words (*jue bi*)
(Liu and Li 1990: 41)

Teenage suicide may represent yet another form of resistance against rural parents who, being socially disadvantaged themselves, invest heavily in and hold high expectations of their children's academic performance. For example, poor peasant Fu and his wife in Sichuan, having suffered from illiteracy themselves, held high hopes for their 14-year-old daughter (*wan zi cheng long*). They saved up money in order to send her to school, with the long-term hope of changing their family's rural status. Unfortunately, Miss Fu failed the entrance examination for junior high school in 1987. Her parents then paid a good sum of money to allow her to resit the examination. Later they warned her, 'if you fail the examination next year, even our ancestors will lose face!' Feeling overburdened, Miss Fu wrote in her room on 9 June 1988: 'A large number of students are sitting the examination this year, but only a small number will be accepted into high school. I really don't have the courage to walk into the examination hall.' She then poisoned herself to death (Liu and Li 1990: 110).

Over nine-tenths of parents in urban China now have only one child, while rural couples are usually allowed to have a maximum of two children. This birth control policy has beneficially reduced the risk of population explosion, but has made a poignant impact on young rural women, whose only opportunity to improve their lowly status may be to produce sons rather than daughters. In a study of sixty-five young rural women (age 20–30) whose first born had been a girl, 67 per cent of them reported suffering from neurasthenia[12] (Zhou 1988). The great majority (82 per cent) experienced a loss of face for having produced female babies, and some felt they were prematurely forced into sterilization, which crushed their longing to give birth to another child. Specifically, they were fearful about not carrying on the lineage, the loss of extra labour power, and not having someone to provide for them in old age. These collective fears were compounded by the abrupt change in attitude of their husbands and parents-in-law, who likewise felt a loss of face, became apathetic and called them 'the devil who extinguishes the family'. Physical abuse and threats of divorce were common.[13] Hostile attitudes were also shown by their neighbours, who shared the patriarchal belief that since daughters would eventually 'marry out', they were *pei qian huo* ('commodities on which the seller stands to lose') – a metaphorical phrase in which rural women's powerlessness finds its most succinct expression. In Zhou's study, one rural woman had the following to say about her oppressive local world:

> I was sterilized after the birth of two girls. My mother-in-law condemned me by saying: 'I have only one son who married a bitch like you. You have extinguished our family. Get out of here and get yourself killed; otherwise we will never turn around.' My husband abused me, beat me, and threatened to divorce me every day. He angrily reproached me: 'If I can get rid of you, you ugly woman, I'll get another woman who can bear me a son. I'll kill you if you don't clear out.'
>
> (Zhou 1988: 98)

We have not found reliable studies of completed suicide caused directly by the birth control policy in China although the latter clearly has deleterious side effects on women. (See chapter 8.) In a patriarchal context, it may interact with marital problems in leading to suicide. For example, elder sister Liu killed herself with poison after discovering that her younger sister had an improper relationship with her husband Zheng. After her elder sister's death, younger sister Liu cohabited with Zheng illegally. She later became pregnant and desired to keep the child. Since Zheng already had a son, he was reluctant to accept this future child for fear of being punished. The younger Liu reacted by poisoning herself (Liu and Li 1990: 93).

Phillips *et al.* (1999) cited one more example of how the low status and limited options of rural women contribute to suicide. A 38-year-old illiterate rural woman killed herself by taking insecticide in 1994 after protesting in vain against her husband's extramarital affair with another woman in a neighbouring village. Her heavy household responsibilities then fell on their 16-year-old daughter, who was unable to stand the hard work and her father's physical abuse. After making seven pairs of cloth shoes for her younger brothers as a parting gift, she 'joined her mother' by taking pesticide as well. Sadly, the main community response to the tragedy was to find the elder son a wife who would once again take up the onerous household chores.

Rural women may use suicide to resist despotism outside the family as well. One issue of 'Democracy and the Legal System' (*Minzhu Yü Fazhi*, 1988: vol. 1) described such a young woman whose wheat wagon accidentally tumbled over and killed a chicken of the wife of the deputy head of a town. She was subsequently tortured until she was unable to work again. The woman tried many times to lodge a complaint with the authorities concerned but was invariably ignored. In the end, she killed the 4-year-old boy of the deputy head and then committed suicide herself. It would seem that this woman was legally liable to provide compensation for the chicken. The tragic act of self-killing can, nonetheless, be understood as a form of rebellion against oppressive officials (*guan bi min fan*).

Another adverse consequence of economic reform in China is the decline of family solidarity, filial values, and status of ageing people, though the weakening of these core commitments is a much longer-term process that reflects the destructiveness of the last century in China, especially the ruinous political movements under radical Maoism. Li and Wan (1987) described a 60-year-old illiterate rural man with three daughters and two sons, all of whom were married. He lived alone as none of the children wanted to support him. They also quarrelled frequently over the responsibility of caring for him, and complained that he simply 'ate the bread of idleness' (*chi bai shi*). After another such quarrel, he killed himself by ingesting pesticide. While there is a historical tradition, supported in the Confucian classics, of elderly people committing suicide as an altruistic act of saving limited resources, in this instance the issue seemed to be angry resentment.

Inequitable access to health care is now a major problem in China. Because of economic reforms, rising cost of health care, and differential state priorities over what to finance, the state budget for health care has been greatly reduced. Health care is now organized less by the socialist spirit of equity than the language of cost. As the SARS crisis shows, the rural health care financing and delivery system of the Maoist years has disappeared. Being uninsured, rural people have to pay for medical services out of pocket. To do this, however, may be for them to invite a financial catastrophe, especially in the poorer rural areas. In the face of competing needs, sick parents may be the first party in the family to be sacrificed. This is illustrated by the case of a 47-year-old rural man with a debilitating neurological disease that required medical treatment. In order to save money (that would otherwise be spent on medical care) for his daughter to enter university (an unusual achievement for a rural female), he killed himself by taking insecticide in 1995. His death as a loving father (*ci fu*) mobilized the local community to help pay for his daughter's education (Phillips *et al.* 1999). From a family-centred perspective, the man's suicide may be considered a triumphant strategy of resistance against inequitable access to health care and limited education for rural people as much as an act of filial concern. Resistance in this sense need not connote resentment or recrimination, but may constitute a practical strategy to protest and mobilize resources.

Although the above case descriptions are selective, lack ethnographic detail of a vital nature, and may be biased towards clinicians' psychosocial framings, they can be rethought as social resistance. To do so means that the infra-politics of the local world be given primacy over the stereotypes routinely applied to individuals. The issue of resistance against the vicious bonds of patriarchal subjugation should perhaps come as little surprise, as it has long been suggested that the weakest part of the Chinese social fabric is the insecurity of the life of woman before she establishes her own 'uterine' family (Wolf 1975). Nonetheless, the nature of patriarchal mistreatment in the above cases is not exactly the same as those classically described in traditional China, such as a woman following a husband loyally in death instead of remarrying (*cong yi er zhong*) and being awarded with tablets of honour because of the familial cohesiveness her death displayed socially, or a woman killing herself in order to become an avenging spirit. The woman worker who was raped (see above), for example, requested in her suicide note that her mother should seek revenge for her. This does not suggest that she operated with the belief that she would become a malicious ghost after her own death. Her suicide cannot be attributed, therefore, to the traditional belief in a vengeful *hun*. Rather than being based on ghostly vengeance (Jeffreys 1952), it suggests an active strategy of soliciting familial retaliation.

Instead of being viewed as 'feudal remains' of religious and moral traditions, as often happens in the ideology of Chinese communism, suicide in contemporary Chinese women can be interpreted in the context of the poignantly gendered impact of economic reforms on a changing patriarchal society. For example, although arranged marriage of an even more oppressive kind was normative in traditional China, the opportunity for more education and the media that glamorize urbanity have raised young rural women's expectations about marriage and life-styles. According to Rubinstein (1992), who studied extremely high rates of suicide among male youth in a matrilineal community in Micronesia, the growth of aspirations and the concurrent blocking of opportunities would lead to a retreatist anger and eventually suicide among the powerless, be they male or female. Such suicide, as Counts (1980) also demonstrated in an ethnography of the suicide of a young Kaliai girl in north-west New Britain, Papua New Guinea, may be institutionalized as a realistic strategy of shaming and revenge against those who drive the powerless to self-killing.

Recent case studies

As part of a collaborative study on the social meanings of suicide in Chinese society, our group's recent case studies on suicide and attempted suicide in rural Hebei, carried out by Wu Fei, a Harvard graduate student from China, support to some extent the continual pattern of suicide as resistance against social, economic and political forces that adversely affect certain individuals. However, we found that even if a suicide can be interpreted as resistance, the suicide subject did not necessarily have a conscious intention to resist. Furthermore, resistance does not always effect microsocial changes in favour of the subject concerned. The case studies attest to the complexity of interpreting what 'causes' suicide in an individual as well as evaluating its impacts. Biomedically defined depression could coexist with suicide as resistance, shame and/or other circumstances that are socially conducive to suicide.

The first subject, like millions of young rural women who have migrated to the cities to strive for a better life these days, came from a poor family in north-east China. During her work as a sex worker in a market town, she fell deeply in love with a married taxi driver and spent most of her money on him. She quit her work in order to marry into his family and leave the shameful status of prostitution. Despite a successful divorce, however, the man refused to marry her. After a heated quarrel that convinced her that he would never marry her, she killed herself via a carefully planned drug overdose. In this case, the suicide would seem to be simultaneously shame, anger, demoralization and resistance.

The second subject indicated impulsive self-harm that was not associated with depression and a real wish to die. She was a married rural woman who was rescued in time by neighbours after drinking insecticide. The attempt was precipitated by her anger at her husband's chronic gambling and physical violence towards her. The suicide attempt did not change his subsequent behaviour. Rather, it made her detach emotionally from the marriage, and pursue a more autonomous life of her own. This suggests that if a subject survives a suicide attempt, her subjective values, but not the local world itself, may change. Historical accounts of suicide in Chinese women suggested that the suicide attempter could be angrily blamed for pretending to die (*zhuang si*) and using the attempt merely as a means to an end (Diamant 2000: 113). Thus, suicide as resistance has to be considered a risky and often weak means of effecting interpersonal change. Nonetheless, since the lethality of suicide in rural

China has been due to the 'impulsive' use of widely available potent pesticides (in the West, overdoses are commonly associated with sleeping pills or analgesics; the suicidal subjects do not kill themselves because an overdose of these medicines is rarely lethal), measures to regulate accessibility to pesticides may have a substantial effect on reducing the high rates of rural suicides that otherwise could have been self-poisoning with no true intention to die.[14]

The third subject was a 76-year-old farmer who killed himself by hanging. He became increasingly bad-tempered after he developed a chronic skin disease that caused itchiness and occupational deterioration. He was frustrated with the fact that people who had been inferior to him surpassed him in work achievement. He was angry not only with himself but also at corruption and unjust policy in the local government that adversely affected his farming work. He wrote a letter to the central government to report the corruption of the local cadres, but to no avail. He developed insomnia that was not relieved by acupuncture as well as interpersonal suspiciousness and chronic suicidal ideation that suggested clinical depression. But his death could also be interpreted as a protest against social injustice.

The fourth subject was a 22-year-old female who killed herself by taking 100 sleeping pills. She was an introverted under-achiever in a rural family that did not value education for girls. She was aware of opportunities in the cities and made two trips there to find out whether she could change her fate. She was impressed by life in the city but only became more hopeless after realizing that her lack of education precluded her from obtaining a good job there. This blocking of opportunity added to her dissatisfaction with rural life and her meagre achievement compared to other family members. Before she killed herself, she left a letter indicating that it was not anyone's responsibility. Resistance was not obvious in this instance.

If suicide represents at best what James Scott considers 'a weapon of the weak', and the social resistance it produces has an uncertain impact in everyday local worlds, is it useful at the macrosocial level? The high rates of suicide among young rural women and the substantial disease burden they engender have begun to draw the attention of the Chinese media, women's associations, the Chinese government, Befrienders International, the global media and other people around the world. Higher rates of suicide among Chinese than Western elderly have also been used as a critique of policy towards old people in East Asian countries (Hu 1995). Thus far, five national conferences on crisis intervention and suicide have been held in China. This was hardly conceivable during the pre-reform era. Institutions such as the Chinese Academy of Preventive Medicine as well as the Ministry of Health have begun to look into suicide as a health problem. The Chinese Association for Crisis Intervention was established in 1994, and the Ministry of Health collaborated with the WHO in holding a workshop on national suicide prevention in March 2000 (Phillips *et al.* 2002). At the third National Mental Health Conference held in Beijing (attended by the first author of this chapter as a Hong Kong representative), on 30 October 2001, Dr Dakui Yin, then Vice-Minister of Health, acknowledged that 250,000 people died from suicide in China each year. These numbers are in keeping with scientifically made estimates. Such an open acknowledgement from a high government official signifies an openness of attitude towards socially sensitive health issues that was simply unimaginable in the past. In China's large cities, limited resources have been made available for suicide prevention, such as the setting up of counselling hotlines and crisis intervention centres. Funded by the Chinese Government, the 'Beijing Suicide Research and Prevention Centre' was formally opened on 4 December 2002, at the Beijing Hui Long Guan Hospital. Whether these efforts will lead to policies that improve the structural disadvantages of vulnerable people remains uncertain.[15] But the fact that suicide is on the agenda and that the search is on for its causes points to a kind of macrosocietal efficacy that none of China's individual suicides could have imagined. As a collective process and cultural production, then, whatever the intentions of individuals, suicide has constituted resistance to the societal forces that for so long have silenced an alternative history of people's despair.

Resistance in wider perspective

There can be no universal theory of suicide, and one needs to be cautious of over-generalizing in a society as many-sided and complex as China. Suicide is not always social resistance, and may be associated with remorse, disgrace and serious mental disorders (Li *et al.* 2001). Despite its high rates, suicide afflicts only a tiny portion of rural Chinese people nowadays. A more common form of resistance adopted by some people is illegal rural–urban migration (see chapters 3, 6 and 7), which may be thought of as rural resistance to a regime that has prioritized the urban and failed to address crucial rural social policy issues.

Driven by a sense of inequality vis-à-vis urbanites as well as a rational search for income and opportunity maximization, many Chinese peasants have reoriented their funds to non-agricultural enterprises, while others have abandoned their fields and streamed to both state and non-state firms in the major urban centres and nearby townships. Currently estimated to have reached 100 million, these migrant workers leave home with a firm destination in mind, and often follow 'chains' set up by fellow villagers that minimize search and transition costs and maximize the probability of success (Solinger 1997; see also chapter 6). Though treated as bumpkins in the cities and often maltreated at work, many of the migrants bring home modern urban ideas, skills and, above all, earnings that strengthen township enterprises and alleviate the poverty of their places of origin (Zhou 1996). Far from being 'blind drifters' (*mangliu*), they are calculating agents who have created one of the largest and most active markets in the world.

Nor do all rural women succumb to arranged marriage. Apart from work migration, they have increasingly used marriage migration as a means of effecting upward social and economic mobility, and many of them have indeed been successful (Gilmartin and Lin 1997). Migration in post-reform China may therefore be considered a collective strategy for several different things. Is resistance among these? We think it is. Resistance against institutionalized mechanisms of discrimination that have been rationalized within state socialism and that place peasants at a great disadvantage create new options and also hearken back to traditional methods of peasant resistance (Bianco 1978). They can be thought of as a thoroughly modern means of taking full advantage of the economic reforms by artfully dodging state barriers, which themselves have become unsupportable, so that the state in turn has come to depend on peasant initiative in the construction industry, for example (Solinger 1997). Zhou (1996) has argued that this endogenous action for empowerment is not merely defensive; by undermining China's socialism as well as the *danwei* system, it is reshaping the very structure of power in Chinese society.

Thus, suicide may be considered one of many forms of action that rural people use to resist, criticize and reverse urban–rural inequity (He 1998). The similarity of the macrosocietal forces notwithstanding, those who are better educated, more skilled and/or have more connections in their *guanxi wang* (social networks) would choose different strategies of resistance (or adaptation) from the much smaller number of people who choose to take their own lives. Recent studies in China have indeed found that suicide is more common in 'illiterate' and 'uneducated' women (Da 1993; He 1996). Although psychiatrists would generally label these women as being at high risk for poor mental health, their lack of education (and social connections) must be seen as one of many kinds of social marginalization. Suicide may then be understood as a rational, if still filled with pathos, means of resistance and an expression of power by otherwise powerless people (Counts 1980).

Resisting medicalization

Family conflict, especially involving in-laws or spouses, is the most commonly cited cause of suicide among both lay and professional people in China (Diamant 2000; Da 1993; Li and Wan 1987; Liu and Li 1990). As reflected in the popular sayings that 'even an upright official finds it hard to settle a family quarrel' (*qing guan nan duan jia wu shi*) and 'domestic shame should not be made public' (*jia chou bu ke wai yang*), state, medical or other external interventions in suicide are exceptional in Chinese society. Viewed in this light, the medicalization of suicide may enable helping professionals to secure resources for establishing suicide treatment and prevention services. For authoritarian regimes that suppress the study of suicide, because of fears of its political implications, medicalization may be the only (albeit still limited) way of bringing about otherwise prohibited social actions, such as the dissemination of more accurate official suicide statistics, research, conferences, media publicity and the promotion of general awareness of the problem.

But even if it accomplishes some of these objectives, medicalization is not without its own distorting effects. For example, while attesting to the social origins of suicide, it emphasizes individual pathology and thereby diverts needed attention from the wider political, economic, social and cultural forces that need to be targeted for intervention to reduce the high rates of suicide. And the gendered social forces in rural China are easily submerged in the homogenizing psychiatric discourse of 'major depression' (Lee 1999). When psychiatric diagnostic criteria are applied to disempowered rural women, they rewrite their social experience in medical terms, and thereby destroy the moral exigencies and infra-politics of personal suffering in public life. In this process, psychiatry supplies the bureaucratic apparatus and expert culture for transforming what is at stake in society into the medical management of individual pathology (Kleinman and Kleinman 1997).

But not all social sources of suffering and suicide among rural women or others can be drugged away by antidepressants. In some societies, in fact, madness would preclude suicide because only a sane person is supposed to be able to choose rationally between life and death (La Fontaine 1975). Although Chinese psychiatrists have begun to liberalize their concept of depression, they have, unlike psychiatrists in the West, attributed only a minor proportion of suicide to depression (Lee 1999); this is one of only a very few major conceptual differences with psychiatry in North America and Europe. In the CCMD-2-R that was the former national system of psychiatric classification used in China, it is stated that 'suicide may be motivated by hopelessness, *protest against injustice*, fear of punishment, superstition and mental disorders … Most people who commit suicide do not suffer from mental disorders' (Chinese Medical Association and Nanjing Medical University 1995: 135). Ironically for the argument developed here, this is only one of very few times in the Chinese diagnostic system that an attempt has been made to offer *resistance* to what otherwise has been an inexorable Westernization of Chinese diagnostic categories. Nonetheless, this interpretation of suicide is no longer obvious in the CCMD-3 that was published in April 2001 (Chinese Psychiatric Society 2001). In connection with suicide, this states that 'there are often underlying grievances, despair, pessimistic thoughts, guilt, superstitious beliefs and mental disorders' (324). The concept that suicide can be protest against injustice has disappeared. This change reflects the power (and, in our view, limitation) of medicalization in China under global change (Lee 1999).

Even where depression is present, and even where suicide is impulsive, the act itself needs to be seen as a social process that requires different kinds of social interventions aimed at structural causes, such as rural women's powerlessness. Likewise, the high rates of suicide among Chinese elderly, especially in the rural areas (e.g., 145 per 100,000 per year for rural males 75 years old and over), compel us not to find another new antidepressant but to re-examine how such Confucian values as filial piety and respect for the elderly lose their salience in the new political economy of the reform era, and may have lost it decades before owing to the delegitimation crisis of the Chinese tradition that radical Maoism brought about. Thus, a study of 1,021 cases of elderly suicide in Changde county, Hunan, found that the common causes were chronic diseases (23.6 per cent), desertion by family members (20.3 per cent), anger due to abuse by children (12.2 per cent) and pessimism caused by children's gambling (9.4 per cent)

(Zhang and Zhang 1998). Clearly, what biomedical research has identified as 'risk factors' and 'causes' of 'successful' suicide are a mere starting point for anthropological research.

Methodological issues

Current medical research on suicide, such as case-controlled studies of risk factors or psychological autopsy studies, uniformly conclude that suicide is a result of depression or other psychiatric disorders. From an anthropological perspective, such studies fail to attend to the layers of privacy and equivocality that typically envelop suicide, or to evaluate the consequences of suicide on the sociomoral processes that maintain suicidal behaviour in a local world. We believe that cursory answers to survey research or lengthy structured interviews that are obtained outside relations of trust cannot be regarded as adequate data. Lin (1990) has suggested that from the angle of vision of the suicide, the act is always 'weightier than Mount Tai' (*zhong yü Taishan*), even if others may consider it 'lighter than a goose feather' (*qing yü hong mao*). This view tallies with the anthropological emphasis on subjectivity and local meanings. Notwithstanding the tensions between biomedical and anthropological methods of analysis, to study suicide as social resistance, validate biomedical research on suicide, and develop effective prevention programmes and policies, ethnography is highly recommended.

Notes

1 Declaration of interest: The Research Grants Council of Hong Kong has supported the authors' work on suicide in Chinese society (Grant #CUHK4380/00H).
2 Translated by D.C. Lau, *Confucius: The Analects*, XV.9 (Hong Kong: The Chinese University Press, 1983), p. 151.
3 For example, the rate of male suicide in the Russian Federation was 74.1 per 100,000 in 1994 (Schmidtke *et al.* 1999).
4 In lay usage, the term *zisha* refers to both completed and attempted suicide. In the health field, *zisha* is completed suicide, whereas *zisha weisui* is attempted suicide.
5 Note that reliable suicide data from Central and South America, Africa, the Middle East and huge Asian countries such as India and Indonesia are still lacking.
6 The higher estimate (by as much as one-third) is due to the ascription of a percentage of accidental deaths of unknown cause to suicide by the Western researchers. This assumption has been questioned.
7 This huge discrepancy is partly a result of difference in the diagnostic criteria used and in the cultural acceptability of experiencing depression.
8 Young rural women, in contrast to university folks and other intellectuals residing in urban areas, were not the predominant group ostracized during the Cultural Revolution.
9 See also Bianco (2001) for an updated account of peasant resistance in China.
10 See Witke (1973) for Mao's critique of arranged marriage and other patriarchal elements of the pre-communist social environment in China that caused women to struggle hopelessly and to commit suicide in a series of articles published in 1911.
11 This can still be interpreted as resistance, inspired by hope as well as by despair, against the current life in favour of an imagined future paradise.

12 Neurasthenia, *shenjing shuairuo*) is a popular illness label for a varying mixture of anxiety, depressive and physical symptoms (Lee 1999). It is a common form of socio-somatic distress in Chinese society that can express disguised criticism and recrimination in bodily terms.

13 Liu and Li (1990: 88) noted that 50 per cent of women who commit suicide because of marital strife do so after being cruelly beaten by their husbands.

14 Poor access to medical resuscitation facilities in rural areas further contributes to the lethality of ingesting pesticides as a means of attempting suicide.

15 A case of suicide as protest that did exert an impact on social policy in Hong Kong is unambiguously exemplified by a 76-year-old jade seller, Mr Wang, who set himself ablaze in court on 7 December 1998 while he was being tried for hawking illegally and obstructing the streets. The judge ruled that he should pay a fine of HK$400, US$50) and have all of his 251 pieces of jade confiscated. Mr Wang pleaded guilty but begged that he should be allowed to keep the jades for his livelihood. When this was turned down, he poured inflammable liquid on to himself and ignited it. As he quickly became a fireball, he walked towards the judge, but soon fell on to the floor, *Ming Pao* (A5), 8 December 1998. Having sustained a 70 per cent deep burn, he died two days later. This incident hit the headlines for several days, and aroused unanimous support from politicians and academics as well as strikes from many hawkers, demanding that the law pertaining to illegal hawking be reviewed and implemented humanely, especially at a time of high unemployment rates. The government then made a positive preliminary response to the collective request.

Bibliography

D.Adityanjee, 'Suicide Attempts and Suicides in India: Cross-cultural Aspects, *International Journal of Social Psychiatry* (1986), 32, pp. 64–73.

R.K Barnhart (ed.), *The Barnhart Concise Dictionary of Etymology* (New York: HarperCollins, 1995).

J.Baechler, *Suicides* (Oxford: Basil Blackwell, 1979).

L. Bianco, 'Peasant Movements', in J.K. Fairbank and A. Feuerwerker (eds), *The Cambridge History of China*, vol. 13, *Republican China 1912–1949* (Cambridge: Cambridge University Press, 1978), pp. 270–328.

—— *Peasants without the Party: Grass-roots Movements in Twentieth-century China* (Armonk: M.E. Sharpe, 2001).

Chinese Medical Association and Nanjing Medical University, *Chinese Classification of Mental Disorders, second edition, revised (CCMD-2-R)* (Nanjing: Dong Nan University Press, 1995) (in Chinese).

Chinese Psychiatric Society, *The Chinese Classification of Mental Disorders, third edition (CCMD-3)* (Shandong: Shandong Publishing House of Science and Technology, 2001).

D.A. Counts, 'Fighting Back is Not the Way: Suicide and the Women of Kaliai', *American Ethnologist*, 7 (1980), pp. 332–51.

Da D., 'A Preliminary Inquiry into Suicide in China', in J. Peng (ed.), *Social Observation in Special Zone* (Shenzhen: Haitian Publishing House, 1993) (in Chinese), pp. 492–510.

R. Desjarlais, L. Eisenberg, B. Good and A. Kleinman, *World Mental Health: Problems and Priorities in Low-income Countries* (Oxford: Oxford University Press, 1995).

N.J. Diamant, *Revolutionizing the Family: Politics, Love, and Divorce in Urban and Rural China*. Berkeley: University of California Press: 2000).

E. Durkheim, *Suicide* (New York: Free Press, [1897] 1966).

N.L. Farberow, 'Cultural History of Suicide', in N.L. Farberow (ed.), *Suicide in Different Cultures* (Baltimore: University Park Press, 1975), chap. 1.

C. Gilmartin and Lin T., 'Where and Why Have all the Women Gone? Women, Marriage Migration, and Social Mobility in China', Paper presented at The International Conference on Gender and Development in Asia, 27–29 November 1997, The Chinese University of Hong Kong, HKSAR, China.

S.K. Goldsmith, T.C. Pellmar, A.M. Kleinman and Bunney (eds), *Reducing Suicide – A National Imperative* (Washington, DC: National Academies Press, 2002).

He Q.L., *Pitfalls of Modernization: Economic and Social Problems in Contemporary China*, (Beijing: China Today Press, 1998) (in Chinese).

He Z.X., *Suicide and Life*, (Guangzhou: Guangzhou Publishing House, 1996) (in Chinese).

Hu Y.H., 'Elderly Suicide Risk in Family Contexts: A Critique of the Asian Family Care Model', *Journal of Cross-cultural Gerontology*, 10 (1995), pp. 199–217.

M.D.W.Jeffreys, 'Samsonic Suicide or Suicide of Revenge Among Africans', *African Studies* (September 1952), pp. 118–22.

Ji J.L., 'Suicide Rates and Mental Health Services in modern China', *Crisis*, 21 (2000), pp. 118–21.

A.Kleinman and J. Kleinman, 'Moral Transformations of Health and Suffering in Chinese Society', in A. Brandt and P. Rozin (eds), *Morality and Health* (New York and London: Routledge, 1997).

J. La Fontaine, 'Anthropology', in S. Perlli (ed.), *A Handbook for the Understanding of Suicide* (Northvale: Jason Aronson Inc., 1975), chap. 4.

S. Lee, 'Diagnosis Postponed: *shenjing shuairuo* and the Transformation of Psychiatry in post-Mao China', *Culture, Medicine and Psychiatry*, 23 (1999), pp. 349–80.

Li J.H. and Wan W.P., 'An Investigation of Suicide in Puning County, Yunnan', *Chinese Mental Health Journal*, 1 (1987), pp. 73–75 (in Chinese).

Li X.Y., Yang R.S., Zhang C., Bian Q.T., Ji H.Y., Wang Y.P., Zheng Y.X., He F.S. and Phillips, M.R., 'A Case-control Study of the Risk Factors in Attempted Suicide', *Chinese Journal of Epidemiology*, 22 (2001), pp. 281–83 (in Chinese).

Lin Y.H., *The Weight of Mount Tai: Patterns of Suicide in Traditional Chinese History and Culture*, PhD thesis, The University of Wiscosin, Madison, 1990.

Liu J.C. and Li Y.Z., *Unravelling the Suicide Riddle*, (Chengdu: Sichuan Publishing House of Science and Technology, 1990) (in Chinese).

Lu Y.W., Lee, S., Liu M.L., Wing Y.K. and Lee T.S., 'Too Costly to be Ill: Psychiatric Disorders among Hospitalized Migrant Workers in Shenzhen', *Transcultural Psychiatry*, 36 (1999), pp. 95–109.

C.J.L. Murray and A.D. Lopez, *Global Health Statistics: A Compendium of Incidence, Prevalence, and Mortality Estimates for over 200 Conditions* (Cambridge, MA: Harvard University Press, 1996).

I.I. Morris, *The Nobility of Failure: Tragic Heroes in the History of Japan* (New York: Holt, Rinehart and Winston, 1975).

M. Phillips, Liu H.Q. and Zhang Y.P., 'Suicide and Social Change in China', *Culture, Medicine and Psychiatry*, 23 (1999), pp. 25–50.

M.R. Phillips, Li X.Y. and Zhang,Y.P., 'Suicide Rates in China, 1995–1999', *Lancet*, 359 (2002), pp. 835–847.

M.R. Phillips, Yang G.H., Zhang Y.P., Wang L.J., Ji H.Y. and Zhao M.G. 'Risk Factors for Suicide in China: A National Case-control Psychological Autopsy Study', *Lancet* (in press).

P.W. Prewitt, 'Dealing with ijime (bullying) among Japanese Students: Current Approaches to the Problem', *School Psychology International* 9 (1988), pp. 189–95.

D.H. Rubinstein, 'Suicide in Micronesia and Samoa: A Critique of Explanations', *Pacific Studies*, 15 (1992), pp. 51–75.

T. Saywell and J. McManus J., 'Behind the Smile: Silent Suffering', *Far East Economic Review* 9 August 2001, pp. 26–30.

M. Scheler, *Man's Place in Nature*, trans. H. Meyerhoff (New York: Noonday Press, [1928] 1971).

A. Schmidtke, B. Weinacker, A. Apter *et al.*, 'Suicide Rates in the World: Update', *Archives of Suicide Research*, 5 (1999), pp. 81–89.

J.C. Scott, *Domination and the Arts of Resistance: The Hidden Transcripts* (New Haven: Yale University Press, 1990).

D. Solinger, 'The Impact of the Floating Population on the *Danwei*: Shifts in the Pattern of Labor Mobility Control and Entitlement Provision', in X.B. Lu and E. J. Perry (eds), *Danwei: The Changing Chinese Workplace in Historical and Comparative Perspective* (Armonk: M.E. Sharpe, 1997), pp.195–222.

Tanaka T., 'The Identity Formation of the Victim of "Shunning"', *School Psychology International*, 22 (2001), pp. 463–76.

S. Taylor, *The Sociology of Suicide*, (London: Longman, 1988).

R. Witke, 'Mao Tse-tung, Women and Suicide', in M.B. Young (ed.), *Women in China. Studies in Social Change and Feminism* (Ann Arbor: Center for Chinese Studies, 1973), pp. 7–31.

M. Wolf, 'Women and Suicide in China', in M. Wolf and R. Witk (eds), *Women in Chinese Society* (Stanford: Stanford University Press, 1975), pp. 111–41.

Wu J.J.J., 'Suicides and Suicide Survivors of the Cultural Revolution', in P. Timothy Bushnell *et al.* (eds), *State Organized Terror: The Case of Violent Internal Repression* (Boulder, CO: Westview Press, 1991), pp. 289–302.

Yip P.S.F, 'Suicides in Hong Kong, Taiwan and Beijing', *British Journal of Psychiatry*, 169 (1996), pp. 495–500.

Zhang H.L. and Zhang J.C., 'Analysis of 1,021 Cases of Elderly Suicide in Chang De County', *US Chinese Psychosomatic Medicine Journal*, 2 (1998), p. 185 (in Chinese).

Zhou J.H., 'A Probe into the Mentality of Sixty-five Rural Young Women Giving Birth to Baby Girls', *Chinese Sociology and Anthropology* (Journal of Translations), 20 (1988), pp. 93–102.

Zhou X.K., *How the Farmers Changed China: Power of the People* (Boulder, CO: Westview Press,1996).

Suggested reading

D.A. Counts, 'Fighting Back is Not the Way: Suicide and the Women of Kaliai', *American Ethnologist*, 7 (1980), pp. 332 51.

S.K. Goldsmith, T.C. Pellmar, A.M. Kleinman and Bunney (eds), *Reducing Suicide – A National Imperative* (Washington, DC: National Academies Press, 2002)

M. Phillips, Liu H.Q. and Zhang Y.P., 'Suicide and Social Change in China', *Culture, Medicine and Psychiatry*, 23 (1999), pp. 25–50.

D.H. Rubinstein, 'Suicide in Micronesia and Samoa: A Critique of Explanations', *Pacific Studies*, 15 (1992), pp. 51–75.

M. Wolf, 'Women and Suicide in China', in M. Wolf and R. Witk (eds), *Women in Chinese Society* (Stanford: Stanford University Press, 1975), pp. 111–41.

Index